# THE WITCH DOCTORS

Also by Adrian Wooldridge:

*Measuring the Mind: Education and Psychology in England, 1860–1990*

# THE WITCH DOCTORS

## MAKING SENSE
## OF THE
## MANAGEMENT GURUS

# JOHN MICKLETHWAIT
# ADRIAN WOOLDRIDGE

TIMES
BUSINESS

Illustration of crystal ball on chapter openers by Ron Leach

Library of Congress Cataloging-in-Publication data is available.

ISBN 0-8129-2988-8

Random House website address: http://www.randomhouse.com/

Printed in the United States of America on acid-free paper

9 8 7 6 5 4 3 2

First U.S. Edition

Book design by Robert Olsson

For Fevronia and Amelia

# Prologue

"You can resist an invading army; you cannot resist an idea whose time has come."

*Victor Hugo*

Yet another cavernous hall—this time in the Southern Californian suburban sprawl; an advance guard of blazered young men with portable telephones; a stand selling T-shirts and bumper stickers; a late candidate; an angry press bus. In many ways, it resembles any other rally during a presidential campaign. The difference is the crowd. If the setting had been a Democratic or Republican rally, people would have been trying to squeeze around barriers, arguing about which regional committee deserved which seats. Instead, despite a conspicuous lack of direction, the audience is eerily disciplined. They clamber out of their station wagons and BMWs, and troop toward the amphitheater as if it is a church or perhaps even a bewitching spacecraft. Occasionally, they are harassed by members of the media. Only one question produces a response.

"Isn't Ross Perot just another politician?"

The man questioned—a tall balding Iowan-turned-Californian who is a supervisor at a defense company—is so angry that he spins around, accidentally yanking his son's arm. "You don't get it, do you," he complains. Then he smiles more confidently. "Mr. Perot is a manager. He knows how to do things."

*Long Beach, California, 1992*

"Only the paranoid survive."

> *Andy Grove, chief executive officer, Intel*

The average big company used 12 of the 25 most common management tools in 1993; in 1994 they used 13; they expect to use 14 tools in 1995. Seventy-two percent of managers believe that companies who use the right tools are more likely to succeed; 70 percent say that the tools promise more than they deliver.

> *A survey of 787 companies around the world by*
> *Bain & Company, April 1995*

"Guru? You find a gem here or there. But most of it's fairly obvious, you know. You go to Doubleday's business section and you see all these wonderful titles and you spend $300 and then you throw them all away."

> *Rupert Murdoch, on being asked whether there was any management guru he followed or admired, March 1996*

"These bold new ideas vault business people *beyond* reengineering, *beyond* total quality management, *beyond* empowerment, and even *beyond* change and toward nothing less than reinvention and revolution. . . . In presenting a radical new view of how businesses can work, Peters offers the following challenge: 'If you're not irate in the first thirty minutes of reading, if you don't throw this book down at least once in the first hour, and if you don't reach for the Maalox by the two-hour mark, then I and this book have utterly failed you.'"

> *Publisher's blurb,* The Tom Peters Seminar: Crazy Times Call for Crazy Organizations *(1994).*
> *For the uninitiated, this is the book with Peters wearing his boxer shorts on the cover.*

"China needs managers more than anything else."

> *Candidate for admission at China Europe International Business School, Shanghai. The school admits 64 students annually. It gets 4,000 applicants.*

"The new authority will be: Member led, Officer driven, Customer focused; a team environment where the whole is greater than the sum of its parts; a flat management structure where employees and managers are fully empowered and decisions are devolved close to the customer; a culture of learning rather than blame; a clear sense of direction and purpose. A firm commitment to delivering high-quality public services through a combination of direct-provision and effective partnerships."

> *Recruitment advertisement, Bath and North East Somerset District Council. Quoted in "Birtspeak," a column in* Private Eye *devoted to "management drivel in all spheres," September 22, 1995*

"Employees will have four primary reactions: Denial, Sadness, Anger, Withdrawal. Be certain to recognize and acknowledge the employee's feelings. However, you may need to restate the message to ensure that the employee knows that the decision is final and has been made at the highest level. Notify your Human Resources Generalist if you anticipate strong reactions. If necessary, he/she will alert Security and Medical."

> *"Communication Guidelines, Manager Meeting with Employees Not Selected for the New Organization," Chase Manhattan Bank, following merger with Chemical Bank that resulted in 10,000 job losses. Chase's directors, all of whom kept their jobs, referred to the jobs eliminated as "saves."*

The management consultancy business generated $11.4 billion worth of fees in 1994; it is on course to bring in $21 billion in 1999. At McKinsey, the biggest strategic consultancy, each partner accounted for $468,000 of revenues. More than half of today's leading consulting firms did not exist five years ago, and only 1 percent existed fifty years ago.

> *The Gartner Group, Management Consultant International*

Even in a city full of surprises and unintentional ironies, the billboard came as something of a shock. There, surrounded by the familiar yellow flags of the Hezbollah and the pockmarked machine-gunned buildings, stood a huge advertisement summoning the faithful of Beirut to a "Total Quality Management" seminar.

Our driver saw our interest.

"Oh yes, management. The future. But only once we get rid of these Syrian pigs."

> *Lebanon, January 1995*

"You know what worries me about your book about management theory: that you'll talk to all the people and read all the books; that you will detail all its incredible effects—the number of jobs lost, the billions of dollars spent, and so on. And you won't say the obvious thing: that it's 99 percent bullshit. And everybody knows that."

*Senior editor,* The Economist, *Summer 1995*

# Acknowledgments

There are two long, equally inglorious traditions in management theory. The first is that books must come complete with a list of acknowledgments long enough to make a chapter in any other sort of book: every person at every conference, every research student, every corporate public relations manager has somehow delivered a valuable insight to the writer. The second tradition is to mention nobody, thereby presumably reiterating the message that the great ideas that await the reader are the author's alone. What follows is something of a compromise.

Our primary thanks go to *The Economist* for giving us the time to write *The Witch Doctors* and also for giving us permission to use articles that we have written for it. In particular, we thank Bill Emmott, the editor of *The Economist,* and Peter David, the business affairs editor, for their tolerance and support. A small squadron of colleagues that included Nick Wiseman, Barbara Beck, Matthew Bishop, Victor Earl, Carol Mawer, and Nick Valery kindly agreed to read all or parts of this book; Victor was particularly helpful in checking facts and Carol in reading proofs. We are also grateful to Jenny Geddes for her invaluable help and to Gideon Rachman for acting as a source of encouragement in the darkest hours.

Three non-*Economist* readers were kind enough to offer their comments when the book was in preparation: Partha Bose, Joel Kurtzman, and Alan Kantrow. They all work for the same "vested interests" that we claim in *The Witch Doctors* make management theory such an unself-critical business. Perhaps seeking to prove us wrong, they were remarkably objective critics, often urging us to be harsher.

When it came to writing the book, we were helped in the first instance by Allegra Huston, who convinced us—perhaps wrongly—that it was not an insane project. We have been enormously lucky to have Gillon Aitken and Andrew Wylie as our agents: we are extremely grateful to both. Our good fortune continued when we ended up with two excellent editors: Peter Smith at Times Books and Tom Weldon at Heinemann. They have not only helped us clarify confusions and cut out nonsense but also contrived to leave us with the impression that we had come up with the improvements in the first place.

Finally, we thank our families, particularly our wives, Fevronia and Amelia. Among the various promises extracted from them on their wedding days, there was no mention of management theory. For that hideous betrayal alone, this book is dedicated to them.

## Authors' Note

Some passages in this book have appeared in different form in articles the authors have written for *The Economist*. They are reprinted by kind permission of the Economist Newspaper Ltd.

One problem with business is that most of the established vocabulary is male (from "businessman" upward). This no longer suits a world in which women outnumber men in many companies. We are well aware of the irritation it causes. However, most of the unisex alternatives, such as "businessperson," jar; and having to add "or she" and "or hers" at every mention of "he" and "his" can make a sentence into an obstacle course. For the most part, we have tried to run away from this problem. When confronted with a choice, we have often opted for the male version. No offense is intended.

# Contents

# THE WITCH DOCTORS

# Introduction:
# The Unacknowledged Legislators

SHELLEY ONCE CLAIMED that poets are "the unacknowledged legislators of mankind." Today that honor belongs to management theorists. Names such as Drucker and Peters may not have the same ring as Wordsworth or Keats; yet, wherever one looks, management theorists are laying down the law, reshaping institutions, refashioning the language, and, above all, reorganizing people's lives. Indeed, at its most extreme fringe, where management theory merges with the self-help industry, gurus are actually ordering people's minds, teaching them how to think about everything from organizing their desk to reassessing their love life. In late 1994, the revelation that the late Princess Diana had sought help from Anthony Robbins, a business-motivation guru who encourages his clients to "unleash the power within" by walking on red hot coals, caused barely a flicker of surprise in Fleet Street. On the other side of the Atlantic, the simultaneous news that Newt Gingrich, the Speaker-elect of the House of Representatives, was preparing for his new job "by reading Peter Drucker" was greeted with relief.

At the same time as the princess and the Speaker were seeking out management theory, millions of more mundane human beings were having it done unto them. Some 43 million jobs were eliminated in America in 1979–95 (though many more were created). By 1997, American manufacturers employed 12 percent fewer workers than in 1979, but production was 51 percent higher. In paternalist Germany, "downsizing" had pushed up the unemployment rate to 11.7 percent by late 1997—the highest level since the Second World War. In Japan, the home of lifetime employment, temporary and part-time workers now account for one in four of the workforce. In Britain, figures from the Department of Employment, leaked in December 1994, showed that 6.6 million men—or 44 percent of the male workforce—had been unemployed at some time since 1990; 3.9 million women—or roughly a third of the female workforce—had suffered the same fate.[1]

Blue-collar workers everywhere are used to being laid off when times get tough. Nowadays, the victims are often managers; and a company does not have to be in dire financial trouble to start slimming. Despite a booming economy, more than 40 percent of the 1200 companies surveyed by the American Management Association in 1997 said that they were eliminating jobs, with organizational restructuring being the main reason.

In America, things came to a head in early 1996 when AT&T, formerly cuddly old Ma Bell, announced 40,000 redundancies. Not only was the company making healthy profits at the time of the announcement, but its share price soared afterward (enriching its then-boss, Bob Allen, by some $5 million). People joked that the abbreviation of the company, which had been a passionate follower of management fads and had already laid off 70,000 people over the past decade, would one day stand for Allen & Two Temps. As various presidential candidates attacked the greed of corporate America, *Business Week's* cover worried about "America's Economic Anxiety."[2] *The New York Times* ran a seven-part series titled "The Downsizing of America."[3] "Firing people has got to be trendy in corporate America," moaned *Newsweek,* in a cover story headlined "Corporate Killers," which contrasted the rising salaries of bosses with their reduced payroll lists. "You can practically smell the fear and anger in white-collar America because nobody in CEO-land seems to care."[4]

From Ohio to Oslo and Osaka, many of those laid off in the 1990s, including a good number of those at AT&T, were "reengineered" out of their jobs. Although ugly names—"downsizing," "outsourcing," and so on—have always been used to disguise routine corporate bloodletting, "business process reengineering" seems to have been at the top of the list in the past few years (as cited by half the firms shedding jobs in the 1997 American Management Association survey). The name was used in a book, *Reengineering the Corporation,* published in 1993 by two management theorists, James Champy and Michael Hammer, to refer to the method of reorganizing businesses around "processes," such as selling, rather than administrative fiefs, such as marketing departments. Since then, the reengineering creed has spread far around the world. In Japan, Nomura's Research Institute keeps an index measuring the use of the word in news stories to chart the country's willingness to change.

So far, *Reengineering the Corporation* has sold almost two million copies, and various lackluster follow-ups, such as James Champy's *Reengineering Management* (1995) and Michael Hammer's *The Reengineering Revolution* (1995), have reached the *New York Times* business best-seller list. The reengineering movement has spawned specialist consultancies, endless conferences, dozens of "do-it-yourself" videotapes, and countless courses at business schools. Now there are signs of a backlash—of reengineering revisionists questioning how easy the theory is to put into practice, complaining about "corporate anorexia" and "dumbsizing," and preaching the virtues of "growth," "trust," and "loyalty." In time, there will doubtless be reengineering re-revisionists reaffirming the faith.

## An Industry Is Born

The reengineering craze is merely the latest, most potent example of the bewildering power of management gurus throughout this century. Although some antiquarians argue that Nicolo Machiavelli was the first management thinker and others assign that honor to whichever Egyptian organized the construction of the pyramids, the first recognizable management guru was Frederick Taylor, the father of stopwatch-based "scientific management." In the early 1900s, his books sold in the millions, and Taylor's consultancy fees were $35 a day—or $630 in today's money. Taylor's worker-as-machine theories always had their critics (Charlie Chaplin, for example, lampooned them memorably in *Modern Times*), but that did not stop them from being adopted by many leading American businessmen, including Henry Ford, or from being spread around the world. A steady procession of management thinkers has followed in Taylor's path. After the Second World War, W. Edwards Deming, who pioneered "total quality management," was dubbed the most revered American in Japan after General Douglas MacArthur.

However, interest in management theory went into overdrive in the 1980s as the rich world in general, and America in particular, tried to come to terms with the rise of Japan, the spread of computers, and radical changes in working patterns. For a new breed of increasingly evangelical management theorists, led by Tom Peters, the accompanying corporate self-analysis proved a bonanza. In the summer of 1982, Peters and another consultant from McKinsey, Robert Waterman, published *In Search of Excellence,* which boldly (and correctly) told American businessmen that they were in better shape than they thought. The book sold more than five million copies, staying at the top of the *New York Times* best-seller list for more than two years and turning its authors into millionaires.

Ever since *In Search of Excellence,* the guru industry has boomed. Some $750 million worth of business books are currently sold in America alone every year, and the market for audio- and videotapes, courses, and seminars is even bigger. Not only are the latest theories, such as reengineering, more rapidly and zealously applied than their predecessors, but the wealth and status accruing to those who promote them have increased exponentially. Peters, now much copied by other gurus, charges $60,000 for a day-long seminar and conducts about 60 such meetings a year. His newspaper column, in which he opines on subjects ranging from personal hygiene to Zen Buddhism, is syndicated around the world. It is rare to meet a guru who has houses on only one continent.

The gurus themselves are only the most visible tip of a much larger management iceberg that incorporates business schools, management consultancies, and much of the business press. It is hard to think of any other academic discipline that can match management theory in having built an industry around itself. American firms alone now spend $20 billion a year on outside advice. Guru breeding grounds, such as McKinsey, have offices wherever firms lose money. Around the world, executives who thought they knew it all are being encouraged to take training courses in everything from assertiveness to ethical management. Even in self-conscious, cynical Britain, some 40 companies provide adventure-based management training courses in which fat merchant bankers and balding bond traders swing across rivers and, around camp fires, tell their colleagues what they really think about them.[5] Every year, more than 75,000 students are awarded master of business administration (MBA) degrees in America—fifteen times the total in 1960. And every year, a quarter of a million people around the world take the Graduate Management Admissions Test (GMAT) for entrance to MBA courses. Business schools are spreading throughout the newly liberated economies of Eastern Europe and Asia; they have reached even Oxford and Cambridge, once regarded as the last preserves of classical education.

As we explain in this book, management theory, more than any other branch of academia, is propelled by two primal human instincts: fear and greed. It is usually one of these two emotions that persuades a middle manager at O'Hare Airport to pick up yet another book on leadership or tempts a chief executive in Ohio to blow yet another million dollars on consulting fees. However, it is also clear that management theory is bound up with three revolutions that directly or indirectly affect all of us: the reinvention of companies, the reinvention of careers, and the reinvention of government.

Nowadays, companies everywhere are going through contortions that their predecessors could scarcely have imagined. The attrition rate of companies is spectacular—only about a third of America's 500 leading companies on a 1970 listing still exist today. Even the best companies, terrified that they will end up in this ever more crowded corporate graveyard, are reorganizing themselves. This applies not only to job slashers such as AT&T but also to fast-growing companies such as Electronic Data Systems (EDS), a computer-services firm that seems to be addicted to management rethinking, despite the fact that it has barely put a foot wrong since Ross Perot founded it with $1,000 in 1962.

Even when such contortions are not directly inspired by management theory, they tend to drive managers back into the gurus' arms. Management theory, after all, is the study of business. It explains not just what this or that firm is doing but what whole groups of firms are doing, and why. The old excuse, that a business person knew his or her own industry and did not need to know about anybody else's, no longer holds water. Industry borders are blurring everywhere: between commercial banking, investment banking, and brokerages; between computer hardware and software vendors; and between publishers, broadcasters, telecommunication companies, and film studios. Even the most hard-headed managers are having to come to grips with ideas like synergy and alliances—and the challenge of managing disparate, multicultural organizations. All these paths lead to management theory.

As companies change, so do careers. Jobs are being reinvented in much the same way that businesses are. Gone are the days when a man (and it usually was a man) could expect to spend his entire career working for the same company, starting as an apprentice, climbing up through the ranks, and retiring, after 40 years of uninterrupted employment, to enjoy an index-linked pension, a corporate carriage-clock, and a mention in the company history. As both companies and employees try to deal with this more unstable age, it is not surprising that they are drawn to books with titles like *The Age of Unreason* (1989, by Charles Handy), *The Change Masters* (1985, by Rosabeth Moss Kanter), and *Managing in a Time of Great Change* (1996, by Peter Drucker).

What is more, the number of people who need to know something about management is growing. Of the 8 million new jobs created in America in 1991–95, 60 percent belonged to the category of "managers and other professionals," now the largest group in the workforce. Nor is it just white-collar workers who have to know their TQM (total-quality management) from their JIT (just in time): nowadays, even the lowliest factory worker in the Western world knows that his most valuable asset is his brain rather than his hands.

Just as companies have been forced by competitors and shareholders to question how they manage themselves, so have governments, prodded by budget deficits and taxpayers. In many cases, this has simply led to privatization. In Argentina, for instance, a group of state-owned businesses that used to cost taxpayers money was sold for over $20 billion. Some governments have moved from privatization to what might be called the next stage of public sector management: trying to reorganize those institutions that have to remain in the government's hands. Britain's former Conservative government redesigned large parts of one of the country's most cherished institutions, the welfare state. It has devolved power to individual schools and hospitals, given doctors and teachers their own budgets, linked those budgets to the number of pupils taught or patients treated, and compiled and published "box scores" of "productivity" (i.e., lives saved and exams passed). These reforms owed much more to management theorists such as Peter Drucker and Alain Enthoven than they did to Tory philosophers such as David Hume and Edmund Burke, which helps to explain why the Labour government has been content to leave the bulk of these changes intact.

Across the Atlantic, the Clinton Administration, obsessed with think tanks, Renaissance weekends, and the like, is even more steeped in management theory. In early 1995, it emerged that Bill Clinton had consulted both Princess Diana's mentor, Anthony Robbins, and Stephen Covey, another motivation expert. Hillary Rodham-Clinton's incomprehensible but apparently omniscient health plan was largely written by a management fanatic, Ira Magaziner. Vice President Al Gore spends most of his time reinventing government in line with the latest management thinking. And a belief in the power of management is one of the few ideas that crosses party lines—as the Drucker-reading Speaker Gingrich bears witness.

## The Age of Anxiety

Wherever management theory has been invoked, fear and anxiety seem to have followed. Ask for an explanation at a shuttered factory in Bavaria or a reorganized hospital in Newcastle, and you will hear an anodyne language that makes laying people off sound more like a scientific decision than a human tragedy: fired workers are "downsized," "separated," "severed," "unassigned," and "proactively outplaced." (AT&T is said to be carrying out a "force management program" to reduce "an imbalance of forces or skills.")

Despite their invariable presence at the scene of the crime, the gurus have not yet been rounded up for questioning. The list of suspects compiled by Pat Buchanan in his populist campaign for the Republican presidential nomination included the fiendish José (the symbolic foreign worker out to steal your

job) and "Goldman and Sachs" (the symbolic Jewish investment bank)—but no Drucker or Peters. More sober commentators have tended to talk about economics.

In one way, this is right. The underlying reasons why people have lost their jobs (or feel more insecure in them) have to
do with competition, technological change, and government
budgets. However, it is not quite enough for the management
gurus to claim that "they were only following orders": that they
were the servants of macroeconomic forces beyond their control. For better or worse, management theory has played an
enormous role in how those forces have affected people. Although American companies would still have shed jobs without
reengineering, the discipline, alongside several other management techniques, probably increased the carnage and certainly
affected the way that the cutting was done.

It cannot have been a coincidence that many of the most
enthusiastic downsizers have also been the most enthusiastic
consumers of management theory. AT&T, for example, has
long been a playground for the gurus, forever calling in consultants or sending staff members on management courses; indeed, the telephone giant is responsible for arguably the most
baffling management slogan of all time—"Putting the moose
on the table"—which had something to do with flattening hierarchies and empowering workers, and was one of several
(disastrous) attempts to inject modern management thinking
into AT&T's NCR subsidiary.

Moreover, a good deal of "anxiety" has nothing to do with
losing one's job but with the way that the workplace is being reorganized. "Delayering," for instance, affects not only those
who are fired. It increases pressure on shop-floor workers who
now have to make more decisions for themselves. It also dis-
rupts people's careers: with fewer rungs to climb, managers
have to be content with moving sideways. Similarly, the gurus
have been unabashed supporters of ways to measure an individual's contribution to a company, from performance pay to
newer devices such as "360-degree evaluation" (whereby people
evaluate each other). Once again, they tend to see these things
as "empowering"; but survey after survey suggests that most
workers find them frightening. Indeed, one of the ironies of
management theory is that although it was invented to make

managers' jobs easier, it has often made their lives much more difficult.

## The Management Theory Paradox

Does the gurus' influence—their apparent status as the unacknowledged legislators of mankind—make sense? One obvious answer is that management theory matters because management matters. Put simply, it changes companies and the way that people work; and in a world where many companies are bigger than some countries and where most people spend more of their waking hours at work rather than at home, that changes lives—often dramatically. While most other academics—even scientists and economists—have to wait decades to see their work have any practical impact, the gurus' ideas are often tested immediately. There are few other academic disciplines that can claim to be so "alive."

Yet there is a catch. As even its foremost thinkers admit, management theory is bedeviled by a paradox: this intellectual discipline that matters so much is still far from respectable. As Peter Drucker puts it, people use the word "guru" only because they do not want to say "charlatan." Another guru, Henry Mintzberg, has a motto, pinned to his wall: "The higher a monkey climbs, the more you see its ass." Even in America, academics at business schools are regarded with condescension—and with suspicion. Outside America, the reaction in common rooms and *Grandes Ecoles* is far more vicious. Management gurus often throw out intellectual grappling hooks to older disciplines, such as economics, philosophy, and history; the other academics seldom return the favor.

At first sight, this looks like a cover for academic jealousy. What underfunded medieval historian, toiling away in an ancient library for an audience of hundreds and a postal worker's salary, could fail to be annoyed by the corporate-jet and speaking-tour lifestyle of a "human-resources management expert"? But this is not enough to explain the management theory paradox. The hard fact remains that most academics are rude about management theory simply because they do not think that it is very profound. And these doubts are not confined to snooty people living in ivory towers. Talk privately to virtually any publisher of management books, and you will probably unearth the attitude: "Isn't it incredible that this stuff sells?" (This is more than just literary prejudice against "boring" business books: by some counts, managers fail to finish four in every five business books they buy.)[6] Nor are those who deal more directly with management theory any more flattering. Corner a consultant, fill him or her up with alcohol, and the chances are that he or she will admit the same thing as the publisher. Even ordinary business people—including those who have fired thousands in the name of one of these theories—will blush awkwardly when asked how "intellectual" management theory is. Sooner or later, in virtually every case, the word "bullshit" appears.

Perhaps a better word would be an older Anglo-Saxon equivalent: management theory lacks what Yorkshire folk used to call "bottom." Even if it is not all "bullshit," then enough of it is to disqualify the rest. In many cases, the blame lies with the dismal range of tub-thumping charlatans ("Transform your company in three days for $10,000") who have jumped onto the management theory bandwagon because there is no longer any room left on the bandwagons peddling advice on sex or dieting. Such people make convenient scapegoats, but (to mix metaphors with the same enthusiasm as they do) they are basically red herrings when it comes to the management theory paradox. There are plenty of appalling economics papers and unspeakable poems published every year, but the thinking world does not turn up its nose at economics or literature. The real problem is that there are grave doubts about the serious canon of management theory.

## Witnesses for the Prosecution

Management theory, according to the case against it, has four defects: it is constitutionally incapable of self-criticism; its terminology usually confuses rather than educates; it rarely rises above basic common sense; and it is faddish and bedeviled by contradictions that would not be allowed in more rigorous disciplines. The implication of all four charges is that management gurus are con artists, the witch doctors of our age, playing on business people's anxieties in order to sell snake oil. The gurus, many of whom have sprung suspiciously from the "great university of life" rather than any orthodox academic discipline, exist largely because people let them get away with it. Modern management theory is no more reliable than tribal medicine. Witch doctors, after all, often got it right—by luck, by instinct, or by trial and error.

The first charge against management theory—its lack of self-criticism—we happily accept. Indeed, one of the points of this book is to provide just such criticism. The second charge—that much of it is incomprehensible gobbledygook—we also happily accept. Another of the purposes of this book is to translate "managementese" into something approaching English. There seems to be something in the water in business schools or at management conferences that destroys people's capacity to speak plainly or write clearly. Read the following paragraph, for example, written by Gary Hamel and C. K. Prahalad, two of the better gurus:

> Wave participants involved their direct reports in the discovery process. Each wave appointed a few "linking pins" responsible for interacting the wave's work with that of the other waves. Change team members acted as coaches to each wave. The output of every wave was thoroughly debated by the other waves and with the Leadership Council. Finally, an "integration team," made up of some of the more "convergent thinkers" across the waves, boiled the work down to its essence and produced a draft strategic architecture that again was widely debated in the company.[7]

Obfuscation and jargon are confined not just to the printed word. The idea for this book sprang out of a symposium held at a Swiss management forum, where a room full of German businessmen endeavored heroically to understand what an American guru was trying to say. Every direct, practical query from the floor received an ever vaguer response from the podium. Specific questions, along the lines of "How should we apply your ideas?" were answered by philosophical musings about what words such as "apply" meant and an invitation to the whole room to discuss "apply." A few incomprehensible diagrams were produced "just as a loose framework." The German businessmen blamed themselves for not understanding.

What, then, of the third, more substantial charge: that, underneath this convenient cloud of obfuscation, most of what the gurus say is blindingly obvious? Too often, to outside eyes, management gurus seem to be dealing in applied common sense ("the customer is king"); many of their catchphrases ("total-quality management") now seem trite. They often claim to be predicting the future when all they are doing is describing the present. Just as Lenin's *Imperialism, the Highest Stage of Capitalism* (1917) predicted the outbreak of the First World War three years after it had actually happened, management gurus are forever prophesying a future that has already arrived.

There is an element of truth in this, but less than critics allege. Some of the things that strike us nowadays as blindingly obvious were anything but obvious when far-sighted management theorists began to talk about them. Peter Drucker, for example, was predicting the decline of the blue-collar worker and the rise of the "knowledge worker" back in the 1950s. People have stopped preaching about total-quality management, not because quality has gone out of fashion, but because everybody is striving for it. Besides, there is nothing inherently wrong with stating the obvious. One of the arguments for hiring management consultants is that they can see what is obvious to an outsider but incomprehensible to an insider.

However, the most common criticism of management theory focuses on the fourth charge: its faddishness. Management theorists have a passion for permanent revolution that would have made Leon Trotsky or Mao Zedong green with envy. Theorists are forever unveiling ideas, christened with some acronym and tarted up in scientific language, which are supposed to "guarantee competitive success." A few months later, with the ideas tried out and "competitive success" still as illusory as ever, the theorists unveil some new idea. The names speak for themselves: theory Z, management by objectives, brainstorming, managerial grid, T groups, intrapreneurship, demassing, excellence, managing by walking around, and so on.

The fashion in theories is mirrored by a fashion in companies. Gurus are forever discovering companies that seem to have stumbled on the secret of competitive success. A few years later, these miracle organizations are faltering, troubled, or even bankrupt. In 1982, *In Search of Excellence* identified 43 excellent American companies and tried to distill the sources of their success. Less than five years after the book's publication, two-thirds of the companies studied had ceased to be excellent. Some, such as Atari and Avon, were in serious trouble; others, like Wang and Du Pont, were no longer outstanding. IBM was well advanced in its serious decline. (On noticing the trend, *Business Week* produced a cover emblazoned with a single word, "Oops!") But, rather than taking a vow of silence, Tom Peters produced yet more books, advocating different solutions to America's problems.

These theories seem to have a large and willing (if confused) audience among managers. In 1995, a survey by Bain & Company, a consultancy, of what use managers around the world made of 25 leading management techniques found that the average company used 11.8 of these techniques in 1993 and 12.7 in 1994. The managers were on course to use 14.1 techniques in 1995.[8] Although Americans are usually singled out as the worst offenders, their consumption rate (12.8) was only slightly higher than that of France (11.4) and Japan (11.5), and it was behind that of the biggest binger, Britain (13.7).

Management fashions seem to be growing ever more fickle; the life cycle of an idea has now shrunk from a decade to a year or less. Humble businessmen trying to keep up with the latest fashion often find that by the time they have implemented the new craze, it looks outdated. The only people who win out are the theorists, who just go on getting richer and richer. Indeed, it is not hard to construct an Oliver Stone movie out of the available evidence for a concerted conspiracy. Established gurus, with jet-set lifestyles to support, are always looking for ways to update their arguments; would-be gurus, be they overworked management consultants dreaming of spending some time with their families or underemployed business professors dreaming of first-class travel, are always trying to invent the revolutionary ideas that will establish their reputations; and everybody in the business is desperate to keep the wheel turning.

## The Contradictory Corporation

All the complaints about faddism miss the point. There is nothing necessarily wrong about trying out ideas. Rather like jogging or pumping iron, a new theory forces companies to exercise their corporate muscles. (General Electric's Jack Welch even dubs one of his management systems "workout," implying that managerial change is good for corporate health.) The problem comes when these ideas contradict each other. The real problem with management theory is that it is pulling institutions and individuals in conflicting directions.

For every theory dragging companies one way, there are two other theories dragging it in another. One moment, the gurus are preaching total-quality management—and the importance of checking quality and reducing defects; the next, they are insisting that what matters is speed (which means being a little less painstaking about checking quality). One moment, they are saying that what gives a company its edge is its corporate culture, the more distinctive the better; the next, they are ordering companies to become more "multicultural" in order to be able to hold a mirror up to the rest of society. One moment, companies are urged to agree on and then follow a single strong "vision"; the next, they are being warned that they live in an "age of uncertainty" where following any single vision can be suicidal. Most management theorists have not worked out whether it is important to be global or local, to be big or small, to be run in the interests of shareholders or stakeholders. Usually, they end up telling managers to do both.

The contradictions are particularly poisonous when they involve a company's relations with its staff. One of the more fashionable words in management theory is "trust"—it is this, the theory holds, that will keep "knowledge workers" loyal and inspire them to come up with ideas. Yet all the gurus also preach the virtue of "flexibility," which is usually shorthand for firing people. Indeed, there is a growing contradiction between the interests of companies and those of their employees. What companies do to make themselves secure—laying off workers, putting them on short-term contracts, or introducing flexible work schedules—is precisely what makes those workers feel insecure. Meanwhile, the only person who could sort out these contradictions is the one who—thanks to all that delayering—has the least time to do it: the boss.

These contradictions within firms reflect a deeper intellectual confusion at the heart of management theory; it has become not so much a coherent discipline as a battleground between two radically opposed philosophies. Management theorists usually belong to one of two rival schools, each of which is inspired by a different philosophy of human nature; and management practice has oscillated wildly between these two positions. *Scientific management* is based on the idea that the average worker is a lazy slob who is only redeemed by greed. The job of the manager is to break down jobs into their component parts, so that even the dumbest persons can master them, and design incentive systems, so that even the laziest will exert themselves. *Humanistic management,* on the other hand, is based on the idea that the average worker is a model human being—intelligent, creative, and self-motivating. The job of the manager is to ensure that the work assigned is interesting enough to bring out the best in the firm's employees, by dint of devolving decisions to shop-floor workers, creating self-managing teams, and encouraging workers to make suggestions about how the company might be improved. This, in essence, is the debate between "hard" and "soft" management.

The first theory, in the guise of scientific management, held sway until the Second World War. The second theory gained ground in the 1950s and 1960s, under the banner of the "human-relations movement." In the 1980s, the humanists pointed to Japan, a country that devolved power to workers and eschewed scientific management. This soft approach was increasingly overshadowed by hard realities: for all their kind words, companies everywhere began to cut back staff. By the early 1990s, the dominant management theory was reengineering, which tried to adapt Taylorism to the age of the computer.

The Contradictory Corporation has had two alarming effects. The first has been to reinforce anxiety, from the boardroom down. American managers have an acronym that captures the effect of all the changes: BOHICA—bend over, here it comes again. *Business Week* quoted one American manager's verdict on management fashion: "Last year it was quality circles . . . this year it will be zero inventories. The truth is, one more fad and we will all go nuts."[9] That was in 1986, and since then the velocity of fads—and their ability to contradict one another—has increased considerably.

The second effect concerns language—and commitment. As contradictory theories zip past them, managers have learned how to pay lip service to theories without really understanding them, let alone bothering to implement them. Like the Soviet bureaucrats of old, many managers are living in a dual world: the real world and the world of officially sanctioned ideology. Thus, they talk about "empowerment" but habitually hoard power, or they proclaim that they are "reengineering" their organizations when they are really just firing a few of the more lackluster workers.

This doublespeak matters because management theory is the language of the international elite. An increasing number of people who rule companies and countries speak in its terms. For the young and ambitious, a business school education is looking more and more like a necessity (and a spell at a consulting firm, more of a probability). Eavesdrop in the business-class lounge of any airport from Shanghai to San Francisco and you will hear a familiar vernacular. In politics, the old battles between left and right no longer seem to matter. Bill Clinton and Tony Blair won office largely by adopting the right's policies on everything from welfare to job creation. Instead, the battleground has become one of managerial efficiency: who will "manage" the economy, who will "restructure" government, who has the necessary "leadership skills," and so on. If this debate is carried out in terms that are contradictory or empty, then everyone suffers.

## With a Scalpel, Not a Hatchet

Some would argue that all these contradictions indicate that management theory is itself a contradiction in terms. We prefer to see it as an immature discipline, prevented from growing up, partly, by its enormous financial success.

Management theory is in roughly the same state that economics was a century ago. Many of its fundamental tenets have yet to be established. The discipline still awaits its John Maynard Keynes, Friedrich Hayek, or Milton Friedman. It lacks rules of debate, so the discipline remains open to anybody with an axe to grind—much as economics was open to the likes of Karl Marx. However, just as anybody wanting to know about economics a hundred years ago could draw on writers such as Alfred Marshall, Adam Smith, and David Ricardo, management theory already has its founding fathers—among them, Alfred Sloan and Peter Drucker. Management theory has also generated debates on such momentous subjects as globalization, the nature of work, and the changing structure of companies. Despite its adolescent excesses, the discipline has generated ideas that work. Japanese manufacturers trounced American ones in the 1980s because they embraced "quality."

Dig into virtually any area of management theory and you will find, eventually, a coherent position of sorts. The problem is that in order to extract that nugget you have to dig through an enormous amount of waffle. This book is an attempt to extract those nuggets.

Needless to say, it would have been much easier (and often far more pleasurable) to have trashed the industry. There is a wealth of material for anybody hoping to produce a "hatchet job." What is actually needed, however, is a "scalpel job," which is what we attempt to do in *The Witch Doctors:* we try to separate the good (or, at any rate, the influential) from the bad and the irrelevant—and to look at its effect on companies and society around the world. By definition, this has been an exclusive rather than an inclusive task. If ideas or thinkers fail the test completely, we have usually left them out, rather than wasting ink on debunking them.

We begin by looking at the life cycle and significance of one of the most influential fads: reengineering (Chapter 1). We then turn to the enormous industry that produces and sells management theory (Chapter 2) and two of its notable gurus: Peter Drucker (Chapter 3) and Tom Peters (Chapter 4). Drucker is the father of modern management and a natural introduction to most of the big debates of our time; Peters has been the most influential guru of the past two decades, not just because of what he has said but also because of the way that he has said it.

It is also important to look at the way that traditional corporate structures have collapsed over the past decade (Chapter 5), as well as the contortions taking place within companies as a result: the difficulties of trying to combine knowledge, learning, and innovation (Chapter 6), and the conflict between "vision" and other forms of strategy (Chapter 7). The question is: Are all these ideas, many of them imposed by bosses, actually putting increasing pressure on the boardroom and making leadership ever more difficult? Above all, what are companies for, and are they responsible to their shareholders alone or to a wider group of stakeholders (Chapter 8)? This section closes with a look at how all these corporate gyrations are changing the world of work and the lives of ordinary people (Chapter 9).

Another growing concern is globalization and the extent to which geography determines what companies do and how they do it (Chapter 10). Management theory itself is now a global industry. Lean production, an idea invented in America but developed in Japan, has changed the way that factories around the world operate; Japanese companies are struggling to learn from the West—but do they still have something to teach the rest of the world (Chapter 11)? On management's new frontier, the developing countries of Asia, the Chinese are pioneering a new sort of organization (Chapter 12), but Western management ideas are still in great demand. Will a new hybrid emerge just as it once did in Japan?

One area where management theory is making fast—and often frightening—headway is the public sector (Chapter 13). Doctors now have to decide whether treating sick people is one of their "core competencies," teachers issue mission statements, and generals talk about war being "the ultimate benchmarking exercise." Another area is the wilder (but extremely profitable) realm of management, where the discipline mixes with self-help, futurology, and downright quackery (Chapter 14).

We have conducted our audit with two groups of readers in mind. The first is the huge number of people who already buy business books, but who find them confusing and faddish—and usually never finish them. More and more people are assuming some sort of managerial responsibility; and managers are more and more frightened of losing their jobs. These people need to know about management—and not just American management. The case studies we use stretch from Stockholm to Shanghai and Seoul. The second group consists of "normal" readers who are only just becoming aware of management theory. This category should encompass virtually every intelligent American, but it could include a government worker in Atlanta who wants to know why his wife has been reengineered out of her job at Coca-Cola (and wonders if he will soon be reengineered out of his job too); a sociology professor at Cornell curious to inspect a wealthy neighboring discipline; or a political activist who wants to know why Bill Clinton and Newt Gingrich keep on mentioning Peter Drucker.

Our aim has been to challenge the specialist readers without confusing the generalists. If any piece of jargon has somehow slipped through our net, we apologize. Time and again, confronted by a theory or a passage in a book, we have returned to three questions: Is it intelligible? Does it add more than mere common sense? Is it relevant? In short, we have tried to judge the gurus on the same terms that the foremost of them—such as Peter Drucker and Michael Porter—have themselves insisted that they wish their theories to be judged: as a serious "intellectual" discipline.

## PART ONE

# HOW IT WORKS

# CHAPTER 1

THE FAD IN PROGRESS: REENGINEERING

THERE IS SOMETHING HEARTENING about the sight of people practicing what they preach and thriving on it: astrologers making millions on lotteries or marriage-guidance counselors wallowing in uxoriousness. So when Michael Treacy, an independent consultant with strong links to CSC Index, an ambitious young consultancy, and Fred Wiersema, a management consultant at the same firm, published a book called *The Discipline of Market Leaders,* in early 1995, it seemed entirely appropriate that, despite indifferent reviews, the book became a market leader in its own right. It stayed on the *New York Times* best-seller list for 15 weeks, climbing as high as number five and selling 250,000 copies.

The success story lasted only until the August 7 edition of *Business Week,* which published a long article alleging that the two consultants, working in conjunction with CSC Index, had used tactics more commonly associated with the grubbier parts of the music industry to get their book into the charts. With *The Discipline of Market Leaders,* shadowy people connected with the consultancy spent $250,000 buying some 10,000 copies of the book in small quantities at bookshops all around the country, paying special attention to those thought to be followed by *The*

*New York Times.* The purchases, according to *Business Week,* were often not made in CSC Index's name or in the names of the two authors; instead, other employees and third parties bought the books and were then reimbursed. Another 40,000 copies that were bought by CSC Index clients were also funneled through hundreds of small bookshops. A database marketing company called Paragon, which bought 10,000 copies of the book (for which it was fully reimbursed by CSC Index), had to store copies in a tractor-trailer parked outside its office. It has long been common for consultancies to buy large quantities of books written by their employees to distribute to their clients and prospective clients as freebies, or just to decorate the office. At about the same time, Gemini Consulting was buying 5,000 copies of *Transforming the Organization* (1995), a book written by two of its own men, Francis Gouillart and James Kelly. However, these purchases are normally done in the open, so that *The New York Times* can take account of such corporate largesse.

Treacy and Wiersema denied taking part in any such scheme, as did CSC Index. But the bad publicity undoubtedly damaged the company. Although at first sight there is little to be gained from spending $250,000 buying one's own book in the most expensive way possible, there are considerable spin-offs from getting a book into the *New York Times* best-seller lists. It increases the value of the book's overseas rights and also of the likely advances on any future books. It also makes the authors a more valuable commodity on the speaker circuit (Treacy was charging $30,000 for a talk when the scandal broke). And the aura of success itself increases sales: people who had earlier dismissed *Discipline of Market Leaders* as trite decided that there must be something in it to justify the fuss. However, the chief potential gainer had been CSC Index, which shared the copyright to the ideas behind the *Market Leaders* with the authors and was just beginning to introduce the theories to its customers. It stood to gain tens of millions of dollars in consulting fees.

*Business Week's* article had a crushing effect. *The New York Times* adjusted its best-seller list. Other newspapers and magazines picked up the story (which might have grown still bigger had Disney not decided to bid for ABC/Capital Cities on the following Monday, monopolizing American business pages for most of the next week). One conference organizer who had booked the authors to speak complained about having to deal with angry telephone calls from participants. *Business Week* also alleged that CSC Index had used similar tactics to buy 7,500 copies of another book published about the same time, called *Reengineering Management* (1995). This time, the author was James Champy, one of the consultancy's founders. To complete a bad month, CSC Index also lost the second phase of a lucrative consulting project at *The New York Times*.

## Reversing the Industrial Revolution

The scandal over *Market Leaders* is actually a chapter— some would call it a comeuppance—in a much bigger story also involving CSC Index and Champy: a story about reengineering. (Champy left Index for Perot Systems in 1996, but was the firm's presiding genius throughout reengineering's glory days.) Reengineering is arguably the most ambitious management theory of recent years. Indeed, the movement's founders, James Champy and Michael Hammer, a mathematician-turned-computer-scientist who now promotes reengineering full-time, insist that reengineering is the most radical change in business thinking since the industrial revolution. Reengineering teaches that managers need to tear up their old blueprints and completely redesign their organizations if they are to stand any chance of surviving. Redesign in the light of reason rather than according to worn-out traditions, say the gurus, and you will be assured of radical improvements in productivity. Asked what he does for a living, Hammer, who combines a mathematician's logic with a proselyte's enthusiasm, replies, quite simply, "Reversing the industrial revolution."[1]

Reengineering was the first great management fad of the 1990s, helping millions of people to lose their jobs, and millions more to work in entirely new ways. Having reorganized corporate America, the discipline's apostles are now carrying its message to the public sector and around the world. By 1996, several surveys showed that more European firms than American ones were engaged in reengineering. The Japanese edition of Champy and Hammer's book, *Reengineering the Corporation*, sold 250,000 copies in its first three months.

Why was reengineering so wildly popular? To answer this question, a little scene-setting is necessary. By the mid-1990s, most managers found themselves in a quandary. They felt let down by two ideas in which they had invested near-blind devotion. The first was technology—particularly the personal computer, a machine that now sat accusingly on every manager's desk. Computers were becoming faster, cheaper, and much easier to use. However, there was a hitch, officially discovered by economists, but long suspected by every corporate treasurer who could count: computers did not make people any more productive. Despite enormous investment in information technology throughout the 1980s, most of the available numbers showed that companies had gained very little from it.

The other treacherous friend was the fad that had preceded reengineering: total-quality management, or TQM. By the time reengineering was preparing to take the world of management by storm, it had become an act of managerial heresy to argue against "quality." To simplify a little, TQM meant getting products and services right the first time, rather than waiting for them to be finished before checking them for errors. As every American manager knows, it was through such "devilish" techniques that Japanese companies, such as Toyota, had built more reliable cars and "stolen" the American market from Detroit. By the early 1990s, Western manufacturers were imitating those methods and beginning to see improvements in customer satisfaction and employee morale.

But "information technology" and "quality" shared a fundamental problem: they seemed to involve doing much the same things as before, with much the same workforce—only doing them with computers and doing them more painstakingly. The machine had not been redesigned; rather, it had simply had a few new gadgets added to it. TQM was a particularly tricky business. Joseph Juran, a quality expert, estimated in 1993 that only 50 of the top 500 American companies had attained "world-class quality." And since virtually everybody was doing it, quality had become more of a basic necessity than a competitive advantage. In such an environment, managers began to sense that continued gains in productivity, market share, and profitability were going to have to come from somewhere else. As it happened, a new management theory had begun to make the rounds of the business schools and consultancies just as this uneasy realization was announcing itself in corporate boardrooms across the United States. The theory had the added virtue of combining technology and quality into one package.

## Disposing of Adam Smith

"Business-process reengineering," as the name implies, is an attempt to break an organization down into its component parts and then put some of them together again to create a new machine. That means asking what the machine is expected to do in the first place—in the jargon, what the "processes" are supposed to achieve. In a typical reengineering project, 10 to 20 young consultants descend on a company, draw up maps of process flows, propose ripping up old accounting procedures, and suggest that people from different departments work together in one team (with a good portion of them losing their jobs). Rather than focusing on what comes out of the machine at the end, a reengineered company's edge comes from its efficiency. Process is more important than product; indeed, good products should naturally follow good processes.

This concept slaughters a number of sacred cows. The first is Adam Smith. In *The Wealth of Nations* (1776), Smith advocated a system of production based on employee specialization and economies of scale. His famous observation is that a group of pin makers who each concentrate on a particular part of the task can make more pins than a group in which each worker makes the whole pin. Industrialists such as Henry Ford and Alfred Sloan perfected this system, building assembly lines and splitting workers into different departmental fiefs, such as marketing and design. Mass production always had its downside, leaving many workers bored and alienated; more recently, its whole *raison d'être* has been questioned by the reengineers, as demand has become more uneven and machines have taken over more and more menial jobs.

One of reengineering's discoveries is that, as a result of information technology, it is often more efficient to turn back to the system Adam Smith rejected. Why should it take six weeks to process a credit form, with each specialist filling out a single line before passing it on to a colleague, when a single clerk, armed with a computer to deal with any specialized problems, could get the job done in just 90 minutes? What matters, argue the reengineers, is the customer: and the customer does not care which departmental manager is supposed to sign a form: all he or she wants is a quick answer and somebody who can be held responsible for it.[2]

Reengineers blame a lot of corporate inertia on the great "functional chimneys," such as marketing departments or information technology departments, that dominate most big organizations. Reengineering consultants have repeatedly discovered that most of the time wasted on any particular process is frittered away during the transfer of information and components from one department to another. Reengineering prefers to group people from different functions into teams dedicated to carrying out processes that span several functions. Thus, people from marketing, design, and research can be gathered together in a team devoted to the "new product development process."

Such a reorganization also gets rid of reengineering's favorite scapegoat, the middle manager. If a firm uses information technology correctly, there is no need to have a connecting layer of people between the powers on high and the shop floor. Information should just zip around "horizontally" rather than filter down "vertically."

## "Don't Automate, Obliterate"

Put in its own strident, devastating tones, reengineering can sound a little mad. However, it is easy to see why even perfectly sane managers have latched onto the idea. At a time when business seems to be getting more complicated and the answers more uncertain, when other gurus order managers to surrender to their circumstances by learning how to live in "an age of unreason" or to "thrive on chaos," reengineering promises certainty and control. Here, at last, is a clear-cut, no-nonsense guide to rebuilding their business and beating the competition. It is also engagingly modern, arguably the first management theory to use computers as a starting point, rather than just a neat addition. And it has been marketed with rare panache.

Reengineering was the product of two institutions that are just around the corner from each other in Cambridge, Massachusetts, and that feed off each other's ideas and personnel: CSC Index, the consulting arm of the giant Computer Sciences Corporation, and the Massachusetts Institute of Technology's Sloan School of Management. Both institutions were obsessed with the implications of the computer revolution for the nature of work and the structure of organizations. The term "reengineering" was first coined in the mid-1980s when a group of young MIT-trained consultants at the Index Group, one of CSC Index's antecedents, masterminded a major restructuring of their own "business processes." Thomas Gerrity, who then held jobs with both Index and MIT and is now Dean of Wharton Business School, recalls dismissing the term as far too "techie" to catch on.[3] But it turned out that "techie" was just what American business wanted.

The first place most businessmen heard about reengineering was in an article by Michael Hammer in the July/August 1990 edition of the *Harvard Business Review,* appropriately entitled "Reengineering Work: Don't Automate, Obliterate." Three years later, Champy and Hammer laid out the ideas more carefully in *Reengineering the Corporation.* With sales of almost 2 million copies in 17 languages, it was one of the biggest-selling business books since *In Search of Excellence.* The business press latched onto the word with extraordinary enthusiasm: the number of articles using "reengineering" in the title increased from 10 in 1990 to well over 800 in 1994.[4]

Soon every consultancy worth its flipchart was marketing some form of reengineering. Arthur D. Little, a management consultancy, called it "high-performance business"; Gemini used the word "transformation." And the business rolled in. A survey in 1994 by Price Waterhouse, an accountancy and consultancy firm, found that 78 percent of Fortune 500 companies and 68 percent of British firms were engaged in some form of reengineering. A survey by CSC Index at the same time produced nearly identical figures, but it also found that the average number of reengineering projects for each company was 3.3 in America and 3.8 in Europe. Nor was the discipline limited to corporate giants. A broader survey of 2,200 American companies by the Institute of Management Accountants' Controllers Council, in October 1994, found that 60 percent were engaged in some kind of reengineering.

Reengineering has also been spreading out of its manufacturing heartland and into service businesses, utilities, and the public sector. One of the boldest apostles of the discipline in America is William Bratton, head of the New York Police Department from 1994 to early 1996. The discipline has spread geographically as well. In Japan, where it spread quickly, it was pioneered by the local subsidiaries of American companies, such as IBM Japan. In December 1993, a lecture session by a

Japanese consultancy, entitled "Proposal for Reengineering—Japanese Style," drew such a large crowd that the consultancy put on two more lectures. In early 1994, the *Yomiuri Shinbun,* a popular newspaper, cited "reengineering" alongside "China" as the two key words for that year.

### Worse than the Disease?

Inevitably, the discipline that made such a fuss about obliteration became associated with one word: downsizing. A survey of chief financial officers at 80 big American companies, in May 1995, found that the main reason for wanting to do reengineering was cost cutting (29 percent), followed closely by "someone important said we should do it" (26 percent). Only a tenth did it primarily to improve service or quality.[5] Other surveys had fairly similar results.

In 1994, corporate America saw its profits rise 11 percent, yet it also eliminated 516,069 jobs and spent $10 billion on restructuring charges.[6] The most dramatic slimmers included some of the biggest money machines: Mobil, Procter & Gamble, American Home Products, and Sara Lee. Edwin Artzt, P&G's chief, said that his firm was cutting 13,000 out of its 106,000 workers to stay competitive—and he scolded the public for thinking that corporate restructuring was a sign of trouble: "That is definitely not our situation."[7] The stock market was certainly no longer skeptical: when Mobil announced its plan to shed a tenth of its workforce in early 1995, the oil company's shares jumped to a 52-week high. The same association of restructuring with corporate virility seemed to be developing in other countries. Britain's stock market reached a new peak in September 1995, in the same week as a blitz of job-loss announcements that affected 9,000 people at Glaxo-Wellcome, a pharmaceutical giant. In France, where the downsizing cult arrived later, shares in Moulinex jumped by 21 percent the day after the appliance maker disclosed plans to cut 2,600 jobs (a fifth of its workforce) in June 1996.

To what extent was reengineering responsible for this bloodletting? Many slimmers cited the discipline directly. That was the case at GTE, an American telephone company. In early 1994, it gave details of a reengineering program that would cut its customer-service centers from 171 to 11, and its revenue-collection centers from 5 to 1. In all, 17,000 jobs would go in the next three years. Some $1.2 billion would be invested in new sorts of technology, but the potential cost savings would be about $1 billion per year.[8] Reengineering had become the predominant management fad of the time and was setting the agenda. Even those companies that were shedding weight in their own way were still thinking about their rivals who were reengineering. Like a pair of omnipresent television-aerobic instructors, Hammer and Champy did not actually need to be at a manager's shoulder to make him or her feel overweight.

The question of responsibility is actually a moot one because, by late 1994, there were doubts in America about just how good for the patient all this slimming was proving to be. True, it had helped make America more competitive, at least for a while. America's unit-labor costs were falling whereas those of Japan and Germany had risen. Unfortunately, by 1994, there were also signs that it had gone too far, with people beginning to talk about "the anorexic corporation." One study, by the American Management Association, showed that two-thirds of firms cutting back in any given year did so again the next year; and a quarter of those surveyed had done so in three or more of the past five years. Another study, by Mitchell & Co., a Massachusetts-based consultancy, found that the shares of downsizing companies outperformed the stock market for six months after a downsizing was announced. Three years later, they lagged.

The first response of any reengineer to such statistics is, of course, a claim that there is a sizable difference between downsizing and reengineering proper. However, the available evidence on reengineering proper is only slightly better than that on downsizing. True, there are examples of confirmed reengineered successes, notably Bell Atlantic, Federal Express, Ford, and Hallmark Cards. There is also plenty of hype from consultants about how much their clients have increased their productivity. From studies of its clients, CSC Index concluded that fundamentally changing a business process produced "an average improvement of 48 percent in costs, 80 percent in time and 60 percent in defects." (In a typical piece of reengineering hyperbole, the consultancy went on to say: "The results are startling—but then reengineering is defined in part by the outrageousness of its goals and the ambition of its scope.")[9]

However, as soon as surveys widen to include other people's clients, such results evaporate. A survey by Arthur D. Little, in the summer of 1994, found that only 16 percent of managers were fully satisfied, and 68 percent were encountering unexpected problems. By late 1994, even Michael Hammer and James Champy were admitting that many attempts at reengineering were falling short of their goals.

## The Quality-Welcome Process

How successful is reengineering? The answer, unsurprisingly, is that the discipline is good at some things and not so good at others. Consider a case study of a company regarded as one of reengineering's successes.

In September 1992, Britain's Lloyds Bank embarked on a massive reengineering effort. By mid-1995, it had changed operations that accounted for two-thirds of the costs at each of its branches and involved nearly all its 29,000 employees.[10] In many ways, Lloyds was a model reengineer (and not just because it was advised by CSC Index, then Champy's consultancy). Although cost cutting was a motive, the bank turned to reengineering principally because of worries about the quality of its service—particularly in comparison with building societies (Britain's equivalent of savings and loan companies). Another related problem was organization—or rather, the lack of it. During the 1980s, countless new services had been bolted on to local branches, simply by adding more staff. "We saw the branch system as an enormous bucket into which things could just be dropped," Gordon Pell, the general manager of Lloyds retail operations, recalls.

As in other industries, reengineering proved a good way to remodel the back office of Lloyds so as to make better use of technology. Under the bank's old system, staff were slotted into narrow jobs in an administrative hierarchy. Countless people and bits of paper were involved in jobs that, from the customer's point of view, were part of the same process. Under the old system of opening an account, for instance, a piece of paper could spend a month being shuffled from desk to desk as different staff ordered bank cards, checked credit details, and so on. Reengineered so that one person was responsible for a largely paperless (though absurdly named) "quality-welcome" process, it took well under a week.

Five other processes were also broken down and reassembled in a mock "laboratory" before being spread across the network in a series of "waves." In some cases, the processes look a little contrived. Before reengineering, customers moving their account to another bank simply told Lloyds where their new account was; under the "customer retention process," they are interviewed and sometimes persuaded to stay. This looks like no more than common-sense marketing, but Lloyds bosses insist that it was only thanks to reengineering that they thought of it.

All the processes are monitored closely (once again, using technology), as Kate Pepper, a young assistant at Lloyds's branch in London's Regent Street, can attest. Pepper used to send out forms for opening an account the day after she met a customer; under the reorganization, she sent them out immediately and thereby increased the branch's computer-generated score for this process from 45 percent to 90 percent. But part of the change was to have her performance closely monitored by "mystery shoppers"—spies sent by Lloyds. And an increasing proportion of Pepper's salary and those of her colleagues is now tied to their performance.

Did the new approach work? The bank's most obvious gain from reengineering has been financial. Lloyds will not give any exact figures, but it claims that the project has comfortably cleared the bank's 12 percent return on capital. Many of the changes introduced by reengineering paid for themselves rapidly. For one thing, the number of faulty checkbook orders fell by 30 percent—enough to pay for all the computers bought to monitor that activity.

For all the timely checkbooks, however, there is much less evidence that Lloyds has met its primary goal of making customers happy. Britain's banks, including Lloyds, were even less loved at the beginning of 1996 than they had been at the start of the decade. One reason for this is that customers increasingly encountered grumpy staff demoralized by downsizing. All the British banks struggled to cut costs and to automate jobs previously done by humans. In so doing, they shed some 80,000 people between 1989 and 1995 and talked of laying off another 70,000.

Did reengineering contribute to this unease? Lloyds avoided using the word "reengineering" ("Too many people associated it with obliteration," admitted one insider), opting instead for a "service quality improvement program," or SQIP. Nevertheless, the pain and worry were obvious. In Regent Street alone, SQIP, combined with other changes, saw the staff decline from 42 to

18 by mid-1995. The total number of branches had been cut from 2,100 to 1,800. As elsewhere, reengineering was particularly tough on middle managers: 41 out of 80 area-manager jobs disappeared.

When will it stop? Reengineering had helped Lloyds reduce the ratio of operating costs to revenues from 64.3 percent in 1990 to 63.6 percent in 1994, but many financial firms have ratios below 60 percent. Just as these ratios have been declining, so has customer satisfaction. In America, some banks are charging people for using human tellers rather than ATMs; in Britain, telephone banking such as First Direct is drawing people away from banks that customers already find no more friendly than a voice at the other end of the telephone. The staff at Lloyds, too, plainly think that they need a breather. What they may not realize is that the next reengineering wave will have to be more fundamental and might even question whether Lloyds needs a branch network at all.

## The Backlash Begins

Although it is stuck in an industry that seems to need fewer and fewer people, Lloyds is, in reengineering terms, not too blood-spattered. In January 1994, NYNEX, the telephone company for New York City and for a good piece of the northeast, embarked on a $3 billion program that got rid of 16,800 people, or 22 percent of its workforce.[11] As with Lloyds, any cost-benefit analysis would show that the exercise paid for itself several times over. As a cover story in *Business Week* in 1995 made clear, however, the changes badly damaged morale. "The officers are in charge of their own fates," said a NYNEX worker. "We're not involved. We're affected." The plan's architect, Robert Thrasher—now known as "Thrasher the slasher"—had to turn off his answering machine at home because he received so many abusive messages. At another telephone company, GTE, employees have been so enraged by cutbacks that they have run radio advertisements detailing its alleged declining service.

It was against this background that many management thinkers started damning reengineering. Calling it "a polite word for downsizing," Charles Handy declared that "blowing organizations apart is not conducive to a state of commitment and euphoria. . . . The trouble with reengineering when it is done badly—which it mostly is—is that it leaves people shattered, even the people left behind."[12] The most influential book of the mid-1990s, *Competing for the Future* (1994) by Gary Hamel and C. K. Prahalad, argues that reengineering has "more to do with shoring up today's businesses than creating tomorrow's industries. . . . Any company that succeeds at restructuring and reengineering, but fails to create the markets of the future, will find itself on a treadmill, trying to keep one step ahead of the steadily declining margins and profits of yesterday's businesses."[13]

The reengineers have tried to fight such criticism. One of their tactics has been to cite statistics in their favor. CSC Index still firmly believes that reengineering itself did not lead to huge job losses. According to a CSC Index study, each reengineering initiative wiped out an average of only 282 jobs (or 22 percent of the total involved in each reorganization). In Europe, the figure was 1,001. In many cases, the jobs were shed voluntarily or the people were moved to other parts of the organization. By the time all these moves are averaged out, CSC Index puts the figure for layoffs at just 336 employees per firm in America and 760 in Europe.

However, a more common defense has been that people were not reengineering properly. Some people were just slashing their workforces and calling it reengineering; others were trying to go by the book but failing to read past the first few chapters. Champy claimed that only about 1 in 10 companies undergoing reengineering was doing it right. "Much of the criticism is based on a misconception of what reengineering really is," Michael Hammer wrote in *The Economist* on November 5, 1994, "and much of the rest reflects a limited assessment of its significance."

Apologias aside, there do appear to be real problems with reengineering. Ironically, one of the biggest is that the discipline is far too close to the type of stopwatch management that the reengineers pretended to despise. Management pioneers such as Frederick Taylor and Henry Ford were fascinated by processes; they were also lousy practitioners of the softer, human side of management. Reengineering—a little like Taylorism—would work well if people were all unthinking automatons, without hearts or souls. However, simply telling a marketing man that he is no longer a member of the marketing department but part of the "product-development process" does not stop him from thinking like a marketing man.

Reengineering's obsession with process rather than product also raises some questions. Trying to shift a firm's competitive advantage from what it makes to how it does so might be a sensible strategy in a mature, stable business—manufacturing milk cartons, for instance. If a firm in a faster-changing industry is making the wrong product, however, then no amount of downsizing is going to help it. IBM's mainframe division may be a case in point. One of the first victims of many reengineering efforts is the strategy department; but without some degree of strategic thought or vision, reengineering always risks building a superb machine whose only purpose is to churn out antiquated products.

If strategy has made something of a comeback, so too has another favorite whipping boy of reengineering, the middle manager. Reengineers see middle managers as barriers to horizontal organizations. Yet they can also be the source of a company's culture, and the repositories of valuable information. Computers, it emerges, are often less successful at connecting the strategists in the boardroom to operational staff in the field than managers with long experience with the organization. In many cases, firms that have downsized and produced big cost savings in the first year have seen those savings evaporate as they have had to train people to do jobs that many middle managers knew by heart.

A study of American companies published in late 1995 by the *California Management Review* found that downsizing had an adverse effect on the innovation record of companies.[14] That does not necessarily mean that reengineering stops research and development departments from producing ideas; the more likely problem is that reengineering destroys the informal network of contacts that allow a product to gain acceptance within an organization. In some cases where jobs have been contracted out, the chief beneficiaries are those same middle managers, now hired as contract labor. Indeed, ripping out middle management has made it hard to get long-term commitment from workers: it is very difficult to devise a career structure if all the middle rungs of the ladder are missing.

Reengineered people feel that their employers have broken the implicit moral contract between bosses and workers—

"We'll work as hard as we can for you just so long as you only fire us if it is absolutely necessary." Xerox saw its reputation for paternalism destroyed when it fired about 1 in 10 of its workers between the beginning of 1994 and the middle of 1995, a period when it was making a profit. At about the same time, one boss at AT&T, an enthusiastic reengineer, confessed to *The Economist* that trust levels at his firm had plummeted: "In the past we said to employees, 'Do as you're told and you have a job for life.' Then we betrayed them." Any warm feeling AT&T's staff felt for Ma Bell would have disappeared in January 1996 when it laid off another 40,000 people (and were hardly restored when it later reduced the figure to 28,000). British Telecom cut its workforce from 232,000 in 1990 to 148,000 in 1995, with devastating effect on morale. Internal surveys in 1995 suggested that only one-fifth of the firm's employees thought that managers could be relied on to do what they said.

Employees in companies that are undergoing reengineering often spend more time discussing potential job losses than they do thinking about their work. In March 1995, CoreStates Financial Corporation of Philadelphia announced it would fire 890 people—or 6 percent of its staff. "Everybody is thinking 'What is my future, what am I doing here?'" one employee told *The Wall Street Journal*. "For the last month, people have been talking more than 50 percent of the time. It's watercooler talk all day long." At good-bye parties at Westinghouse, people joked that "the winners get to leave; the losers get to stay." A survey by the American Management Association, in mid-1995, found that more than half the respondents felt more overwhelmed by work than they had in 1993, before the recovery really started. A similar poll in Britain found that 70 percent of workers felt less secure than they had two years before; 44 percent felt pressure to work late, and 31 percent said people were afraid to take time off if they were sick.[15]

In other words, reengineering is less than it was originally cracked up to be. But that does not mean it is useless. Reengineering tends to work particularly well in logistics and order fulfillment; it forces a company to concentrate on speed and service—the two factors that most interest its customers. Thus, through reengineering, the manufacturing and distribution side of EMI Records in North America managed to increase the number of compact discs (CDs) being delivered on time to retailers during their peak selling period from 90 percent to over 99 percent. (The peak selling time matters because, as in the case of *The Discipline of Market Leaders,* many people will only buy a record, or book, when it is a hit.) EMI also claimed that the annual cost of transporting CD units fell by 30 percent, and that labor productivity at the distribution sites increased by 70 percent.

Occasionally, reengineering can galvanize an entire industry. Thanks to the discipline, America's freight-carrying railway companies recast themselves as the logistical arm of their customers. Rather than just ferrying boxes from one point to another, the railroads keep their customers informed about the whereabouts of each box with the aid of computers. Some also link up with their old foes, the truckers, to provide a more seamless service. Companies such as Chrysler hire railway companies to take their cars all the way from the factory gate to the dealer's doors.

Even when critics consider reengineering at its most bloody, they tend to forget what the alternatives are. British Telecom, AT&T, and NYNEX may be bruised, but they are surely in a better state than France Télécom or NTT. It was easy to chuckle at Lou Gerstner, IBM's chairman, for declaring that "we enter 1995 with the bulk of our right sizing behind us" (which was his way of describing 1994's 35,000 redundancies at IBM); but IBM still looked in better shape than, say, France's Bull. And Big Blue also illustrates another point that critics of reengineering may have exaggerated. The computer maker is often included alongside firms such as General Motors and Digital in lists of firms that have downsized and still not solved their problems. That is true. But the real reason that they got into trouble in the first place had nothing to do with reengineering.

### Reengineering Reengineered

What is needed is refinement of reengineering, not complete abandonment of it. By 1996, there was talk of taking a more "holistic" or "organic" approach to the discipline, involving managers and even workers. Such compromises do not come easily to an all-encompassing discipline. However, an example of a holistic version of reengineering can be seen at Corning, a technology company headquartered in the small town of the same name in the foothills of the Appalachian mountain chain, in upstate New York.[16]

Corning is the quintessential paternalist company (though the term "paternalist" is frowned on by Corningites as being too politically incorrect). The company chairman from 1983 to 1996 was James Houghton, the great-grandson of the founder; his brother, Amory, preceded him as chairman and now represents the surrounding area in Congress. (If you get a haircut on Main Street, you stare up at a poster of "Amo's" smiling face.) Half the town's 12,000 adult inhabitants work for Corning. Whole families have worked for the company for decades and cannot remember a time when Corning did not pay their salaries. Everything about Corning ("the biggest company in the smallest town in the United States," according to Jamie Houghton) proclaims its commitment to good corporate citizenship, from its splendid new headquarters, deliberately built low so as not to overshadow the town, to the leaflets in the lavatories warning of the dangers of herpes, smoking, and bulimia nervosa.

Houghton refused categorically to consider reengineering if it meant destroying his hometown. But by the end of 1993, senior managers, some of whom also sat on the boards of companies that were undergoing reengineering, felt that Corning could not ignore the new management theory any longer. The company's share price had fallen by one fourth. The ostensible problem was Dow Corning, a separate joint venture with The Dow Chemical Company, a producer of silicone breast-implants. This company was being sued by thousands of women for alleged damage from implants. But Corning's underlying problems were twofold: (1) organizationally, it was a mess—it had some 150 different businesses, each with its own legal status; and (2) those businesses—fiber optics, medical services, catalytic converters, and so on—were not making money.

In the past, Corning, which is notorious for its enthusiasm for management theories, had had surprisingly little difficulty in combining its zest for profits with its commitment to paternalism. The company had avoided laying off local workers by transforming itself from a glassmaker (it once made the glass for Edison's electric lights) into a technology company. Recent fashions such as total-quality management, high-performance workplaces, and employee empowerment had essentially meant

being nice to workers. Reengineering had a very different reputation. The challenge for Corning's management was to see
whether they could reengineer without destroying their small
town's economy and breaking a century-long commitment to
enlightened industrial relations.

By coming to the discipline fairly late, Corning had a huge
amount of experience to draw on—including the numerous
examples of reengineering efforts that even Michael Hammer
admits have failed. It thus took a different approach. One of
the biggest causes of failure in other companies has been the
lack of consistent involvement from the top; Corning made
sure that senior managers sponsored each group of reengineers and that the company's president, Roger Ackerman
(who became chairman when Jamie Houghton retired in early
1996), took personal responsibility for each program. Reengineering has often failed because companies are keener on
slaking the stock market's thirst for quick fixes, usually by
firing workers, than on introducing structural changes. To
Wall Street's chagrin, Corning refused, point blank, to an-
nounce any immediate redundancies.

Elsewhere, reengineering had been imposed by computer-
wielding consultants. At Corning, the consultants were told to
stay in the background. Indeed, rather than imposing reengineering on a hostile workforce, Corning got the workers to do
their own reengineering. In January 1994, it asked key employees, many of them from middle management (a group normally
despised by reengineers), to forsake their proper jobs for a few
months in order to redesign their company from top to bottom.
The company put a building at their disposal (known as the
"Donut U.," because it was next to a Dunkin' Donuts store), told
them to turn up in casual clothes (now policy throughout the
company), and divide themselves into teams to look at processes
such as "manufacturing" and "innovation."

Corning made sure that the reengineers had easy access to
senior management. It also put a huge amount of effort into
explaining to the workforce what was going on. Roger Ackerman held regular town meetings at which he and his colleagues
explained what was happening and why. (The meetings were
videotaped and distributed to those who could not attend.)
The company magazine ran frequent articles on the process.
Workers were encouraged to express their worries by e-mail—

anonymously, if they preferred—and they were offered "stress counseling."

The reengineers introduced a number of changes that are almost par for the course in reengineering, such as reorganizing its tangle of businesses (they found that 95 percent of sales came from only half of Corning's products). Reengineering cut the number of levels of managers between Houghton and the shop floor from seven to five, simplified decision making, and got rid of two senior vice presidents and their staffs. Though it is always difficult to put a figure on such things, the company calculated that reengineering could produce $50 million to $60 million in savings in 1996–97.

But the Corning reengineers also used their freedom to introduce two important modifications to the discipline. First, they made sure that reengineering applied in the boardroom just as much as on the factory floor. The bulk of the cuts in manpower came from management, and one of the biggest structural changes took place at the corporate headquarters: more power was handed over to the operating units. Second, the Corning reengineers made sure that change was evolutionary rather than revolutionary. Far from starting with Hammer and Champy's clean sheet of paper, the Corningites tried to build on what the company was already doing right.

Nobody at Corning pretends that reengineering has been free of friction. The word has been the subject of nervous, often angry, discussions in the town's churches and bars. When one of the authors jokingly asked what would happen if he went into one of the local bars posing as a management consultant, he was flatly told not to entertain the thought. The two local newspapers have repeatedly hinted that the company has a secret plan to reengineer the community out of existence. The local union sees reengineering hanging over the valley like a skull and crossbones. An in-house survey concluded that 33 percent of the firm's workers were suffering from stress, and only 12 percent of those were coping with it.

Still, by mid-1995, when we visited the company, the overall feeling was one of relief. Corningites were acutely conscious that they had introduced the most feared management technique of their time without suffering the massive layoffs or bitter industrial disputes that often accompanied it. Yes, the company had been forced to get rid of some workers, but most of them had gone through early retirement. Profits were improving, meaning that the jobs of those who remained were much more secure. A century's worth of paternalism may have meant that Houghton and Ackerman started with a considerable advantage over other reengineers. All the same, they did seem to have found a middle way where words such as "obliteration" were not necessary.

Above all, they had rejected one of the fundamental parts of the reengineering creed that had first made the discipline so appealing to other managers: the idea that it is a mechanical, scientific process. Rather than regarding it as a retooling manual on how to reorganize a company, Houghton and Ackerman had looked on it more as a form of background music. Sometimes they listened to it, and sometimes they turned it off.

### The Desperation of Fading Market Leaders

The reinvention of reengineering as a discipline in places like Corning may not be enough to save reengineering as a business. After all, it is much easier to sell a medicine with a label saying "This will cure you, no matter what your complaint," than one with a label saying "This treatment may or may not succeed, depending on your circumstances. It is likely to be painful and could well have unintended side effects."

To make things worse, by 1995, the year when *The Discipline of Market Leaders* appeared, reengineering had become a commodity business. Big consultancy firms—particularly Andersen Consulting—had moved into the market. By mid-1995, CSC Index was only the fourth largest reengineering specialist in America.

It was against this background that CSC Index threw its weight behind both Champy's lackluster follow-up, *Reengineering Management* (1995), and the ill-fated *Discipline of Market Leaders.* But even with unusual marketing methods, neither book filled the gap. What was needed was a new fad, a new idea that could be branded, preached, sold, and spread all around the world. But then, with the management theory industry, that is always the case.

# CHAPTER 2

## THE MANAGEMENT THEORY INDUSTRY

ANYONE WHO MEETS the dean of the Wharton School of Business at the University of Pennsylvania and is expecting an unworldly academic who lives for nothing but ideas is in for a surprise. Thomas Gerrity is as smooth as they come, immaculately tailored and perfectly coiffed. He litters his conversation not with scholarly references but with business buzzwords, even referring to his university's president as "the CEO."

Gerrity's business patois is not an affectation. He is one of a new breed of deans: businessmen who have been roped back into academia in order to force business schools to practice what they preach. In his previous life, Gerrity was s of CSC Index, the consultancy that invented reengineering (see Chapter 1). As dean of Wharton, Gerrity has tried to put his own creed into practice, dividing both his students and his professors into specially varied teams. Each team includes at least two non-Americans; each faculty team includes professors from different academic disciplines. He has also changed the system for gaining tenure and awarding annual pay raises, in order to shift the emphasis from publishing academic articles (once the only road to success) to teaching and "leadership."

Many of these changes cost money, but with an annual budget of $135 million, Gerrity can afford to experiment. At Harvard Business School, where the annual budget is $195 million, a new dean, Kim Clark, is implementing similar reforms of his own, including a plan to put 500 case studies online. (Harvard is spending $11 million on upgrading its information technology.) Ever since *Business Week* started publishing a ranking of business schools, in November 1988, deans like Gerrity and Clark have had a license to tamper with the syllabus, throw up plush new buildings, and recruit expensive "star" professors. Thanks to Gerrity's reforms, Wharton, a financially minded school where the students have been known to throw dollar bills rather than caps into the air at the end of their graduation ceremony, has powered its way to the top of these tables.

As Gerrity's own career suggests, business schools, consultancies, and the ideas they trade in are really part of the same prosperous industry. Virtually everybody involved in management theory is making money out of it in one way or another. Indeed, the "management theory industry" seems immune to economic cycles: consultancies take on ever more staff as their clients employ fewer, and business schools become more ornate and numerous as the universities around them crumble.

This success, as we shall see, is largely a reflection of the seemingly endless demand for the industry's product. Management theory has always appealed to thousands of people who want to get ahead; now it has tapped into the market of the millions who are scared of being left behind. However, the success and scope of the industry have also had an effect on the sort of ideas it produces. With such huge vested interests, self-criticism is almost unheard of. And the industry's relentless appetite for more ideas to process, print, sell, and regurgitate has helped to make it a peculiarly faddish discipline where ideas are grabbed at, rather than matured. In other words, the industry has often driven the theory, rather than the other way around.

### The Breadth of the Industry

The management industry can be divided more or less into three parts. The most obvious of these is the management consulting business, which employs at least 100,000 people full-time around the world and has been growing more than twice as fast as the world economy for the past decade. In 1996, according to *Consultant's News,* an industry newsletter, it generated about $40 billion in revenues. The biggest firm, Andersen Consulting, brought in just under $3.1 billion in 1996—not counting another $1.3 billion of consultancy fees booked by its sister accountancy firm, Arthur Andersen.[1] Four other consultancy-accountancy combines collected over $1 billion in consultancy fees: Ernst & Young, Coopers & Lybrand, KPMG Peat Marwick, and Deloitte & Touche. However, the most profitable (and also the second biggest with revenues of $2.6 billion) is McKinsey: its revenue per consultant was $532,000—compared with Andersen's $71,000. The other big "strategic consultants"—Booz, Allen & Hamilton; Gemini Consulting; Mercer Management; the Boston Consulting Group; Arthur D. Little; Bain & Company—all booked over $200,000 per partner. A measure of the youthful vitality of the industry is that more than half of today's leading consulting firms did not exist five years ago.

Consultancies have replaced Oxbridge and the Ivy League as the nurseries of the powerful. Indeed, students from the latter jostle to get into the former, and with good reason. The list of companies headed by ex-McKinseyites stretches from America's IBM, Levi Strauss, and American Express to France's Bull and Britain's Asda. Even Ben & Jerry's, that symbol of countercultural commerce, was run for a while by a former consultant from the firm. In Britain, the consultancy's old-boy list includes the present head of the Confederation of British Industry (and both his immediate predecessors), the boss of the City of London's new securities regulator, and William Hague, the new leader of the Conservative Party (who also went to Insead Business School). Alumni are encouraged to go out of their way to keep in touch, with the result that McKinsey has an even broader reach than its office network, which stretches across 35 countries, would suggest.

The second part of the management industry is made up of the business schools. There are about 700 business schools in the United States alone. All these institutions are teeming with academics desperate to make their name as management theorists: the 1996 meeting of the American Academy of Management, the discipline's annual jamboree, attracted no fewer than 4,500 people. Journals such as *Harvard Business Review* and *California Management Review* have an influence and an

audience far beyond the universities that spawned them. The
GMAT examination, which practically every business school in
the world compels prospective students to sit for, is a huge business in its own right. Four times a year, 60,000 people sit down
in 700 centers in over 100 countries to try to prove themselves
worthy of studying management.

The MBA's popularity is easy to explain. The typical members of Harvard Business School's class of 1974 now look set to
retire with a net worth of $8 million, and the chances are good
that their successors will look down on them as paupers.[2] In
1997, the median starting pay for graduates from Wharton was
$130,000. Nowadays, the keenest recruiters, led by banks and
management consultancies, dazzle the students with offers of
bonuses of $30,000, interest-free loans, stock options, tuition
reimbursements, free cars, and moving allowances. Invitations
to a recent reunion of Stanford graduates from the early 1990s
included a request that attendees "chip in" for a small gift from
the grateful students to their alma mater; it was only after he
had booked his airline ticket that one graduate, who had fool-
ishly taken a low-paying job in the British civil service, realized
that the chipping in amounted to $1,000 a head.

Despite this bonanza for the best students from the best
schools, there are doubts about how much the average MBA
is worth. After all, for many students, the combined costs of
two years of tuition and forgone salary can easily come to
$100,000; and the proper way to measure the gain from a busi-
ness school education is not just to take the starting salary but
to compare it against what one would have earned without the
MBA. One academic who constructed an economic model of
the costs and benefits of going to business school, Ronald
Yeaple of Rochester Business School, found that in nearly all
cases it took several years for students to make a profit.[3] After
seven years, a Harvard Business School student could claim a
positive net value of nearly $150,000, but average students
from 5 of the top 20 schools were all sitting on losses.

The third and least well defined part of the management
industry is what might be called the guru business. There are
plenty of ways for individual management thinkers to make
money. The most obvious is by writing business books, which
have gone from being an exotic species selling in small numbers
in the mid-1970s to a mainstream cash cow today. About 2,000

business books appear each year in America, and the best of these can sell in the millions. Until the 1980s, business books were a fairly obscure specialty, selling in little more than academic numbers. All this changed with the publication of *In Search of Excellence* by Tom Peters and Robert Waterman, which sold a million copies in one year and turned both its authors into celebrities. At one point in 1983, the top three slots in the *New York Times* best-seller list were filled by business authors (who, incidentally, had all studied at Cornell University together): Tom Peters (*In Search of Excellence,* 1982), John Naisbitt (*Megatrends,* 1983), and Kenneth Blanchard (*The One Minute Manager,* 1983). Two years later, Lee Iacocca's autobiography became the best-selling business book of all time, and one of the best-selling hardbacks ever. From then on, every publisher worth his or her salt set out to discover, nurture, and promote talented business writers.

Nevertheless, for many management theorists, books are largely a form of advertising for even more profitable activities. Many of these involve speaking of one kind or another. Nowadays, no business conference is complete without at least one guru. Not only do such authors give the event an intellectual edge, but they will probably be the only speakers who do not try to turn their speech into a commercial for their own company. These presentations also give the audience a chance to catch up on the latest theories without having to plough through a book. The business speaking-circuit is expanding quickly. America's Conference Board alone now holds 100 events a year (double the number five years ago); that means it calls on at least 2,000 speakers a year.[4] In 1996, the biggest earner was probably Harvey MacKay, the boss of an envelope-manufacturing firm and a motivational guru best known for *Swim with the Sharks without Being Eaten Alive,* who charged $50,000 a speech—and gave about 50 of them a year. This put MacKay on the same level as Henry Kissinger and General Colin Powell. A clutch of other gurus, including the persistently popular Tom Peters, charged not much less. All-day seminars or workshops with individual companies can be even more remunerative.

Like the Hollywood studios, the gurus have discovered how to sell their ideas through a range of outlets, including diaries, audio- and videocassettes, and training camps. The Tom Peters Group, three training and communication companies headquartered in Palo Alto, California, produces videos, churns out a regular newsletter, and generally helps to stretch his brand. One of its more recent offerings is "The Tom Peters Business School in a Box," which comes complete with 42 "personal agenda cards," 14 "time cards," and two dice, one colored, one white. Significantly, perhaps, the "Business School" was the work of three of his employees and has only a foreword by Peters. Meanwhile, Peter Senge, a prophet of "the learning organization," seems to have introduced franchising: he has allowed a Taiwanese follower, Young Show-ing, to translate his books and popularize his ideas in the Chinese-speaking world.

### Overpaid and Over Here

These rough divisions—into consultancies, business schools, and gurus—imply that the management industry is much more structured and narrowly defined than it really is. Where, for instance, should one include "MBA-ware" sellers—software companies that make teach-yourself-management programs with names such as "Negotiator Pro" and "ManagePro"? Or more orthodox software makers that design their products specifically to help companies implement management fads? (The rapid rise of Germany's SAP can be attributed largely to its products for companies conducting reengineering exercises.) And what about companies that take groups of executives to the African bush or to the Scottish highlands so that they can hone their leadership skills? Or the firms that specialize in counseling outsourced workers? Or the growing numbers of management psychologists–psychometrists who draw up profiles of desirable recruits? Or the psychiatrists who, although trained to deal with suicidal teenagers, have found it more remunerative to "facilitate" team meetings and tell top executives how to cope with the pressures of life among the elite?

What makes the management industry even more complicated is that it is now a global entity. Not so long ago, anyone who wanted to understand management went to an American university, studied American gurus, argued about American corporations, and probably joined an American consultancy. The great debates in the subject—such as the one about the relative merits of scientific and humanistic management—were almost all conducted among Americans. But in the past two decades the rest of the world has started to catch up.

From Bradford to Barcelona to Berlin, the cities of Europe are now littered with business schools. A few—Insead, just outside Paris; the London Business School (LBS); and Switzerland's Institute for Management Development—deserve a place in America's first division. Britons alone spent about £50 million on MBA fees at 100 schools in 1994—and about half that figure on business books. Continental Europeans, particularly the French, remain a little more skeptical, but most of the leading American gurus have broken through. *In Search of Excellence* sold 100,000 copies in three years in France and did even better in Germany, Holland, Spain, and Sweden. This was quite an achievement given that *In Search of Excellence* barely mentioned Europe; in *Liberation Management,* published almost a decade later, the canny Peters devoted whole chapters to ASEA Brown Boveri (ABB), a Swiss-Swedish industrial giant, and Germany's medium-size companies. Nowadays, leading North American gurus such as Gary Hamel and Henry Mintzberg spend at least part of the year in Europe (at LBS and Insead, respectively).

And Europe is beginning to produce gurus of its own. There is as yet only one European guru who ranks in the first division by American standards: Britain's Charles Handy. However, a cluster of other names, including John Kay (head of the Oxford Business School), Sumantra Ghoshal (LBS), and Yves Doz (Insead), are knocking on the door. There are also several areas in which European gurus look as if they are ahead of their American counterparts, particularly the cultural side of managing multinationals. Any big firm in Europe becomes multinational very quickly. Geert Hofstede of the Netherlands' Institute of International Culture more or less invented cultural diversity as a management subject, pointing out that attitudes toward pay and hierarchy can vary enormously from country to country. Fons Trompenaars, also of the Netherlands, is one of the leading writers on corporate culture.

Indeed, in many "soft" management areas, Europeans have a much stronger tradition than the more scientifically based Americans. Many gurus are now reexamining work done on human motivation at Britain's Tavistock Institute back in the 1950s by a team of psychologists led by Elliot Jacques. And at a time when the younger American gurus seem to spend half their lives studying more and more esoteric subdisciplines, the Europeans' comparative lack of specialization may be an advantage. One reason that Peter Drucker has described Charles Handy as "the most interesting management writer today" is that he sees shades of himself: both had comparatively little formal management education, both served time in the real world (Handy as an oil executive, Drucker as a banker), and both are generalists, as interested in sociology and politics as they are in management. Drucker, it should not be forgotten, was once a European.

With Western Europe firmly within its orbit, the management industry is now moving east and south. By introducing management theory to the former Soviet bloc, Western governments and business schools hope to create a cadre of people who are familiar with the language and techniques of Western management. The Stockholm School of Economics has an outpost in Riga that teaches economics and business to 100 students a year from Estonia, Latvia, and Lithuania. Even in Moscow, business schools are starting to appear, although many of the graduates seem wrapped up in their puppy-like enthusiasm for buzzwords. One Western entrepreneur recalls having to shout at his new recruit that relentlessly mouthing acronyms such as EBIT (business school speak for "earnings before interest and taxes") was doubly pointless: first, the entrepreneur did not know what EBIT meant; and, second, it was based on meaningless figures. Even South Africa has made a contribution with something called ubuntu management, which blends Western ideas with African traditions, such as tribal loyalty.

However, the biggest growth is in the Far East (see Chapter 12). The region has long sent its bright young people to American business schools—Taiwan's government is stuffed with people with American MBAs. Now Asia is producing schools of its own, though nowhere near enough to meet the demand for them. In China, a country that is desperately short of trained managers, the China Europe International Business School plans to move from its present temporary home on the outskirts of Shanghai into a huge new campus in Pudong, the city's as-yet-unbuilt financial center, in 1997. It will also double its annual intake to 120 students (it already gets 4,000 applicants a year). Despite the fact that most of the big Asian businesses remain family-run operations, the consultancies have already made impressive progress. McKinsey's Indian office is the company's fastest-growing branch. As the younger business-school-educated generation of Asians takes over, the consultants can expect a bonanza.

Step onto any of Hong Kong's crowded trams and you will find a young Chinese puzzling over the latest offering from Tom Peters or John Naisbitt. In a mammoth pan-Asian survey of business people in 1995, roughly half of the respondents had bought a book by a Western management writer in the previous two years (nearly the same proportion admitted that they had not finished reading it).[5] For many Western gurus, Asian speaking tours offer much the same enticements that musical tours do for elderly rock stars. The money is good ($25,000 a seminar), the audience is large and relatively uncritical, and an Asian anecdote or two will turn up to spice up their performances back home. The only question is how long they will be able to survive with so little local competition. At present, there is only one well-known Asian guru, Kenichi Ohmae of Japan, but there are plenty of rising stars. One of the best thinkers at Insead is Chan Kim, a South Korean.

## The Importance of Theory

What keeps the management industry together and provides much of its vitality is management theory. Theory and industry feed off each other—and both grow bigger as a result. For three groups of people, the link between theory and money is particularly important: professors, consultants, and managers.

Increasingly, academics are keen not just on thinking up striking new ideas, but on selling them. In earlier times, such a taste for publicity might have provoked academic ostracism. Now, with house prices in the more desirable university towns soaring, every young professor dreams of writing a best-seller; and, with even the best business schools desperately competing for students, every business school dean encourages him. Business school professors used to pride themselves on cloaking incomprehensible ideas in impenetrable prose for a tiny audience. Now, the likes of Rosabeth Moss Kanter, of Harvard Business School, and Jeffrey Pfeffer, of Stanford, write in deliberately accessible prose and allow their publishers to mount jazzy advertising campaigns, with press kits, book signings, and endorsements by leading businessmen. Although it is difficult to condemn any management theorist who can write books in English, it is hard to imagine the same hoopla surrounding the launch of, say, an economics textbook.

Significantly, business school academics are setting up their own consultancies. Michael Porter is a director of Monitor; Rosabeth Moss Kanter is a founder of Goodmeasure, another Boston-based consultancy. Just to show that the British can play the same game, John Kay is a founder of London Economics. Indeed, the lines between academia and commerce are often so blurred that it is hard to categorize people. Should Kenichi Ohmae—long head of McKinsey's Tokyo operation and now head of his own consultancy, who gives packed lectures at business schools around the world and edits Harvard Business School books on subjects such as globalization—be counted as an academic or a consultant? Is a "CEO thought summit" held at the Massachusetts Institute of Technology and sponsored by Price Waterhouse an academic get-together or a corporate public relations ploy?

For consultancies, the link between new ideas and profit is even clearer. As one consultant puts it, "Customers expect you to add to their intellectual capital." McKinsey spends $50 million to $100 million a year on research. The *McKinsey Quarterly* (which looks as if it is trying to best the *Harvard Business Review,* and occasionally does) and the McKinsey Global Institute have long given the firm a quasi-academic glow. Virtually every other consultancy nowadays produces a magazine with a name like *Prism* or *Insights Quarterly.* One of the more flaky products, *Transformations,* from Gemini, comes with significant passages already highlighted or underlined. The most determined attempt to catch up with McKinsey has been made by Booz, Allen & Hamilton, which has appointed sundry knowledge officers. It has also brought in Joel Kurtzman, a former editor of the *Harvard Business Review,* to run a new periodical, *Strategy & Business.*

Few things reflect as well on a consultancy as a best-selling business book. *Reengineering the Corporation* helped CSC Index raise its annual revenues from $70 million before the book appeared to more than $160 million in 1994. Arthur D. Little aims to produce at least one big book a year, and offers consultants time off for writing if they can come up with a good enough proposal. *Product Juggernauts: How Companies Mobilize to Generate a Stream of Market Winners* (1995), an excellent study of product innovation, was one result.[6] Consultancies happily arrange for such books to be serialized in magazines, advertised in newspapers, and endorsed by well-known businessmen. A few of them even arrange for the books to be bought in bulk—as in the case of *The Discipline of Market Leaders.*

The scramble to produce the next management blockbuster shows how competitive consulting has become. Consulting used to be something of a cozy business. Now, giants such as Andersen Consulting and Electronic Data Systems (EDS) are pouring resources into the area. EDS has already gobbled up one of the oldest firms in the business, A. T. Kearney. Two of the leading strategist companies, Gemini and Mercer, are themselves the products of the consolidation of several smaller firms. Despite this increased pressure, there remains a clear difference between consultancies eager to be seen as originators of the latest trend and those wary of becoming its slaves, though they may be keen on keeping up to date. The first camp includes most of the later arrivals on the scene, such as CSC Index and Gemini. By contrast, McKinsey has produced several blockbuster books—Tom Peters, Robert Waterman, and Kenichi Ohmae have all worked for the firm—but it has shied away from the sort of concerted "this is our new idea" approach of its younger rivals. This is partly a function of size: even if the firm wanted to force a single idea down its clients' throats, its partners might not all agree to the move. But it is also because McKinsey, with its impressive array of contacts, does not need jazzy new products to act as calling cards. Interestingly, the Boston Consulting Group, which originally made its name with ideas such as growth-share management and time-based management, also takes a similar approach.

That does not mean that consultants at the more established firms are any less keen on writing books themselves. McKinsey has churned out over 50 books since 1980, compared with only two between 1960 and 1980. Despite famously long hours, there is no shortage of consultants who are willing to sacrifice their evenings, weekends, and holidays to write on management. Ever since Tom Peters transformed himself from an unknown

McKinseyite (named Thomas J. Peters) to the middle manager's pinup by publicizing an internal research project, consultants have daydreamed about writing a business blockbuster. At worst, a successful book can win clients and project the consultant up through the ranks; at best, it can allow one to launch a career as an independent consultant and speaker.

Much the same thoughts seem to be going through the minds of corporate chairmen. More and more retired businessmen are carving out second careers—and piling up second fortunes—as management pundits. Sir John Harvey-Jones, the amiable former boss of Britain's ICI, has starred in a television series, "Troubleshooter," in which he wanders the world dispensing advice to other managers; he has also turned himself into one of the most familiar figures on the business lecture circuit. The days when practicing bosses had time to come up with new theories may be over, but they are still trying to influence academic opinion. Percy Barnevik, the boss of Investor, is a regular guest at business schools and has written the introduction to a Harvard Business School book on globalization. The *Harvard Business Review* regularly subjects leading businessmen to searching interrogations and has no shortage of willing victims. Anita Roddick, the founder of Britain's Body Shop, was so frustrated by her few weeks as a guest lecturer at Stanford Business School that she tried to shake up the 1995 conference of America's Academy of Management with a passionate lecture on the socially responsible company. She is also founding a New Academy of Management, a sort of new-age business school with a spot of social do-goodery thrown in.

It is tempting to damn chief executives for spending so much time chasing will-o'-the-wisp theories when they should be looking after their shareholders. In many cases, however, the chief beneficiary is the company they head. A taste for management theory allows companies to present themselves as "go ahead"—and even gives them a chance to earn money. One way for a company to get noticed is to promote itself as a "center of excellence"—and charge people for watching it perform. Every year, 2,400 management pilgrims trek to Springfield Manufacturing, a diesel-engine assembler based in Missouri, to watch it practice something called "open-book management." The company earns $1.4 million from the tours, and assorted videotapes, books, and audiotapes. Other meccas include Walt Disney

World, home to a "people-management seminar," and AT&T's Universal Card service center, where guests pay $375 a day to watch the telephone giant demonstrate its skills in customer service.[7] Quite apart from the money such demonstrations earn, they spread the word that Motorola and Federal Express, for instance, are the last thing in quality.

Another similar tactic is to promote oneself as a small business school in one's own right. Companies such as Merck, 3M, Procter & Gamble, Disney, Marriott, IBM, McDonald's, and Motorola in the United States, and Unipart in Britain have all dignified their in-house training programs with the title of "university." As befits their newfound status, the "faculty" members of these universities are keen on developing new ideas, not just transmitting received wisdom, in order to seem up to date.

One is almost tempted to praise the breadth of the management industry. One result of having so many different sorts of people, with such diverse styles and perspectives, eager to contribute to management theory, is that it helps to widen the discipline's audience. There is something there for most readers, from fantasists who dream of getting rich quick to social scientists who want to understand the way organizations operate. Retired businessmen usually write anecdotal books, showing how their own careers demonstrate general business principles; academics have a weakness for powerful analytical techniques, such as regression analysis. Flourishing creativity also creates an expanding cornucopia of management tools for companies.

On the other hand, looking at the management industry's various fiefs—the teachers, consultants, business people, publishers, software makers, and so on—also suggests a worrying conclusion: a veritable army of people have a vested interest in hyping the gurus, and almost nobody gains by criticizing them. Even the press has, to some extent, been coopted. Gurus regularly write articles for business magazines and newspapers. News organizations such as the *Financial Times, Business Week,* and, yes, *The Economist,* are all expanding their conference business, turning themselves into both purveyors of management thought and critics of it. In general, we would argue that the mainstream business press is, at last, getting a little less tolerant of the gurus. Some of the management industry's more recent offerings—notably, *The Discipline of Market Leaders* and

*Transforming the Organization*—were given a (deservedly) hard
time by reviewers. Various columnists, such as Lucy Kellaway in
the *Financial Times,* make a specialty of scurrying around the
rubbish tip of daily press releases from consultancies and publishers that now gathers outside every management journalist's
door, and finding some particularly absurd new fad to ridicule.
However, given our vested interest, it is only fair to record that
many other people reckon that the critical instincts of the media
are fading even further. "How many requests do you think we
receive from publications doing yet another survey of fads like
reengineering?" moans one senior consultant, who thinks that
"the pack mentality" among journalists increases with each and
every new management page or management correspondent.
Journalists, he argues, are more interested in being the first to
write about an apparent trend than in investigating whether the
trend actually works.

## Thriving on Anxiety

If all these vested interests transform the management industry into an impressive marketing machine, they do not completely explain why customers fling themselves under its
wheels. What drives a man who is already working himself into
an early grave to read some screed on organizational transformation? And what drives a company that is staring oblivion in
the face to send key employees to expensive seminars on liberation management?

Andrzej Huczynski, a student of management gurus, argues that part of the answer lies in managers' anxiety about
their status. The first American business schools were built so
that managers could look graduates from the great schools
of law and medicine straight in the eye. Managers went on
executive-education programs and international conferences
because that was the sort of thing that professional people did.
Managers lapped up "scientific management" because everybody who was anybody seemed to have a branch of science to
support them.

Some of the most successful gurus have been shameless
flatterers of managerial egos. Peter Drucker subtitled his classic *The Practice of Management* "a study of the most important
function in American society." "The manager," he argued, "is

the dynamic, life-giving element in every business." Henry Mintzberg has repeatedly stressed the difficulty and complexity of managers' jobs, reinforcing the idea that managers are special people, grappling with intractable problems. Tom Peters tries a slightly different tactic, telling managers not just that they are important but also that they are rather wacky. Their children may call them squares. Their wives may despair that they are not as much fun as they used to be. But, listening to Tom Peters, they become crazy guys who dream impossible dreams and make unbelievable things happen.

The average struggling doctor or university professor might be surprised to discover that managers are socially insecure people. The gleaming buildings and carefully manicured lawns of business schools bespeak the arrogance of wealth. Top managers have seen their incomes increase substantially over the past decade, at a time when the income of shop-floor workers has stagnated or even declined. Surely the people who are really anxious about their status are members of the traditional elites, such as civil servants and academics? The answer is that, in social terms, the managerial class is probably more secure than it used to be. But today's managers have a lot of other things to be worried about, and management theorists have become virtuosos at discovering and calming these worries.

Managers are much more fearful of the future than they have ever been before. They know that they are living through momentous changes in the global economy—the rise of Asia, the fall of blue-chip companies like IBM, the collapse of career ladders—and they do not know whether those changes will make them rich or turn them into casualties. At the most basic level, they are terrified of losing their jobs. First in the United States, then in Britain, and now in Europe and Japan, companies have broken with the convention that a job in management is a job for life.

Even if they have survived the latest round of restructuring, managers still have to come to terms with radically redesigned jobs. What, after all, are they actually supposed to do when they "manage"? Are they strategy setters? Sergeant majors in business suits? Coaches? Amateur psychotherapists? In the old days of steep hierarchies and deferential workers, such heretical questions never arose. Senior managers set strategy, subdivided tasks into their component parts, and designed incentive schemes, and their juniors supervised workers and bawled them out if they slacked off. But now that computers are putting information in the hands of more and more employees, and decision making is being devolved to front-line workers, the traditional sources of managerial authority are disappearing. Some "lean" factories have even introduced a quasi-Maoist device called "360-degree assessment," whereby managers have to listen to frank reports on their personal foibles and failings from the people they are supposed to be managing.

Allan Katcher, an American psychologist, has asked senior American executives what they would least want their subordinates to know about them. In 19 out of the 20 cases, the answer was the same. They feared that their subordinates would learn how inadequate they felt in their jobs. These trembling Chihuahuas were professional managers, groomed throughout their careers to become top dogs. Yet, many people who end up in such managerial positions are promoted not for their managerial skills but for their excellence in other jobs—as engineers or lawyers or editorial writers. In their former jobs, they no doubt despised management theory. Perhaps, they despise it still; but now that they are going to be evaluated on the basis of their managerial abilities, they reluctantly fall under its spell. They turn to the people who "know." Guiltily, they buy a book on management, then organize a conference with, say, a consultant from McKinsey to act as a "facilitator."

To these anxiety-ridden men and women, management books offer a rare source of security. The most obvious beneficiaries are those fringe thinkers who concentrate on the individual rather than the organization—hence the charm of Stephen Covey's new-age psychotherapy (*The Seven Habits of Highly Effective People,* 1989) and of motivational gurus such as Anthony Robbins. However, managerial angst has also helped brass-tacks authors who provide their readers with a more general explanation of what exactly is happening to them. For instance, Charles Handy's *The Age of Unreason* (1989) addresses the disappearance of jobs for life. A follow-up, *The Empty Raincoat* (1995), looks at the widespread feeling that life is out of balance, with some people working round the clock and others having nothing to do. Even fairly straightforward management books often come in packages designed to appeal to the nervous. Who would have guessed

that *Control Your Destiny or Somebody Else Will* (1993) is actually a (fairly good) business biography of Jack Welch? One
book by Tom Peters begins with a quotation from Andy Grove,
the boss of Intel: "Only the paranoid survive"; another is
called *Thriving on Chaos* (1989). The ideal "unique selling
proposition" for a management book is something along the
lines of "Buy me or else you will not be among the elite who
will avoid being downsized out of a job or put on a short-term
contract."

Often, the gurus offer the illusion that, for all the complexities of the world, the answers are really rather straightforward,
provided the guru is one's guide. *In Search of Excellence* is full of
reassurances that "the answer is surprisingly simple, albeit ignored by most managers."[8] To find the truth, one needs neither a
gigantic brain nor a magic wand. Peters even argued that it was
the book's relentlessly commonsensical nature that made it a
best-seller: "The absence of magic—practical common sense—
turned out to be its biggest selling point." The first chapter of
his subsequent book, *A Passion for Excellence* (1985), was called
"A flash of the obvious." Another way to make ideas seem simple
is to translate them into formulas, such as Douglas McGregor's
"theory X and theory Y." Nowadays, alliterative formulas are so
rampant that a reader does not know whether the "three Cs"
refers to commitment, creativity, and competition, as Kenichi
Ohmae preaches, or competence, connections, and concepts, as
Rosabeth Moss Kanter would have it.

When such charms are not soothing managers' fears, they
are usually firing their ambitions. A taste for management theory can help bright young executives to steal a march on their
colleagues. Being chosen to attend an expensive management
seminar means that they are in favor with their immediate superiors. Attending the seminar gives them access to a trendy
language and helps them to network with similarly ambitious
colleagues from other companies. (It also makes a welcome
break from doing any real work.) Championing an idea suggests
that a manager is open to change, willing to take risks, and in
touch with the latest thinking. The chance to put the fad into
practice gives him much higher visibility throughout the company, tests his mettle as an agent of change and not just a stooge
of the status quo, and generally increases his chances of winning promotion.

Another reason that managers are keen on management theory is defensive: What better way to defend your turf than to clothe your specialism with the dignity of scientific theory? Peter Drucker's "management by objectives" strengthened the position of general managers. Total-quality management reinforced the role of production chiefs. The training department is forever on the lookout for ideas that will help inflate the training budget, while the "human resource specialists" are suckers for any theorist who argues for "putting people first" (to borrow the title of a book by a professor at Stanford Business School, Jeffrey Pfeffer).

## The Importance of Being Faddish

Why do managers flit from theory to theory rather than settling for just one or, as their disappointment mounts, rejecting the whole guru business entirely? And why do management gurus keep tearing up the sacred texts and starting from scratch? The glimmer of an answer should already be apparent. The sheer number of would-be gurus means that there are always numerous ideas in the marketplace. The prevalence of fear and ambition among the consumers of management ideas means that the market is always unstable.

Arguably, the ground for the current frenzy of management fads was prepared by the professionalization of management in America in the wake of the Second World War. The premise behind this change was that a set of general concepts and generic principles could be applied in all circumstances. Belief in these universal ideas weaned managers from their earlier reliance on improvised in-house management practices and prepared them to become consumers of mass-produced and mass-marketed managerial techniques.

This regimented system, which allowed for fads but was not built around them, lasted only as long as the 1980s. Suddenly, most of its fixed points were called into question. The mass-production model no longer seemed to be working. The paragons of good management—companies such as General Motors and IBM—were slipping. Ideas that had been invented outside the system—foreign notions such as "lean production" and "customer–supplier" partnerships—appeared to have the edge. American companies now had to consult Tom Peters and Toyota rather than just the Harvard Business School and McKinsey. What might be called the velocity of management faddism increased exponentially just about everywhere. The more companies panicked, the more they flitted from technique to technique in search of salvation. Of the 27 fads highlighted by Richard Pascale in *Managing on the Edge* in 1990, two-thirds were spawned during the 1980s. Since then, the process has only speeded up.

And, from the management industry's viewpoint, the beauty of the system is that none of the formulas works—or, at least, none works as completely as the anguished or greedy buyers had hoped. The result is enormous profits for the gurus but confusion for their clients. "In the past 18 months," one Midwestern equipment manufacturer told Pascale, "we have heard that profit is more important than revenue, that quality is more important than profit, that people are more important than profit, that customers are more important than our people, that big customers are more important than our small customers, and that growth is the key to our success. No wonder our performance is inconsistent."

One thing that the management industry deserves to be flagellated for repeatedly is that it so often sells its ideas as permanent solutions. Close study indicates that management remains an art rather than a science, its aspirations to the contrary notwithstanding. With that in mind, we will now look at the ideas themselves, beginning with the work of the two best-known witch doctors: Peter Drucker and Tom Peters.

# PART TWO

# PROPHET AND EVANGELIST

# CHAPTER 3

PETER DRUCKER: THE GURU'S GURU

IN MOST AREAS of intellectual life, nobody can quite decide who is the top dog—sometimes because rival schools of thought have rival champions, sometimes because there are so many fine specimens to choose from. In the world of management gurus, however, there is no debate. Peter Drucker is undisputed alpha male. He is also one of the few thinkers from any discipline who can claim to have changed the world: he is the inventor of privatization, the apostle of a new class of knowledge workers, the champion of management as a serious intellectual discipline. One South Korean businessman has even gone so far as to adopt Drucker as his Christian name, in deference to the great man. This is perhaps a little extreme, even sad, but Drucker is the one management theorist whose writings every reasonably well-educated person, however contemptuous of business or infuriated by jargon, really ought to read.

This unrivaled position has a lot to do with age and output. Now in his late 80s, Drucker was a leading management pundit when today's management pundits were reengineering their train sets. Since discovering the discipline back in the 1940s, he has produced an astonishing quantity of work: 26 books, thousands of articles, tens of thousands of lectures, and goodness

knows how much practical advice for managers. Not all of it
has stood the test of time; and some of Drucker's later work is a
little thin, padded out with immodest references to his early
work. Yet what makes all this effort worthwhile is the sheer
quality of his intellect. No matter how many blind alleys
Drucker heads up, his relentlessly curious mind always makes
the reader think. Drucker will say that he hates the word
"guru," thinking it synonymous with charlatan. But, in truth,
he is the one management thinker who genuinely deserves the
accolade.

## The Road to Drucker

According to Tom Peters, "no true discipline of management" existed before Drucker.[1] Yet it has become fashionable to
trace virtually any modern management idea to the "pioneers
and prophets" of the early twentieth century—and sometimes
even further back. But, for the modern reader (let alone the
modern manager), the academic squabbles over who first said
what are of limited interest. Even if Cato's list of job descriptions for provincial administrators in the Roman empire is a
distant ancestor of Charles Handy's theories about the workplace 2,000 years later, the logical response of every sane modern manager should be: "So what?"

Peter Drucker, thanks in part to his own talents and in part
to the era in which he began to write about management, is the
first management thinker consistently to pass this relevancy
test. Like his biblical namesake, he is the rock on which the
current church is founded, as the voices crying in the wilderness who preceded him will confirm.

Management, in one sense, is as old as humans. Drucker
himself has pointed out that "all the great business builders—
from the Medici of Renaissance Florence and the founders of the
Bank of England in the late seventeenth century down to IBM's
Thomas Watson in our day—had a clear theory of the business
which informed all their actions and decisions." One history of
management has traced the craft back to the Sumerians of 5000
B.C.[2] Organizing either the construction of the pyramids or Julius
Caesar's invasion of Britain must have required basic skills and
talents that might be described as management.

Many would say Niccolo Machiavelli (1469–1527) was the first Western management theorist. The *Financial Times* once dubbed Machiavelli's *The Prince* the sixteenth-century equivalent of Dale Carnegie's *How to Win Friends and Influence People*.[3] Any executive exposed to corporate politics (i.e., every manager in the world) could do worse than read *The Prince* and take to heart its advice about being "a great dissembler and pretender."

Management archaeologists find more significant individuals appearing during the Industrial Revolution. There were not only economic theorists such as Adam Smith (1723–90) and Jean Baptiste Say (1767–1832), both of whom devoted many pages to the running of enterprises, but also practitioners such as Eli Whitney (1765–1835), an American gun maker who built his rifles from interchangeable parts and thus, arguably, invented the assembly line, and Robert Owen (1771–1858), a Scottish mill owner who thought there was money to be made by treating workers as if they were human beings (he would not employ any child under the age of ten) and thus has been deemed "the pioneer of personnel management."[4] However, it was only with the introduction of mass production around the beginning of the twentieth century that business demanded the creation of a new elite of managers and a new, formal science of management theory.

The principal inspiration for this new science, in America at least, was Frederick Winslow Taylor, an engineer who invented carbon-steel machine tools. Taylor believed that there was a single best method of organizing work, and that this method could be discovered through a detailed study of the time and motion involved in doing each job. The stopwatch, the motion picture camera, the slide rule, and psycho-physiological tests—these were the tools of the trade of Taylor and his acolytes. The principles at the heart of scientific management were clear: break jobs down into their simplest parts; select the most suitable workers to fit the available jobs; turn those workers into specialists, each an expert in his own appointed task; arrange these specialized jobs along an assembly line; and design the right package of incentives (including bonuses and prizes) to ensure that the workers did indeed work.

In Taylor's world, "managers" were not just unthinking sergeants carrying out the owner's instructions. They played two vital roles in turning factories into "smoothly running machines." The first was to coordinate the various specialized tasks (after all, the workers themselves could hardly be expected to understand how their specialty fitted into the larger enterprise); the second was to monitor and motivate the workers (who might easily weary of their tedious routine). The principle of the division of labor also applied to managers: there were specialists in accounting, recruiting, and so on. At the top of the pyramid sat the elite, Taylor's version of Plato's guardians, whose job it was to design and regulate the entire system, to monitor the behavior of competitors, and, above all, to plan ahead.

Taylor's ideas were translated into practice remarkably quickly—particularly by Henry Ford, a self-made mechanic just like Taylor, at his new factory in Highland Park, a suburb of Detroit. At the same time, Taylorism helped shape the curriculum at a new sort of educational institution, the business school. The first business school, Wharton, was set up at the University of Pennsylvania in 1881. The University of Chicago and the University of California both established undergraduate schools of commerce in 1899. New York University's Stern School of Business Administration, Dartmouth's Amos Tuck School of Business Administration, and Harvard's Graduate School of Business Administration followed in the next decade. The *Management Review* was founded in 1918, and the American Management Association, in 1925. By the end of the Great War, Arthur D. Little, originally an engineering firm, included management advice among its services. James McKinsey set up his consultancy firm in 1925.

Ironically, given Henry Ford's patronage of Taylor's ideas, one of the first results of scientific management was the success of General Motors, where Alfred Sloan turned himself into a professional manager, detached from the hurly-burly of the shop floor. (In contrast, Henry Ford was an inveterate meddler, keeping his firm in a state of near chaos.) Many of Taylor's disciples found their way into state and local government and tried to apply scientific management to places like the schoolroom and the operating theater.[5] Congress held hearings on the subject as early as 1912, giving publicity to the new idea. Herbert Hoover, an engineer by training, tried to use scientific management to make government more efficient.

But the apostles of scientific management did not have it all their own way. A rival group of theorists, who became known as the human-relations school, wanted to see workers involved in managerial decisions. Mary Parker Follett, a pioneering female management theorist, stressed that "we can never wholly separate the human from the mechanical side."[6] Elton Mayo, a psychologist based at the Harvard Business School, emphasized noneconomic rewards for productivity: "So long as commerce specializes in business methods which take no account of human nature and social motives, so long may we expect strikes and sabotage to be the ordinary accompaniment of industry."

This humanistic school of management was at its most influential in Europe, particularly in Britain, where the powerful craft unions faced off with Taylorism, and leading businessmen sought a gentler approach. Quaker businessmen such as the Cadburys and the Rowntrees urged other employers to treat their workers like human beings rather than machines. William Richard Morris, the father of Britain's automobile industry, was so dismayed by the difficulties of introducing the new system that he christened it "mess production."[7] C. S. Myers, a psychologist, criticized scientific management for taking a simplistic view of human motives. Elliot Jacques, another psychologist, focused on the social dynamics of group behavior and, after the Second World War, turned Tavistock Institute in London into the headquarters of humanistic management.

A fair number of Europe's leading intellectuals became caught up in the struggle between scientific and humanistic management. In Germany, avant-garde thinkers made a cult of scientific management. Bauhaus architects like Walter Gropius and Ludwig Hilberseimer tried to marry design with scientific management; Bertolt Brecht and Fritz Lang briefly sang the praises of the new craze; and Max Weber, the father of organizational theory, studied different types of bureaucracies to see which would be the most efficient. In Britain, intellectuals usually sided with the humanists. Aldous Huxley in his book *Brave New World* (1932), English-born Charlie Chaplin in his film *Modern Times* (1936), George Orwell in his 1946 essay "James Burnham and the Managerial Revolution" and his novel *Nineteen Eighty-Four* (1949)—all expressed their fear of mass production, scientific management, and the reduction of the individual into a cog in a vast industrial machine.

### An Intellectual Refugee

This, then, was the slightly schizophrenic discipline that Peter Drucker stumbled upon on the eve of the Second World War. Drucker scorns the idea that he was the man who invented management (although there is a book about him with that title). Instead, he argues that, by the mid-1930s, "nothing had come together." Nobody had asked the question "What is management?"

Drucker was born in 1909 into the Austrian upper middle class. His father, a cosmopolitan government official, introduced young Drucker to Sigmund Freud when he was eight or nine years old. As a student, he got to know such illustrious intellectuals as Karl Polanyi, a historian, and Fritz Kraemer, a military strategist. He earned a doctorate in international and public law from Frankfurt University in 1931 and published articles in German economics journals.

The events that led this Viennese intellectual to write about something then as removed from the mainstream as management were complicated and largely accidental. He spent his 20s trying to avoid Adolf Hitler and drifted among a number of jobs, including banking, consultancy, academic law, and journalism. (His journalistic training included a spell as the acting editor of a women's page.) He finally found a home in an American university, teaching politics, philosophy, and economics. His first book, *The End of Economic Man* (1939), concentrated on politics and economics and warned about the Holocaust. His second book, *The Future of Industrial Man* (1942), annoyed academic critics because it mixed economics with various social sciences. In it, Drucker argued that companies had a social dimension as well as an economic purpose. This unorthodox idea also attracted the attention of General Motors.

The American car giant, then the biggest company in the world, invited Drucker to draw its portrait and gave him unrestricted access to GMers, from Alfred Sloan down. The result, *The Concept of the Corporation*, sealed Drucker's fate. The book immediately became a best-seller, in Japan as well as in America, and has been in print ever since. However, it further alienated turf-minded American academics: economists regarded it as vulgar sociology, and political scientists dismissed it as economics gone mad. One reviewer hoped that "this promising young scholar will now devote his considerable talents to a more respectable subject."[8] Shunned by his natural allies, Drucker was forced to write about management.

Since then, Drucker has either invented or influenced virtually every part of management theory (his name will thus crop up in this book with infuriating frequency). Many of the themes that have dominated his work were present in *The Concept of the Corporation*. Like all Drucker's books, *The Concept of the Corporation* is a roaming narrative: it begins with a story from China and, at different times, worries about the percentage of Victorian Englishmen who were gentlemen (a minute fraction, in Drucker's view) and the efficiency of Russian industrial management. The book's central purpose was to treat a company as a social system as well as an economic organization. The two longest sections in the book are entitled "The Corporation as Human Effort" and "The Corporation as a Social Institution." Drucker found the way that people worked together interesting in its own right rather than merely a means to make profits.

All the same, the subject that most of Drucker's readers seized on was decentralization. Drucker showed how GM's decentralized structure enabled it to respond to challenges such as the transition from war to peace—and concluded that the car firm "realized its concept of decentralization sufficiently to obtain from it an overall pattern of behavior and a basis for the successful solution of the most difficult concrete problems of economic life."[9] Although Drucker made it clear that he had doubts about the value of decentralization for organizations in general, other big American companies, such as Ford and General Electric, rushed to copy it. By the 1980s, Drucker was credited with "moving 75–80 percent of the Fortune 500 to radical decentralization."[10]

## Drucker's People

The two most interesting issues that have come out of Drucker's dissection of the car company—and that have dominated his work ever since—have only a marginal connection with decentralization. One has to do with empowering workers (or "creating the self-governing plant community," as Drucker somewhat clumsily put it at the time), and the other, with the rise of the knowledge worker (i.e., the worker's whose value lies in what he has in his head, not in what he can do with his hands).

For all its dry academic language, *The Concept of the Corporation* was essentially a passionate plea for GM to treat labor as a resource rather than just as a cost. Drucker insisted that industrial relations ought to be based on people's desire to be engaged in their job and proud of their product. He was also a stern critic of the assembly line, even though at the time it was regarded as the most advanced form of manufacturing. In "the assembly-line mentality," he said, "the more efficient a worker is, the more machine-like and the less human he is."[11] Drucker charged that the monotony of assembly-line production actually made it an inefficient process—partly because the line had to adjust to the speed of the slowest member and partly because workers never got any job satisfaction from seeing the finished product.

This enthusiasm for self-management was ahead of its time. Nowadays, team-manufacturing techniques such as cell-manufacturing are commonplace, and many companies are handing more power to their workers. When Japanese car makers set up shop in Britain in the 1980s and told Geordie factory workers that they were supposed to think as well as rivet, weld, and hammer, many of Britain's car bosses scoffed at the foreigners' naïveté. Today, every car factory in Europe imitates their methods. The tragedy for GM was that it rejected Drucker's advice about using teams in the 1940s—only to have the same lesson rammed down its throat by the Japanese in the 1970s.

A second great theme of Drucker's work has been that the old industrial proletariat needs to be replaced with knowledge workers. The advanced world is moving from "an economy of goods" to "a knowledge economy," he argues, and management is being transformed as a result. Managers are having to learn how to engage the minds, rather than simply control the hands, of their workers. This softer approach is a direct challenge to Taylor's stopwatch theories and their fans in business. But the idea of "a knowledge worker" (a term that Drucker coined in 1959) also poses questions for politicians. It suggests that a country's raw materials are really its educated workers; hence the importance of training and education. And rather than try to defend dying industries against cheaper, less "knowledgeable" workers abroad, governments should concentrate on improving the country's stock of knowledge, but otherwise keep well out of the way.

Typically, Drucker has not confined himself to the question of how managers and governments ought to handle these new knowledge workers. He has spent much of his career looking at how the knowledge workers themselves can come to terms with this new world in which they are neither workers nor bosses. Since they, rather than their employers, control the key productive asset of modern society—that is to say, brain power—they have considerably more freedom than their predecessors. Workers are free, or, in the jargon that Drucker did not invent but unfortunately helped to legitimize, are "empowered" to shape their own careers, hopping from firm to firm in pursuit of the highest salary or the most interesting job. But Drucker was also quick to spot that this freedom could be destabilizing as well as liberating: knowledge workers needed more training, new pension arrangements, and other kinds of attention.

Drucker's ideas about the changing nature of work have since inspired a whole generation of writers to look in more detail at the subject. Today, few would dispute that changes have taken place, but they might argue that the transformation has not been as fundamental as predicted. Still, most people would admit, along with Charles Handy, a prominent member of this generation, that "virtually everything can be traced back to Drucker."[12] Furthermore, Drucker, who started his career by turning down opportunities to become a banker and has always enjoyed a somewhat ambivalent relationship with academia, is himself an archetypal knowledge worker.

## The Rational Temptation

At the same time, Drucker was not simply another exponent of the human relations school of management, a "soft" inspirer always looking for the human angle. In fact, there has always been a hard, "Taylorist" side to his thinking.

Drucker invented one of the rational school of management's most successful products, "management by objectives," an approach that dominated "strategic thinking" in the postwar decades. *The Practice of Management* (1954) emphasized clear objectives, both for the corporation and the manager, and urged translating long-term strategy into short-term goals. In particular, Drucker believed that a firm should have an elite group of general managers determining strategy and setting objectives for more specialized managers. The structure of the firm, he argued, should follow its strategy: "Organization is not an end in itself, but a means to the end of business performance and business results. . . . Organization structure must be designed so as to make possible the achievement of the objectives of the business five, ten, fifteen years hence."

Management by objectives has been under a cloud since the early 1980s. The best modern companies, such as 3M and Motorola, allow ideas—including ideas for long-term strategies—to emerge from the bottom of the organization rather than from on high (see Chapter 8). Those companies that have stuck with the system of command and control—notably General Motors— have looked hopelessly inflexible. The problem is that command-and-control management cuts senior management off from the people who know both their markets and their products best: the ordinary workers. Hence the current fashion for that other great Drucker theme, handing decisions back to workers through delayering and empowerment.

On balance, management by objectives looks like a fad that will remain in the graveyard. The question is, why did the prophet of empowerment take such a rigid approach to management? His critics say that Drucker lost his way, faddishly endorsing two incompatible approaches. But a more generous interpretation is also possible.

Drucker was trying—as he has done ever since—to create a balance between what was best in both the humanist and rationalist schools. Management by objectives is not incompatible with empowerment, he argued: senior managers should set general goals for their subordinates but allow them to decide how to reach those goals. And throughout his management-by-objectives phase, he continued to lay heavy emphasis on the importance of corporate culture. He was one of the first people to realize that companies are held together by a shared vision of the future—and that it is the boss's job to come up with that vision.

Drucker's suspicion—that if society is to avoid both anarchy and alienation, soft ideas like empowerment need to be mixed with harder ones, like management by objectives—is proving prescient. Anybody who studies the collapse of Barings will find it hard to be an uncritical supporter of empowerment. But simply restoring the old command-and-control system risks alienating the knowledge workers, on whom the success of most companies depends. Druckerish compromise looks like the best way forward.

## New Worlds to Management

Drucker was one of the first people to realize that good management is not restricted to the United States. In the 1950s, when most people dismissed Japan as nothing more than a maker of cheap knickknacks, Drucker became fascinated by Japan's idiosyncratic approach to management. Following the publication of *The Concept of the Corporation,* the Japanese treated him almost like a sage—as they still do. His influence is now felt in the rest of Asia.

Perhaps Drucker's most insightful observation is that management plays a vital role in all spheres of life, not just in business. It is as important for universities, churches, hospitals, or charities as it is for the manufacturers of soap powder. Indeed, he refused chairs at Stanford and Harvard because both schools wanted him to concentrate on business case studies in his teaching, business organizations in his consulting work, and business examples in his writing. But, he responded, management is not only a business concern; it is "the defining organ of all modern institutions." In keeping with this approach, his own clients include voluntary organizations such as the Girl Scouts of America as well as large companies, and the management school that Claremont College in California founded in his honor recruits about a third of its students from outside the business world.

Drucker's enthusiasm for taking management theory to the public sector should not be mistaken for enthusiasm for government. It was Drucker who gave the world the idea of "privatization"—and he has always complained about the inability of government to run just about anything. In *The Age of Discontinuity* (1969), he argues that the job of governments is to govern rather than try to do things that could be done by the private sector. In Drucker's view, things that lie outside the government's scope extend well beyond telephone companies and utilities. Even in one of his later books, *Post Capitalist Society* (1993), where he questions shibboleths of shareholder capitalism, he still insists that the best way for governments to avoid depressions is to stop meddling with the economy. Warfare, Drucker has argued, is the only example of a modern government program that has achieved its objectives.

## Does He Still Matter?

Drucker either led the way or cleared the path for others in countless smaller ways as well. Thanks to the broad scope of his ideas and his longevity, Drucker has exercised the sort of influence that leaves other gurus bursting with envy. Even when criticizing him, his peers approach him with reverence—which verges on relief at the thought that their much maligned industry has at least one class act. "Our debt to Peter Drucker knows no limit," Tom Peters once admitted.

This respect is echoed in the corporate world. When asked which management books he has paid attention to, Bill Gates replies, "Well, Drucker, of course," before citing other lesser mortals.[13] Drucker has also had the satisfaction of seeing many of his ideas put into practice. The younger Henry Ford took *The Concept of the Corporation* as his text when he tried to rebuild his company after the war. As Drucker himself has boasted, the book "had an immediate impact on American business, on public service institutions, on government agencies—and none at all on General Motors." (If a GM manager was found with a copy of the book, Drucker noted, his career was over.) Institutions as diverse as Michigan University and the Archdiocese of New York have used the book to restructure themselves. It was the first book to be prescribed for students entering Charles de Gaulle's elite Ecole Nationale d'Administration. *The Concept of the Corporation* also set the Japanese thinking about devolving power to their workers. One of Drucker's more recent fans is the Reverend Bill Hybels, senior pastor of Willow Creek Community Church in South Barrington, Illinois, and one of America's most successful "megaministers." He has a quotation from Peter Drucker hanging outside his office: "What is your business? Who is your customer? What does the customer consider value?" Hybels has got to know Drucker well and regards him as "a wisdom figure."[14]

Yet, even around the management industry's great totem, doubts swirl. Drucker has never enjoyed quite as much adulation from academia as he has from either guruland or his public. ("I have never been quite respectable in the eyes of academia," he himself confesses.)[15] There is no single area of academic management theory that he has made his own, as Michael Porter did with strategy and Theodore Levitt did with marketing. Some academics regard him as a journalist rather than a scholar, and, twisting the knife, as a glib generalizer rather than a first-class reporter. Tom Peters recalls that he never saw Drucker's name on any reading list when he was a student at Stanford Business School.

The least persuasive criticism is that Drucker does little more than state the obvious, that his persistent themes—about the rise of the knowledge worker, the importance of clear objectives, the fact that firms are social as well as economic institutions—are all too obvious to bear mentioning, let alone repeating over and over again. The trouble with this argument, as mentioned earlier, is that most of his observations are obvious only because Drucker has made them so. Drucker is a victim of his own success in popularizing a way of looking at the world. And obvious or not, some of his insights do not seem to have gotten through to the managerial elite just yet. Would America's bosses be sacking their workers with one hand, while awarding themselves huge pay raises with the other, if they understood Drucker's arguments about the social nature of firms?

Other criticisms have had more force. Drucker sometimes manages to be both simplistic and obscure at the same time. He repeatedly states that humans live in a society of organizations but fails to make clear what this means. In *Post-Capitalist Society,* he complains that America has embraced pension-fund socialism, but his comments are presented more as a play on words than a deep analysis of American society. In a broad sense, he is right that the real bosses are not the likes of John D. Rockefeller and J. P. Morgan, but the workers themselves. They are the ones who own most of society's capital, through their pension rights, and who receive most of society's rewards, through their wages and social benefits. But would it not be better to call this popular capitalism?

Drucker's work may also be criticized for its unevenness. Whereas *The Concept of the Corporation* may be considered a model monograph that is tightly argued and based on original research, some of his later books can be rambling and repetitive, full of recycled examples. His voice has also become less distinctive. Although it is true that as early as 1954 he was arguing that an "organization structure should contain the least possible number of management levels," his enthusiasm in the 1980s for "information-based organizations" and for stripping out layers of management seemed not much different from the voices of the baying pack following Tom Peters.

In general, he is not as good on small firms as big ones. In *The Concept of the Corporation,* he asserted, flatly, "We know today that in modern industrial production, particularly in modern mass production, the small unit is not only inefficient, it cannot produce at all."[16] Indeed, the book helped to launch the "big organization boom" that lasted for the next 20 years. Drucker has since recanted: he now believes that "the Fortune 500 is over" and has written progressively more about the importance of entrepreneurship, as in his 1985 book, *Innovation and Entrepreneurship.* (Anybody who accuses Drucker in print of being a fan of big companies is in for a long letter, chronicling his enthusiasm for decentralization.) All the same, Drucker still seems much more at home with the giant corporations that dominated the United States under Dwight Eisenhower than with the small to medium-size businesses that regalvanized the country under Ronald Reagan. He has written nothing as good as *The Concept of the Corporation* about a small company.

On the other hand, the charge that Drucker is a jack-of-all-trades rather than a master of one reveals more about the limitations of academia than it does about Drucker's shortcomings. Remember that Drucker was expelled from the ivory towers of economics and political science because his work would not fit into their narrow classifications. As for charges that he resorts to the dark art of journalism, that may be just another way of saying that he is readable. Drucker was—and still is—too idiosyncratic a figure to fit in with the turf-conscious conformists who make up modern academia.

In a business that is dominated by American business school specialists with nanosecond memories, Drucker is happy to range across the centuries and use a reference to China of the Tang dynasty, or seventh-century Byzantium, or eighteenth-century France. His historical knowledge allows him to throw a shaft of light on contemporary debates. Commenting on globalization, for example, he points out that a larger share of manufacturing was "multinational" before the First World War than it is today. Companies such as Fiat (founded in 1899) and Siemens (founded in 1847) produced more abroad than at home almost as soon as they got off the ground. Henry Ford, although a notorious xenophobe, started his English subsidiary before he began to expand his original automobile plant in Detroit.[17]

In writing about business alliances, Drucker usually throws in a reference to his heroine, Jane Austen, and her obsession with dynastic alliances; in commenting on the latest bout of speculative fever on Wall Street, he is soon regurgitating bits of Charles Dickens's *Little Dorrit;* and, most surprisingly of all, he illustrates an article on the rise of the knowledge-based organization with a reference to the civil service in British India. What is more, this is not garden-variety erudition. He quotes from Volume 3 rather than Volume 1 of Marx's *Das Kapital,* from Harrington rather than Locke. Among other activities, he has written two novels and held a chair in Oriental Art at Claremont Graduate School.

Drucker's is not the sort of history that can be found in the textbooks: his interest lies neither in the kings and queens of the old history nor in the capitalists and proletarians of the new, but in managers and organization. His heroes are the likes of Jean Bodin, who (according to Drucker at least) invented the nation-state, and August Borsig, who invented the German apprenticeship system. His trademark is his ability to cut between panoramic views and striking close-ups. One moment he is churning out broad generalizations about the rise of the car industry; the next he is relating an anecdote about Henry Ford's forgotten partner. He is not afraid to predict the future as well as to generalize about the past. He has had his share of failures (remember his admiration for large companies), but his batting average is higher than most (notably in the case of privatization and the collapse of the Soviet Union).

### The Last Encyclopaedist

Arguably, Drucker is not a management theorist at all, but a cosmopolitan intellectual in the European tradition. Drucker is one of the last of the encyclopaedists, contemptuous of the hyperspecialization of modern academia and determined to know everything about everything. He illustrates his writings with a wide range of references, from psychoanalysis and musicology to economics and sociology, from real-life case studies to academic literature.

Why, one might well ask, did this polymath concentrate so much of his energy on management? The glib answer, "because it is important," is probably the truthful one. Discovering management had much the same effect on Drucker as discovering God (or Marx) has on lesser mortals. "Management is the organ of institutions," he hymns, "the organ that converts a mob into an organization, and human efforts into performance."[18]

If there is a core theme running through Drucker's writings, it is this: at best, good management will bring economic progress and social harmony in its wake. Marx based his prediction of the imminent demise of capitalism on the "inexorable law of the diminishing productivity of capital"; and it is because managers have succeeded in outfoxing this law, by realizing that the key to improved productivity lies in working smarter rather than working longer, that the modern economy goes from success to success. The real reason, Drucker argues, that some countries made the breakthrough into sustained growth is not because they discovered new technologies but because they invented new organizations. Thus, Alfred Sloan's General Motors is a more awesome creation than the combustion engine, and the hospital is a more important medical breakthrough than any newfangled medicine.

Drucker has no illusions about how difficult management is. In *Managing in a Time of Great Change,* a collection of essays published in 1995, he focuses on three problems that are making the modern manager's life hell. The first is the sheer scale of contemporary managerial change, as vertically integrated companies give way to networked organizations. The second is the frequency of managerial failure. Most managers, he points out, have failed to understand what it means to manage in revolutionary times, and they spend their time tinkering with their business when they should really be rethinking the whole theory on which it is based. The third is the growing tension between business and its environment: between business's need for perpetual innovation and the community's need for stability; between the rapidly changing nature of knowledge and the limited capacity of the human mind; between business' need to compete internationally and society's interest in the common good.

Good management means doing the decent thing by both workers and consumers, not just amassing profits for bosses. "An organization is a human, a social, indeed a moral phenomenon," Drucker notes, in a phrase that today's reengineers ought to be forced to learn. Drucker has argued that the best managers are driven by the desire to create value for customers, and that the best way to do this is to treat workers not just as costs of production, but as resources, capable of making a sustained and valued contribution. This enthusiasm for the well-being of workers led Rosabeth Moss Kanter, a professor at Harvard Business School, to compare Drucker to Robert Owen, the nineteenth-century Scotsman who ordered his factory managers to show the same due care to their vital human machines as they did to the new iron and steel that they so lovingly burnished.

Is Drucker right? Moss Kanter classifies Drucker as "a management utopian." Perhaps he is, but then there are worse sorts of dreamers.

# CHAPTER 4

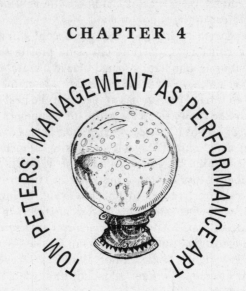

TOM PETERS: MANAGEMENT AS PERFORMANCE ART

W HEN MOST PEOPLE HEAR the term "management guru," they think of Tom Peters. His first book, *In Search of Excellence*, cowritten with Robert Waterman, was the original management blockbuster: it sold a million copies on its first printing in 1982, went through numerous reprintings, and turned both of its authors into millionaires. It has now sold more than five million copies. More books have followed. Peters pours out a constant stream of tapes, videos, articles, and, together with his army of assistants, a quirky but readable newsletter. On the international lecture circuit, Peters has outlasted and outearned such shooting stars as Ronald Reagan, Norman Schwarzkopf, and Oliver North. Every year, thousands of middle managers gape in awe as Peters, arms flailing, brow sweating, voice hoarse with preaching, urges them to nuke hierarchy and learn to thrive on chaos.

An all-day Tom Peters seminar remains an event. Against a backdrop of slides with messages such as "The Most Important Sentence in the English Language!?" he orders the befuddled young watchers in suits to make mistakes and to have fun.[1] "You advertise for a marketing job. Luciano Benetton walks in. He's wearing no clothes. Do you hire him?" Then he adds as an afterthought: "Don't worry: *he* wouldn't want to work for *you* anyway." One moment you are being told to learn from the threaded needle in a complimentary sewing kit in London's Four Seasons hotel; the next moment Peters is praising a car dealer who put flowers rather than automobiles in his showroom. Questions about practicalities only push him to new extremes. "I see no reason why you need to spend more than six minutes every three months in your office," he tells the head of the Eurostar London–Paris train service. "Get on that railroad."

## The Llama Factor

Peters's extraordinary prominence is a mixed blessing for his profession. Many people only have to read one of his columns or watch one of his television performances to have their prejudices about management theory redoubled. How can a man in his 50s parade around like that? How can a self-respecting columnist run on about his penchant for power-walking or his wife's Zen Buddhism? How can somebody finish a day by wishing a group of senior managers "loud times and lots of screw-ups"? As if to taunt his critics, Peters illustrated the cover of one of his books, *The Tom Peters Seminar: Crazy Times Call for Crazy Organizations* (1994), with a picture of himself in his boxer shorts. He also dedicated the book to his mother, "a talker who raised a talker." Peters's books are littered with phrases like "wow," "yikes," and "ho-hum." "Prosewise, he is no Edward Gibbon," as he himself might put it.

There is, however, a lot more to Peters than his peculiarities. Admittedly, he has contradicted himself spectacularly over the past decade, but that is partly because the corporate world has changed spectacularly over the past decade. True, he has a penchant for dashing off fairly flimsy newspaper columns (who else would use a guest spot in the *Financial Times* to teach readers breathing-relaxation exercises?); yet he also wrote an admirably obscure Ph.D. dissertation and continues to churn out articles for heavyweight (and unremunerative) academic periodicals like the *California Management Review.* He is willing to rant and rave to get his point across, but he has persuaded more managers to think a little bit more carefully about what they are doing than almost anyone else alive.

Even Peters's harshest critics should be willing to concede two things in his favor. First, he has a remarkable talent for making a dull subject like management sound interesting. What is noticeable about all the titles of his books—*Liberation Management, A Passion for Excellence, Thriving on Chaos*—is that they convey his fascination with his subject. Second, he has an intimate knowledge of corporate life, not just in the United States but also in Europe and around the Pacific Rim; not just in the boardroom, but also in the marketing department and in the machine shop; not just in the giants like Sony and IBM, but also in countless small companies that nobody else seems able to track down. He cannot book into a hotel, fly in an aircraft, or park his car without finding an interesting management angle. One of the best stories in *Crazy Times* is about Valerio's, an eccentric Italian restaurant he stumbled across in New Zealand that refuses to post menus outside and frames complaints from disappointed customers.

Before becoming a management guru, Peters managed to fight in Vietnam and work for both the Pentagon and the Office of Management and Budget, in Washington DC. He also picked up an MBA from Stanford Business School. But the two most important parts of his training were his undergraduate degree in engineering and then the time he spent as a consultant with McKinsey. Peters has always retained a consultant's ability to inveigle his way into hundreds of companies and an engineer's curiosity about how things actually work.

In other words, Peters is a much more complicated and accomplished man than he first seems. All the same, if the normally peaceful herd of llamas that roam around his Vermont farm were to turn nasty and trample their owner to death, Peters would have an uncomfortable epitaph: that what he did—launching, leading, and defining the current guru boom—was more significant than what he actually said, much of which was subsequently either proved wrong or contradicted by Peters himself. That judgment contains a fairly damning criticism of Peters, which we will try to substantiate later in this chapter. But it also contains a compliment. Few of the business heroes Peters worships have changed their industry in the same way that Peters has his. Insofar as the current management theory boom has a starting date, it is with the publication of *In Search of Excellence;* and insofar as it has a presiding genius who keeps the arguments rolling and the pretenders coming, it is Tom Peters.

## An Excellent Beginning

In the late 1970s, McKinsey decided to pour a substantial amount of money into a research project on the "excellent company." Peters and another consultant, Jim Bennett, were chosen to review the existing literature on "organizational effectiveness." The emphasis that theorists had traditionally placed on strategy and structure, they concluded, had gone beyond the point of diminishing returns, and other, softer factors, such as management style and "culture," were also crucial to success. This was relatively controversial stuff since most McKinsey men were steeped in the lore of strategy and structure. The young researchers' project only took off when three other people joined: Robert Waterman, a more experienced McKinseyite, and two business school professors, Anthony Athos, a specialist on corporate culture, and Richard Pascale, who had for years been conducting comparative research on American and Japanese companies. Peters and Waterman decided to write up the project as a book.

Why did *In Search of Excellence* do so well? For one thing, it was based on a formidable amount of evidence, at least by the far-from-exacting standards of management science. But it also acted as a showcase for the four main ingredients of what might be called the "Peters phenomenon": an uncanny sense of timing, an extraordinary ability to articulate the mood of the moment, the skill to dispense advice that sounds practical, and a breathtaking talent for marketing. As Peters readily admits, the timing was "pure luck."[2] The book appeared in October 1982, the month that American unemployment hit 10 percent and the first time it had broken the double-digit barrier since the Great Depression. *In Search of Excellence* also came out after a glut of books on the wonders of Japanese management.

Indeed, the book seemed perfectly designed to appeal to an America that was worried about its declining competitiveness but tired of being told about the Japanese miracle. Like many other pundits, Peters and Waterman agreed that American managers bore much of the blame for their country's plight, thanks to their obsession with the short term and their indifference to quality and service.[3] However, they argued that Americans did not have to look all the way to Japan for models of how to run excellent companies and revive national competitiveness. America, they pointed out, possessed a host of companies that were producing new products, pioneering new processes, and working overtime to satisfy all their constituents—customers, employees, shareholders, and the public at large.[4] Peters and Waterman thus sounded the "morning in America" theme two years before Ronald Reagan used it to seal his reelection. And like "the great communicator," they trumpeted the abilities of Americans, relying on their own grit and brains, to solve any problem.

> The findings from the excellent companies amount to an up-beat message. There is good news from America. Good management practice today is not resident only in Japan. But, more important, the good news comes from treating people decently and asking them to shine, and from producing things that work. Scale efficiencies give way to small units with turned-on people. Precisely planned R&D efforts aimed at big bang products are replaced by armies of dedicated champions. A numbing focus on cost gives way to an enhancing focus on quality. Hierarchy and three-piece suits give way to first names, shirtsleeves, hoopla, and project-based flexibility. Working according to fat rule books is replaced by everyone's contributing.[5]

The book had another virtue: simplicity. For all the research that went into it, *In Search of Excellence* sometimes reads like a popular how-to book. For example, Peters and Waterman list eight easily identifiable (and memorably expressed) characteristics of excellent companies, such as "sticking to the knitting" (i.e., concentrating on what the firm does best and contracting out everything else to other specialists), creating simultaneous loose–tight control systems (i.e., centralizing core values but decentralizing the way they are achieved), and staying close to the customer. As Peter Drucker has put it, *In Search of Excellence* made management sound "incredibly easy. All you had to do was put that book under your pillow and it will get done."[6]

Peters and Waterman democratized management theory, turning it from a monopoly of chief executives and their boards into something that junior managers needed to master. Significantly for a business book, examples were plucked from all levels of big companies and from several small ones as well. As Drucker conceded: "When Aunt Mary has to give that nephew of hers a high school graduation present and she gives him *In Search of Excellence,* you know that management has become part of the general culture."[7]

The book reached the Aunt Marys of this world not just because it was preaching a simple, relevant message, but largely because of Peters's marketing acumen. He publicized the book with an almost missionary zeal (certainly at a pace that his more laid-back collaborator, Robert Waterman, has found difficult to follow). No conference was left unaddressed, no article unwritten, no talk show untalked. Three years later, Peters could boast that between 100,000 and 200,000 people had been through his "excellence" seminars. The source of his extraordinary stamina is still being debated even within the ranks of the gurus. Henry Mintzberg, a friend, thinks that Peters welcomed the publicity so vigorously because he was convinced that the boom would not last—something that Peters admits was probably true.

Whatever the explanation, Peters brought a new evangelical edge to the profession. He treated "excellence" as a crusade. The truest believers were "skunks"—innovative outsiders who worked on the fringes of companies (the name came from a well-known inventive part of Lockheed, called the Skunk Works). In September 1984, Peters held his first annual Skunk Camp: "40 brave souls who have been going their own way met in California and swapped tales about the battles fought, the scars accumulated, and the personal and soul-satisfying experiences that have come from watching their people become winners." It was vital to have this hard core of true believers because, as Peters is the first to admit, *In Search of Excellence* was more bought than read. Three years after its publication, Peters calculated that 5 million people had bought the book; 2 million to 3 million opened it; around 500,000 read five chapters; 100,000 read it all; and 5,000 made detailed notes. As he put it, "The number with bent pages and heavy underlining is dispiritingly low."[8]

Peters completed his next book, *A Passion for Excellence,* with a new collaborator, Nancy Austin. From a marketing point of view, it amounted to brand reinforcement. It was, he declared from the outset, about the skunks and their battles. The message was expanded (Peters now stressed leadership), but it was also simplified. The eight "excellent" characteristics were boiled down to a triangle of virtues. The three sides of the triangle represented care for customers, innovation, and people. At the center was leadership, exercised largely by what Peters calls "management by walking around" (MBWA)—arguably the first of his great zany slogans. Once again, the book was peppered with intriguing examples. To emphasize the point that "quality is not a technique," Peters and Austin cited a $250,000 industrial "blow dryer" bought by Frank Perdue because the chicken seller reckoned that "the most obnoxious thing in the world is the eight hairs that stick up on a typical wing when it is barbecued." The new blow dryer fluffed up the hairs and burnt most of them off before the chicken went to the stores. "The new technique," Peters and Austin tell us admiringly, "on average reduces the eight hairs to two. Frank doesn't think it is enough."[9]

## Thriving on Silicon Valley

In pop music terms, *A Passion for Excellence* was the classic second album: it sounded like the debut blockbuster, but it was a neater, more professional product. With the third book, *Thriving on Chaos* (1987), the star felt the need to reinvent himself. Now clad in his "crazy times for crazy people" clothes, Peters announced: "There are no excellent companies." This must have been as much a shock for the skunks as Bob Dylan's turning electric was for folk music fans. Once again, the timing was eerily perfect. *Thriving on Chaos* appeared in the same week that the stock market crash of 1987 threatened to unleash chaos on the Western economies.

In the book, Peters articulated a widespread feeling that the world was in the grip of a revolution running out of control, and that businesses needed to introduce drastic changes if they were to have any chance of surviving. Traditional companies, he argued, were terrifyingly like East European economies: tightly controlled from the center; grotesquely overmanned; and obsessed with financial planning. Modern information technology was allowing companies to bypass middle managers (whose main role in life was to collect and control information) and to hand over decision making to the people who assembled the machines or stocked the shelves. The pace of innovation and the fickleness of consumer tastes were making long-range planning redundant. And increased competition from poorer countries was forcing companies in the rich countries to slash their labor costs, either by replacing men with machines or by inventing cleverer production processes.

Once again, Peters was attractively certain about what to do: shrink your company, get rid of your middle managers, and devolve power to the lowest possible level. And above all, keep on changing. "If you aren't reorganizing, pretty substantially, once every six to twelve months," Peters warned bosses, "you're probably out of step with the times." Again, Peters made it clear that this was an attitude even the humblest workers had to embrace. Taking the idea of the permanent revolution to its logical conclusion, he advised people to ask themselves at the end of each day, "What exactly and precisely and explicitly is being done in my work area differently from the way it was done when I came to work in the morning."

*Thriving on Chaos* spent 60 weeks on the *New York Times* best-seller list, which was half as long as *In Search of Excellence,* but longer than any of its successors. Peters's more recent books, such as *Liberation Management* and the *Pursuit of Wow,* have repeated the antirationalist message of *Thriving on Chaos,* reinforcing the brand in the same way that *A Passion for Excellence* reinforced *In Search of Excellence.* In general, the arguments get zanier and the prose more high-octane. The layers of management that need to be eradicated now seem to include everything between the chief executive and the messenger boy. Peters's lists of things managers have to do now stretch for pages (there were 45 precepts for managers of all levels in *Thriving for Chaos* alone). *Liberation Management* includes a list of maxims for modern management that advises: "get fired," "take off your shoes," and "race yaks."[10] He concludes *Crazy Times* with nine "beyonds," among them, "beyond change: towards the abandonment of everything" and "beyond TQM: toward wow!" Peters now preaches "the sublime pleasures of modestly organized anarchy."

Peters's later writing (it might be stretching a point to describe it as "mature") can be read as a long hymn of praise to his adopted home, California's Silicon Valley. California's computer industry has generated an extraordinarily entrepreneurial, free-wheeling, convention-busting management style. The area sees more than 300 businesses founded every year. Each time scientists and entrepreneurs get a bright idea, they form a company to test it on the market and then move on, either because the idea has flopped or because the technology has changed; as a result, people and capital are recycled quickly and efficiently to take advantage of changes in fashion or breakthroughs in technology.[11] Bankruptcy is a badge of honor. As Peters puts it himself: "Through luck I ended up in Santa Clara county—a big godawful mess populated by failures."[12]

The inhabitants of Silicon Valley are happier in sneakers and jeans than in suits and ties, and appalled at the idea of people spending their entire lives working for the same organization. They happily hop from job to job, confident that their value lies in the quality of their ideas rather than their track record of loyalty. Such people like to work in companies that are structured around projects and are as free from bureaucracy as possible. Even a fairly large company, such as Intel, is a free-flowing collection of "chip squads"—a series of ever-changing teams working on different generations of microprocessors. Valley people hop not just from job to job but also from career to career, with scientists becoming entrepreneurs, entrepreneurs becoming managers, and managers becoming venture capitalists. In other words, they thrive on chaos.

### The Point of Peters

All this explains why Peters is a multimillionaire. But is he any good? Even if he knows a huge amount about companies, two potentially fatal flaws mar his work: first, he has got it wrong too often (two-thirds of the companies singled out as excellent in 1982 have now fallen from grace); and, second, he has contradicted himself even more often than the average politician. Add them together and the canon of Peters's work looks worryingly insubstantial and ephemeral—hence the suspicion that what he has done is more interesting than what he has said.

This charge can partly be answered by saying that Peters writes his books for the real world, for people to use, and that the real world changes fairly quickly. Although he has not quite stooped to writing get-rich-quick books, he has always made it clear that, far from being exercises in academic analysis, his books are intended to help people prosper, or at least survive. *Thriving on Chaos* is subtitled *Handbook for a Management Revolution.* From this perspective—from the perspective of the manager (one is tempted to say the skunk) in the field—an unfailing nose for business trends is one of Peters's strengths rather than his weaknesses, even if those trends often do not last long.

Peters's modus operandi is to sense where the corporate world is heading, usually correctly, and then shout it from the rooftops. *Liberation Management* is, among other things, a feisty guide to the latest management fads, each amply illustrated with case studies, such as flexible organizations (CNN virtually reinvents itself at the start of every news day), learning organizations (Quad/Graphics insists that its employees keep on educating themselves), and a relentless focus on customers (Britain's Joshua Tetley pub chain offers prizes to bar staff who can recite the names and drinking habits of 100 customers). The list could go on for pages. One of the faults of *Liberation Management,* and some of Peters's later books, is that it does.

In other words, criticizing Peters for giving out advice that was only relevant for, say, five years, misses the point. Peter's readers need advice that they can use *now*. Many of the companies that Peters selected as excellent in 1982 were indeed so at the time; their decline cannot be blamed on him. What mattered from the reader's point of view back in 1982 was "What can I learn now?" In a recent newspaper article, Peters regretted having dismissed two even more unconventional writers, Stephen Covey (*The Seven Habits of Highly Effective People*) and Ken Blanchard (*The One Minute Manager*) for not being rigorous enough.[13] Yet the books by Covey and Blanchard, argues Peters, "give ordinary people (like me) practical things to do this afternoon to make the world of work a little better." Surely some part of Peters was writing about himself.

All this may get Peters off the hook for being disproved by events. Even by the standards of one-minute managers, however, there have been some fairly substantial contradictions. Remember that this was the man who, having launched the "excellence movement" in 1982, was willing to claim "Excellence isn't" in 1987. All the same, the charges against him are often exaggerated. One of the most frequently voiced objections is that, having started his career genuflecting before big companies, Peters now preaches that small is beautiful. Though *In Search of Excellence* is devoted to giant companies—which, incidentally, were the only companies that could afford to pay McKinsey's exorbitant fees—it is, on closer reading, remarkably sensitive to the ills of gigantism and the advantages of staying small:

> The message from the excellent companies we reviewed was invariably the same. Small, independent new venture teams at 3M (by the hundred); small divisions at Johnson & Johnson (over 150 in a $5 billion firm); ninety PCCs at TI; the product champion-led teams at IBM; "bootlegging" teams at GE; small, ever-shifting segments at Digital; new boutiques monthly at Bloomingdale's. . . . Small is beautiful.[14]

Such decentralization cut down on the need for layer upon layer of middle managers. It also ensured that companies were committed to innovation and that they focused on their customers.[15]

## Still Crazy after All These Years

However, there is a deeper consistency to Peters's work. Everything he has written, from *In Search of Excellence* to his latest *Crazy Times* ramblings, can be read as an extended critique of scientific management. One of his most characteristic phrases, about creating a "technology of foolishness," came from his first book.[16] Peters is the Michel Foucault of the management world: a scourge of the rationalist tradition and a celebrant of the creative necessity of chaos and craziness.

When Peters went to business school, management was still dominated by numbers: "The only facts that many of us considered 'real data' were the ones we could put numbers on."[17] Management education celebrated the virtues of quantitative analysis, pooh-poohed "soft-headed humanism" and unscientific intuition, and sought detached, analytical justifications for all decisions.[18] In short, it made damn sure that the "technical jocks" were in charge.

The rationalist model found its most influential exponents in "the whiz kids," a group of strategic analysts who helped mastermind America's victory in the Second World War and then went on to reshape the Ford Motor Company.[19] For Peters and his generation, the horrific weaknesses of this approach to management were demonstrated not just in America's ailing industries but in its hopeless foreign policy: the brightest whiz kid of them all, Robert McNamara, left the chairmanship of Ford to become Secretary of Defense, and then tried to win the Vietnam War by escalating enemy kills. The rationalist model "is right enough to be dangerously wrong," Peters and Waterman mused in 1982, "and it has arguably led us seriously astray."

*In Search of Excellence* advances three arguments against the rationalist model. First, the model puts too much emphasis on financial analysis and too little on motivating workers or satisfying customers. The obsession with cost persuades firms to undervalue quality and value, to patch up old products rather than invent new ones, to treat workers as costs of production rather than sources of value. The authors quote their colleague, Anthony Athos, approvingly: "Good managers make meanings for people, as well as money."

Second, the rationalist model encouraged bureaucratic conformity at the expense of entrepreneurial innovation. Rationalist managers believe that big is best, because it brings economies of scale; that messiness is disastrous, because it means waste and confusion; and that planning is essential, because it allows firms to control the future. For Peters and Waterman, the best firms, such as 3M, an office-products giant, were almost exactly the opposite: they were hotbeds of experimentation, happy with irrationality and chaos.[20]

Third, the rationalist model rests on a misunderstanding of human nature. "The central problem with the rationalist view of organizing people is that people are not very rational," the authors argue. "To fit Taylor's old model, or today's organizational charts, man is simply designed wrong."[21] Scientific managers overestimate the importance of financial rewards in motivating workers: people are much more interested in intangible things, like winning the praise of colleagues or working for an organization they admire. "All the companies we interviewed," the authors note, "from Boeing to McDonald's, were quite simply rich tapestries of anecdote, myth, and fairy tale."[22]

Peters and Waterman were hardly the first people (and hardly the last) to draw attention to the limitations of the rationalist model of management. As already noted, there is a long tradition of bashing scientific management stretching back to the human-relations school of management theorists who devoted themselves to demonstrating that man is a social animal, not just a rational calculating machine. In *The Human Side of Enterprise*, published in 1960, Douglas McGregor argued that management theory paid too much attention to "theory X," which holds that workers are lazy and need to be driven by financial incentives, and not enough to "theory Y," which holds that, on the contrary, workers are creative and need to be given responsibility. The business press was not indifferent to the softer side of business thinking either: *Business Week* even ran a cover story on corporate culture in the late summer of 1980.[23]

Even so, Peters has taken his antirationalist stand to extremes hardly dreamed of by his predecessors. The world has gone bonkers, he rants, and to cope with it managers must go bonkers too. It is no longer enough for them to pay attention to the intuitive as well as the rational side of their jobs. They must go mad: throw away their slide rules, forget about climbing the career ladder, and turn themselves into zany entrepreneurs. It is no longer enough for companies to slim their headquarters and thin the ranks of middle management. Firms should use internal markets to turn their employees into mini-entrepreneurs, and external markets to make sure that they are not wasting their time doing things like cooking and computing, which could be done better elsewhere. For Peters, "crazy" organizations are more efficient as well as more fun than their sane rivals.

But is this really true? The critical question to ask about Tom Peters is not whether he is consistent but whether his extreme and relentless antirationalism makes sense. Peters is blind to the importance of such humdrum virtues as stability and continuity. For instance, in Peters's chaotic world, there is no room for schedules or middle managers; in the real world, middle managers are often the people who hold organizations together, and schedules are the framework around which most "uncrazy" people build their days. Indeed, Peters fatally underestimates the need in even the craziest organizations for some stability if they are to thrive.

Even Peters's beloved Silicon Valley is fortunate to possess two islands of stability in Stanford University and Hewlett-Packard, both of which have trained entrepreneurs and provided them with a network of contacts. As for the relentless reconfiguration of other organizations in the area, this has not come without costs. In *The Breakthrough Illusion* (1990), Richard Florida and Martin Kenney pointed out that "hypermobility" can lead to waste, as research studies are disrupted and creative individuals burn themselves out, ending their careers before they are 40. In his book on the company man, Anthony Sampson quotes Frank O'Mahoney, a spokesman for Apple, lamenting the company's amnesia:

> There's not much institutional memory at Apple. When we celebrated the tenth anniversary of the Macintosh it was hard to find people who remembered it. We wanted to have an Apple museum but not enough early products had been kept. The consultants seem to know more about the history of Apple than we do.[24]

Indeed, the history of Apple over the past decade might be read as a sermon on why following a crazy dream is not enough. Anarchy is a provocative idea; it is not a business strategy. Having said all this, it would be churlish not to concede that Peters-the-provocateur is on to something, even if Peters-the-prophet is not.

### Far Enough Out to Be Interesting

The world may never go as "crazy" as Peters predicts; but it is definitely moving in his direction, as product cycle times collapse, command-and-control systems buckle, and the pace of innovation increases. Companies such as Apple may perish, but Silicon Valley will survive precisely because its business culture is more fluid and its companies more entrepreneurial than those with inflexible systems of management. Middle managers may be reinvented as "coaches" and so on, but they will never be the bureaucratic pen pushers of old.

Peters concedes that the firms he celebrates may have got a little ahead of the norm. *In Search of Excellence* talked about the likes of Hewlett-Packard, Johnson & Johnson, and 3M. In later works, he also has case studies on well-known firms such as ABB and Union Pacific. But alongside these sturdy beasts are more exotic creatures, including "virtual" firms such as Verifone, Oticon, and 3.00 (yes, this is a company's name). Peters's ambition is to be an agent of change: "far enough out to be interesting, close enough in to be plausible."[25]

Does he pass this test? At the lunch break of a Tom Peters seminar, two British businessmen—one in pet foods, the other in brewing—are asked privately whether the likes of Verifone, a credit-card authorization firm that has no head office and that bans the use of paper, are really relevant to their fairly stable industries. The two managers both admit that they see Peters primarily as a provocateur. But they insist that his ideas do help. As the pet food manager explains, the main effect is psychological: "It's in the way I look at the world . . . the way I treat people." The brewer looks stumped; then he says: "We're just about to empower our draymen—to let them negotiate with the pubs to which they deliver. That was an idea that we got from a Peters seminar three years ago." Three years sounds like quite a long time in the "nanosecond nineties." The world is going in Peters's direction. It is just not moving as quickly as he would like.

# PART THREE

# THE GREAT DEBATES

# CHAPTER 5

RETHINKING THE COMPANY

THE SHELL CENTRE, on the south bank of the Thames in the heart of London, is a striking monument to corporate self-confidence. Solid and imposing, it serenely surveys all that surrounds it, including the Palace of Westminster and a dozen Whitehall departments. With its labyrinthine corridors, hundreds of meeting rooms, and all-pervasive sense of bureaucratic permanence, the building has been a perfect habitat for Shell Man—as the company's employees were once mockingly known the world over. By tradition, Shell Man was a bureaucrat in all but name, differing from the civil servants and paper pushers who accompanied him on the daily commute from the suburbs to Waterloo Station in only one thing—the size of his paycheck. He looked forward to a lifetime of secure employment and an index-linked pension at the end of it. The company provided country-club membership not just for him but for his children. When he was posted to Asia and Africa—as he often was as part of his carefully planned progression up the company—he competed in pomp and circumstance with the British ambassador and was not above doing a little spying on the side for his friends in the British Secret Service.

In Washington State, the headquarters of Microsoft could hardly be more different. To reach the software giant, you have to drive out of Seattle into the surrounding redwood forests until you come to Microsoft Way. The company has dispensed with corporate skyscrapers and awe-inspiring reception areas. Instead, the visitor is confronted with groups of white buildings, as modest and low as traditional head offices are tall and imposing. Microsoft employees look more like graduate students than successful businessmen: they are dressed in sweatshirts and sneakers, and they sport long hair and pony tails. The average age is only 32; and there are noticeably more women around the place than at Shell. But these Microrerfs are as dedicated as their counterparts at Shell, often working late into the night, sustained by pizza and free Coca-Cola; and, for the most part, they are a great deal richer. Those who have stayed the course—and a great many have fallen by the wayside—have often ended up as millionaires.

At first sight, an outsider might conclude that Royal Dutch/Shell and Microsoft are in two separate worlds, one designed for an industry where the basic product often takes a decade of hard prospecting just to locate, the other for a business where change is measured in weeks. The outsider might add that Shell looks a bit more like the "classical" model of a company—the sort of thing that other firms would try to copy and that, one day, Microsoft would mature into. However, rather than Microsoft evolving into Shell, it is Shell that has recently been trying to become more like Microsoft. Over the past decade, the oil company has strived, among other things, to become more entrepreneurial and to hire more female staff. In March 1995, this Microsoftization was speeded up when Shell announced that it was shedding 1,200 jobs in its headquarters, in an attempt to cut bureaucracy and rid itself of its "committee culture."

Management theory is currently trying to understand the seismic shift in corporate organization that has driven Shell and companies like it to become more like Microsoft. This effort is the starting point for Chapters 5 to 9, which are about "the great debates" of modern management. This chapter is concerned with the uncertainty that has forced the modern company to question its old assumptions about size, strength, and structure. Chapter 6 considers how these new, more flexible companies try to use knowledge. And Chapters 7 and 8 focus on the implications of these changes for the leaders of companies. How should they now set strategies? How should they govern themselves? And to whom are they answerable? Finally, Chapter 9 examines what all these corporate changes mean for the world of work.

## The End of Certainty

Over the past decade, companies have been forced to rethink almost every tenet of managerial wisdom. Once companies prided themselves on the size of their headquarters and the length of their payrolls. Now they are renting out space in their head offices and cutting their corporate staff to the bone. Once companies prided themselves on "vertical integration" and were run like self-contained empires with as little recourse to outsiders as possible. Now they are "sticking to their knitting" in a different sense, focusing on their core businesses and contracting everything else out to independent specialists. Once they had a clear line of command and control, starting with the chairman at the top and stretching to the lowliest menial. Now they are turning themselves into "inverted pyramids," encouraging workplace democracy and handing power to front-line workers. Once they had a clear idea of to whom they were responsible—their shareholders—and what they were supposed to be chasing—ever higher profits. Now they are being urged to think about their stakeholders and to increase "well-being" rather than just profits.

What forces have unleashed this maelstrom? A computer scientist might say that the world is struggling through a transition, from the machine age to the information age. An investment banker would point to the mobility of capital. But the fundamental cause of the change facing managers everywhere is probably two factors, both first identified by Peter Drucker: uncertainty and knowledge.

Nowadays, change is discontinuous—or, perhaps more accurately, more discontinuous than it has ever been before. If history was ever a guide to success in the commercial world, it certainly is not any longer. Industries can be shaken overnight, giants felled by a single blow. In the space of five years, one can go from being frightened of IBM to pitying it; in the space of a few days, a centuries-old bank such as Barings can disappear.

Thanks to globalization, a company can be surprised or outwitted by unknown competitors in countries on the other side of the world. Technology is changing so quickly that a Nintendo Game Boy now contains as much computing power as the supercomputers that used to control America's missile defense system. As a result, Niccolo Machiavelli's maxim, "Whoever desires constant success must change his conduct with the times," has emerged from relative obscurity to become a daily mantra.

In this more frantic world, the only currency that really matters is knowledge. Brute force, huge factories, distribution networks, mineral resources, even money—all count for far less. By early 1997, the stock market valued General Motors and Ford (two companies with combined sales of more than $300 billion) at about $80 billion; by contrast, two ideas-based companies—Microsoft and Intel—could muster combined sales of only $30 billion and a combined workforce of one million people and just 70,000 employees but their stock was worth three times as much as the two Detroit juggernauts. As Tom Peters puts it, "The age of lumps is gone; the age of ephemera has just begun." Witness the enormous value of fantasy and star quality: the $6 billion that Seagram, a beverage company, bid to enter the entertainment industry; the $2.3 billion rise in the value of shares of companies that sponsored Michael Jordan just on the rumor that he might return to basketball; and the $1.3 billion fall in IBM's value when its chief financial officer, Jerome York, announced he was leaving.

Globalization only makes knowledge more important. As the price of communication drops to close to zero (it will soon be as cheap to telephone Delhi from Manhattan as it is to call the Bronx), bringing millions of cheap hands and brains into competition with Western ones, the only sustainable advantage is likely to be the capacity to produce ideas. Nor is "knowledge" just something that firms in Silicon Valley and Hollywood need to be worried about. Even smokestack firms like America's Chaparral Steel, a small mill that has repeatedly broken productivity records, have shown that brains are more important than iron ore. One of America's most admired companies is Rubbermaid— a firm that makes an endless supply of low-tech housewares and the like, but does so in an outstandingly intelligent way.

## Reasons to Panic

Modern management theory is obsessed with "change" of one sort or another: how to generate it, how to respond to it, how to avoid being swept away by it. This is perhaps not surprising, given the number of celebrated companies that have either ended up in the boneyard or at least got a good look over the fence. At one time or another over the past decade, doubts have been raised about the likes of Mettallgesellschaft, Daimler-Benz, Mazda, Nissan, Caterpillar, Philips, Bull, Olivetti, Du Pont, Salomon Brothers, and Westinghouse.

Rather than celebrating their size, large companies seem to be trying to hide it, imitating their smaller rivals by shrinking their headquarters, slashing layers of management, and subdividing themselves into smaller, more manageable units. ABB, the Swiss-Swedish engineering giant, has a corporate headquarters of 171 people and has divided itself into 1,300 local companies, each one a separate legal entity. Percy Barnevik, the company's founder, famously followed a 30 percent rule: whenever he took over a company, he reduced the size of its bureaucracy by a third. Some firms have even gone the whole hog and broken themselves up into separate companies. Both AT&T, America's biggest telephone company, and ITT, its quintessential conglomerate, split themselves into three in 1995. "It has become clear to me that the best way to take advantage of the incredible opportunities springing up in the communications industry is to separate into smaller, more focused enterprises," explained Bob Allen, AT&T's boss: "Our integrated structure worked very well for us. But it is an idea whose time has passed." The stock market agreed: the market capitalization of the new broken-up AT&T skyrocketed, as did that of ITT. In the early 1990s, Courtaulds, a British textile company, and ICI, a British chemical company, divided into two. Within three years of announcing the breakup, the combined value of ICI and Zeneca was two-and-a-half times that of the old ICI.

Even the Germans have been forced to join in all this "unbundling." Since Jurgen Schrempp took over Daimler-Benz, Europe's biggest company, in May 1995, it has been offloading businesses almost as quickly as it once went about acquiring them. In March 1996, Schrempp let Fokker, a Dutch aircraft maker that he had advised Daimler to buy in 1993, go bank-rupt. In Japan, Toyota has eliminated three of its seven layers of management and decoupled pay from titles.

This change of thinking has also had dramatic conse-quences for firms' sense of social responsibility. Even the most paternalistic companies, which ran themselves rather like pri-vatized welfare states, have been forced to join the bloodletting, ruthlessly sacrificing managers as well as workers. Some IBM employees feel so misused by their once benevolent employer that they have formed IBM Workers United, which publishes a monthly newsletter called *The Resistor*.[1] And the cutting looks as though it will continue. Despite a panic about "corporate anorexia," some American companies have recently introduced a practice known as "pruning"—cutting the workforce regu-larly in order to promote the health of those who survive.

## The Virtues of Virtuality

Management theorists have produced wildly differing diag-noses of this corporate malaise. Many of them revolve around the size of the companies concerned. In general, this is a mis-take. Neither bigness nor smallness confers an inherent advan-tage; it depends enormously on what sort of market a company is in, what sort of product it provides, and how it is structured (as we shall see, there are plenty of ways for a giant to act small and for a small company to act big). So why is the debate im-portant? First, until recently, bigness was a sign of success: the traditional company was based on the doctrine of economies of scale. Second, the size debate opens up most of the other issues about the modern company.

One widely held view is that big companies have had their day and are rapidly being displaced by much smaller, nimbler or-ganizations; in its most extreme form, this argument holds that the future lies with "virtual" companies—small, fast-changing, amoebalike organizations that come together to get a job done and then break apart, only to reconfigure in a different form around another project. Peter Drucker has announced that "The Fortune 500 is over." Tom Peters argues that "smaller firms are gaining in almost every market."[2] Charles Handy talks about or-ganizations becoming corporate condominiums—temporary col-lections of knowledge workers. Both *Inc* Magazine and *The*

*Economist* have at various times been aggressive promoters of the "small is beautiful" argument and cautioned governments for supporting dying monoliths.[3]

The prophets of virtual organizations point out that such firms have few of the fixed costs of their bigger rivals—head offices, company perks, pensions, and the like—but can still use modern communication tools to imitate their global reach. From this point of view, the craze for downsizing and delayering can do little more than stave off the death of the big companies. In the end, the only way that they will be able to compete with small companies is to join them and break themselves up into a thousand parts.

Critics of big companies also point out that economies of scale have been falling dramatically since the 1970s. "Lean manufacturing" and "just-in-time production" have shifted the emphasis from size to timeliness; freer capital markets and cheaper, better communications have radically reduced barriers of entry into industries; and the spread of affluence has generated a demand for customized goods and services, fragmenting mass markets into thousands of niches. At the same time, the "diseconomies of scale" have loomed ever larger. Giant companies generate bureaucratic bloat; giant factories create shop-floor alienation; and many giant corporations fail to attract creative workers, or to make good use of them if they do get hold of them. Worse still, the standardized, homogenized products that pour out of these factories are suffering from a double squeeze: fashion-conscious customers are opting for goods that are tailored to their specific needs (or passing whims), and value-conscious ones are less and less willing to pay a premium price for a global brand.

## Big Is Back

The average size of both companies and workplaces has certainly been falling steadily throughout the industrial world since the late 1960s, with Europe leading the way and America struggling to catch up. But size (or the lack of it) is in itself no guarantee of failure. IBM and Daimler-Benz may have run into trouble, but other big firms—such as McDonald's, Marks and Spencer, and Toyota—have prospered. *Fortune's* 1997 list of America's 10 most admired companies was headed by Coca-Cola, and included such stalwarts as Merck, United Parcel Service, Johnson & Johnson, Pfizer, and Procter & Gamble, as well as more recent creations such as Mirage Resorts, Microsoft, Intel, and Berkshire Hathaway. The most vigorous challengers to established big businesses are often other big businesses. Sears Roebuck has lost market share in America principally to other big retailers such as Wal-Mart, which increased its payroll by 182,000 in 1992–94.

Indeed, there has recently been a backlash in favor of big firms. In industries such as banking, health care, and media, bosses have convinced themselves that size, integration, and synergy are wonderful attributes and embarked on enormous mergers to prove it. Their logic looked faulty. In banking, the only justification for mergers such as Chase-Chemical and Lloyds-TSB is cost reductions—something unlikely to improve the industry's already low standards in customer service. ("Why anybody thinks that they will produce a gazelle by mating two dinosaurs is beyond me," commented Tom Peters with respect to the Chase-Chemical tie-up.) In health care, the mergers may provide a way for the industry to cope with the new cost-consciousness of its customers; but they could also stifle the innovative parts of companies that are responsible for most of the drug industry's profits. In entertainment, it makes more sense for a distribution channel, such as a television network, to buy shows and films from as many producers as possible, rather than to just take its parent's offerings. As for size, although a studio needs to be big enough to produce enough hits to cover the multitude of duds, nobody has yet proved that there is any gain from being as big as the new Disney-ABC combine. Its closest rival, Time Warner, is hardly an inspiring example of vertical integration.

A 1995 study by *Business Week* and Mercer Management examined 150 deals worth more than $500 million completed in the early 1990s and found that only 17 percent created substantial returns in comparison with other companies in their sectors; and "nonacquirers"—companies that did not take part in big takeovers—outperformed acquirers.[4] This was in line with a host of studies of takeovers in the 1980s by academics such as Michael Jensen at Harvard, most of which showed that leveraged buyouts and mergers did create value—but mainly for shareholders in the companies that were bought. In other words, buyers paid too much. Why? One delightful study released in 1995 by Mathew Hayward and Donald Hambrick of Columbia University found a statistical way of confirming what we all knew already: there was a link between the premiums paid by bosses and their own inflated self-esteem, which the academics measured by things such as the boss's salary in comparison with that of his peers and the acres of flattering press coverage. The moment any boss appears on the cover of an American business magazine fondling his golf clubs alongside a headline such as "Hurricane Jack Lands on the Green," sell the stock.

However, the dubious arguments for megamergers should not obscure the fact that another quieter group of big companies has proved that size can have more solid advantages. The best big firms—such as Coca-Cola, Levi Strauss, Nestlé, and Philip Morris—have shown that it is possible to have both: the weight that comes with size and the nimbleness that used to be associated with smallness.

Can small firms really stand up to competition from these "lean and mean" big firms? Bennett Harrison, a professor at Carnegie-Mellon University in Pittsburgh, has looked at the way that small firms cluster around big ones and argued that, even if such small firms count as separate entities, their workers are in fact no less reliant on these corporate hubs than their peers working at the big firms.[5] Far from reveling in their nimbleness, the chief preoccupation of many small firms in Silicon Valley is structuring alliances and mergers so that they can gain the necessary scale. According to Broadview Associates, an American consultancy, there were 2,913 mergers and acquisitions worth a staggering $134 billion in the world's high-tech industry in 1995 (compared with 1,861 deals worth $90.5 billion in 1994). Much the same thing is going on in another part of the world much praised for its smallness: Germany's *Mittelstand*. Some 25,000 medium-size companies went bust in Germany in 1995. In a time of cost cutting, small and midsize firms in industries such as machine tools found it harder to "outsource" things than big companies, and felt that they lacked clout when it came to distributing products—particularly overseas. "The notion of a critical company size holds true in our industry too," admits one prominent *Mittelstand* leader.[6] In Japan, although a few upstarts have managed to steal a march on the giant *keiretsu* in businesses such as retailing, most small independent firms feel incredibly exposed, particularly because of their lack of capital. The bankruptcy, in August 1995, of Nishiki Finance, one of the few banks prepared to lend to small businesses, led to the bankruptcy of over 400 companies.

## The Death of a Model

The arguments about size will no doubt continue. But if size per se is no more a portent of disaster than it once was of success, then it seems fair to ask whether all this talk about a corporate revolution is justified. One school of gurus takes an increasingly skeptical view of the apocalyptic visions offered by the likes of Tom Peters. Henry Mintzberg, a Canadian of contrarian bent who holds managerial chairs on both sides of the Atlantic, at McGill University and Insead, likes to point out that there is nothing new about "turbulence": every generation believes that it is living through an unprecedented spate of corporate births and deaths.

Accept this point of view, as many managers secretly do, exaggerate it a little, and you reach one of two conclusions. The first is that all the traditional company needs to do is refine itself—make its strategies more far-seeing, its structures more elaborate, its control mechanisms more comprehensive. Indeed, many of the most successful management tools of the past two decades, such as the Boston Consulting Group's "growth-share matrix"—which divides markets into cash cows, stars, and dogs—are intended to supercharge existing managerial systems. The second muddle-through solution is to keep the firm's basic structure but build or acquire an "entrepreneurial" wing, crammed with computers and T-shirted people. This approach combines the virtues of bureaucratic solidity with those of entrepreneurial zeal.

Both solutions are dangerously complacent. Nostalgia may add a glow to the postwar period, but it certainly was much stabler than the 1980s and 1990s. N. C. Churchill and D. F. Muzyka, two academics at Insead, have calculated that the "death rate" (the percentage of names that do not reappear from one year to the next) of the Fortune 500 companies was four times as high in 1990 as it was in 1970.[7] Even the best managers have found that fine-tuning traditional command-and-control systems is subject to the law of diminishing returns. Similarly, crafting an entrepreneurial wing onto a hierarchical company works only for a short time, if at all. Part of IBM's problem in the 1980s was that the comparatively free-thinking mentality of its personal computer division never reached the other parts of the company. One of General Motors's ideas behind buying Electronic Data Systems was to absorb a little of the computer-service company's entrepreneurial culture; it never did, and was forced to sell the company.

## Who Killed Alfred Sloan?

Companies are indeed undergoing a revolution, but the explanation lies in something other than the (debatable) demise of size. A growing band of management thinkers believes that companies of all sizes are living through a transition from one corporate model based on control to another based on entrepreneurialism. The current leaders of this school are Christopher Bartlett, of Harvard Business School, and Sumantra Ghoshal, of London Business School, but its members also include Yves Doz and Chan Kim of Insead, Gary Hamel and John Stopford of London Business School, and C. K. Prahalad of Michigan.

The departing ideology is Sloanism, a managerial philosophy named after Alfred Sloan, who took over as president of General Motors in 1923. Sloan's great achievement was to do for management what Henry Ford had done for labor—turn it into a reliable, efficient, machinelike process. Indeed, to a large extent, Sloan's system was supposed to be an antidote to temperamental pioneers like Ford, whose irrational dislike of producing anything other than the Model "T" (he once kicked to pieces a slightly modified version) nearly bankrupted his company. Sloan wanted to invent a company that could run itself. He thus invented the modern multidivisional firm, in which businesses are divided into a set of semiautonomous operating units, each responsible for maintaining the market share and profits of a single business or market and each having its division heads reporting to a group headquarters in charge of setting long-term strategy and allocating capital. Although the Sloanist firm was decentralized, there was a rigid (and formal) command-and-control system. And there was even a professional class of managers to run it—the people that sociologists once dismissed as "organization men"[8] and that commentators now remember with growing nostalgia.[9]

Sloanism inspired some of American capitalism's greatest achievements. It was also an unsurpassed way of producing standardized goods. General Motors, for example, raised its share of the American market from 18 percent in the early 1920s, when Sloan took over, to upward of 45 percent by the late 1970s, to make it by far the largest car company in the world.[10]

For the past 30 years, however, the Sloanist model has been under attack. As already pointed out, its noisiest critic has probably been Tom Peters. But, even if Sloan had never become a megaguru, Sloanism was destined to be undermined in the real world by four antagonists. First came the Japanese businessmen who relentlessly inundated Western markets with better, cheaper, more reliable goods through "lean" production based on teamwork, which avoided both the alienation and the waste of Sloan's system. The second front was opened up by Michael Milken and Ivan Boesky, who, for all their faults, demonstrated that Sloanism had allowed many American firms to be hijacked by managers more interested in their pay and perks than in shareholder value. The third attack came from Silicon Valley, where Apple's Steve Jobs and others there have repeatedly demonstrated that you can succeed in business without growing a giant bureaucracy. The last attack came from the reengineers who ripped apart all the old Sloanist functional departments such as "marketing," "production," and "research" and pushed workers into cross-functional teams, forcing them to use computers to bridge the gaps.

All of these changes—and a hundred smaller ones—can be traced back to uncertainty and knowledge. Under pressure from them, the Sloanist system has disintegrated—or, more accurately, an extreme version of one of Sloan's beliefs, decentralization, has triumphed over two of his other tenets: emphasis on formal controls, and self-sufficiency.

Consider, first, the weak aspects of Sloan's formula, most notably his belief in an elaborately structured hierarchy in which the most senior managers concentrate only on long-term planning, and the most junior focus on day-to-day problem solving. The hierarchy was a slowly moving conveyor belt, relaying information (ground into statistics and reinterpreted by middle managers) to strategy makers at the top. However, modern companies have to be driven by their customers, not their bureaucracies. Jack Welch, chairman of General Electric, once vilified the Sloanist company for having "its face toward the CEO and its ass toward the customer."

As for the data conveyor belt, markets today are so like quicksilver that information that arrives late is not worth having. Rather than worrying about rationality and the importance of being "an objective organization, as distinguished from the type that gets lost in the subjectivity of personalities," as Sloan once put it, modern business has a craving for the instinctive. Richard Branson, for example, had the idea of setting up an airline when he spent three days trying to get through to People Express and found the phone permanently engaged. There had to be a severe shortage of any product for which there was such demand, he reasoned, and so he founded Virgin Airlines. Indeed, the idea of allotting people permanently into departments of any sort seems strange. Even if the departments are industry-specific, such as "our computer division," they can still be caught out by new markets and products that often spring up between the cracks of old industries.

### Inside the Walls

The next casualty is the idea of each company as a completely self-sufficient organization. Sloanist firms were fortresses, making many of their own raw materials. Now, managers are smashing down barriers—not only with suppliers but also with competitors. More than 20,000 new alliances were formed in the United States between 1987 and 1992, compared with just 750 during the 1970s, according to Booz, Allen & Hamilton. Xerox alone has 300 alliances—50 of them with IBM. There are now more than 400 airline alliances around the world, many of them designed to get around national boundaries. Europe has also caught the alliance bug. France Télécom and Deutsche Telekom spend half their time hopping into bed with each other (and the other half trying to entice various American firms to join them).

The success rate of alliances is still very low. Surveys put it at about one in five. They also have a low life expectancy, rarely lasting longer than four years. A third of the managers

questioned by Booz, Allen described alliances as dangerous.
The same forces of change that make a company look like an
ideal partner one day can turn it into a competitor the next.
And even when alliances work, there can be problems about
how to share the spoils or about things quite apart from the
way the companies work together in the field. By early 1997,
the marketing alliance between KLM and Northwest Airlines
was generally deemed to be the most successful in the airline
industry, bringing in some $150 million of extra revenue to
each partner, but, despite their obvious compatibility, the two
carriers have often come close to divorce over nonoperational
issues, such as shareholder rights.

All the same, most companies see alliances as a way to gain
outside expertise without having to go through the rigmarole of
a full takeover. They also let a company dip its toe into a new industry that it does not yet fully understand. Through corporate
venturing and the like, big drug firms such as Glaxo-Wellcome
and Merck now have research agreements with strings of tiny
cousins in the biotechnology industry.

The old corporate wall has also been breached in the relationship between a company and its suppliers. Around the
world, companies are reducing the number of suppliers and
forging closer relations with those who survive: showing them
sensitive information, helping them improve their procedures,
and including them in company bonus schemes. As part of its
huge reorganization, designated Ford 2000, the Detroit car
maker hopes to halve its number of suppliers (currently 1,600);
it is also handing them various engineering tasks it previously
did in-house. The motive is partly to reduce costs; but it is also
to get better performance. After all, a trusted supplier is more
likely to come up with ideas for new products (as Marks and
Spencer's food suppliers do) or to allocate good people to the
job. Ford and Chrysler have always got better performance from
their suppliers than General Motors because they have promised
them long-term deals. One of ABB's suppliers knocked 30 percent off its costs once it was given design responsibility.[11]

The basic assumption behind such "connected corporations" is that, far from being the prerogative of a particular
company, any product or service is the responsibility of an entire chain of firms, starting with suppliers and ending with distributors. France's Renault even got its suppliers to design the

headlights, instrument panel, and other parts of its Twingo model. Procter & Gamble, a consumer goods company, and Wal-Mart, a retail giant, have invested in a joint information system in a bid to coordinate production with sales.

As with the vogue for alliances, the charms of "supply-chain management" may have been exaggerated. Japanese manufacturers who pioneered the idea are noticeably trying to extricate themselves from these marriages now that it is cheaper to find parts abroad. A host of problems can arise when the invited partner turns out to be a competitor. Nevertheless, as Jordan Lewis, an author who specializes in the subject, points out, managers can no longer think about their particular firm in isolation. Even if their firm is not already entwined in a cat's cradle of alliances with other firms, its own internal structure is probably beginning to resemble a network of alliances among different parts of the company.

## From Decentralization to Empowerment

Inviting lots of suppliers and rivals inside Sloan's fortress is a blatant attack on everything that the great man held most dear. So, too, is the current penchant for flattening hierarchies. Yet another way in which modern management has turned against Sloan is perhaps the most cruel. Critics of Sloan have accepted one of his ideas, decentralization, and then taken it to extremes that he would never have countenanced.

Sloan divided General Motors into separate arms, such as Buick, Pontiac, and Chevrolet. Today, some big companies are trying to break themselves into thousands of small firms—thereby hoping to "empower" the workers in the front line. The theory is that, in today's frantic business world, it is often better to make the wrong decision quickly than the right one slowly. (Asked to explain his strategy, Bert Roberts of MCI, one of America's biggest telephone companies, replied, "We run like mad, and then we change direction.") Some companies, such as Britain's Virgin, make a point of breaking up subsidiaries once they reach a certain size; Acer, a Taiwanese computer company, is splitting itself into 21 subsidiaries, each of which it intends to float on the stock market.

As GE's Jack Welch has pointed out, each big company has to give its subsidiaries power until it hurts—and then give them more. For some management theorists, even this level of decentralization is inadequate. Tom Peters, for instance, thinks that companies should treat each worker as a small company in his or her own right. He praises the Ritz-Carlton group, which has given even its lowliest bellhops the power to spend up to $2,000 on the spot to solve a customer's problem. One of Peters's business heroes is Virginia Azuela, the housekeeper on the fourth floor of the Ritz-Carlton in San Francisco, who "owns" that floor because she makes all the decisions involved in maintaining it.

The problem with decentralization on this scale is that it may seem only a step away from anarchy. The natural reply of some Peters acolytes might be: "Fine. Step on the gas!" On the other hand, a whole range of big companies, such as Procter & Gamble and McDonald's, seem just as capable of thriving in the new chaotic world as virtual companies. And even the trendier, flatter companies, such as Microsoft, Intel, or McKinsey, are not so much disorganized as organized in a different way. Such firms may be flat and flexible, but they are also more than just a collection of individuals. There is something holding them together. It is a new kind of building block.

### The New Building Blocks: 1. Core Competencies

With the collapse of the Sloanist system, the natural inclination is to look for another structure to replace it—a new set of departments, divisions, and teams. Unfortunately, there is no universal answer of that sort. Rather, management theory has tended to focus on techniques by which a horizontal company can stretch across its many divisions in order to define itself. These include network building and entrepreneurialism. But the starting point for every company is one of management theory's ugliest but most important buzzwords: "core competencies."

"Core competencies," as defined by Gary Hamel and C. K. Prahalad, are the skills and capabilities, codified and uncodified, that give a company its unique flavor and that cannot be easily imitated by a rival. These collections of knowledge constitute its expertise, which is what gives the company its competitive edge. Sony's core competence in miniaturization, for example, allows the company to make everything from the Sony Walkman to videocameras to notebook computers; Canon's core competencies in optics, imaging, and microprocessor controls have allowed it to enter such seemingly diverse markets as copiers, laser printers, cameras, and image scanners.

However, the whole point of core competencies is not so much what a firm does as what it decides not to do (which it then contracts out to specialists). Often, selecting a core competence means excluding itself from parts of the production process it performs poorly. Canon may be good at making photocopiers, but the Japanese firm buys 75 percent of the components from outside the company. Nintendo lets others design its video games. Nike designs and sells sports shoes but does not assemble anything itself. In the semiconductor industry, "fabless" (or fabricationless) firms, such as America's Cirrus Logic, have stuck to design; that has left room for companies such as Taiwan Semiconductor Manufacturing Corporation to sell their services as "foundries"—manufacturers who will work to order.

In an age when Brooks Brothers contracts out its tailoring, nothing is sacred where "outsourcing" is concerned. By one estimate, small subcontractors accounted for nearly half the production costs of large American firms at the end of the 1980s. Even fairly small companies are hollowing themselves out so that they can concentrate on their core competencies. At the 42 companies in the Boston area that Rosabeth Moss Kanter visited for her most recent book, *World Class: Thriving Locally in the Global Economy* (1995), the most likely things to be outsourced were food, the payroll, cleaning, building maintenance, mail, security, local transportation, travel arrangements, public relations, child care, training, technical writing, and printing. In addition, manufacturing companies were outsourcing activities such as metal fabrication, painting, die cutting, and even assembly.

In general, this seems to benefit the companies concerned. A 1993 survey by Coopers & Lybrand of nearly 400 fast-growing companies showed that the 65 percent that outsourced performed better than those that did not. A quick look at the car industry shows that Toyota and BMW (which buy about 75 percent of their car parts) have done better than Ford (50 percent), which in turn has done better than General Motors (25 percent). Meanwhile, the outsourcing industry has grown like Topsy, fattening not only giants such as Pitney Bowes and EDS, but also countless smaller firms. Even monasteries have gotten in on the act. The Holy Cross Abbey in Virginia and Gethsemani

Abbey in Kentucky have computerized various technical and intellectual databases, selling their services through a data services broker called the Electronic Scriptorium.[12]

The core competencies of successful companies are somewhat easier to spot than those of one's own firm. Many old-fashioned conglomerates cheat by covering wide areas. In South Korea, when the government tried to restrict companies to a few core businesses, the *chaebol* (as the country's conglomerates are called) responded by choosing broad areas such as technology, industry, and energy. In France, water companies seem to have persuaded themselves that cable television is a natural business for them to be in, because, like water, it involves pipes and has a complicated billing system. Even in America, many big diversified companies, such as Rockwell and General Electric, base their core competencies around objectives such as being number one or number two in an industry.

Another problem with core competencies, as Hamel and Prahalad admit, is that, if the market changes and managers get stuck in a rut, they can easily degenerate into "core rigidities." One common problem is complacency. Until well into the 1980s, Sears's internal position papers did not even mention Wal-Mart as a competitor to be watched. Another problem is making too much of a good thing. By the mid-1990s, Sony's obsession with churning out new variations on products was beginning to tire customers. Perhaps the biggest problem, however, is the basic conservatism of human nature: most people go on thinking about problems in the same way, using the same old technologies, and satisfying the same old customers.

### The New Building Blocks: 2. Renewal

It is dangerous, therefore, to treat core competencies as though they were set in stone. That is why modern management theorists are always looking for ways to keep a company on its toes (to practice "renewal," in the jargon).

In most cases, the responsibility for shaking up the company falls on the company chairman. The best leaders are often subversives who enjoy blowing up their own creations. However, this is hardly a solution that can be applied too often. The theorists have also come up with two other ways of making sure that companies stay alive. Once again, the whole organization has to be treated, for these are not just optional extras that can be bolted onto some department.

The first of these is entrepreneurialism. Entrepreneurship, which Tom Peters once defined as "unreasonable conviction based on inadequate evidence," was precisely what Sloan's system was supposed to eradicate. Yet one of the biggest problems for Sloanist companies was their conservatism: the cloistered elite in charge of innovation were too far removed from the market and too bound by conventional wisdom to recognize the new demands arising in the marketplace. The link between entrepreneurialism and innovation is examined more closely in Chapter 6. Suffice it to say here that basically entrepreneurialism means creating small units, giving them the power to try out ideas, and, perhaps most important, allowing them to make mistakes. This does not mean throwing money at them. As Peters often points out, 75 percent of the firms on *Inc* Magazine's list of the 500 fastest-growing small firms in America in 1992 were started with less than $100,000, and 50 percent began with less than $50,000.

The other process is networking, to make sure these entrepreneurial ideas spread throughout the company. Wal-Mart has a video link connecting all the stores to corporate headquarters and to each other. Store managers frequently hold videoconferences to swap information on which products are selling and which promotions are working. At Kao, a Japanese consumer products company, an internal information network allows everybody to find out about everything to do with the company, and its laboratories frequently fly company scientists from the other end of the world to attend meetings. Sweden's Ericsson has linked 17,000 engineers in 40 research centers in 20 countries into the same computer network. Xerox encourages technical representatives to make videos of themselves talking about their achievements in solving tricky problems and then distribute them all over the world, just as scientists distribute research papers. Ford has an internal television network that keeps employees informed about everything from the stock prices of the world's car companies to the latest motor racing results.

Often, however, electronic networking is not enough. Managers still need to meet face to face. William Bruns, a professor at Harvard Business School, points out that it is not uncommon for senior managers to spend three out of every four weeks on business trips—or to have their timetables worked out 12 to 15 months in advance in color-coded diaries: red for Europe, blue for South America, green for the home office.

But one man's crowded schedule does not make a networked corporation. Companies such as Nestlé, Unilever, and ABB constantly throw people from different parts of the organization together, in the hope that they will generate electricity. ("Technology transfer is more than just a piece of kit," remarks one senior Unilever figure.) Wal-Mart uses its private air force to ferry store managers to its headquarters in Bentonville, Arkansas. Most companies get their money's worth from seemingly extravagant arrangements such as regular retreats for senior managers and global get-togethers for the marketing department. Motorola even sent workers from Singapore and Florida to a mountain resort to help them get along better.

If nothing else, networking means getting rid of exclusive departments—encouraging what Jack Welch calls boundaryless behavior: "Every time you meet somebody, you're looking for a better and newer and bigger idea. You are open to ideas from anywhere."[13] The importance of ideas and knowledge to corporate success means that everybody must be willing to share the fruits of their thinking. At Verifone there is a saying, "Share, or screw you."

## Culture as Glue

Core competencies, renewal, networking, and entrepreneurialism: a cynic might say that this sounds like a fairly vague list around which to build a company. And the cynic would be right. Indeed, rather than trying to construct a horizontal company out of these building blocks, it might seem intellectually more honest to argue that the perfect post-Sloanist company is almost structureless. All that holds it together is its culture—that intangible thing that inspires employees to be self-disciplined and allows managers and their workers (to use two outdated terms) to trust each other. In fact, culture is not as ephemeral as it sounds.

Arguing that the most successful companies are those with the strongest corporate cultures is something of a self-fulfilling prophecy. Most managers can only dream of working for a company in which most of the employees know instinctively what they should be doing. However, a few do exist. At Johnson & Johnson, for instance, the "Credo"—a sort of formalized mission statement—is emblazoned in the company's factories throughout the world. The Credo has not only helped keep an increasingly diverse company together, but it is also credited with guiding the company's principled response to the Tylenol crisis, when a lunatic laced some of the company's Tylenol tablets with cyanide.

In most cases, a company's culture cannot be captured in some anodyne mission statement. At Nordstrom, an American retailer, the entire employee manual amounts to one piece of paper saying "Use your good judgment in all situations," but everybody who works there is obsessed with customer service. Similarly, when people at Hewlett-Packard talk about something called "the HP way," they are not referring to a rule book. In *Built to Last: Successful Habits of Visionary Companies* (1995), Jerry Porras and James Collins argued that the most successful companies have stuck to their core values—a sort of cultural version of core competencies. Thus, though its empire now stretches from theme parks to network television, Disney has basically stood by its core values of wholesomeness and making people happy. IBM stumbled because it paid less attention to its core value (customer service) than to a business strategy (dominating mainframe computers). Back at HP, Bill Hewlett and David Packard refused to take on big government contracts because they thought it would force them to adopt a hire-and-fire mentality, which would destroy the respect for the individual that is part of the HP way.

Corporate culture is not something that just appears. Companies—and bosses in particular—have to work at it. It is noticeable that many of today's business heroes, such as Richard Branson of Virgin, Anita Roddick of the Body Shop, or Herb Kelleher of Southwest Airlines, are particularly talented at generating enthusiasm—and even passion—among their staff. But even "inspirational" leadership involves perspiration, too. Roddick spends much of her time meeting her employees; she has installed bulletin boards, faxes, and videocassette recorders in each of her 700 shops. Senior managers everywhere are spending more time on what Goran Lidahl, ABB's executive vice president, calls "human engineering": getting to know workers.

However, the most obvious place for companies to perpetu-
ate their culture is in recruitment and training. One aim of
modern corporate education is to encourage self-discipline
(which, in the ideal post-Sloanist organization, is supposed to
replace authority from above). Throughout the 1980s, Ingvar
Kamprad, the founder of IKEA, led week-long training sessions
for hand-picked managers on the company's history, culture,
and values. Andersen Consulting, has such a thorough training
program that its employees are often mocked as "Andersen Androids." The Androids start off with six weeks of intensive
training that resembles nothing so much as an army boot camp,
with 80-hour weeks and a strict dress code. In their first five
years with the company, they receive about 1,000 hours of formal training. On being recruited, all Androids are assigned to a
"counseling partner" who meets with them every six months to
discuss their performance.

However, self-discipline only operates when people trust
one another. Even before Francis Fukuyama turned "trust"
into a talking point, management theorists had been putting
more and more emphasis on the concept, and rightly so. Junior
managers will only obey their seniors in these much looser organizations if they feel that their seniors have the company's
best interests at heart; and senior managers will only hand
power over to their juniors if they feel that they can trust them.
On the basis of a survey of 3,500 companies and follow-up interviews with 10 leading companies, Chan Kim, a professor at
Insead, and his colleague, Renée Mauborgne, have demonstrated that trust only flourishes if top management builds fair-
ness ("procedural justice," in their terms) into the heart of the
firm. Senior managers must go to great lengths to ensure that
decisions are fair, and seen to be fair particularly in sprawling
companies, where lines of control are vague and suspicion of
political infighting is rife.

## But Is It Stable?

Today's business school academics are perhaps a little hard
on Alfred Sloan. Always worried that his ideas would be misused by bores and bureaucrats, Sloan was not quite the advocate
of machinelike obedience that people now imagine. He argued
that managers should see themselves as workers' servants rather

than their masters, and he tried to encourage intellectual independence. On being told that one of GM's top committees was in complete agreement on a subject, he proposed postponing the meeting until people had cultivated some independent opinions.[14]

If Sloan could be presented with the post-Sloanist company, he might with reason point to at least three protruding fault lines in the model that has replaced his. The first is the enormous importance the model ascribes to charismatic leaders. As Chapter 9 points out, the modern boss is seriously overworked. Companies are also having to confront problems that Sloanism banished: the risk that an all-powerful boss will gently go off the rails, and the difficulty of finding an equally charismatic successor. Two companies that have popped up several times in this chapter, ABB and General Electric (GE), have both been built up by charismatic monarchs whose reigns are now ending. The fact that powerful leaders have a habit of grooming second-rate people to succeed them means that succession crises are likely to become more common on the corporate scene.

The second problem is that, as companies grow more complicated, the job of managers becomes more ill-defined. Once managers could simply tell their subordinates what to do. Now, people have to report laterally as well as vertically, across borders as well as within countries, and they have to do so in conditions of mounting ambiguity, where competitors are suddenly allies and where the supplier the manager used to boot around is now given a bigger office than the manager's, in the same factory. Or the manager might be made "team leader" of a group that has thrown German researchers together with Californian designers.

However, Sloan's biggest concern would probably be over the area of control. Companies are finding that the shift from formal to informal management structures is rife with risks. The weakening of formal structures has clearly led to some spectacular disasters. The Barings family lost its bank because the management overempowered one individual, Nick Leeson. Two of Japan's biggest banks, Daiwa and Sumitomo, have also lost small fortunes by failing to control traders. In Hollywood, Japan's Sony did what one was supposed to do with creative knowledge workers: it gave them billions of dollars and oodles of trust—and got kicked in the face. One senior figure at

Unilever now blames its Persil Power fiasco (it produced a stronger version of its detergent that unfortunately damaged clothes), in part, on its decision to hand responsibility for the product to a self-governing team.

In theory, all these external sources of control are supposed to be replaced by "trust" and "self-discipline." Even if he had found these concepts palatable, Sloan would have pointed out that their effectiveness as controlling agents has been dramatically reduced by all the other things modern management is up to. The system that has replaced his own is fraught with contradictions.

Because of the popularity of downsizing and delayering, no workers can be sure of their long-term futures. The fluidity of alliances means that friends are rapidly transformed into enemies. With the emphasis on speed, people have less time to develop long-term trusting relationships. The pressure of time and money is forcing companies to compress training courses in which people meet each other. The arrival of multicultural companies means that people can no longer rely on shared backgrounds and tacit understanding to bind them together. Worst of all, many managers are expected to act as willing participants in their own destruction. Company bosses are asked to transform themselves from local barons into loyal lieutenants, and middle managers are being told to develop systems that will make middle management unnecessary.

These contradictions are already forcing some firms to reintroduce some of the command and control modern gurus despise. Note, too, that some of the companies that make a great fuss about being democratic to the outside world are also among the most hierarchical. Park your car in somebody else's space outside a Hollywood studio and you will soon discover that all the Armani casual wear disguises a rigid class system. When on tour, the Rolling Stones have 17 grades of security pass. Even at Microsoft, there is one automatic form of control: everything of any value goes through Bill Gates's office.

This is a correcting impulse rather than a reversal. Even if modern "informal" companies are somewhat less robust than their Sloanist predecessors, there seems little doubt that they are the organizational form of the future. Once again, the manager has to return to those old concepts: uncertainty and, particularly, knowledge. Companies used to think that their most precious resource was capital and all they needed was a small elite to allocate that capital and boss around workers. "How come when I want a pair of hands I get a human being as well," Henry Ford once remarked. Now firms realize that their most important asset is knowledge. The trouble with knowledge is that it is so much more difficult to manage than capital: not only is it fixed in the heads of pesky employees rather than stored in the bank, but it is infuriatingly volatile and short-lived to boot, as explained in Chapter 6.

# CHAPTER 6

## KNOWLEDGE, LEARNING, AND INNOVATION

SOUTH KOREA'S CAPITAL CITY is a dismal place at the best of times, a mess of building sites, standard-issue apartment towers, and poky corner shops, all touting ginseng and shiny "hand-made" suits. But in the depth of winter, Seoul can be positively hellish. Freezing winds chill the bones; icy pavements make walking all but impossible. You spend much of your time scrambling for a taxi to take you from one well-heated hotel to another. The only consolation is that the bars are well-stocked with whisky, and the locals, who revel in being called "the Irish of Asia," encourage you to drink late into the night.

So it was a strange city for Steven Spielberg and Jeffrey Katzenberg, two of Los Angeles's wealthier inhabitants, neither of whom is famed for his whisky consumption, to have chosen to visit for four days in November 1995. Even odder perhaps was the two moguls' choice of host: Cheil Food and Chemicals, one of Korea's stodgiest companies, better known for making things like seaweed soup than movies.

This unusual rendezvous came about because Cheil had invested $300 million in DreamWorks, the film studio founded by Spielberg, Katzenberg, and David Geffen. The investment gives Cheil an 11 percent stake in DreamWorks and makes it the single largest outside investor after Paul Allen, the cofounder of Microsoft. The deal was masterminded by Miky Lee, a granddaughter of the founder of Samsung, one of Korea's most powerful companies, and head of Cheil's new multimedia division, Lee Entertainment. In return for its investment, Cheil got the rights to distribute DreamWorks' products throughout much of Asia, a seat on DreamWorks' five-member executive committee for Ms. Lee, and a chance to draw on DreamWorks' expertise for Cheil's new film studio, J-Com. Cheil is also forming several joint ventures with Raymond Chow, a Hong Kong film tycoon, to distribute Western and Asian films in Asia, and to build large numbers of multiplex cinemas. "Five years from now," a spokesman for Cheil predicts, "we'll be the first major multimedia entertainment group in Asia."

What is going on here? Part of the explanation lies in family politics. Cheil's boss, Jay Lee (Miky's brother), had expected eventually to inherit the top job at Samsung from his grandfather. But his branch of the family was passed over. As a consolation prize, it received the group's food and chemical business. Jay Lee severed Cheil's connections with Samsung in 1993 and then set about getting his revenge. Seeing that DreamWorks had already rebuffed an offer by Samsung to invest $800 million in the new Hollywood studio, Cheil's coup in securing the partnership seemed all the more enjoyable. Cheil rammed home its triumph over Samsung by festooning all the leading hotels with banners welcoming DreamWorks and putting on a banquet fit more for Henry VIII than the scrawny visitors from Tinseltown.

But there was a deeper, more strategic reason for the alliance: the younger Lees sincerely believe that Cheil has to become "a knowledge company." Like many of their generation, Miky and Jay Lee are cosmopolitan Americanophiles. (The latter, who is a new-age manager by Korean standards, makes a point of wandering unannounced into midlevel meetings and has put the company cafeteria on the top floor of its headquarters, a position normally reserved for the chairman's office.) Korean firms have always been adept at buying knowhow from the West. Miky Lee points out that her grandfather started in the flour business and ended up in semiconductors. Now, she thinks it is time to import the latest Western industry, multimedia, adding that the sort of management skills that can be learned from managing film companies—the ability to weave networks and create vivid images—will be increasingly useful in managing the food and chemical businesses.

On the surface, the Lees' decisions may seem difficult to fathom. There are no synergies between food and films (other than the fact that cinemas are good places to sell hot dogs and popcorn). South Korea, with a language that is spoken by only 46 million people and a native film industry that is one of the weakest on the continent, appears to be an unlikely Hollywood of Asia. Furthermore, Cheil is staffing its multimedia division with stolid company men who cut their teeth on selling food products and expect to spend the rest of their lives with the company—hardly the right sort of culture for the networking, deal-a-minute world of multimedia.

Although their solution may be a little wacky, the Lees' diagnosis is surely right: we are in the middle of the transition to an information age, in which the most important resources are not physical but intellectual; and given the difficulty of making this transition, it is best to start early.

## Knowing Me, Knowing You

As already mentioned, knowledge—alongside uncertainty—has forced companies to change their structure dramatically. But managers' problems with knowledge go much deeper. Not only do they have to learn how to husband knowledge—to "grow" it as they once grew their capital—but they also need to learn how to handle the people who possess it. The modern masters of the universe are those people who have had the good fortune to be born bright: lawyers, scientists, stockbrokers, skilled mechanics—indeed, anypeople who can make connections and generate ideas more rapidly and imaginatively than their peers. Nor can the problem of "knowledge" be solved just by throwing money at technology. In the 1980s, General Motors plowed nearly $80 billion into new factories and equipment to reduce its dependence on its troublesome workers, yet its productivity gains were minuscule. By contrast, Ford, which concentrated on knocking down barriers between the boardroom and the shop floor, achieved noticeable growth.

The result has been a ferment in management thinking. Most firms are accustomed to measuring relatively simple things like the amount of stock in their warehouses, or their income flows. But how should they be measuring knowledge, which is something they cannot even define? In the traditional managerial system, a primary concern was to persuade bored workers to keep their noses to the grindstone. Today, those workers are seen as the company's most valuable resources because of the knowledge in their heads. To harness that knowledge, the manager needs to be able to understand it, define it, locate it, measure it, and encourage it to grow. Above all, the manager must be able to turn that abstract phenomenon into winning products.

As a result, consultancies, for one, have spent long hours telling companies how to maximize not profit but the "self-respect" of their employees. Management theory also has sensible things to say about how to turn a company into a place where knowledge is encouraged ("a learning organization") and how to transform that knowledge into new products ("innovation"). In neither case does management theory offer a blueprint for success, but it does describe the proper foundations.

## The Beginning of Wisdom

In Henry Ford's time, it was already clear that a company's assets consisted not only of physical things, such as factories, but also of the accumulated skills of workers. Intellectual capital is now considered to be of paramount importance. In more and more cases, the ratio of a company's market value to the book value of its fixed assets is reaching double figures. Even in fairly boring manufacturing companies, three-quarters of the value added comes from knowledge, in its various forms, according to one calculation by James Brian Quinn of the Tuck School of Business at Dartmouth.[1]

The first person to notice the rise of the knowledge-based society was the ever-prescient Peter Drucker. Since the 1960s, management thinkers have been conducting detailed academic research on how individuals and organizations learn. Three decades ago, Herbert Simon, a professor of computer science at Pittsburgh's Carnegie-Mellon University and a Nobel Prize-winner in economics, used computers to simulate and analyze the way that organizations reach decisions. Chris Argyris, a psychologist based at Harvard Business School, found that failure is a better teacher than success. Success can only generate what

Argyris calls "single-loop" learning (I did X and it worked), whereas failure can generate "double-loop learning," which leads people to question their failures and the assumptions behind them. Walter Wriston, former chairman of Citibank, puts the same point rather more succinctly: "Good judgment is the result of experience, and experience is the result of bad judgment."

Such discoveries were not confined to universities. Royal Dutch/Shell pioneered the use of "planning as learning" in the 1970s. The firm's scenario planning division, invented by Pierre Wack and headed for many years by Arie De Geus, acted as a sort of think tank in which managers used various versions of the future to test their assumptions about their company, their competitors, and the market. The "total-quality" movement indirectly promoted learning by encouraging workers to monitor their own progress and solve their own problems, rather than simply defer to managers.

By the mid-1980s, "learning" and "knowledge" had both become buzzwords that conferred instant modernity on the user. Even General Motors got in on the act. One of the features of its innovative Saturn division, announced in 1985, was a "learning laboratory" built next door to Saturn's factory in Springhill, Tennessee. Called the Workplace Development Center, it included a complete mock-up of an assembly line, which was used to videotape and study workplace procedures.

Mainstream gurus then began turning their attention to the role of knowledge in the workplace. Shoshana Zuboff, a professor at Harvard Business School, argued that, in the age of the smart machine, "learning is the new form of labor . . . the heart of productive activity." Others warned that those who depended on brawn would be impoverished and marginalized. Robert Reich, then a Harvard professor, who went on to become Bill Clinton's first Secretary of Labor, predicted a growing tension between knowledge workers (whom he rather grandly dubbed "symbolic analysts") and manual workers, because the former would be able to take advantage of globalization whereas the latter would become stuck in parochial poverty. Rosabeth Moss Kanter, also from Harvard, observed more optimistically that, in a knowledge-based economy, companies would have to share more power with their employees.

The consensus in the business world seems to be that learning is a good thing. And most people seem to know broadly what an organization focused on learning should be able to do. Many quote the example of the Honda motorcycle managers who went to America on a mission to sell big bikes but found that the Californians they met were more impressed by the small 50-cc Hondas the managers were using to visit their prospective customers. Despite having invested a lot of time and money in the big bikes, Honda switched to the small ones—and made a fortune. Other frequently cited examples of ideas factories are 3M and Rubbermaid. The problem with such companies, management writers point out, is that too many think of themselves as a product rather than as a process (which is a more accurate way of envisaging them).[2] And the managers who can explain how to create a learning organization are few and far between.

## Peter Senge and the Fifth Discipline

Even the management thinker widely known as a prophet of the "learning organization" is hard to pin down. Peter Senge, head of the Centre for Organizational Learning at the Massachusetts Institute of Technology and author of the best-selling *The Fifth Discipline* (1990), believes that today's companies owe their competitive edge to their ability to learn and to keep on learning. In brief, Senge argues that people who are keen to learn should embrace five disciplines: they should put aside their old "mental models," learn to be open with others ("personal mastery"), understand how their organization really works ("systems thinking"), agree on a "shared vision," and then work together to achieve a common purpose ("team learning").

Senge argues that managers will only be able to make the leap from the machine age, with its narrow, compartmentalized view of jobs, to the information age if they undergo a "personal transformation," which will leave them at once more open to their fellow men and better equipped to understand the world as a coherent system. And he provides a set of mental tools to help people to make the leap, emotionally as well as intellectually. One tool, intended to improve communication, is "the container"—an imaginary receptacle into which all the participants in a meeting place their fears and frustrations. As the container fills up, the meeting begins to achieve results unhampered by "negative" feelings. Another tool, intended to break down preconceptions, is the "ladder of inference." To climb the ladder, people must base their decisions on empirical observation rather than prejudice. Senge recommends that, after a particularly stressful meeting, executives should all sit down together and meditate in order to restore their inner calm. The most powerful tool of all, however, is "systems thinking," which enables one to "see" the structures driving behavior.

To be frank, *The Fifth Discipline's* huge success is puzzling. Not only is the book hard to understand but, at the time of its publication, dozens of other consultants were arguing that the West was in the middle of a "paradigm shift" (to use a well-worn term beloved of the management theory industry) from an industrial to a knowledge-based economy, and that the knowledge-based economy needed a "new man," equipped with new ways of thinking. By his own admission, Senge drew his inspiration from a number of "extraordinary people," notably Jay Forrester, who supervised his PhD dissertation on systems dynamics, and Chris Argyris. Systems dynamics, Senge said, taught him to look at things as parts of a system rather than just as independent entities—hence he placed equal emphasis on all five of his disciplines.

Senge's contribution to management theory has been twofold. First, all this thinking has exhibited a fashionable New Age slant. (Senge is a devotee of Zen.) Second, his ideas have a practical edge that has been missing from academic discussions. Although much of his thinking sounds like psychobabble, Senge has been able to persuade companies to adopt his ideas. In 1994, Senge and a group of consultants published *The Fifth Discipline Handbook,* a collection of case studies and essays that illustrate how his ideas worked at companies such as Ford, Federal Express, and Intel—and is, in general, a much more helpful book than its predecessor. His research center, started in 1990, has 18 corporate sponsors, including AT&T, Ford, Motorola, and Federal Express. Each pays the center $80,000 a year to try out ideas that might help organizations learn. Senge has set up his own consulting and training firm, Innovation Associates, which was recently bought up by Arthur D. Little. He is also connected with the Learning Circle, a sort of club for devotees of "learning organizations."

If they are lucky, these devotees will be invited to one of Senge's regular management retreats. Usually held in a rural backwater, these meetings take place against a background of tinkling piano music or beating drums (depending on the time of day) and consist of outdoor events at which people bond through shared physical suffering. The objective is to overcome the fragmentation of modern society and appreciate the world as a connected system. Senge thinks that the West is suffering from an advanced case of fragmentation: physical health has broken away from mental health; education has fragmented into a collection of banal facts; and government has splintered into a battle of special interests. Nowhere is the harmful effect of all this fragmentation more evident than in management: marketing departments are at war with manufacturing, front-line managers with corporate headquarters, workers with bosses. The goal of the management guru, according to Senge, is to overcome this fragmentation and see the world as a whole once again.

## What Is Knowledge?

Given his long list of satisfied corporate clients, it is hard not to believe that Senge is better at putting his ideas into practice than he is at explaining them on paper or at conferences. ("This isn't management; it's abstract art," one infuriated *Mittelstand* businessman confessed, having attended a sold-out Senge speech in Switzerland.) Fortunately for those who find Senge's New Age thinking a little fuzzy, the past couple of years have seen a succession of much more weighty books on how companies create and use knowledge, including *Competing for the Future* (1994), by Gary Hamel and C. K. Prahalad; *Wellsprings of Knowledge* (1995), by Dorothy Leonard-Barton, a professor at Harvard Business School; and *The Knowledge-Creating Company* (1995), by Ikujiro Nonaka and Hirotaka Takeuchi, two Japanese management theorists.

Most discussions of the learning organization begin with the sort of knowledge it wants to cultivate, which immediately brings to mind "core competencies"—the skills and traditions that give the firm its competitive advantage (see Chapter 5). Core competencies revolve around learning. They reside in the heads of the firm's employees—which is what all this saccharine talk about people being "a company's most precious resource" really means. Three kinds of knowledge, says Dorothy Leonard-Barton, are at the heart of every core competence:

public knowledge, industry-specific knowledge, and firm-specific knowledge.[3]

Thus, from a learning organization's point of view, the collected degrees and qualifications of workers represent only part of its knowledge base. Knowledge and competencies also reside in various traditions of collective behavior—in the factory's physical layout and databases.[4] That is why theorists are studying "tacit knowledge"—the informal, occupational lore that is generated by workers grappling with everyday problems and passed on in cafeterias, as opposed to the official rules recorded in company manuals and transmitted in compulsory training sessions.

The leaders in the use of tacit knowledge may be the Japanese. Visit a Japanese factory and you will see plenty of employees communicating without actually talking. Nonaka and Takeuchi argue that Japanese firms are past masters at tapping into the tacit insights and hunches of the mass of employees. Indeed, Japanese companies have been more reluctant to get rid of middle managers than Western ones, in part because they acknowledge the vital role played by middle managers in bringing different sorts of tacit knowledge together. These managers are the real "knowledge engineers" of the knowledge-creating company, according to Nonaka and Takeuchi.

## Sucking in Ideas . . .

The hallmark of a learning organization is that it keeps adding to its treasure trove of knowledge. It can do this in two ways: by sucking in ideas from outside its frontiers, and by making sure that they circulate inside the company.

Learning organizations, by definition, should be scouring the world for ideas that might be adapted to suit their particular ends.[5] It is surprising how much commercially valuable knowledge exists in the public domain, and more and more of it is being generated every day. John Kao, a professor at Harvard Business School, points out that a growing number of companies hire teenagers to surf the World Wide Web and bring back new ideas.[6] Japanese firms post researchers abroad for years on end and send representatives to an extraordinary number of conferences. (Any visitor to a scientific conference will be familiar with the Japanese delegate in the front row, carefully photographing each and every slide.)[7] Japanese companies have established research laboratories as close as possible to American universities: Hitachi's Chemical Research Centre even shares premises with the University of California at Irvine. Korea's Samsung regularly sends managers to spend time in the offices of IDEO, a design company based in Palo Alto, in the hope that they will pick up some of Silicon Valley's talent for innovation.

Although this tactic sounds a little sneaky, the ability to absorb knowledge from outside is becoming an important source of competitive advantage now that even the biggest firms admit that research is too expensive for them to fund on their own. Once-lavish research facilities like AT&T's Bell Labs and Xerox's Palo Alto Research Center face a future of contracting resources or collective funding.

In many cases, this means forming institutional relationships with firms that would normally be regarded as enemies. Ford and Chrysler have formed a dozen consortia to collaborate in the design of items such as dummies for crashes, and electric batteries. The Power PC chip was developed by IBM, Motorola, and Apple. These arrangements have proved so popular, points out the U.S. Department of Justice, that the country had 325 research consortia by the early 1990s. But perhaps an even better way of encouraging an organization to share information and gain access to another company's "core competencies" is through alliances, joint ventures, or mergers. In the automobile industry, for example, joint ventures between American and Japanese firms, such as Chrysler and Honda, or Ford and Mazda, are one reason why the American firms have all but eliminated the productivity gap between themselves and the Japanese.

In Detroit's case, the reason for forming alliances was simply to build better cars—and the choice of a partner was fairly obvious. But in technological industries, where the boundaries between many businesses are collapsing, firms often form alliances or joint ventures just to keep in touch with industries on which their future may depend. This often means consorting with companies from industries that one never considered compatible. For instance, Electronic Data Systems (EDS), whose basic business of servicing customers' mainframe computers is starting to look feeble, has pushed into interactive media through innumerable alliances: with Spectradyne, to provide movies in hotel rooms; with Video Lottery Technologies, to provide gambling; with USTravel, to dispense tickets from automated machines for everything from airline flights to Broadway shows; and with USWest and France Télécom, to provide home banking.

## . . . And Making Sure They Circulate

Ideas from the outside world are of little use if they get stuck as soon as they enter the firm. A true learning organization is one in which knowledge ricochets around the system like a ball in a pinball machine. In other words, networks need to be built to shunt formal information from one end of the company to the other; moreover, barriers to tacit knowledge need to be discovered and removed.

Virtually any companywide information system, however mundane, will help a company to learn. Most big companies use Lotus Notes or a similar groupware program. Management consultancies have set up special learning networks with names such as "Knowledge On-Line" and "Knowledge Xchange," which allow consultants to pool expertise, swap ideas, and browse through a library of case studies.

However, machines can only do so much. Hence, the fashion is to appoint knowledge officers and "mentors"—senior workers whose job, like that of the fag masters of old-fashioned British private schools, is to watch over the progress of younger workers. Some companies, Dorothy Leonard-Barton points out, look for people who possess "T-shaped" skills—that is, deep expertise in one discipline (the stem of the T) combined with a sufficient intellectual range to relate that expertise to many other areas of corporate activity (the crossbar).[8]

It makes good sense to set up formal networks for the diffusion of knowledge. Perhaps the biggest advantage of such systems is that the information put into them by consultant $X$ or worker $Y$ will stay there long after he or she has left the company. But perhaps what workers need most to prosper is not structure but freedom—and many more opportunities to keep their minds sharp and their skills up to date. Many software companies have started to organize themselves like universities. When Lars Kolind took over as head of Oticon, a Danish hearing-aid manufacturer, he dissolved the entire formal organization, abolishing job titles. His aim was to create a "spaghetti organization" in which everybody was connected to everybody else. Microsoft calls its headquarters, in Redmond, Washington, a campus. In his heyday, Steve Jobs, the founder of Apple, cultivated the style of a professor at an alternative university, conducting free-flowing arguments with his sneakered staff. Imagination, a British design company, boasts an in-house restaurant and bar where employees hang around and socialize after work, in much the same spirit as students do in college bars.

## Bold Experimentation

The other characteristic of a learning organization is a passion for experimentation—and a willingness to fail. Experiments allow companies to broaden their portfolio of products—they are the key to a firm's long-term survival in periods of great uncertainty. They also help firms shake up established ways of doing things and thus prevent core competencies from degenerating into core rigidities. Recently, many such experiments have been elaborate "top-down" ventures in which senior managers have tried to change the direction of the entire company by, for example, taking over other firms. On the whole, however, it is much better for bosses to take a back seat and encourage a culture where experiments are frequent. Seemingly insignificant projects can sometimes end up changing the entire nature of the company. Hewlett-Packard pioneered the pocket calculator business because one of the firm's cofounders, Bill Hewlett, wanted an "electronic slide rule" for his own use. Corning broke into the fiber-optics business because some of its researchers had the idea of introducing an impurity into glass so as to make its inner core more refractive than its outer layer and thus better able to transmit light. Most successful innovations seem to happen in the office farthest away from the corporate headquarters.

One of the main faults of would-be learning organizations is their habit of suppressing or even punishing unsuccessful innovations. In science, failed experiments can be as instructive as successful ones; most business organizations are poor at acknowledging failure and have difficulty learning from it. This bias toward success may have a dulling effect on the learning ability of most organizations (remember Chris Argyris's conclusions). Learning organizations should not only be willing to admit their mistakes, they should be prepared to promote them. This is something that most creative industries understand better than manufacturing ones. The policy of Steve Ross, who built up Warner Bros., was: "People get fired who do not make mistakes."

Another bold way to experiment is to recruit people who are not "one of us." Tom Peters likes to describe visiting a typical corporate retreat (either at Palm Springs or Palm Beach), having read yet another long description of a company that wants to become a learning organization but still finds itself turning out too many me-too products. The moment he walks into the seminar, he discovers the reason why: "150 people, 147 of whom will be White, male, and around 48 years old, and 144 will be wearing lime-green polyester golf-trousers."[9]

The jibe carries a serious point. The secret of managing knowledge workers, like the secret of making a martini, lies in the mixing. The group that produced Hitachi's high-capacity computer disk drive included nuclear engineers and chemical engineers, as well as computer scientists. In its search for what its director, Gerald Hirshberg, has called "creative abrasion," Nissan Design International deliberately hires people in contrasting pairs, balancing, say, nerds with hippies.[10] It even encourages workers to display a color chart of their "personalysis" on their desk so that managers can mix and match staff more easily.[11]

Much of Microsoft's success stems from its recruitment policy. Microsoft cultivates relations with leading professors so that it can spot talent as early as possible. It also targets people with what it calls "bandwidth" (i.e., those who show a breadth of interest), and it looks out for "crossovers"—people whose academic background might have been in something like music but who have invested time mastering computers. After that, it throws together superlogical "bit heads" with artistically sensitive designers. As one insider describes it: "Designers are invariably female, are talkative, live in lofts, have vegetarian diets, and wear found objects in their ears. Developers are invariably male, eat fast food and don't talk except to say, 'Not True.'"[12]

But will all this create a learning organization? The answer is "not for long." No matter how many weirdos an organization recruits, no matter how much it forgets, no matter how knowledgeable its chief knowledge officers are or how T-shaped their skills, most companies will still find it a hard target. Even if a company keeps its eyes and ears open, forms alliances with the most unexpected partners, and routinely executes one out of every three directors, the chances are that it will still find it manages "knowledge" less effectively than it had hoped.

The reason for this is simple: learning is difficult—and, like individuals, organizations can suffer from learning disabilities. Even when a company appears to have mastered one challenge, technology or competitors throw up another one. There is no magic single answer that enables a company to become a learning organization. The management theorists, however, do seem to be showing managers where to look for the right answers. Much the same can be said when it comes to innovation, the area where all this accumulated knowledge and learning should bubble to the surface.

## The Challenge of Innovation

Most management theorists now agree that the ability to produce good new products is not just a matter of luck and prayer. It can be planned, managed, and taught, just like any other aspect of a company's work. The art of innovation, management theory tells us, is really a series of balancing acts: be obsessive about developing new products, but make sure that they fit into your long-term vision; build new products in self-governing teams, but set demanding targets for those teams; listen to, but do not follow, what your customers say; and so on. If mastered, these habits can make the art of generating an endless stream of new products a little closer to a science.

The first step in pursuing innovation is to decide what you want out of it. For Japan's Sony and for Rubbermaid, the American household goods maker, innovation means product proliferation. "Our objective," says Wolf Schmitt of Rubbermaid, "is to bury competitors in such a profusion of products that they can't copy us." Sony realized that it could not prevent its Walkman from being copied. So it flooded the market with different types of Walkmen—170 models by 1989 alone. Speed is also essential for clothes companies: many Hong Kong tailors can get copies of the latest Paris fashions on the backs of their customers faster than the Paris fashion houses that dreamed up the ideas.

For a car manufacturer such as Toyota or a specialist retailer such as IKEA, success means offering value-for-money: a
minivan or a sofa will sell if it offers the best quality within that
price range. For elevator companies like Otis and Westinghouse,
it means outstanding after-sales service. Today, elevator companies make most of their money out of servicing their products,
not building them. For Intel, a chip maker, the goal is continual
technological improvement, or, as its chief executive, Andy
Grove, puts it, "Double machine performance at every price
point every year."[13] Even as Intel launched the 486 chip in
1989, a new team was at work on the fifth-generation chip, the
Pentium; and by the time the Pentium appeared, another team
had already started on the P-7, the seventh-generation chip.

Their aims may be different, but most innovative companies
are obsessed with their product. The character in the film *The
Graduate* who keeps talking to Dustin Hoffman about plastics
may not have been a particularly interesting man, but he was
ahead of his time in his devotion to what he produced. The hallmark of a "product juggernaut," or a succession of winning
products, is an unnatural obsession with what a company makes,
say Arthur D. Little consultants Jean-Philippe Deschamps
and P. Ranganath Nayak.[14] The product is the glue that keeps the
company together, the subject that dominates the corridor
gossip. Companies can instill this obsession in different ways.
Rubbermaid instructs rival business teams to get as many new
products to market as possible. The teams meet to discuss their
plans and compare their performance at an annual companywide
products fair. Hewlett-Packard, an American computer company, links the pay of some managers to the number of new products they introduce. Merck, a pharmaceutical company, prods its
research staff to win governmental approval for one major thera-
peutic drug each year. Many Japanese companies try to outper-
form their most feared rivals—an attitude vividly captured in
Sony's "BMW" slogan: "Beat Matsushita Whatsoever."

In many of the best companies, the chairman is responsible
for creating a culture of obsession: an obsessive individual himself, he recruits other obsessives and encourages them to devote
their lives to their products. Sony's Akio Morita kept proto-
types in his pocket and demonstrated them to hapless visitors.
Rubbermaid's chairman, Wolf Schmitt, confesses that he is
"probably the biggest pain to our people in sending out notes

with ideas and clippings. I'm probably on every mailing list in the world because I buy a lot of products I find in catalogues. I send them to people to stimulate new ideas."[15] Microsoft's two founders, Bill Gates and Paul Allen, used to sleep under their computer terminals as adolescents, so as to be able to get back to the machines as soon as they woke up. For decades, some of Gillette's male employees have come to work unshaven so that they can try out new razors—a different one on each side of the face.

However, an obsession without a target can end up as wasted energy; hence, the importance of vision. Vision, which might be dubbed the modern version of strategy, is discussed in more detail in Chapter 8. For the purposes of innovation, vision is an idea of how the market will look (or could be made to look) in the future and thus inspires and focuses workers. This may sound banal, but it is actually a formidable weapon. Japan's Canon saw a vision of a future in which photocopiers were small, cheap, and ubiquitous and persisted in producing its personal copier against all outside advice. In the view of Hamel and Prahalad, Motorola's greatest asset is its vision of a wireless world with everybody owning a personal telephone, programmed with a lifelong personal number. One reason why IBM, which spent $6 billion on R&D, was beaten to the punch by Steve Jobs and Steve Wozniak working from a California garage is that Apple's founders had a dream of a computer for "every man, woman, and child in America."

### It's a Team Game

Teams—particularly when they span functional and even national boundaries—can be vital for innovation. Members of teams focus more readily on the matter at hand. The first people to make this discovery were the Japanese. Firms such as Canon and Sharp made a habit of setting rival teams to work on the same project and asking one team to design the successor to a project that is still on the drawing board. Nowadays, teams are regarded as de rigueur just about everywhere—and firms lay on special facilities to encourage them. Sun Microsystems offers laundry and dry cleaning services to members of teams who work round the clock. One of Ford's facilities contains a barber shop, a laundry, and several restaurants.

Perhaps the most valuable aspect of this team-based approach is that it cuts down on the wastage created by dividing firms into functional fiefs. Under the old system, designers paid little attention to whether the products they envisioned could be made. Fundamental engineering errors were often only discovered after months or even years of work. This was one reason why, when it came to building the 777, Boeing formed some 200 "design–build" teams, forcing engineers, designers, and even customers to use the same computers. Not only were mistakes spotted sooner, but Boeing's huge factory seemed more tightly knit ("it was no longer a case of air conditioning over here, finance over there, and manufacturing over there," observes one engineer).

Even when companies do not divide people into teams, workers can still be persuaded to team up in less formal ways. Silicon Graphics provides white boards in the (spacious) cafeterias in its Hong Kong research center so that its staff can exchange ideas while they eat. One of Glaxo-Wellcome's facilities, in Cambridge, England, is designed to force researchers to talk to each other: all the chemicals are kept in a common store; newspapers and journals are put in people's rooms so that others have to ask to borrow them.

Devolving power to teams may sound fine and dandy, but teams have to be given strict goals (if not strict instructions on how to reach them). Perhaps the most widely studied ideas factory in the world is 3M, which registered 543 patents in 1993 and has a portfolio of 60,000 products, including everything from stationery to reflecting road signs. The company encourages its workers to spend 15 percent of their time "bootlegging"—that is, working on their own inventions. At the same time, it demands that 30 percent of its annual revenues come from products less than four years old. And the targets are being tightened. 3M's eventual goal is for 10 percent of revenues to come from products that are less than a year old.[16]

Other companies are similarly exacting. Microsoft grades employee productivity: "They review your progress twice a year, with marks from one to five," a Microsoftie told Anthony Sampson. "Four means exceptional; one means you're out." Many leading companies, including Motorola and Ford, "benchmark" their product development skills against those of their rivals and of other market leaders. Analog Devices, a Massachusetts-based manufacturer of integrated circuits, publishes figures on how long it takes each business unit to halve its product development time or defect rates. Toshiba tracks both the technical and managerial accomplishments of its employees. Hewlett-Packard produces graphs measuring the contribution of each team member in terms of time and money.

Japanese companies seem to be particularly demanding. Ikujiro Nonaka and Hirotaka Takeuchi quote an executive at Honda: "It's like putting the team members on the second floor, removing the ladder, and telling them to jump, or else. I believe creativity is born by pushing people against the wall and pressurizing them almost to the extreme."

## The Customer Is Almost King

An innovative company also has to strike a balance with its customers. A survey of innovation conducted by Arthur D. Little showed that the greatest number of good ideas comes from customers, not marketing, sales, or top management. Once again the Japanese have led the way. A favorite approach is "product churning": putting hundreds of different products on the market and then backing the ones that the consumers prefer. About a thousand new soft drinks are brought out every year in Japan, but only a handful survive more than a year. Sony puts realistic-looking mock-ups of new products in its showroom in Tokyo's Ginza district and watches the reaction of shoppers.

This technique of turning consumers into codevelopers has now been copied in the West. Boeing asked eight airlines to participate in the planning and design of its twin-engine 777; British Airways alone made more than 200 changes to the aircraft's basic specifications. A laboratory run by Hewlett-Packard in Bristol sent its researchers to hospital emergency rooms to determine how doctors could use the company's mobile communications gear. Epson, which makes small printers, asks its young development engineers to spend six months in the field as salespeople, and six months in the service department. Harley-Davidson's boss spends more than half his time hanging around with his customers—in stores, at motorcycle rallies, and burning up the freeway. Xerox has even employed anthropologists to observe people using its photocopying machines.[17]

But companies can also go too far in this direction. Customers are usually very conservative; they want better, cheaper versions of what they already have rather than innovative products. No customer could have come up with 3M's Post-it notes; indeed, people showed little appetite for them when they first appeared—just as they initially scorned both the fax machine and CNN. Chrysler pushed through its Minivan despite research showing that customers thought it was strange looking; its developers bet correctly that people would like it once they got used to it. If Compaq had listened to its mainframe-loving customers, it would never have entered the market for PC-network servers. As Hajime Mitarai, Canon's president, once explained to *Forbes:* "We *are* crazy. . . . We should do something when people say it is crazy. If people say something is 'good,' it means that someone else is already doing it."[18]

Perhaps the most worrying aspect of the current trend toward innovation is that it seems to produce a proliferation of similar products rather than startling new ones. Close to 30,000 new food products appear each year in American supermarkets, yet, from soap to coffee, most of the brand leaders date back to the turn of the century. When products such as Snapple have awakened markets in soft drinks or Ben & Jerry's in ice cream, they have tended to come from small "countercultural" firms. In its recent history, 3M has seen a string of advances such as the Scotch Brite Never Rust Wool Soap Pad, but not another completely new item like Post-it.

During the 1980s, gurus such as Kenichi Ohmae used to scold American companies for always chasing "home runs" in innovation, while Japanese firms, guided by their doctrine of continual improvement, notched up a succession of singles. Now that Sony and Matsushita are watching the more innovative parts of the consumer electronics industry migrate to Silicon Valley, people are reassessing this idea. "Incrementalism is innovation's worst enemy," argues Nicholas Negroponte, the high priest of multimedia.[19] Tom Peters points out, correctly, that too many cars look the same. You can't tell the difference between the Nissans, the Hondas, and the Toyotas, and now that quality is close to perfect (when was it that the last car you bought broke down?), people are increasingly likely to choose things on the basis of style. If there is one area in which all Peters's predictions about craziness, ephemera, and consistent change are likely to pay off, it is innovation.

## A Kindergarten or a Barracks?

As the debate about innovation shows, one of the biggest issues in any company nowadays is control. Most management theorists have followed Peter Drucker's lead and argued that the new knowledge-based economy is doing what Marx and Mao tried to do but failed: shifting power from "the bosses" to "the workers." The reality is more depressing.

It is certainly true that employers who behave in a high-handed manner will soon go out of business for lack of talent. Employees who feel unhappy can simply take their brains to another employer—or else set up on their own. As Gary Hamel has observed:

> In the knowledge economy the only employees that are worth having are those with many other choices of employment. The most capable knowledge workers are less inclined to think of themselves as sought-after faculty members. It's not HQ any more, it's the corporate campus. . . . Beavis and Butthead are not the only ones who have a problem with authority—try winning the fealty of a whip-smart 32-year-old bond trader or brand manager on the basis of raw, positional authority.[20]

The most successful knowledge workers can indeed dictate terms to their employers—or else set up as freelancers or consultants if they get the urge. Companies woo intellectual stars in much the same way that sports teams woo sports stars. The announcement that a star researcher or columnist is moving to a rival firm can be enough to depress a company's share price and set off a migration of talent in the bargain. At the British advertising firm Saatchi & Saatchi, shareholders drove out the brothers at the helm—and then watched them set up a new agency that lured away many of the old firm's clients.

Nor is it just a case of a few talented individuals being given the red carpet treatment. Companies everywhere are treating workers of all sorts with more respect than they used to. Yesterday's "hired hands" have become today's "associates" or "colleagues." More firms encourage employees to use their facilities to work on their own projects, as 3M does. More and more companies give their employees sabbaticals to write books or just recharge their batteries. (*The Economist* is fortunately one of these, or this book might never have been written.)

As the word "empowerment" implies, bosses have had to hand over power to people lower down on the chain. Companies have to market membership just as aggressively as they market products and services—and perhaps more so. The best employers go out of their way to earn the loyalty of their workers by looking after their welfare (particularly their educational welfare) and providing them with opportunities to put their knowledge to work.

For all that, the "knowledge economy" is not going to be the workers' paradise that many people envisage. Companies owe their success to a whole host of things other than the combined IQs of their employees: their underlying values, their managerial systems, their traditional routines, their customized factories, and their local traditions. In other words, a great deal depends on their organizational memories, laboriously built up over their corporate lifetimes. Some of the most valuable knowledge is highly company-specific: you need to join the company in order to acquire it (because it is only passed on to initiates, rather like Masonic lore), and you need to remain part of the company if you want to use it (because it only makes sense when it is combined with the skills of your fellow employees).

Learning organizations are successful precisely because they are so good at generating knowledge in ways that others cannot imitate. Successful companies recruit people when they are young and impressionable, and they devote a lot of effort to turning these raw recruits into company men and women. They send them on in-house training courses (Motorola, Disney, and numerous other companies have their own "universities"), influence the way they speak and dress, and encourage them to spend their time with other company people. The training programs for high-flyers will often last for years and will shuttle them from job to job and from country to country in order to give them an overall view of how the company operates.

Companies can put heavy emphasis on knowledge while still leaving their employees with no doubt where the real power lies. Wal-Mart, a discount retailer that has been repeatedly praised by management theorists as a model learning organization, gets its new recruits to raise their right hand and swear that "every time a customer comes within 10 feet of me, I will smile, look him in the eye, and greet him. So help me Sam." Until recently, IBM expected all its employees to wear a white shirt and sober tie. People who work for Nordstrom happily refer to themselves as "Nordies" and start every day by chanting "We want to do it for Nordstrom."

For many workers, perhaps even most, the fundamental division in modern society will not be between capital and labor but between insiders and outsiders—between those who are part of knowledge-intensive companies and thus have a chance to sharpen their intellects and hone their skills, on the one hand, and those who are left out in the cold, on the other. This is particularly bad news for two sorts of people. First, people who leave school or university in the middle of a recession and who are judged too old when the next round of hiring comes along will find that no amount of government-sponsored training or general education can make up for the lack of company-specific skills. Second, middle-age workers who become victims of the downsizing or delayering fashion, and whose skills and values have been finely tuned by their previous employer, will find, however hard they try, they cannot fit in elsewhere.

Does a model exist to show how a knowledge-based economy might look? It may stick in the gullet to think of, say, Sylvester Stallone as a knowledge worker, but Hollywood's star system does suggest how the most talented people in other industries may one day strike deals with their employers. Once contract workers bound to studios, actors are now free agents. And the studios are no longer vertically integrated companies owning everything they produce. Rather, every film is made by a complex alliance in which the studio is no more than the banker: virtually all the important aspects of making a film—from casting and producing it to special effects—are contracted out. Another moral to be drawn from Hollywood is that the studios have survived. Studios may not be able to push around Stallone, but the vast majority of entertainment workers cross the studios at their peril. The studios' web of production deals and alliances continually creates and disperses more knowledge. They are learning organizations par excellence; but they have given away power only where they have had to.

# CHAPTER 7

STRATEGY: FROM PLANNING TO VISION

IN THE WITCH DOCTORS' world, one talent is prized above all others: the ability to predict and control the future. In the old days, soothsayers donned strange clothes, performed exotic gyrations, and sacrificed unfortunate animals. In return, tribal chiefs put luxurious huts and a large supply of young virgins at their disposal. Naturally enough, the witch doctors did everything possible to protect the secrets of soothsaying from the curious gaze of outsiders or the critical questions of cynics.

Management theorists may not wear a feathered headdress or pore over the entrails of dead animals—at least not in public. But in their bid to predict and control the future, they have developed exotic-sounding techniques, such as SBUs, PIMs, PPBSs, and 3 × 3 matrices (to name only the most comprehensible); and they have kept those techniques as mysterious as possible, protected from the prying eyes of laymen by complicated mathematical formulas and labyrinthine diagrams. One business school student recalls attending a 15-part course on "strategy" given by one of the leading names in the field: "I learned a great deal about military history and Confucian metaphors. But the only practical advice that we were given was that every company should send teams of people from different disciplines to country hotels every year to think about the future."

Indeed, strategy has become an ever more obtuse art. For most of this century, "strategic planning" was regarded as the very kernel of management thought; it often had an entire department devoted to it. Planning—a neat, definite, military concept—was adapted and refined into what seemed to be a precise science. Since the 1980s, however, strategic planning—like many other management nostrums—has been discredited. In uncertain times, when few businesses feel happy predicting their next month's profits, the idea of five-year plans strikes many managers as a little, well, socialist. Yet the appeal of having some goal to aim for—even a less attainable, more ephemeral one—remains. Strategy has thus been recast in new terms, most prominently as "vision." The question at the heart of this chapter is whether this is really an improvement.

## Building the Planning Machine

The organization that was most susceptible to the claim that management theory can confer control over the future was the multidivisional firm that achieved its finest flowering in America in the 1960s and 1970s. Technically, the credit for putting planning at the center of corporate life should probably go to writers such as Igor Ansoff and Harvard Business School's Alfred Chandler, who both, in their different ways, spent the 1950s and 1960s insisting that all companies needed an overall corporate strategy.[1] However, the trail had already been blazed by a familiar duo—Frederick Taylor and Alfred Sloan. By separating the performance of a task from its coordination, Taylor prepared the way for the arrival of a new class of professional strategic planners. At Sloan's General Motors, managers sitting in the corporate headquarters were responsible for crafting long-term strategy for the entire organization.[2]

Arguably, managers' fascination with planning goes even deeper than Sloan and Taylor. Virtually any book about strategy contains a string of military metaphors about the importance of "reconnaissance" or "good intelligence." Managers have always fancied themselves an officer class. Strategy is what separates them from the sergeants. The planning department was as close as many of them came to an officers' mess. In

America, there was an explicit military connection. The American army embraced planning with a rare fervor in Vietnam: one of the architects of America's policy of "strategic bombing" had been an architect of strategic planning at Ford in the 1950s, Robert McNamara. Meanwhile, in France, strategic planners tried to run the whole country, public as well as private.

By the early 1960s, planning was still a fairly simple process.[3] It usually involved three stages: designing a blueprint setting out a company's or a division's future; agreeing on the plan; and finally implementing it. Each part of the process, which in total took about a year, had its own dedicated workers. Ideas were the province of the planning department. Agreement was left to senior management and the board. Implementation was the job of the other managers who had been specially trained for this role (at places like General Electric's Crotonville center) and were issued weighty manuals (such as GE's famous "blue books") to tell them how to perform the task. The function of an organization, in the eyes of Ansoff, was to implement strategy: everything—its structure, its hierarchy—followed from the plan.

Flattered by the success of their brainchild, management theorists tried to turn planning into a rigorous and sophisticated science. The academics deconstructed strategy making into its constituent parts: mission, objectives, external analysis, internal analysis, and so on. Confronted with objections to the rigmarole, they simply made the strategy-making process even more complicated: management theorist George Steiner took almost 800 pages to explain the rudiments of planning in *Top Management Planning* (1969).[4] Ten years later, in *Strategic Planning* (tellingly subtitled *What Every Manager Must Know*), Steiner even introduced a new phase, the "plan to plan."[5]

By the end of the 1960s, firms such as General Electric found that they needed at least three levels of strategy makers: first, the managers of particular products or divisions; then, a layer of "strategic business units" that looked after several related areas of business; and finally, a layer of corporate strategists who acted as "portfolio planners" and decided how to allocate the company's resources among the various strategic business units. Tools that helped planners through this maze were soon all the rage. GE itself developed an "industry-attractiveness-business-position matrix," but the most successful aid was the Boston Consulting Group's "growth-share matrix," which, as explained in Chapter 5, classified businesses into cash cows, stars, question marks, and dogs. The aim of all these devices was the same: to tell managers whether to invest, harvest, or divest, depending on where their business fell on the chart.[6] By 1979, 45 percent of the Fortune 500 companies were using some form of portfolio planning.[7]

## Porter the Planner

All this complexity might have been tolerable had the strategy gurus agreed on what they were trying to do. But they had not. The biggest split was between the Harvard Business School, which emphasized case studies and argued that each problem had a particular solution, and the Boston Consulting Group (BCG), which always tried to provide a universal explanation of the way that companies operated. For instance, the BCG believed that successfully identifying your business as, say, a cash cow was as useful to a coffin maker as to an advertising agency. For a while it looked as if these disputes might be solved by Michael Porter, who churned out a series of books on corporate strategy during the 1980s, before turning his attention to globalization (see Chapter 10). Porter brought to the subject the intellectual vigor of somebody who has both an MBA from the business school and a PhD from the economics faculty that sits glowering at the business school across the Charles River. However, he is not known for his brevity.

In his first book, *Competitive Strategy* (1980), Porter tried to plot a middle way between the two approaches, arguing that there were both individual and general lessons to be learned about strategy. Thus, he studied individual companies but set them in the context of their relevant industries, and he outlined "generic strategies" but emphasized that different firms must choose different paths to success. In his next book, *Competitive Advantage* (1985), Porter became more prescriptive, outlining generic strategies that firms could take. Before deciding on what strategy to pick, he argued, a firm needed to do a lot of homework. This included analyzing the "five competitive forces" that determine an industry's attractiveness (potential entrants, buyers, suppliers, substitutes, and competitors) and deciding what sort of industry it was (growing or declining, ripening or mature, and so on). Porter also argued that a company should think of itself not as a single unit but as a "value chain" of discrete activities (designing, producing, marketing, etc.).

This love of analysis explains why Porter became something of a god to planners. Porter's work does not lend itself to one-line summaries; yet, underneath all his lists and copious examples, there is a fairly simple message. In essence, strategy is about making a choice between two ways of competing. One choice is market differentiation, competing on the basis of value added to customers, so that people will pay a premium to cover higher costs. The other choice is cost-based leadership, offering products or services at the lowest cost. Porter's data showed that firms with a clear strategy performed better than those that either lacked a clear strategy or that consciously tried to follow both paths and lead the way on price and quality.

## Why the Planning Machine Stalled

All this was marvelous for Porter, whose big, square books on strategy remain standard texts in many business schools. But it was not enough to rescue the idea of planning from collapse. Even as Porter was refining his ideas, the Japanese car companies were demolishing his arguments, beating the Americans at both cost and quality. The result was that planning quickly went out of fashion.

Not only did the Japanese manage to combine things that Porter thought were incompatible, they did so without bothering to prepare strategic plans. The American addiction to corporate planning struck Japanese thinkers such as Kenichi Ohmae as a private-sector version of the Soviet addiction to central planning, with the same disastrous impact on innovation and enterprise. The attacks on strategic planning came not only from overseas. Even in the Harvard Business School, frustration with planning had been growing. Robert Hayes pointed out that many line managers found strategic planning an impediment to good management.[8] Amir Bhide noted that two-thirds of the founders of fast-growing companies he had interviewed had started their companies with either back-of-the-envelope business plans or no business plans at all.[9]

Companies have now shifted their attention from planning the future to getting the most out of the present through disciplines like reengineering. Many companies have disbanded their strategy departments entirely; and strategic consultancies, starved of work, have had to bone up on reengineering. One leading management thinker, Henry Mintzberg, has even written a long but excellent obituary called *The Rise and Fall of Strategic Planning* (1994).

So what exactly is wrong with strategy and planning? The charge sheet is a long one, but it essentially divides into two complaints: practical difficulties and theoretical impossibilities. Topping the list of difficulties is the fact that strategic planning never really amounts to strategic thinking. Instead, it becomes a pedantic annual ritual in which representatives of each department try to grab whatever resources are being doled out. That not only leads to fights (the marketing strategy contradicts the manufacturing strategy); it also means that the company's strategy often takes no account of the interdepartmental connections that can lead the way to the markets of the future.

Strategic planning soon becomes a numbers game. The real substance of General Electric's round of meetings was about making the numbers add up rather than discussing the company's future. And in this world, where increasing a department's budget by 1 percent in real terms is seen as a drastic move, incrementalism is king. True, IBM's planners did gradually allocate more money to the company's personal computer division, but they never grasped how radically their industry had changed. One reason why Rupert Murdoch has consistently beaten the world's other media giants to the punch is that he relies on instinct rather than committees.

Paradoxically, when a company's planners do decide (usually too late) to do something, they often blunder into a big acquisition or diversification that proves to be anything but strategic. Think of Westinghouse's decision to enter the financial services business in the late 1980s, or AT&T's attempt to break into the computer business with its acquisition of NCR, or any of Daimler-Benz's catastrophic forays into aerospace and electronic goods. Fine, someone might argue, but surely all that this proves is that strategy can be poorly executed. The point is, planning can frequently be a pointless activity, even in the hands of the most talented managers. The most obvious problem is that, since the future is, sensibly enough, *in* the future, we have no way of knowing it. Strategic planning is usually hopelessly conservative, projecting current practices into the future and ignoring the way that innovations are constantly changing the rules of the game. This conservatism may have been appropriate in, say, America in the 1950s (though many would dispute even that), but it has no place in a business world where the environment can change radically and where the greatest source of competitive advantage is not really "cost" or "quality" but "creativity." Planning preserves existing categories of thought, whereas creativity blows them apart.

Even the best planners can get things completely wrong. Consider two fairly predictable industries. Five years ago, most Western financial institutions were still terrified that Japan's banks would take over their business and drew up complicated strategies and briefing documents on how to cope with the Japanization of their markets. Today, the same banks and securities houses are still worried about Tokyo's bankers—but only because they might go bust. Similarly, for most of the past decade, British Airways (BA) has been obsessed with stopping American carriers such as United and Delta from establishing competing "fortress hubs" at Heathrow. Now, Virgin Atlantic— an upstart founded by a man BA refused to take seriously because he did not wear a tie—is BA's chief competitor on the Atlantic route. Nor have United, Delta, and American been that smart: they have spent most of the past decade fighting each other while small airlines such as Southwest stole their customers. And, remember, both airlines and banking are highly regulated, capital-intensive businesses. Who would want to be a strategic planner at an Internet pioneer like Netscape?

The second objection is that statistics are by no means as reliable as the planners believe. (Planners tend to resemble the Lilliputian tailors in Jonathan Swift's *Gulliver's Travels,* who measure Gulliver with a quadrant and sextant, perform a set of complex computations, and return several days later with a suit of clothes "very ill made.") Far from being objective and trustworthy, statistics are often based on flimsy data and shaped by the prejudices of those who collect them. Even in the late 1980s, the U.S. Central Intelligence Agency's planners argued that the Soviet Union possessed one of the world's biggest economies—despite the fact that any Moscow taxi driver could have told them this was nonsense. Henry Mintzberg has repeatedly pointed out that the most important knowledge in any organization is not what is written down in formal reports and expressed in numbers but what is exchanged in informal conversations, with customers, suppliers, and other workers.[10]

The last objection is that strategic planning separates thinking from doing. The strategy makers—usually a tiny elite—think; the workers—everybody else—acts. Strategists lack the detailed knowledge of organizations that is needed to make informed decisions. And the front-line workers who possess that intimate knowledge are too far removed from strategy making to have any impact. If all the piffle about learning organizations and so on means anything at all, it is that a company's strategic intelligence should involve all its workers; it is not just the preserve of a small group of planners.

### Growth Is Back

Strategy is clearly in trouble. But the announcement of its death is somewhat exaggerated. The past few years have seen more and more managers pining for the halcyon days of strategic thinking, if not quite strategic planning. To a large extent, this is a reaction against reengineering. Managers have started to realize that restructuring is not in itself a strategy, but a means of dealing with the failure of earlier strategies. More often than not, downsizing leads not to long-term growth but to yet more downsizing, and the obsession with the short term leads not to organizational mastery but to drift and panic. The urgent drives out the important, and the fleetingly fashionable distracts attention from the real opportunity. Driven to produce short-term profits, managers forget to ask whether their industry has a long-term future; determined to squeeze more out of less, they fail to spot new markets or invent new products.

In *Grow to Be Great: Breaking the Downsizing Cycle* (1995), two consultants from Mercer Management, Dwight Gertz and Joao Baptista, looked at some 1,000 American companies and found that only 7 percent of the best-performing ones in 1988–93 had cut costs in the previous five-year period. Companies that invested in growth were awarded with a compound 15 percent annual rise in their share price while those that invested in cost savings saw only an 11 percent rise.

The real successes of American business of the past decade are not those companies such as General Electric and Xerox that have completed heroically bloody turnarounds, but those that never went in the wrong direction in the first place—and kept on growing. Venerable old Hewlett-Packard, for instance, has quadrupled in size. By mid-1995, even those companies that had cut back hard realized that future profits would come from growth. "Union Pacific used to have 80,000 employees. Today we have fewer than 50,000," Drew Lewis, the company's chief executive, declared to the periodical *Strategy & Business.* "There is still room to cut costs, but we're not going anywhere unless we grow our revenues through improved services and satisfactory margins."[11] And as bosses' thoughts have turned to growth, their time horizons have lengthened. In late 1995, Brian Dickie, a consultant at Booz, Allen & Hamilton, estimated that his clients' "strategic focus" had lengthened considerably to around seven years ("on earlier occasions 18 months was not unusual").

With "growth" suddenly back in fashion, management theorists have reinvestigated strategy—and reached two general conclusions. The first is that, for all its faults, planning was not an unmitigated disaster. Royal Dutch/Shell pioneered a system of scenario planning that was meant to be more of a learning exercise than an attempt to make accurate predictions. However, by asking a succession of "what if" questions, scenario planning gave the oil company a better understanding of its strengths and weaknesses. It also produced some fairly accurate predictions: Shell was the only major oil company to predict the 1973 oil crisis and to have a ready-made strategy for coping with it.

The other, more general conclusion is that, even if they have ditched planning, the most successful companies remain intensely interested in thinking about the future. Microsoft has an Advanced Technology Group, Toshiba boasts a Lifestyle Research Institute, and Yamaha has a "listening post" in London, chock-full of all the latest musical gadgetry, which it makes available to Europe's most talented musicians. The most adventurous companies are indulging in what Disney calls "imagineering." Electronic Data Systems hired Disney alumni to help the company put together an exhibit demonstrating how information technology would reshape people's lives. Some leading businessmen, including Olivier Lecerf, former head of Lafarge, a large cement manufacturer, and Frank Carruba, the chief technology officer of Philips, have started taking sabbaticals in order to reflect on the future.[12]

Management consultancies have also started to develop new techniques for thinking ahead. Arthur D. Little encourages its clients to imagine a future in which a particular technology—virtual reality (VR), say—has become commonplace.[13] Children spend their time in VR playgrounds; clothes buyers "try" on clothes in VR mirrors before asking for them to be made; students "tour the world" looking for the best VR classroom. Clients have to think about what all this means for their own businesses. They also have to "write a history of the future" in order to see what technological breakthroughs and regulatory changes are needed to make this "history" possible. The consultancy argues that this technique provides a way of thinking about the future without either extrapolating from the present or indulging in the pseudoscience of prediction. The point, a little like Shell's scenario planning, is simply to ask "What if . . . ?"

## The Importance of Science Fiction

But can all this futuristic thought be translated into a strategy without falling back on the (generally bad) idea of planning? The answer, according to many theorists, is to come up with a strategic vision—something that provides a company with a sense of mission without the costs and constraints of central planning. Visions, according to their advocates, define a few outstanding goals around which companies can organize their resources; and they help to inspire the workforce to pursue common aims. Think of the way that John F. Kennedy used his vision of putting a man on the moon within a decade to galvanize America's space program; or Apple's dream of a computer for every man, woman, and child in America. Microsoft's clearly articulated dream of "owning the desktop," which dates back to the early 1980s, has helped it to dominate first operating systems and then applications software, and now seems to be pushing it toward the Internet. Sun Microsystems has reaped great benefits from sticking by its idea that "the network is the computer" for almost a decade.

Nor are visions confined to sneakered entrepreneurs. In Japan, even the dowdiest managers spend some of their time gazing into crystal balls. Ever since he published *The Mind of the Strategist* in 1982, Kenichi Ohmae has been pointing out that Japanese companies organize themselves around common visions—visions, moreover, that emerge from a continual process of negotiation, rather than from the mind of a single domineering leader. Perhaps the only creature more admired in American business during the 1980s than the generic Japanese manager was Jack Welch. Welch, too, has an obsession with visions.[14] When he dispensed with all GE's strategic planning apparatus, he set a fairly simple goal instead: "Be one or two in an industry—or else get out." This idea was easy to understand but hardly an inspiring vision. For much of the early 1980s, all that GE's workers knew about strategy was the pain of Neutron Jack announcing yet more redundancies. Welch's first attempt at a loftier theme—trying to persuade GE's staff that they owned the business—flopped. He had a little more success with his idea that GE was like a "business engine," but his message did not get through until late 1988 when he launched "Work Out"—an empowerment program that began with a series of meetings in which GEers could air their grievances.

Once Welch's new vision caught on, ideas started coming from the very middle managers who had been most hostile to him. For years, Welch returned every month to "The Pit"—the amphitheater at GE's Management Development Center in Crotonville where Work Out was conceived—to deliver a sermon on Work Out to employees. Already—like all the best visions—it has acquired its own language. "Low-hanging fruit," for instance, are easy-to-make savings in factories; a "python" is an entwining bureaucracy. Now Welch has changed his message again; he dreams of turning GE into a "boundaryless organization." "Companies need overarching themes to create change," Welch has argued. "If it's just somebody pushing a gimmick or a program, without an overarching theme, you can't get through the wall."[15]

All this has been enough to turn dreaming up visions into a management industry in its own right. Virtually every firm now has a mission statement that purports to articulate its view of the future. An increasing number of companies assemble "vision task forces." Even bosses who took the same dismissive attitude to "the vision thing" as George Bush have had to knuckle under. Lou Gerstner came into IBM declaring that the one thing that the computer giant did not need was another vision; by 1995, he had begun mumbling about "building a networked future."

Even accountants now feel the urge to dream. In 1994, Arthur Andersen's auditing arm, which five years earlier had embarked on a project called Vision 2000, decided it was time for a fresh message called Creating Our Future. The vision task force was made up of 100 people: 75 partners and 25 young high-flyers. It met in Chicago, Lisbon, Berlin, and Singapore, and the "visionaries" chattered away online between these gatherings. Andersen also consulted clients, such as Jack Welch, and gurus, such as Charles Handy. Having played around with propositions such as "By 2005, Arthur Andersen has become the biggest accounting firm in the world," the dreamer-accountants decided that the company's aim should be to change from auditing the books of its clients to auditing their businesses. To meet this more consultative role, the accountants came up with an equation and a slogan. The equation was $K = (P + I)S$, where $K$ is knowledge; $P$, our people; $I$, information; and $S$, the power of sharing. The slogan for Andersen was: "The World's Greatest Place to do Great Work." Although this must surely count among the shabbiest battle cries in history, Andersen's accountants swear that the process has helped redirect their company—and that five years is too long to wait for another dream because "Visioning has to be an ongoing process."

## The New Synthesis

Can visions really be fleshed out into meaty strategies? To generalize slightly, academics have tended to split into two groups. The first group wants to push the subject of strategy into more ephemeral fields. John Kao, a professor at Harvard Business School (and a successful entrepreneur in his own right), argues that the chief strategic aim of a company should be to encourage creativity. In the old days, planners used to hand out sheet music with exact descriptions of what each person should play; now, according to Kao, strategy is like jazz. The strategists should set the overall direction, but let individuals improvise. This creative approach is proving so popular that one "paper" at the 1995 American Management Association convention consisted of a bunch of jazz musicians, jamming for all they were worth.

A second group of thinkers still hearkens after a more disciplined, Porterish approach. For instance, in *Foundations of*

*Corporate Success* (1993), John Kay, a British economist-turned-management-theorist, takes an approach almost as complicated as Porter's. Kay argues that strategy should be built around identifying each firm's strength in four fields: its reputation (which can include brands), its ability to innovate, its strategic assets (such as a drug patent or a government-sanctioned monopoly), and its "architecture," by which he means the network of relationships within and outside a firm (he is particularly keen on Marks and Spencer's supplier network). Kay offers an excellent analysis of why particular firms have succeeded, but he remains adamant that each firm's position is different, and that there are no generic answers to strategic success. This may well be an intellectually rigorous approach, but it is hardly designed to win him readers.

The book that has had the biggest impact on strategy, *Competing for the Future,* published in September 1994 by Gary Hamel and C. K. Prahalad, combines elements of both approaches. Prahalad has helped turn his employer, the University of Michigan Business School, into one of the foremost centers of thinking on business strategy in America. Hamel is arguably the brightest (and, according to his peers, the richest) business thinker of his generation. In 1997, he launched a new consultancy called Strategos. The success of *Competing for the Future* also owed something to the marketing savvy of the book's publisher, Harvard Business School Press, which spent $75,000 marketing the book, secured serialization in *Fortune,* and sent the authors on a national tour to publicize their ideas.

The central claim of *Competing for the Future* is that the most important form of competition is the battle to create and dominate emerging opportunities, and that the whole of traditional strategic thinking, from the role of senior managers to the nature of strategy itself, needs to be rethought in the light of this insight. Traditional strategists looked on companies as collections of products and business units; Hamel and Prahalad look on them as collections of skills. Traditional strategists tried to position their organization as cleverly as possible in existing markets; Hamel and Prahalad argue that a company should try to reinvent its whole industry by following a vision. As one example, Hamel and Prahalad cite Motorola's dream of a "wireless" world in which telephone numbers are assigned to people rather than places, and everybody has a portable phone.

The best way of dealing with an increasingly uncertain world is not to take refuge in short-termism but to imagine what the market will be like 10 or more years hence and then try desperately to get there. The winners can reap benefits in numerous ways: by establishing a monopoly, however briefly, of a particular product (Chrysler with minivans, and Sony with the Walkman); by setting standards or owning intellectual property rights (Matsushita with VCRs, and Microsoft with DOS); or by establishing the rules of the game (Wal-Mart with out-of-town hypermarkets). As for the losers, they are consigned to a perpetual cycle of downsizing.

One obvious response to this argument is that visionary companies may earn the applause of management theorists, but it is the plodders who come after them who make the real money. Why not let the leaders make all the investments and take all the risks and then simply copy or buy their product, just as Bill Gates did? Until recently, most academic research tended to hint that "first movers" had a big advantage (by one count, 19 of the 25 firms that were market leaders in various consumer products in 1923 were still on top 60 years later). However, such surveys often tend to deal only with surviving companies and surviving brands. For instance, everybody (including Procter & Gamble) tends to believe that the firm invented the disposable diaper business when it launched Pampers in 1961. In fact, another brand, the inelegantly named and now defunct Chux, had already been going for a quarter of a century, though it had concentrated on wealthy households and people who were traveling. Pampers was not a new product; it was just cheaper and aimed at a wider market. The same story can be told about videocassette recorders. An American firm, Ampex, pioneered the product in 1956 but was swept out of the way 20 years later by cheaper models from Japanese manufacturers such as Matsushita and Sony. Gerard Tellis of the University of California and Peter Golder of New York University's Stern School of Business have completed a detailed study of over 50 markets in which they look at the brands that have perished as well as those that survived: the pioneers, they have discovered, are leaders in only 1 in 10 of the markets, and, on average, the current leaders entered the market 13 years after the "first mover."[16]

On balance, this sort of research challenges but does not invalidate Hamel and Prahalad's argument. In many cases, the follower's product was sufficiently different that it could almost count as a new one. And even if some copiers may have won in the past, it does not look like a tempting strategy for the future. The problem with copying the leaders is that dozens of other companies are trying to do the same thing, on ever narrower profit margins. In most branded-goods businesses, nearly all the profits are chewed up by the leading two products. Besides, following companies not only have to imitate a product; they also have to copy the core competencies that helped produce it. Having let Japanese competitors take the lead in camcorders, Philips, Thomson, and Zenith have simply found it impossible to catch up. Much the same has happened to the Japanese producers of cellular phones: they are still chasing Motorola, Ericsson, and Nokia. An alternative line of attack on Hamel and Prahalad is that visions do not mean a fig if one does not have the resources to back them up. An entire school of management thinkers supports the "resource-based theory of the firm," which argues that what really matters is the physical firepower a company brings to the battle. In fact, physical resources are becoming less and less important for competitive advantage. All the money and accumulated brainpower in the world will not save a company if it fails to think carefully about where it will be a decade hence. IBM spent $6 billion a year on research and development but failed to see that the market was shifting from mainframes to personal computers. As late as 1991, a third of its R&D budget was spent on "big iron." Returning to cellular telephones, all of Matsushita's and Sony's clout have not stopped tiny Nokia from running rings around them.

### Stretch Yourself

Besides, Hamel and Prahalad are more than just ethereal futurists. They insist that companies should first spend money on thinking about the future (as Microsoft, Toshiba, Yamaha, Disney, Motorola, and EDS do); and that firms need what they call a "strategic architecture"—a sense of what benefits they want to deliver to their customers and what mechanisms they should use to deliver those benefits. Two concepts are crucial to strategic architecture.

The first is "stretch"—trying for huge gains without telling people how to get there. Traditional planning departments were preoccupied with engineering a tight fit between goals and resources; Hamel and Prahalad argue that strategy is about "stretch"—about using a vision of the future to inspire workers to go that little bit further. This sort of ambition and sense of purpose is most common in start-ups. (Tracy Kidder's gripping account of Data General, *The Soul of a New Machine* [1981], shows how managers can happily impose 80-hour work weeks and impossible deadlines if they can inspire their workers with a vision of greatness.) But big firms have also pulled off the same trick, especially in Japan. Toshiba told its employees to design a new VCR using half the number of parts and taking half the time at half the cost. A team was dispatched—and the job was done. As an admiring Jack Welch has pointed out: "Nobody in Japan asks 'How much productivity can you get?' as if it were a finite element."

On the other hand, there seems to be a very thin line between stretching employees and destroying them. When chief executives set their own targets (for instance, the "strike price" at which their share options become profitable), they rarely stretch themselves. Steve Kerr, General Electric's Learning Officer, warned *Fortune* in November 1995 that the discipline can be destructive: "To meet stretch targets, people use the one resource that is not constrained, which is their personal time. I think that's immoral. . . . 'm seeing all around this country people working evenings, working Saturdays, working Sundays to achieve stretch targets."

Hamel and Prahalad's other concept is our old friend core competencies (see Chapters 5 and 6). For Hamel and Prahalad, defining core competencies is the first step in designing a strategy. If a firm knows what it is good at—logistics management in the case of Federal Express—it can then choose something to aim at—like "on-time delivery." Competencies also form the basis for the modern equivalent of portfolio management: if a firm knows what it is good at, it will venture only into new areas where its core skills can be applied to create new products, and it will buy only the companies that can add substantially to its portfolio of skills.

As already mentioned, one problem with core competencies is that they can easily become just as unbending as five-year plans. Moreover, they are not the only answer. Some of the world's most admired companies—such as ABB and America's

General Electric—have followed deliberate "multibusiness" strategies. Three British academics—Andrew Campbell, Michael Goold, and Marcus Alexander—have argued that strategy should be based on the "parenting" skills of the holding company rather than on any links between the skills of its subsidiaries.[17] In its heyday, Britain's Hanson spotted mature businesses that were being appallingly managed and then subjected them to fierce financial management. A good parent knows when to get out of a particular line of business as well as when to get in. In 1995, 3M decided to get out of the tape business, even though it was profitable and fitted in quite nicely with its other subsidiaries. The skills of 3M's senior managers lie in fostering growing technical businesses: it would have been a bad parent for a business in which efficiency was becoming more important than technology.

One could argue that the distinction between core competencies and parenting is often one of semantics: one man's parenting skill is another's core competence. On the face of it, "economic value added" (EVA) or "market value added" (MVA) are radically different approaches, since they are based on the efficiency with which a company uses its capital rather than on any abstract ideas about synergy. Under EVA, a company judges whether something is worth doing by taking the net operating profit from that business and then deducting the cost of the capital deployed to make that profit; MVA, which has been championed by Stern Stewart, a New York–based consulting firm, basically calculates the amount of money shareholders have invested in a business—and then subtracts that sum from its market value.

The idea is to encourage managers and even shop-floor workers to think exactly like shareholders. Britain's ICI has sent some 1,000 managers on a course designed to persuade them to "pull levers that create shareholder value," which has forced factory bosses to learn about beta factors and free cash flow. The late Roberto Goizueta, who used the MVA formula to become America's most successful boss—he added $59 billion to Coca-Cola's value (narrowly beating Jack Welch, who added $52 billion to GE's)—always used his own pocket version of EVA that his grandfather taught him: "You borrow money at a certain rate and invest it at a higher rate and pocket the difference." It is this formula that led Goizueta into Hollywood (Coke briefly owned Columbia Pictures). More successfully, it guided Coca-Cola's strategy of concentrating on its soft drinks business; even without Goizueta as long as Coke can continue to borrow money at 10 percent and earn returns of 30 percent, its strategy will stay the same.

Interestingly, the discipline is also spreading to areas where shareholders have less weight. Veba, a huge German utility, used an EVA system to restructure itself into a mere 50 pieces. Led by the Mitsubishi Corporation, leading Japanese companies are taking a much harder, more mathematical line to portfolio management, judging the performance of their divisions by their return on equity.

Core competencies and economic value added are not as incompatible as they seem at first glance. It turns out that the best way for companies to improve their returns to shareholders is to focus on their core businesses. Researchers at the J.P. Morgan investment bank have constructed an index measuring a company's focus on a scale of 1 to 100. American companies that "clarified" their businesses outperformed the market by 11 percent in the following two years; firms that diversified underperformed by about 4 percent. Institutional investors would prefer to do their own diversification by buying a range of shares in different specialists rather than investing in a conglomerate. And focused firms are usually easier to manage than diversified firms. It is this sort of gainful clarity that AT&T was pursuing when it split itself up into three separate businesses in 1996.

## Competing for the Past

*Competing for the Future* is probably as close to required reading as any management book in the 1990s. But, for all its virtues, *Competing for the Future* is not free of two of the maladies afflicting management theory. The first is the discipline's enthusiasm for pulling companies in opposite directions. It would be nice to think that Hamel and Prahalad's concept of "stretch" sits well with all those other theories about "empowerment" and "trust": one imagines a team of cheery souls setting off together in search of their dream, watched over by a kindly father figure. In practice, for most workers, "stretch" means being told to work their butts off in pursuit of an unattainable goal—something that most people would describe as

hell. The second problem is the industry's propensity for reinventing the wheel. In 1960, Theodore Levitt, a professor at
Harvard Business School, wrote an article called "Marketing
Myopia," which argued that companies should define themselves in terms of their broad orientation rather than their specific products. This led to a great deal of waffle as railroads
redefined themselves as "transportation companies" and oil re-
fineries reclassified themselves as "energy processors" and
began to think about buying other mineral companies. But it
did not produce much clarity of thinking, and the practice eventually went out of fashion.

Supporters of *Competing for the Future* would argue that it
is a much more complicated, more sophisticated approach than
Levitt's. However, that does not make modern core competencies any easier to find than their 1960s' equivalent. In both financial services and the jumble of industries that pass for
multimedia, companies are having trouble deciding which businesses match their skills. Are banks really in the same industry
as stockbrokers and insurers? Would a newspaper baron's skills
be more useful in Hollywood or in electronic publishing, or neither? Even when companies have to make a move, they often go
in the wrong direction. Henry Mintzberg points out that, if
horse-drawn carriage companies had decided, at the turn of the
century, that they needed to start thinking of themselves as
transport companies and moved into cars, they would probably
have still been wiped out by the likes of Ford, because they had
no expertise in making combustion engines; instead they would
have been better advised to capitalize on their operating skills,
such as making wooden toys for children or turning out horse
whips for the flagellation market.[18]

In the end, all strategy is gambling on the future. Visions—
no less than plans—are only as good as those who make them.
Even the dumbest lottery player can figure out that companies
that predict the future correctly do better than those that do
not. Hamel and Prahalad hardly strengthen their argument by
focusing on companies that have bet on a possible future and
won (Canon, Motorola, Microsoft, etc.) rather than on companies that have made the same bet and lost. Apple lost to Microsoft because all the vision in the world cannot make up for
the lack of more mundane business skills. Arguably, one of the
company's misfortunes was that the skilled administrator who

was brought in to add some mundane professionalism to the company, John Sculley, also spent too much of his time musing on the long-term future of the industry.[19] As chairman of General Motors in 1981–90, Roger Smith did everything right in Hamel and Prahalad's terms, dreaming of making GM "the car company of the twenty-first century" and spending billions to improve the company's technological skills, but he still saw his company's share of the domestic market fall from 46 percent to 35 percent.

Nor is "poor visioning" confined to perennial losers like GM. Texas Instruments tried to exploit the core competencies it had developed in its semiconductor business in areas such as calculators, watches, and home computers. But its managers lacked the necessary experience in managing such consumer-oriented businesses. The Saatchi brothers decided that banking and consultancy were both "people businesses" that would respond to the same management techniques that had served them so well in advertising. Airlines, on the whole, have made a hash of running hotels, even though it seemed sensible to combine the two.

Looking forward, it is easy to see quite a few visions ending in tears. Some of the richest people in Hollywood are about to lose spectacular amounts of money on multimedia, thanks to a combination of overwhelming greed and overheated imagination. America's two most successful software billionaires have diametrically opposite visions of how their industry will develop. Larry Ellison of Oracle believes that the personal computer will give way to cheap, easy-to-use network terminals, which will be able to pull down information from a central database. To Bill Gates, this is just "the latest in a string of misconceived visions that Larry has been coming up with"; his own vision remains centered on the personal computer.[20] Doubtless, in 10 years, some son-of-Hamel and son-of-Prahalad will write a book saying that vision was correct, and make it seem an easy choice; today, any normal mortal confronted by Gates and Ellison is reminded of the old jibe: "Two men say they're Jesus; one of them must be wrong."

# CHAPTER 8

## STORM IN THE BOARDROOM

THE ANNUAL GENERAL MEETING of British Gas, in May 1995, was an unusual affair. Not only did it attract some 4,000 shareholders—a record—but it was also a tale of two Cedrics. The first was Cedric Brown, then the chief executive of the privatized utility, a slightly worthy and anonymous man who had suddenly found himself dubbed by the tabloids "the most hated man in Britain" for awarding himself a compensation package of £492,000; the second was a pig, also called Cedric, who had distinguished himself to his owner by being the greediest in his sty. While the human Cedric tried to keep order in the hall, his swinish namesake sat outside, guzzling potato peelings from overflowing troughs labeled "share options."

Perhaps Brown had only himself to blame for this charade. However, he is only one of several bosses around the world to suffer the wrath of the outside world recently. Outsiders in the business community, pension funds, even individual shareholders, have begun asking painful questions: Who owns a company? Who is accountable for running it? What responsibility does a company have to the community, to the environment, to equal opportunities? These questions—particularly those concerning corporate governance and ethics—used to be something of a sideshow. Now they are discussed at every board meeting.

Corporate insiders have not proven themselves any less heretical of late, posing disturbing questions about the nature and conduct of leadership. Apply the question "Who?" to virtually any unsolved problem of management theory—as in "Who will choose the company's vision?" or "Who will unleash the organization's entrepreneurs?"—and the answer is nearly always "the chief executive." Indeed, this unfortunate soul's responsibilities have grown all the greater the flatter organizations have become and the more empowered and uppity their "intrapreneurs" feel. The man, or occasionally the woman, at the top may often be the only one with the authority and reach needed to hold the entire organization together. "No institution can possibly survive," Peter Drucker once argued, "if it needs geniuses or supermen to manage it. It must be organized in such a way as to be able to get along under a leadership of perfectly normal human beings." One might have thought that, after nearly a century, management theory would have removed some of the superhuman element from leadership. Instead, the latest managerial fashion is just the opposite: more onerous responsibilities than ever are being heaped on the head of the organization.

So how should the leader lead? Unfortunately, the books on leadership offer contradictory answers to this question. Some say that leadership is fairly easy to pick up: that it involves no more than setting clear goals, being honest with one's employees, saying "We" not "I," and so on. Others preach that leadership is so damned esoteric and instinctive that it is a gift only a few are born with. No number of bulletin boards and mission statements, no amount of "human engineering" is going to turn Joe Public into Jack Welch.

This debate is management's equivalent of psychology's nature-versus-nurture debate. The notable scarcity of leaders who can change organizations, and the unorthodox ways in which those few people persuade others to follow them, is a powerful argument on the side of nature. Nevertheless, some thinkers, including Warren Bennis and John Adair, insist that leadership can be taught—a view that harkens back to the military idea that men can be trained to do anything. Which school of thought will prevail? Those readers whose appetite for words of wisdom from the gurus must be slaked immediately can jump ahead to the next section of this chapter. For those who can tolerate a small diversion for scene setting, it may be useful to consider the standing of the modern boss, and the strangely unproductive relationship between the current generation of superbosses and management theory.

## The Mind of the Practitioner

For most of this century, successful bosses tended to fill two entirely negative roles in the public imagination. In one role, they were evil capitalists who tried to make money by any means possible, who sewed up markets, and who ganged up against the little guy. This was the many-headed serpent Rockefeller that appeared in newspaper cartoons and the William Randolph Hearst whom Orson Welles lampooned in *Citizen Kane*. Alternatively, business people were just, well, boring: they were suited company men like Jack Lemmon in *The Apartment*. "The office" was a metaphor for tediousness. During the 1960s, both images were taken to extremes.

More recently, the popular imagination has begun to conceive of the businessman in a more favorable light. Antibusiness sentiment has not disappeared entirely: Pat Buchanan managed to fan some of the embers in the 1996 campaign. But most liberal parties, such as America's Democratic Party and Britain's Labour Party, have never seemed more pro-business. Modern entrepreneurs, particularly those in the computer industry, such as Bill Gates and Steve Jobs, are regarded as surprisingly "cool," even though their business practices are sometimes just as ruthless as John D. Rockefeller's. In America's 1992 presidential election, a businessman, Ross Perot, at one stage led both George Bush and Bill Clinton in the opinion polls, and there are still people in Washington who believe that the former boss of Electronic Data Systems could have won if he had proved a less eccentric campaigner. Four years later, despite a public backlash against Big Business and downsizing, another eccentric businessman, Steve Forbes, also made a mark.

At lower levels of government, American voters have found managerial competence—or at least the appearance of it—an irresistible asset. In the aftermath of the riots, Los Angeles turned to Richard Riordan, a businessman schooled in the real world, to reorganize the scarred city. Meanwhile, outside the United States, Italians trusted Silvio Berlusconi because he came from the lean, modern, private sector. Rather than daubing the walls with Marxist slogans, left-wing students took to sticking up critical articles from heavyweight financial publications about Berlusconi's balance sheet.

This phenomenon may be principally a reflection of voters' frustration with modern professional politicians. But it also seems to represent a craving for management, for efficiency, for the type of leadership that had been tested in the private sector. Much more revealing than the list of those businessmen who have run is the increasingly long "What-if?" list of those bosses who could mount a political challenge if they wanted to. Would America, in the 1996 election rather have chosen between Bill Clinton and Bob Dole—or between Jack Welch and Bill Gates? Would Britain rather have chosen between John Major, Paddy Ashdown, and Tony Blair—or between Lord Hanson, Sir John Harvey-Jones, and Richard Branson? In Finland, would any politician willingly campaign against Jorma Ollia of Nokia, or in Ireland against Tony O'Reilly of Heinz? Even in bombed-out Beirut one can find a billboard for a "total-quality management" conference standing proudly next to a cluster of yellow Hezbollah banners.

Given the weight of public expectations, one might have expected business people to be great generators of new management theories. The reality is more disappointing. In the early days of management, men such as the gun maker Eli Whitney and the mill owner Robert Owen were indeed management thinkers. As already mentioned, two of the most important thinkers of the early twentieth century were businessmen: Henry Ford and Alfred Sloan. Over at IBM, the company's founder, Thomas Watson, helped define what customer service meant. "The beliefs that mould great organizations," his son (and successor as head of IBM) Thomas Watson Junior once wrote, "frequently grow out of the character, the experience and the convictions of a single person." In Japan today, people still look to businessmen for theories about business, as explained in Chapter 11. In Korea, Lee Kun Hee, the boss of Samsung, has invented a "new management philosophy" that can roughly be described as one part Californian new-ageism and two parts Korean autocracy. Another example of the modern boss-theorist is Ricardo Semler, a Brazilian businessman and author, who has taken his family firm, a pump- and propeller-making company called Semco, to extremes of empowerment that even Tom Peters at his most wowish has not dreamed of. Semco used to be the sort of place where even visits to the lavatory were timed. Now, workers choose their own bosses; a third of them select their own pay.

In Europe and America, however, boss-theorists are few on the ground. ABB's Percy Barnevik may be an exception (see Chapter 10). Most practicing bosses like to be seen as *au fait* with the latest thinking but do not have time to put their own thoughts on paper. When Noel Tichy, a respected professor at the Michigan School of Business, recently claimed that the twentieth century had produced "only two business leaders who will be remembered for their ideas: Alfred Sloan of General Motors and Jack Welch of General Electric," the first instinct of many readers may have been to question whether Welch counted.[1] Despite his near divine status in American management, Welch's management theory is arguably more anecdotal than revolutionary. Yes, he empowered workers, but so did a lot of other people. His maxims—"Don't manage, lead," "Control your own destiny or somebody else will"—are punchy rather than profound. Massive though Welch's achievement is, it cannot be compared to Sloan's.

In truth, many of our most esteemed and successful businessmen seem to manage instinctively, and without having been particularly influenced by a formal study of the discipline. There are exceptions, such as David Packard, who says in *The HP Way* that "no other operating policy has contributed more to Hewlett-Packard's success than management by objectives" and then goes on to quote Drucker enthusiastically.[2] But most managers are less modest. Percy Barnevik says that everybody agrees on what makes for a good company, from empowerment to decentralization. The tricky part is putting these ideas into practice, and no theory can tell a firm how to do that. Bill Gates admits to an admiration for Peter Drucker but otherwise treats the genre with suspicion. He points out that in the early 1980s most management writers were raving about IBM at just the same time that he, as a young entrepreneur, was discovering that the giant had feet of clay.[3]

Gates's own book, *The Road Ahead* (1995), has virtually nothing to say about management; it is about information technology. Most books by (or about) bosses are not, strictly speaking, works of management theory. Instead, they tend to fall into one of three categories. The first might be described as "tips from the top." One of the first business best-sellers was *Think and Grow Rich* (1937) by Napoleon Hill.[4] Although subsequent writers have cast doubts on Hill's ability to tell the truth, the author always claimed that the book began when, as a cub reporter, he was sent to interview Andrew Carnegie in 1908 and the steel baron suggested that he interview other business leaders to find the secret of their success. In the end, Hill collared over 500 people, including Rockefeller, Ford, George Eastman, and Frank W. Woolworth: the result, published in 1937, has since sold 7 million copies.

A more recent "tips from the top" book is Mark McCormack's *What They Don't Teach You at Harvard Business School* (1984). McCormack runs a successful sports-promotion business—a trade he revolutionized. Yet any reader looking in the book for some Druckerish insight on how to transform a services industry will come away frustrated. Rather, it is an apparently random list of thoughts, most of them illustrated by a couple of anecdotes featuring its name-dropping author: be punctual, listen "aggressively," "once you've sold, shut up." Having introduced the idea of time management by saying that he is one of the best time managers around, McCormack gives hints on how to save those seconds, such as knowing which elevators are the quickest in a building you visit frequently, or, if you are arriving by plane at an airport, getting your driver to pick you up at the less crowded departures gate.[5] Useful, but not, one suspects, the stuff of which record profits are made.

By contrast, the other great manager-writer of the 1980s, Lee Iacocca, belongs to the "I did it my way" school. His tome, modestly titled *Iacocca* (1985), is probably better remembered for the line, "Henry Ford made my kids suffer, and for that I'll never forgive him," than for any management insight.[6] A chapter near the end of the book, called "The Key to Management," reduces the skills of his trade to three essentials: have quarterly meetings with your executives, be decisive, and concentrate on people rather than information. The whole point of the book seems to be that Iacocca has a unique collection of unteachable skills.

It is worth adding that other writers, who have since taken a cooler look at the Iacocca myth, have depicted the car baron as somebody who spent too much time hunting subsidies and promoting himself, and too little building better cars.[7] Nevertheless, there are genuinely successful bosses whose achievements seem to be built on similarly nontransferable business skills. Read any biography of Rupert Murdoch, and one of the most lasting impressions is that "none of this can work without him." Nearly all News Corporation's most successful gambles have been personal hunches of Murdoch; it is hard to imagine his successor inheriting his management style.

Yet that does not mean that the careers of either Murdoch or Iacocca are alien to management theory. News Corporation's history could be rewritten as a case study in globalization—a subject about which Murdoch can talk as fluently as any guru (particularly when he is raising money). Scratch away at Iacocca's time at Chrysler and you will find plenty of Japanese management techniques—particularly ones concerning customer service and lean production. It was arguably Iacocca's failure to do such things more thoroughly that forced his successors to re-rescue the American car giant.

The last category of manager books, "the fixer," is close to the spirit of the Perot campaign: namely, that a good manager can draw on experience and instinct rather than any great theory to fix problems. The prime example of the fixer is Sir John Harvey-Jones. After a long and fairly successful spell as chairman of ICI (and also a stint as chairman of *The Economist*), he discovered a second life as the star of *Troubleshooter*—a popular BBC series in which Sir John visited companies and tried to fix them. Although Sir John is not afraid to invoke gurus (particularly in later books such as *Managing to Survive*, 1993), his approach is that of a pragmatist. His whole style, from his outlandish tie to his elderly-footballer haircut, is that of a man who will give it to you straight. Which he does. Sir John's advice tends to be along the lines of "You should sell this plant" or "You should stop making these" rather than "You should reengineer this business." Any manager can learn a great deal from *Troubleshooter*—more than from most management books written by theorists—but once again it does not offer a blueprint in the same way that, say, Alfred Sloan did.

The general separation of theory from practice is, arguably, a reflection of the maturity of management theory. To use a parallel example from economics, people expect their finance ministers to know their way around monetarism and Keynesianism; they do not expect them to spend their spare time experimenting with complicated new formulas on blackboards. Yet, there is no getting away from the fact that the relationship between great managers and articulable management theory is not always direct, perhaps in part because management theory has done little to help most bosses in their jobs.

## That Leadership Thing

Even in the wayward, word-sputtering world of management theory, no subject has produced more waffle than leadership. By one count, there are 130 definitions of leadership. "Never have so many labored for so long to say so little," argued Warren Bennis and Burt Nanus in *Leaders: The Strategies for Taking Charge* (1985). "Time and again the old military analogies are rolled out from Alexander the Great to Nelson, Montgomery and in due course no doubt General Norman Schwarzkopf," Carol Kennedy complained in 1994. "Business leadership is evidently harder to recognize and define than the 'follow me' qualities on a battlefield."[8] To borrow one of these military metaphors, writing about leadership is a little like invading Russia. Even writers of Drucker's class tend to run into deep snow.

As any new boss will immediately learn, management fashion has made the top job immensely more difficult. Part of the problem is structural: there are not as many layers of management between top and bottom. Many head offices now contain fewer than 100 people, and decisions have to be made more quickly. At the same time, the modern boss is no longer supposed to be bossy. Leadership is no longer about issuing instructions but about releasing other people's energies. In Charles Handy's Federalist model of the company, "the centre does not run the corporation except in times of war or its equivalent." It is time now to look at the chaotic knowledge-based organization from the boss's point of view.

Although Alfred Sloan built his system in part to cage unruly bosses like Henry Ford, it was a structure most bosses felt happy with. It had firm rules. The boss had a threefold job: to set the strategy, design a management structure, and install effective controls. Many of the management fads in the 1960s and

1970s—particularly management by objectives—gave bosses a good excuse to stick with Sloan's model rather than to question it. Setting an objective for a manager was, after all, just another way of determining the "strategy" part of Sloan's model. If the business world appeared to be moving faster, that just meant that strategies, structures, and controls had to be that little bit more complicated and comprehensive. Today's bosses wearily seem to have admitted defeat: The Sloanist model "was right for the 1970s," argues Jack Welch. "A growing handicap in the 1980s and it would have been a ticket to the boneyard in the 1990s."

No one wants to end up in the boneyard, of course, and it is hard to find any modern boss who has a bad word to say about empowerment. But should we believe them?

Recent management literature on leadership has tended to praise people such as Jean Kvasnica, a Hewlett-Packard manager who has led several successful projects by getting out of the way, or Jaguar's North American managers, who, after a troubled restructuring, actually put the most difficult people in charge of employee involvement groups—again with successful results. However, most bosses would have sent Kvasnica to the company doctor and fired the troublemakers at Jaguar. It is hard to tell which Jack Welch is the more genuine person: the one who preached the virtues of empowering General Electric's employees, or the one who went ballistic when his "empowered" traders at Kidder Peabody ran up huge losses. In reality, most bosses would much rather see themselves as generals at the head of an army, rather than as the teacher-facilitators that gurus such as Peter Senge would like them to be. Lord Sheppard of Britain's Grand Metropolitan once described his own style as "management by a light grip on the throat."

To make things worse, at many companies, the new freedom means freedom to criticize the boss. In Britain, companies such as British Petroleum, British Telecom, BMW, and even the English rugby team have experimented with "360-degree feedback"—letting the workers tell the bosses what they think of them. In some cases, the answers are given directly; in others (usually more successful cases), the answers are filtered anonymously through a third party who then tells the boss the good or bad news.

However, bosses' problems with "learning organizations" are not purely ones of ego. Bringing out the best in others (particularly thousands of others) is more difficult than just absorbing information and sending out commands. As already pointed out, it is devilishly difficult to devise a structure that allows people to come up with new ideas while giving an organization a common purpose. All the current talk about the importance of being a coach rather than a general tends to overlook how difficult being a coach is. "Managing is like holding a dove in your hand," argued Tommy Lasorda of the Los Angeles Dodgers. "Squeeze too tight, you kill it. Open your hand too much, you let it go."[9]

## Nature versus Nurture

Whatever their problems with empowerment, bosses are clearly putting more emphasis on the "leadership" part of their job and less on the purely "managerial" part. The difference between the two was set out by Warren Bennis in a famous but long list. ("The manager maintains; the leader develops. The manager focuses on systems and structure; the leader focuses on people. The manager relies on control; the leader inspires trust."[10]) However, being able to tell the difference between managers and leaders is not the same as finding a way to turn the former into the latter.

Recently, companies have set about trying to develop leadership in a systematic way, aiming perhaps not so much at teaching leadership as at honing it. Not surprisingly, one of the leaders in making "the soft stuff hard" is Hewlett-Packard, which measures people's leadership potential against a list of 26 characteristics, then sends staff on a coaching course. Each January, some 80,000 people at General Electric fill out internal résumé forms. GE monitors employees' "boundarylessness" on a scale of 1 to 5 (you score low points for blocking ideas traveling around the company). It also has a formal process called "Session C," matching managers to jobs, which occupies a whole month of Welch's time every year.

All the same, leadership training remains an imprecise and wasteful business. To find 25 leaders likely to run its big operations, PepsiCo trained some 100 people. At one time, the Bank of America tracked the progress of 1,000 potential leaders; six years later, more than 80 percent of them had left. And sometimes even the best-regarded training systems can turn out to be flawed. In the early 1980s, IBM was thought of as being the ideal cradle to develop leaders; today, it is dismissed as a graveyard of corporate bureaucrats.

Indeed, it is possible to argue that even the combined powers of nature and nurture are not enough: like Napoleon's generals, modern leaders need to be lucky—particularly when it comes to timing. One of America's most widely admired bosses, Lawrence Bossidy of Allied Signal, was asked how a single person can change a large organization; he replied by enunciating the "burning platform" theory of change: "When the roustabouts are standing on the offshore oil rig and the foreman yells, 'Jump into the water,' not only won't they jump, but also they won't feel too kindly towards the foreman. There may be sharks in the water. They'll jump only when they see the flames shooting up from the platform. Chrysler's platform was visibly burning; the company changed. IBM's platform was not visibly burning; it didn't."[11] In other words, a boss's ability to turn a company around depends more on the state of the company than on the boss's character.

Even so, leadership can contribute a great deal to a company's success. First, vision is crucial. In order to change organizations, it helps to be identified with a particular set of ideas or values. The point is not that the vision should be right or even particularly profound, but that it should be a rallying point for a diverse group of people. In some cases, the theory does not even have to be spelled out. What Richard Branson has actually said about Virgin has been fairly flaccid; what really matters is that he stands for a certain way of doing things.

Second, the gulf between "transactional leadership" and "transformational leadership" has widened. These two terms were devised, ironically, by an unsuccessful politician, James McGregor Burns, who was an adviser to John F. Kennedy and then ran for Congress. Transactional leaders, he decided, were ones who dealt with their followers on a tit-for-tat basis: you give me your vote, I will get you a job. A transformational leader is somebody who spots a profound need that the follower had not realized existed and sets out to meet it. This latter approach engenders far greater loyalty. As sociologists have pointed out, "normative" organizational power is a strong force: it leads people to do what you want them to do because they share the same values rather than because they are responding to sticks and carrots.

The final point to make about modern business leadership is more of a hunch: being a maverick seems to be a decided advantage. "Out-of-the-box thinking," to use the new jargon, has become more valuable now that most companies can do perfectly the basic things, and mundane products can be copied instantaneously. In a world in which most bosses are doing the same things—flattening their command structures, turning their workers into entrepreneurs—it is often the quirky individuals who stand out, attracting better employees and dreaming up more exciting products. Fewer and fewer bright business school graduates want to join big companies—unless those big companies are themselves mavericks like Microsoft and Virgin. In 1989, 70 percent of Stanford's MBA graduates joined big companies; in 1994, only 50 percent did.

Talk to Bill Gates, Rupert Murdoch, or Richard Branson and the first impression you get is one of relentless curiosity. Yet most leadership programs concentrate on the nuts and bolts of management, and most managers are depressingly narrow people (as a glance at the hobbies listed in any Business Who's Who demonstrates). Some inspirational managers have made a point of encouraging young high-flyers to broaden their minds. Yotaro Kobayashi, Fuji Xerox's boss, was surprised when, as an up-and-coming manager, he was sent off by his hero, Joe Wilson, to the Aspen Institute in Colorado to learn about Plato and Aristotle; Kobayashi has now set up a similar center in Japan, in an attempt to encourage Japan's ultraconformist businessmen to broaden their minds. Tom Peters takes the same message to thousands of middle managers, when he encourages them to throw away their management books and read novels—or even race yaks.

Another maverick asset that current management structures do little to cultivate is the experience of failure. Welch was first noticed at General Electric in the 1960s because he ran a plastics plant that blew up. As a youthful entrepreneur, Richard Branson spent a night in a police cell after smuggling some records into Britain from France. Rupert Murdoch nearly went bust at the beginning of the 1990s. Babe Ruth may have been best known for his home runs, but he also set a record for strikeouts. Thanks to those flatter management structures, however, the chance of having one of these constructive experiences of failure is limited.

So where does that leave the modern boss? The simple answer is: *overworked*. He (or she) faces a far more complex challenge than his predecessors: today's boss is expected to give away power while keeping some form of control, and to tap the creative talents of his employees while creating a common culture within the company. He has to spend far more time meeting and motivating those irritating knowledge workers, who are now spread across an increasingly wide range of countries. On top of all this, he has to be a maverick who may have failed in the past and who knows his Aristotle as well as his Drucker. It is hardly surprising that the executive search market is growing at 15 percent a year, and that it is now normal for bosses to be divorced or married to their secretaries.

In other words, management theory seems to have flunked Drucker's challenge: to come up with an institution that does not need to be led "by geniuses or supermen." Far from easing the job of a leader, management theory seems to have made it more difficult—in fact, well nigh impossible. Even the hallowed excuse of looking back to great leaders of the past seems increasingly self-defeating. Would Winston Churchill have been a good "teacher-leader" in a multicultural corporation? Would Alexander the Great have been prepared to let squadrons of T-shirted knowledge workers disappear to follow their own ideas for a couple of years?

### Unaccountable, Sexist, and under Siege

Although management theorists have piled all these responsibilities on the boss and the boardroom, they have, until recently, been less keen on developing ways of holding these newly visionary leaders accountable for their visions. This is a serious flaw. To call in Drucker once again: "Any government, whether that of a company or of a nation, degenerates into mediocrity and malperformance if it is not clearly accountable for results and not clearly accountable to someone."[12] It cannot be entirely coincidental that, although virtually every other part of the company has been redesigned, reengineered, and reinvented, the gurus and consultants have left alone the people who have sanctioned these revolutions. No witch doctor ever advanced his career by suggesting a change of ruling family.

According to the old joke, a company's board is like "the parsley on the fish"—there for ornamental purposes rather than anything more substantial. Even accepting this description, most boards no longer make a particularly appetizing garnish.

White men constitute 43 percent of America's workforce, but hold 95 percent of its senior management positions. The only area in which women have done well—middle-management jobs such as assistant vice presidents and office managers—is the one that has been hardest hit by reengineering. One of America's best-known women chief executives, Loida Lewis of Beatrice, a food and retailing conglomerate, got the job principally because she inherited stock from her late husband. In France, the senior layers of management are even more deftly snapped up by the "Enarques" who have come from the tiny civil service school, ENA. In 1993, almost half the bosses of France's 125 largest companies were former civil servants.

In 1970, *Management Today* looked at the composition of the boardrooms of 200 big British companies. In 1995, the magazine repeated the exercise with 2,000 companies.[13] After a quarter of a century of radical economic and social change, the typical inhabitant of the British boardroom remains an Oxbridge-educated male in his early 50s. Only 3.7 percent of the directors were women—and many of these held nonexecutive posts. The most obvious sign of change was that, at FTSE-100 companies, pay packets in the boardroom had risen threefold in real terms (to £248,000) in a period when average wages were up only 50 percent.

This exclusiveness matters. America's WASP elite lacks the range of experience to deal with an increasingly multicultural home market, let alone to mastermind the conquest of world markets. France has bred an elite that is good at certain types of management, such as long-range planning or big infrastructure projects, but out of its depth in fast-moving industries such as computers. Worse, the very similarity among the middle-aged, blue-suited, white-shirted men who are directors and chief executives around the world increases the "parsley effect." Tom Peters has pointed out that the homogeneity of America's senior managers makes a nonsense of high-falutin' plans to divide companies into autonomous, competing units. It also means that companies grow out of touch with their consumers. Surveys have shown that, even when it comes to fairly chunky products such as cars or life insurance, the decision about what to buy is now often—if not mostly—made by a woman. There are very few female directors of car companies or insurers—and no prominent chief executives.

## Shareholders at the Gate

The chief pressure on boards to change their ways has not come from the gurus but from a new class of shareholders-rights activists. These include individuals such as Robert Monks, a genial American who, in early 1992, took out a full-page advertisement about Sears in *The Wall Street Journal,* under the title "Nonperforming assets," and Ekkehard Wenger, a German economics professor who specializes in causing grief at annual meetings and who defends his often unsubtle style by quoting Schiller: "One must tell the Germans the truth as coarsely as possible."

However, most of the clout has come from institutions such as the California Public Employees Retirement System (Calpers), the state workers' pension fund, which has taken a vigorous approach to its portfolio, building up big blocks of shares in companies and then trying to force them to change. In America, pension-fund managers and other fiduciary organizations are obliged to vote at annual general meetings. But they have also been spurred into action by the way that boss-friendly states in America, such as Delaware, allow lumbering giants such as Time Warner to choose lower takeover offers or adopt "poison pills" and "golden parachutes," which make takeovers more expensive for acquirers and protect the board's own salaries.

General shareholder pressure has led to a spate of public inquiries, including the Cadbury and Greenbury reports in Britain and the Vienot report in France. A string of studies has shown that interventionist shareholders, such as Calpers and Warren Buffett, have got better returns on their investments. And in America, at least, angry shareholders have persuaded boards to boot out the bosses of some of America's biggest companies, including American Express, IBM, and WR Grace. They have also forced directors to get their act together by suing them. There were 347 suits filed against directors by shareholders in America in 1994; the average payout was $7.7 million.

Few countries insist on accountability from boards and bosses when it comes to executive pay, succession, and nonexecutive directors. The hardest-to-swallow item on this list is executive pay. By virtually any measure, directors in general—and bosses in particular—have been paying themselves generously. In 1996, the "winner" in America was Lawrence Cass of Green Tree Financial, who made $102 million in 1996, compared with the meager $65 million he earned in 1995. Between 1990 and 1995, the average American chief executive's pay rose 92 percent (to $3.75 million); over the same period, corporate profits rose 75 percent and workers' pay 16 percent (to $26,652).[14] Shares authorized for management equity now account for 10 percent of the outstanding shares of America's biggest 200 firms. But the real problem is not so much one of scale as of performance. Most of the high payments come from share-option deals that reward bosses generously if they succeed but fail to punish them if they do not. Although Disney share-holders have been happy to pay the company's chairman, Michael Eisner, hundreds of millions of dollars in salary, many of them expressed outrage in 1997 at the $90 million pay-off awarded to Michael Ovitz, who served only eighteen far-from-successful months as the company's president.

Similar one-way bets are now common for other senior managers, too. The "value-sharing" deal that tempted Jerry York, IBM's chief financial officer (CFO), to the same post at Kirk Kerkorian's Tracinda Corporation in 1995 was worth $25 million. A survey by *CFO* magazine concluded that "although more CFOs are taking risks with their compensation, only a few are sharing downside risk as well as upside reward with their shareholders."[15] One of the most interesting parts of the Barings scandal was the pyramid of bonuses constructed on top of Nick Leeson's performance. The trader himself was on a £420,000 bonus; those above him got much more.

The problem with pay is that, although it annoys some shareholders intensely, one man's undeserved million-dollar salary in a multibillion-dollar company is seldom a big enough issue to persuade shareholders to revolt—particularly when the financial world itself is hardly known for parsimony when it comes to paychecks. At British Gas's shareholder meeting, the institutions actually voted in favor of the besieged Cedric Brown. Critics of the boardroom have consequently concentrated on getting bosses to reveal more about what they are paid and why, hoping to shame them into good behavior.

Most bosses still regard it as their privilege to choose their successor. The abuse is worst in continental Europe: in France, for example, it is still normal for the stewardship of a large company to pass from one Enarque to another with barely a word to the company's owners. The two General Electrics—America's GE and Britain's GEC—have both dithered over the choice of a new boss. But what can be done about bosses who have simply held on to power too long and refuse to retire? So far, the most radical solution has come from John Kay of the London Business School: he has pleaded for fixed terms for bosses on the grounds that authoritarian structures are "insidiously corrupting" for all but the most remarkable men and women.

A better solution would be to force the board to do its job and represent shareholders' interests. Nonexecutive directors and, particularly, nonexecutive chairmen are a vital part of this process: after all, a chief executive who is also chairman is a bit like a student who marks his own exam papers. In Britain, in the wake of the Cadbury Report in December 1992, over 80 percent of the country's biggest companies have a nonexecutive chairman. In America, power has shifted slightly toward the nonexecutive members of the board who are now taking their job much more seriously. There are now even "director schools" such as the Directors College at Stanford Law School. Three-quarters of the 1,000 directors quizzed by headhunter Korn/Ferry in 1995 said that their boards had clear objectives for measuring the performance of chief executive officers (CEOs); two-thirds had formal annual reviews. The coup at General Motors that got rid of Robert Stempel in 1992 was organized by a group of nonexecutive directors led by John Smale, who then became nonexecutive chairman.

This is not to say that nonexecutive directors are infallible. Many of the same names keep popping up on the boards of companies associated with lousy performance and poor corporate governance. In 1995, Lilyan Affinito, a retired manager at a sewing-pattern company, earned $300,000 a year for sitting on the boards of the likes of Kmart and Tambrands.[16] Such directors have a habit of emerging unscathed from the worst corporate wrecks. It was also Smale who persuaded Stempel's successor, Jack Smith, to offer José Ignacio López de Arriortúa the job as head of North American operations because his cost cutting had such a big effect on the car giant's bottom line. (López then took off to Volkswagen.) And, in December 1995, Smale handed back the chairmanship to Smith, making it clear that, like many other directors in America, he regarded splitting the two posts as an emergency procedure.

However unhappy they may be, American shareholders can at least thank God that they do not have to deal with French firms. In 1966, a law allowed French companies to adopt a two-tier German style of supervisory board. Fewer than 1 in 50 have bothered to do so. Despite evidence of poor management at Suez, Air France, and Crédit Lyonnais, French companies have resisted attempts to divide the président from the directeur général. The idea of collective board responsibility is not enshrined in French law. In a 1994 survey of independent directors in France, over half said that they did not have enough information to exercise control over bosses.[17] "In the Anglo-Saxon model there is a very strong degree of control exercised by the market," Jean Peyrelevade, chairman of Crédit Lyonnais has pointed out. "The French market is too weak to fulfill that role."[18] Even when members of France's narrow business elite do fall out, the boss can usually shrug off the challenge. When Jacques Calvet, the head of Peugeot, threatened to resign as a director of Générale des Eaux over the selection of a new chief executive, Guy Dejounay, the water utility's boss, ignored him, and Calvet stayed anyway.

## A Question of Ethics

Interestingly, the French bosses caught in the corruption scandals of the mid-1990s (known locally as *les affaires*) were usually charged with *abus des biens sociaux,* abuse of corporate funds. This underscores the general link between ethics and corporate governance. For companies no less than debutantes, a good name is easy to lose and very hard to rebuild. The study of corporate ethics is one of the fastest-growing areas in management theory.

Royal Dutch/Shell's hard-earned image as a kinder, gentler sort of oil company, conscious of its social responsibilities and fashionably multicultural, was quickly destroyed in 1995—first by its attempt to dump the Brent Spar oil rig in the North Sea (the correct decision, as it happened, though poorly explained), and then by its association with the Nigerian government that executed Ben Sarowiwa, a poet who had caused a fuss in his country by investigating the oil giant's environmental record.

Shell's dilemma may strike many as extreme. But nowadays companies can end up in the headlines for milder things. In October 1995, Bausch & Lomb was the subject of an October 1995 cover story in *Business Week* headlined "Blind Ambition," which argued that in its go-getting quest for profits the company had jumped over certain commercial niceties such as selling its supposedly exclusive Ray-ban glasses to grey-market distributors. The issue dominated the company's subsequent board meetings. Politicians have also discovered that companies are easy to embarrass. In 1995, Robert Reich, then America's labor secretary, made a point of taking journalists to a Californian sweatshop, recently raided by the police, to show them goods bound for retailers such as Montgomery Ward and Dayton Hudson.

Nowadays, a company's board has to think about a different sort of accountability. Many of the assets that boards are charged with looking after are intangible ones—notably, the firm's reputation. In an environment where more and more consumers in the developed world make commercial decisions on "noncommercial" grounds, Milton Friedman's maxim that a company's only responsibility is to make money legally looks ever less defensible. A firm that does not break the law but is seen as socially irresponsible has a tough time. By the same token, firms such as Levi Strauss, Johnson & Johnson, Body Shop, and Ben & Jerry's have all prospered from their "ethical" reputations.

There are two problems with ethics from a management theorist's point of view. The first is that, like motherhood and apple pie, nobody is against ethics. There are over 500 courses in "ethics" at American business schools (one even sends its students off to a monastery). By 1995, about two-thirds of American companies had formal codes of ethics; a third had ethics offices or ombudsmen. Commentators have not, however, noted a wave of ethical activity sweeping the country as a result.

The second problem is more serious: there is a yawning gap between what people say and what they do. One of the prime examples of this is a series of recent whistleblower cases in which managers who tried to report alleged "unethical" behavior were hounded out of their jobs. (In one case involving American agribusiness Archer Midland Daniels, the whistleblower was even pilloried by a preacher in the company's hometown.) Few firms are prepared to go as far as Ben & Jerry's and allow outsiders to publish audits of their performance. Even ethical firms have trouble sticking to their own high standards. In January 1995, Johnson & Johnson, which had earlier earned plaudits for its honest behavior over the Tylenol cyanide scandal, had to pay out $7.5 million in fines and costs after admitting that a subsidiary had shredded documents relating to a federal investigation.

In some cases, the lapses have more to do with image than with substance—though that can be damaging enough. Body Shop was forced to rephrase a claim that its products were not tested on animals after documents revealed that some of the ingredients that went into its cosmetics had been tested on animals by other firms in the past. However, there is also evidence that many firms have only a skin-deep approach to ethics. In a survey of young managers by Joseph Badaracco of Harvard Business School and Allen Webb of McKinsey, most of the respondents thought that "overinvesting" in ethics was not the way to get ahead: only a third thought that their companies would respect whistleblowers.[19] Like many other theorists, Badaracco and Webb believe that responsibility lies with the board: first, to set up strict ethical codes with clear sanctions; and second, to set a good example themselves.

But on whose behalf are these directors acting? So far in this chapter, the general assumption has been: the shareholders. But an increasingly noisy group of theorists argues that the modern firm is "accountable" to a wider group of people—including its local community and its workers. Who, in the end, should own a company?

## That Stakeholder Thing

"It is time we killed a myth," Charles Handy has declared, "the myth that it is the shareholders who run the business, and that it is for them that we all work."[20] Britain's leading management theorist argues that shareholder capitalism was designed for an era when the owners of a business were also its managers. Nowadays, most individual shareholders are punters rather than owners, swapping between companies as if they were racegoers picking horses. By dint of their size, pension funds take a slightly longer-term view, but, according to Handy, their role is more akin to that of financiers rather than owners. At the first whiff of a takeover, they usually sell out. Besides, argues Handy, shareholder capitalism is basically a "machine-age model," designed for the days when the chief asset of a firm was its property; now that the value in most companies resides in the heads of its employees, it is not appropriate "for anonymous outsiders to own or trade collections of people."

Corporate governance, in Handy's eyes, is essentially a political problem; it should thus be settled in a political way through some kind of separation of powers, so that the executive part (the managers) is separated from the legislative part (the shareholders), while "a judiciary" of accountants and other observers sets the rules. Rather than being formal corporations, companies should be "membership communities"—the members being all persons, from workers to customers, who have a stake in the enterprise. Money should still be raised through shares, Handy argues, and the shares should still entitle shareholders to some say in the way the company is run—but they should not entitle them to fire its board or sell the company over the heads of its employees. Shareholders with, say, a 1 percent stake in a company would get membership rights.

There are several strong traditions of corporate governance around the world, and almost all of them are now under fire in their own countries. In the interest of simplicity, we concentrate on the two most discussed models: the American system, which is similar to the British one; and the German one, which is broadly similar to that in Japan and others in Continental Europe.

Under the American system, a great deal of power ultimately rests with the shareholders. Takeovers are fairly common, and shareholders can also pester directors through "proxy" resolutions by which they force "their" managers to do ast, the German model gives a much greater voice to stakeholders—particularly banks and workers. Germany has a two-tier board system in which the managerial board is monitored by a supervisory board. Under a 1976 law, shareholders' representatives (nearly always banks) and workers have equal power on the supervisory board—but the chairman (usually chosen by the shareholders) has the casting vote.

Over time, both systems have changed more than their adherents like to admit. Many Wall Streeters would argue that the stakeholder–shareholder debate in America was settled earlier this century when the Dodge brothers sued Henry Ford for keeping back too much profit from the car company in which they all had shareholdings, and the Michigan Supreme Court ruled that "a business corporation is organized and carried on primarily for the profit of the stockholders." But it is clear that the modern American company—particularly the multibusiness conglomerate—barely resembles the original joint-stock companies of the nineteenth century. Rather than being one family's property, a company has become a lot of people's investment.

Peter Drucker's original solution to this problem, back in the 1950s, was to argue that a company's management was a trustee, accountable to no single group of shareholders or stakeholders. This sounded like a comfortable solution. But, as Drucker admits, American bosses did pretty much what they wanted until the 1980s. In the takeover boom of those years, shareholders' rights were fiercely restated, with the owners often selling off the company from under the managers' feet. Now, there is a great deal of talk in America about "maximizing shareholder value," but this will not wash either, according to Drucker, because it forces the company to be managed for the shortest term. "Long-term results," argues Drucker, "cannot be gained by piling short-term results on short-term results."[21]

Moreover, like Handy, Drucker has doubts about whether this is a sensible way to inspire knowledge workers: "An engineer will not be motivated to make a speculator rich." Drucker is more enthusiastic about shareholders' rights than Handy, but he still believes that some kind of formal separation of powers is necessary to give managers room to manage. He thinks that there should be some sort of formal "business audit," which would allow long-term owners to set the managers' public performance targets, and then let them get on with it.

The criticisms that Drucker and, particularly, Handy have been voicing for some time have now reached the political mainstream. In 1995, Will Hutton, the editor of the *Observer* newspaper, had a surprise best-seller in Britain with *The State We're In,* a polemic that blamed shareholder capitalism for Britain's presumed social ills and argued that the solution lies in stakeholding. In early 1996, Tony Blair, the leader of the Labour Party, also declared himself a believer in a "stakeholder society"—though he was tantalizingly vague about what the phrase meant. In private briefings, he made it clear that his thinking was influenced not by Hutton but by John Kay of the London Business School, another prominent advocate of stakeholder values.

In his State of the Union Address at the start of 1996, Bill Clinton asked American firms to put "long-term prosperity above short-term gain." Robert Reich, his then-labor secretary and a long-term admirer of stakeholder societies such as Germany, wrote an article in *The New York Times* accusing companies of abandoning their responsibilities to communities and employees. In the old days, Reich argued, gentlemanly capitalists took care to balance the interests of shareholders, employees, and the public at large; in the age of "electronic capitalism," footloose investors simply look for the lowest wages and the laxest regulations. His solution is to encourage firms to maintain jobs and neighborhoods through tax penalties.

### The German Question

But have the advocates of stakeholding proved their case? So far, the stakeholder lobby in both Britain and America has been much better at pointing to the inadequacies of shareholder capitalism than at coming up with robust sounding systems of their own.

Much of their argument relies on gazing admiringly at Germany (or Japan) and deciding that its impressive performance since the war "proves" the case for stakeholder capitalism. This does not hold water. First, many other factors explain Germany and Japan's "success," such as the strength of their education systems and their long-established manufacturing skills. And, second, that success looks more questionable now that the Japanese and German economies have stumbled.

Many of the peculiarities in the German system owe more to circumstance than to deliberate strategy. Very few German companies are quoted: the country's stock market capitalization amounts to less than a third of its gross domestic product (GDP). The German stock market is much less liquid than its counterparts in London and New York, and this makes it difficult for German investors to trade out of their shares. Note, too, that many of those investors are banks.

This system is changing, partly because financial deregulation is creating a new, more critical class of fund manager, but mostly because it has not worked very well. A supervisory board stuffed with bankers did little to prevent Daimler-Benz's woeful diversification in the 1980s or Metallgesellschaft's disastrous flirtation with oil futures. Bankers and shareholders have different priorities: shareholders want the company to make as big a profit as possible, whereas bankers are content if it makes enough profit to pay off its loans. Employees, too, have different priorities from shareholders. Inviting workers into the boardroom is surely one reason why Germany's manufacturers are now battling with high wages and comparatively low productivity.

Stakeholder capitalism looks even less impressive when it comes to dealing with knowledge workers. So far, cruel old shareholder capitalism has proved a far more effective nursery for the industries of the future. Silicon Valley is in California, not the Ruhr. Germany can muster only three software companies of any significance: Software AG, SAP, and Siemens. An interesting game to play with any advocate of stakeholder capitalism who starts prattling on about emancipating knowledge workers is to ask him or her to name any German high-technology firms that do not begin with "S."

### Gekko versus Reich

An alternative argument in favor of stakeholder capitalism is that there is really no contradiction between stakeholders' interests and those of shareholders. Indeed, a stakeholding approach is in the best long-term interest of shareholders. Robert Waterman reckons that "corporate cultures that tend to put three constituencies—shareholders, customers and employees—on the same plane, as opposed to putting shareholders first, are perversely the ones that do best for shareholders."[22] "You're accountable to more than one constituency," John Kotter at Harvard has warned bosses.

This sounds like a temptingly fluffy compromise. After all, in most normal circumstances, the interests of the various stakeholding groups coincide with those of the shareholders. Contented workers deliver better services; contented customers make for a profitable company. It is indeed in shareholders' interest to treat workers—particularly knowledge ones—well. However, treating all the constituencies as equals does not work when times get tough. The lack of clear accountability makes it difficult for managers to make tough decisions—as both the Germans and Japanese have recently discovered.

For most of the postwar era, the economies of Germany and Japan boomed, and the interests of the various stakeholders have coincided. But in the mid-1990s, the decisions became more pressing, and managers' habit of fudging or delaying them became more damaging. The result was that companies kept workers who might be better employed elsewhere; and in both countries, the economy failed to move into higher value-added industries and services. By contrast, Anglo-Saxon capitalism, with its clearer lines of authority and constant pressure from the stock market to perform, forced managers to make unpalatable decisions. The downsizing and restructuring that followed may have been painful, but they increased economic efficiency.

This defense of shareholding may sound horribly complacent. What about all those fat cats paying themselves gigantic salaries? And what about the golden parachutes that allow these weighty felines to get rich on failure? In fact, the best way to deal with the anxieties that have given rise to the recent stakeholder debate is to give more power to shareholders, not less. Study almost any corporate disaster—from the collapse of Maxwell Communications to the decision by Japanese firms to overpay for American property in the 1980s—and you find a board acting without anybody looking over its shoulder.

As Matthew Bishop concluded in a survey of Corporate Governance in *The Economist*, "Few if any woes have stemmed from too much shareholder interference."[23] An ideal system, argued Bishop, would do three things. "It would, first, give a boss enough freedom to manage well. It would ensure that he used that freedom to manage the firm in the interests of shareholders. And if somebody else could do a better job it would let him." The key concept, from an economist's point of view, is contestability—the ability for shareholders to be able to change managers if they are not doing a good job. The best way to solve the problem of corporate governance, then, is to create a market in it.

Nobody can deny that shareholders are sometimes a little quick to sell out in takeovers, but that does not obscure the fact that the biggest losers in most takeovers are usually the shareholders in the acquiring company. When the shareholders in Saatchi & Saatchi finally forced Maurice Saatchi out at the end of 1994, they may well have made a tactical mistake (Saatchi founded a rival agency that then won many of his previous employer's clients). But the real reason why "Old Saatchi" reached its parlous state was that the Saatchi brothers had spent their shareholders' money on a wild acquisition spree.

It may not be a popular way to end a section on stakeholders and shareholders, but perhaps the last word should belong to Gordon Gekko—the fictional raider in *Wall Street*. His "greed-is-good" speech to a group of shareholders is every liberal's nightmare. But it also contained the following passage:

> Now in the days of the free market when our country was a top industrial power there was accountability. The Carnegies, the Mellons, the men who built this great industrial empire made sure it was because it was their money at stake. Today management has no stake in the company. All together those men sitting up there own less than three percent of the company. You own the company, that's right, you, the stockholders, and you are being royally screwed by these bureaucrats with their stock lunches, their hunting and fishing trips, their corporate jets and their golden parachutes.

Trying to change shareholder capitalism into stakeholder capitalism assumes that the former has been given a chance to work and has failed. Most of the evidence suggests it has not.

# CHAPTER 9

## THE FUTURE OF WORK

YASUYUKI NAMBU, THE BOSS of Pasona, Japan's biggest manpower-services agency, has covered the walls of his office, from floor to ceiling, with photographs. They all feature Nambu posing with the world's best-known politicians: Margaret Thatcher (several times), Ronald Reagan, Bill Clinton, and Mikhail Gorbachev, not to mention royal persons such as Prince Charles. (Asked how he got to know Prince Charles, Nambu replies that Ronald Reagan introduced them.) The whole office exudes, by Japanese standards, an ostentatious air: the colors bold and bright, the secretaries (of whom there are an impressive number) all strikingly pretty and impeccably dressed.

The Japanese establishment might have been able to forgive Nambu all these things—even perhaps the scarlet shorts he wears to bicycle to work—if he had chosen a different career and founded a different sort of company. In a country in which the ideal is to become a salaryman chained for life to some big, safe corporation, Nambu is an entrepreneur. He started his first company, a Buddhist-style kindergarten, when he was still at university, employing his fellow students as teachers. Noticing that Japan was filled with bored mothers who had nothing to do all day and frustrated companies with too few staff to meet surges in demand, he decided to start Japan's first temporary worker agency: the Pasona Group. The business grew rapidly: by late 1995, it had 120,000 employees and some 28,000 clients, and Nambu had become a multimillionaire.

Nambu's wealth is a striking reminder of how much the nature of "work" has changed. In 1995, for the first time ever, the Japanese questioned in an annual survey by the Ministry of Labor, decided that job satisfaction was more important than company loyalty. Even the Japanese, it seems, no longer want to spend their lives doing the bidding of a single employer; and employers can no longer afford to keep people on the books regardless of how much value they are adding. Part-time and temporary workers already make up more than a quarter of Japan's workforce.

To the Japanese establishment, however, temporary workers spell anarchy. The Ministry of Labor has blocked Nambu's relatively innocuous scheme to help move middle managers from big firms that are trying to slim down to smaller ones that would like to expand but cannot afford to pay much. His strategy is to get the big companies to subsidize the wage bills of the smaller firms. One serious obstacle to this scheme is that the ministry allows temps to work in only 16 categories of jobs. Those "protected" by the current rules include nurses, telephone marketers, receptionists, and even janitors—in other words, the stalwarts of manpower agencies in the rest of the world.

Nambu clearly relishes his status as an outsider and showers visitors with press cuttings about his struggles with the Japanese bureaucracy. But he is also determined to keep his operation going. Japanese firms, he argues, will sink in today's cutthroat world unless they get rid of their hidebound business practices. The move toward temporary work, he continues, will not necessarily produce anarchy, so long as it is handled correctly. Nambu prides himself on Pasona's modernity—and its success with the younger generation. He has even set up a junior executive board, elected from among the younger employees, to generate ideas and offer him advice. Every year, on the anniversary of the company's creation, he holds a "challenge day," when all employees are encouraged to suggest new ideas.

Nambu's biggest concern is to ensure that temporary workers feel they belong to Pasona. Senior managers sit at desks on a raised platform in the middle of the company's giant open-plan office, so they can meet temps coming to collect their paychecks. Nambu sends out 30 or more "herograms" a day: elegant, hand-written notes that express his appreciation for outstanding work. Much of the top floor is taken up with a stylish café where workers can socialize and a health center where they can get a checkup or a $3 massage. Temporary work does not mean going unappreciated or being left out in the cold, argues Nambu. His temps can feel just as needed and secure as any salaryman; moreover, they have the advantage of being able to go when they want to. They are not just chattel.

## The End of Your Job?

Nambu is just one participant, albeit a rather flamboyant one, in a worldwide debate about the changing nature of work. If Freud was right, and work, like love, is a prime source of self-esteem, then most modern managers have been on a psychological assault course. Sacking surplus shop-floor workers has always been a managerial chore. Now it is the managers themselves who are getting the sack. Having been celebrated for much of the postwar period as the visible hand that made capitalism so successful, they are now often dismissed as so much unnecessary flab. Many theorists argue that something even more profound and frightening is upon them: the job itself—their unit of power, the place where they manage others—is facing extinction.

In an article called "The Temping of America" (March 19, 1993), *TIME* magazine warned that "America has entered the age of the contingent or temporary worker, of the consultant and subcontractor, of the just-in-time workforce—fluid, flexible, disposable. This is the future. Its message is this: 'You are on your own.'" A year later, in a cover story entitled "The End of the Job" (September 19, 1994), *Fortune* was even more pessimistic. "What is disappearing is not just a certain number of jobs—or jobs in certain industries or jobs in some parts of the country or even jobs in America as a whole. What is disappearing is the very thing itself: the job. That much sought after, much maligned social entity, is vanishing like a species that has outlived its evolutionary time."

The *Fortune* article was an extract from a book called *Job-shift: How to Prosper in a Workplace without Jobs* (1994), by

William Bridges, which argues that in a fast-moving economy the traditional job is a fixed, artificial solution to a fluid problem. Before the late eighteenth century, Bridges points out, a "job" referred to a specific undertaking rather than a fixed position, not unlike the word "gig" today. Soon, he reckons, it will return to that original meaning. And *Jobshift* is positively optimistic compared with *The End of Work,* by Jeremy Rifkin, which predicts a future of mass unemployment and social unrest.

> In the past when new technologies have replaced workers in a given sector, new sectors have always emerged to absorb the displaced laborers. Today all three of the traditional sectors of the economy—agriculture, manufacturing, and services—are experiencing technological displacement, forcing millions onto the unemployment rolls. The only expanding sector is the knowledge sector, made up of a small elite of entrepreneurs, scientists, technicians, computer programmers, professionals, educators, and consultants. While this sector is growing, it is not expected to absorb more than a fraction of the hundreds of millions [of jobs] eliminated in the next several decades.[1]

Politicians have discussed "the future of work" at meetings of the G7 countries. Writing papers on the subject is a growth industry in both Brussels and Washington. Throughout the rich world, increased anxiety at the workplace has been blamed for "voteless recoveries" where economies improve but people still feel miserable. The idea that the basic laws of employment are being turned upside down has encouraged mavericks such as Pat Buchanan and the late Sir James Goldsmith to raise protectionist banners, calling for barriers to be erected to protect jobs.

A cynic might argue that, as far as the poor are concerned, jobs have always been "nasty, brutish, and short." What is different about the current furor is that it has affected the managerial class. There is now a tidal wave of middle-class angst about the information age. The general feeling is that, 30 years ago, most managers had a reasonable chance of building a safe career. They went to work for a firm they referred to by an abbreviation like GM or GE and stayed there for about 40 years, doing progressively less work. Getting older meant getting a bigger office, more power, a better title. Today, downsizing, outsourcing, subcontracting, "the home office movement," and so on, are all turning people into temporary workers. Even famously paternal middle-class organizations such as the BBC and IBM have dispensed with the idea of a job for life. This has come as a blow for a generation who idled away their university years reading about the expected effect of demographic shortages and technology on work: fewer hours for more pay.

Is all this really true? Or has a subject that rightfully deserves contemplation been whipped up into one that incites paranoia? The more mundane truth is that jobs are not so much coming to an end as just changing. Yes, some aspects of the transition to a knowledge society (which is what we are really talking about) will be painful; but the change should by and large be beneficial. Above all, the victims, such as they are, will be primarily the poor and the uneducated—not managers who pore over books about the future of work.

## The Sage of Putney

The best place to begin any discussion about the future of work is a large, elegant flat in Putney, a prosperous suburb in West London and the home of Britain's best-known guru. Charles Handy stands out not only because he has been quietly saying for some time what many writers are now screaming from the hilltops, but also because some of his prophecies have been proved right. His forecast a decade ago that fewer than half the workforce would be in "proper" full-time jobs by the turn of the century has just about come true in Western Europe; in America, the proportion of people who are unemployed, self-employed, or on short-term contracts is currently about 35 percent.

Technology and competition, Handy has argued, are ushering in a new era in which "work is something you do rather than something you go to." Companies will survive, but in a much diminished state. The core of a company (which he has at various times likened to the center of a doughnut and the heart of a shamrock) will be staffed by a small squad of entrepreneurs and bureaucrats, and governed by the "½-by-2-by-3" rule of corporate fitness: half as many people will be paid twice as much for doing three times as much work. Two sorts of people will try to sell their services to this inner ring. The first will be the general, unskilled "somebodies" (as in "somebody can do that"). The second class will be "portfolio people"—knowledge workers who have assembled a portfolio of skills that they can sell to a variety of companies. It will not be unusual for individuals to be portfolio workers when they are in their 20s, to join the core of an organization for the next two or three decades, then to return to being a portfolio worker in their "troisième age." Indeed, one of Handy's recurring themes is that workers will continue working much longer in life (albeit on a part-time basis) partly to earn more money and partly to give themselves something to do.

Handy's diagnosis may be harsh, but his prescriptions are usually fairly soft—some would say too soft. Handy believes that the pursuit of profit is not everything and that companies should change their ownership structure to give stakeholders, such as workers and customers, more power in relation to shareholders. Training, education, and voluntary work remain important Handy themes.

Handy may be better at provoking thought than prescribing solutions (a fault or virtue that he shares with Drucker). But it is worth noting that his philosophy is rooted in at least one reality: his own. Should we be surprised that the prophet of the portfolio worker and the troisième age is himself a man in his mid-60s who "sells" his services to a variety of clients (including the London Business School and several charities); drifts among Putney, the English countryside, and Tuscany; and spends only six months a year working on his own projects? The idea that there is more to life than profit is easier to take from a thinker who limits himself to about a dozen high-paying "cabarets" a year and does the rest of his speaking assignments either for free or for charity. In many ways, the questions that need to be asked about Handy are not just whether his prediction of the future and his suggestions for change are correct, but also whether he is a fair representative of his audience.

## What Is Not Changing

Any manager who thinks that there is something new about technology threatening jobs should read George Eliot's *Middlemarch*. As the railway moved ever closer to the Victorian market town at the center of this novel, panic mounted about what the new technology would mean for its inhabitants. But was the fear justified? The railway changed people's lives dramatically, but not necessarily for the worse. For every stagecoach driver the iron horse put out of work, it created many other jobs, not only on the railway itself but also in businesses and shops that were now connected to the outside world. Even if some of these changes were painful, in the longer run jobs were surely safer in a town such as Middlemarch that was connected to the railway, than in towns that were not.

There are three reasons for believing that this optimistic version of history will repeat itself: one is rooted in basic market economics, and two in (slightly more suspect) statistics. They do not disprove theories predicting "the end of work," but they do suggest that their ideas should be taken with a pinch of salt.

Ever since the Luddites rose up and smashed their looms in the early nineteenth century, market economics has had a long, unbroken record of disproving warnings about new technology.[2] Over the past two centuries, countless jobs have been pushed aside by machines, but more have been created on the way. The pessimists counter by claiming that the computer—or, more accurately, the computer-plus-telephone—will have a far wider effect than machines like the Spinning Jenny that so annoyed the Luddites. By some calculations, three out of four jobs in the industrial world are the sort of repetitive tasks that might be automated. There is something in this: many economists reckon that there may be a short delay while the labor market invents new jobs. It is hard to imagine a displaced railroad engineer (the biggest predicted job decline in America) rapidly picking up work as a home health aide (the biggest increase).[3]

But this is a quibble over timing. So far, at least, there seem to be far more similarities than differences between this wave of technological change and previous ones. If past experience is any guide, protectionist measures only look impracticable. (How on earth do Goldsmith and Buchanan imagine that they will keep out cheap Third World products and technology anyway?) Such measures are also counterproductive: barriers against technology will simply produce economic decline, as in the towns of Victorian England that were not connected to the railway.

The two sets of statistics referred to above should also be of some comfort to worried managers (though neither is conclusive). The first is that, although managers are now more likely to lose their jobs than before, they are also much more likely to find them. In America, "managerial and professional" jobs now make up the biggest slice of the workforce—and they are growing fast. In Britain, a study published in 1995 by the University of Warwick's Institute for Employment Research found that, despite a decade of headlines about downsizing, 1.35 million new managerial jobs were created in Britain in 1981–94; it also predicted that another 630,000 new managerial posts would be created by 2001, bringing the total up to 4.9 million people, or 18.5 percent of the employed labor force. As usual, the losers are the poor and the unskilled.

The standard retort to statistics like these is that it is simply a matter of labeling: in factories, team leaders and work supervisors are now managers; in the high street, a video store attendant can often be a manager too. This point is a fair one, but it does not completely invalidate the statistics. For example, the researchers at Warwick were convinced that even allowing for this trend, the number of managers "is going to grow hand over fist."

The second set of statistics that the worried manager ought to bear in mind suggests that—so far—the job for life is not becoming any rarer. The proportion of Americans who stayed in one job for more than eight years hardly changed at all between 1971 and 1991; if anything, the average length of time middle-aged Americans spend with one employer has actually edged up, from a little over six years in 1966 to just over seven years in 1991. Similar figures have been recorded in most other countries.

Once again, it would be unwise to read too much into these numbers. For one thing, it is doubtful that they include all temporary workers, and the most recent figures date back only as far as the early 1990s, before the full effects of downsizing had been felt. For another, signs of change are evident: there has been an increase in the number of people who have retired (or been pushed out) at the age of 55 or earlier. And the overall figures can hide considerable turbulence within companies as they switch employees around all over the place.

Those predicting the end of work tend to think of the traditional job as an inflexible eight-hour block dedicated to doing one thing. The truth is that jobs—particularly managerial ones—have always involved doing "a bit of this" and "a bit of that." People endlessly cover for each other as a result of holidays and illnesses. Projects are assigned on the basis of whoever comes through the door next. Reading an inflated description of, say, CNN as "a virtual organization" in which people are assigned to projects that may not even be connected with their field of experience, one tends to forget that news organizations have always been chaotic places in which nature writers are sometimes sent off to cover the latest war in Abyssinia. If William Randolph Hearst wandered into CNN, he would be bemused by the gadgets and nonplussed by the absence of alcohol, but he would recognize a world in which the big story dominates everybody's lives, and in which editors throw people at stories regardless of their previous experience.

Nevertheless, the statistics (not to mention economics) imply that the managerial Armageddon is a little further off than some have feared, and that work is changing less radically than many people have claimed. The "job," like other maligned institutions, such as the company and even the city, is not going to disappear in the immediate future. In 20 years' time, you will still be able to walk into any office and discover a group of greying employees gathered around a decaffeinated coffee machine bitching about their superiors, discussing who is sleeping with whom, and complaining about the coffee.

### Listen to Bangalore

The point is that the management theorists have exaggerated their case when they talk about the end of the job. The more honest among them admit as much. That does not mean that the workplace is not changing.

Any Western trade unionist wanting to visit the dusty office of Wipro Infotech, an Indian software firm, in Bangalore would risk a heart attack—and not just because of the climb up four flights of stairs. All three forces of change—technology, communication, and global competition—are there on display. Here are Indian hands and brains doing the work that Western ones used to do—redesigning General Electric's internal software system—and doing so for a fifth of what it would cost in the West. After the Indian engineers have finished, their product will be transmitted to America via the satellite dish on the building's roof. In other corners of India, people are doing back-office work for companies such as Swissair, and some are even studying videoscreens, acting as security guards for premises in America.

Even the countrysides of Western Europe and America are being repopulated by a new kind of worker. An old smithy in Exmoor is now home to a company that uses components from as far afield as Japan to make expensive microscopes with computer-controlled manipulators for customers in 80 countries.[4] It is not difficult to see why people might get dreamy about the possible impact of all these things. As Handy says:

> Our world is about to see a change as significant as the technological event which, in many ways, launched Europe into a new age 600 years ago when the printing press was invented and developed. For the first time then people were able to read the Bible in their own language in their own home in their own time. . . . They could now make up their own minds about right and wrong, God and devil. As a result, the authority of the Church crumbled, and with it the authority of most institutions. Individual freedom led to creativity, which led to the Renaissance. . . . The television set and the telephone, with the computer at the end of it, the wired and unwired world which we now contemplate, are the modern equivalents of the printing press. When Motorola achieves its dream of a personal number for each of us at birth, then a telephone will truly belong to a person not a place. Insignificant as that sounds, it means that the office will become as unnecessary as the churches became.[5]

Once again, it is easy to quibble with Handy over details: five hundred years after Gutenberg, churches remain "necessary" for many people, including Handy. Yet the world of work is clearly changing, if not quite as much as some people claim. The undercurrents upsetting the old order—and troubling managers in particular—raise three general questions: Where do we work? Whom do we work for? And what do we do?

## Ring Me at Home

Handy's argument that work is becoming something we do, rather than the place where we go, is slowly coming true. Close to 43 million Americans do some portion of their work at home—a figure that is 75 percent higher than in 1988. Twelve million of these are full-timers. In many cases, the force for change is demography as much as technology or high office prices: everywhere, women are accounting for a larger share of both the fully employed workforce and the part-time one. According to the researchers at Warwick University, 46 percent of Britain's employed labor force in 2001 will be female. They also predict that by then there will be an extra 1.3 million part-time jobs, and the number of self-employed will rise by 436,000 to 3.7 million, or 14 percent of the total employed labor force. All these sorts of workers tend to do some of their work at home. America's AT&T has guessed that by the end of the decade one of every two Americans will do at least some of their work from home.

In America and many parts of Europe, there is a growing "SoHo" (or single-operator home office) movement. One in three American homes already has a computer; some 40 percent of these have modems allowing their computers to talk to the outside world. Virtually every salesperson has a portable telephone. Within five years, most modems will in all likelihood be cellular, meaning that a salesperson visiting a client will not even have to find a phone-jack to download the latest sales information. Enthusiasts claim that not only is working at home more convenient—especially for women—but it is also more efficient. Numerous studies have shown that people in office jobs spend half their time working by themselves. By some calculations, a worker's productivity rises by 15 to 20 percent if he or she stays at home.

Is this true? The best argument for the efficiency of staying at home is usually the inefficiency of going to work. One study of 90,000 managers by Booz, Allen & Hamilton found that people waste a quarter of their time at work. Add up the hours spent in pointless meetings, commuting, and hanging around the coffee machine and you should find this is an underestimate. Plenty of companies have allowed people to stay at home and found that productivity improved. In one experiment, Compaq gave all its salespeople personal computers connected to its main network (so that they had instant access to all the latest information and prices) and told them to work from home. Not only did Compaq save on office space; it also found it could get by with two-thirds of the original salesforce, largely because each salesman sold six times as many computers. At *The Economist,* it is noticeable that all but the laziest foreign correspondents are more productive than their London counterparts: one reason is that they gain roughly a day a week in terms of meetings that they do not have to attend.

But is working at home really such a charmed, productive life? In many countries, it is either impossible or complicated for home-office workers to claim their full expenses against their income taxes. In Japan, Toshiba, an electronics group, has begun to experiment with letting software researchers stay at home. But most houses in Japan are too small for people to live in comfortably, let alone work there; and telephone costs can make the whole exercise punitively expensive. Moreover, the motives of those replying to surveys look suspect. If you were a mother with three small children, would you not claim that working at home was more productive? Anecdotal evidence suggests that many of the home-office fanatics are loners with formidable powers of concentration. Most "normal" workers, particularly managers, worry that being at home means being out of the loop. In any normal home there are plenty of distractions, ranging from athletic events on the television to sex, that are not usually available in the office (try sitting at home and writing a book, particularly on management).

The supporters of the SoHo movement are also selective with their examples. They make a great fuss about the number of young companies that have sprung from domestic surroundings, such as Apple and Mrs. Fields Cookies. But this is hardly a new trend. Companies as big as Disney and Ford both started as home-based businesses. Similarly, the suggestion that just about any type of worker can now work at home is nonsense. Time after time, the same groups of home workers pop up—management consultants, writers, and so on. Such portfolio workers are rare on the ground. As John Kay, a British guru who also flits between various comfortable careers, observed when reviewing one of Handy's books, "There is Charles Handy, and me, but not many others."[6]

## It's a Temp's World

Temporary workers are not a new phenomenon, particularly in Europe, but they are becoming more common. A report in October 1995 by Britain's Institute of Management found that nearly 9 out of 10 British companies used part-time and temporary workers (a rise of 15 and 8 percent, respectively, over the previous year). In the period 1990–95, the number of temporary workers in Britain increased by 350,000 at the same time that the overall workforce declined by 750,000. And an increasing proportion of these temporary workers were employed in factories.

In America, part-timers, leased employees, and the self-employed now account for one-quarter of the workforce. America's biggest private employer is no longer General Motors but Manpower, a temporary employment agency with 600,000 people on its books. There are now about 6,000 temp agencies in America—double the figure of 10 years ago. In 1995, 38 out of the 500 firms on *Inc* Magazine's list of fast-growing companies reported staffing concerns of one sort or another. Even in Japan, that temple of lifetime employment, heretics such as Yasuyuki Nambu are appearing in unprecedented numbers, despite a highly regulated system. "You can work at the place of your choice at the time you like and the job you like," says Nambu, "without being bound to one company."[7]

From an employer's point of view, Nambu's optimism about the virtues of temporary work may be justified. Enthusiasts in America talk about there being "a contingency spot market."[8] In *Jobshift,* Bridges gives the example of Home Corporation, a Montgomery, Alabama, firm that owns apartment complexes and that decided to lease its entire 500-strong property management staff from a temporary agency called Action Staffing.[9] Temporary workers do not need the same benefits that full-timers do; they are also much easier to lay off. Blue Cross/Blue Shield of Rhode Island cut its workforce by 40 percent over five years without having to sack one "real" worker. A report published in October 1995 by Reed Personnel Services, a British employment agency, indicated that demand for temporary staff was at an all-time high but warned that too many employers were short-changing temps when it came to holidays, training, sick pay, and so on.

This sort of problem explains why the "corporate condominiums" and "virtual corporations" that Handy, Drucker, and Peters find so exciting may be some time in coming. Far from being invigorated by the choice now open to them, most temporary workers feel insecure—and their work shows it. There are ample examples of quality declining when temporary workers are brought in. At one condom factory, the managers could tell when the temporary workers had arrived by the number of faulty products tripping off the other end of the assembly line. Surveys have shown that roughly 60 percent of the people in the contingency labor force would rather have full-time jobs.

However, there are some signs of hope. The higher the skill of the temps (i.e., the closer they get to becoming "portfolio workers" rather than just "somebodies"), the more likely they are to be doing what they do out of choice. At the top level of companies, there has been a long tradition of bringing in company doctors. (One example from the public sector is David Gergen, who was called in to mend President Clinton's press relations.) In America, a growing number of agencies are hiring out bosses and project managers or skilled workers such as lawyers and copy writers. Hiring out high-technology specialists is the fastest-growing part of Manpower's business. Companies such as Microsoft and Silicon Graphics rely heavily on this short-term help—and pay them well. White-collar temps often earn more than permanent staff.

## Small Is Fragile

Ask working people about their employer nowadays, and the answer is likely to be "a small company." Whatever the relative merits of big and small companies, one is more likely to work for a smaller company—and that company is more likely to go bust.

Of the 21 million business enterprises in the United States, only 14,000 have more than 500 employees.[10] By some counts, businesses of this size are growing about two to three percentage points faster than the economy as a whole. Even in economies where small firms are less numerous, they are often the prime source of new jobs. For instance, in semisocialist Sweden, where 70 percent of the country's manufacturing employees toil for big companies like Volvo, the only type of company to add jobs in 1985–92 employed fewer than 20 people.

However, small companies remain fragile creatures. Studies of employment growth in states such as California have pointed to the importance of "gazelle" companies: firms, not necessarily new ones but usually fairly small ones, that suddenly leap forward but can also trip up. Californians are both more likely to be sacked and more likely to be hired than workers in most other states. A similar story emerges if one looks at industries instead of regions. Some 60 percent of high-tech start-ups die before their fifth birthday.

Working in the midst of all this creative destruction may not be to everybody's taste, but it appears to attract the best and the brightest. In *The New Rules: How to Succeed in Today's Post-Corporate World* (1995), John Kotter tracked 115 members of the Harvard Business School's class of 1974. Only 23 percent were employed at companies with 10,000 people. Most worked for companies with less than 1,000—and 40 percent of them claimed to be entrepreneurs. By 1991, those employed at the smaller businesses were paid an average of $450,000—twice as much as their classmates at the bigger firms.

Even employees who work for big companies are not free from this sort of uncertainty. As already noted, the most success-ful big companies have become more entrepreneurial, pushing decision making down the ranks and restructuring themselves around teams. The difference nowadays between working for one part of a large federated engineering group, such as ASEA Brown Boveri (ABB), and working for a small company, such as one in the network of small clothing suppliers around Benetton in northern Italy, is becoming more and more unclear. In the old days, if a subsidiary asked for more independence, it would prob-ably have been told to go to hell; nowadays, it is more likely to be encouraged with lots of warm and fuzzy talk about the need "to create villages within our cities."

This approach has an effect on the way people work. Even in a big company, people can no longer afford to see a career as a ladder leading straight from the humblest office to the board-room. Rather, it has become a series of islands connected by causeways, loosely governed by a small floating flagship. In many ways, hopping from one corner of General Electric to an-other can be just as terrifying as leaving one Silicon Valley start-up and going to another.

## What We Do

Whether a manager's job is at a big firm or a small one, a striking number of characteristics of that job are changing—from the kind of people the manager supervises to what hours they work and whether they have an office, or even a desk. This explains why managerial insecurity runs much deeper than mere fear of losing a job.

As fewer people take on more and more tasks, conventional job descriptions have to be thrown out. Suddenly, managers are being told what to do by people they once considered their juniors, and they have to share information that was once theirs exclusively. Managers have to supervise not only temporary workers but also people who work for other companies. Call up your computer department and someone from Electronic Data Systems or Computer Services Corporation may come to fix your problem; ring down to the mailroom and you may be talking to a Pitney Bowes postman.

Even if you shout at somebody on the assembly line, it might turn out to be a subcontractor's representative. As for your own workers, they may well be outside your control. Ten out of the 120 employees at Walters Hexagon, a small British company that supplies different types of screws and fasteners, are "engineering envoys" who sit in customers' factories and ferry goods from Walters delivery people to the correct customer department.[11]

Managers are even losing those traditional symbols of their status, their offices and desks. The trendiest companies are introducing "hotdesking" and "just-in-time desks." Some companies are doing this to reduce clutter and to make more imaginative use of their space. (Digital Equipment's Finnish office has used the resulting space to build a sauna for the use of its clients.) Others find that it encourages workers to become less preoccupied with status and hierarchy, and that it forces them to get on the road. Gemini refuses to give its consultants their own desks because it wants them to spend most of their time with clients rather than hanging around the office. The fashion for replacing individual offices with open-plan cubicles has also spread to more staid industrial firms. At the Aluminum Company of America, the chief executive, Paul O'Neill, has removed all the permanent walls and doors in the executive suite. The industrial titans at Alcoa now apparently hang out together in a "communications center" or cook food together in the kitchenette.[12]

But the real reason in many cases is cost. By changing its person-to-desk ratio from 2:1 to 12:1, Digital Equipment's

British arm saved £3.5 million a year. By reorganizing its real estate (and forcing 20,000 managers to share offices), IBM saved $14 billion. As Charles Handy points out, people are much less efficient at using office space than machines, which can work for a full 168 hours a week whereas humans rarely get beyond 60. Worse, an increasing number of people are not even in the office during the hours when they could be there. According to Franklin Becker, director of the International Workplace Studies Program at Cornell University, "About 70 percent of the people who work in management consultancy, sales and customer service are usually not at their desks."[13]

However, it is not clear whether all this hotdesking is popular with employees. Ironically enough, Herman Miller, an American furniture design company, gives its employees carts in which to carry around their individual belongings so that they can personalize their workstation while they are there. Similarly, the current vogue for open-plan "networking" offices can deprive people of having a place to think. At one part of Asda, a British supermarket chain, employees who want space to themselves have to wear red caps.

This might seem disorienting enough for any manager. Yet, at hip technology companies such as Intel and Microsoft, managers have to get used to being a member of a temporary task force rather than the leader of a permanent division: there are often no precise physical locations or jobs. And the pace is different. Rather than working a regular 9-to-5 day, the project tends to build to a pizzas-at-midnight, you-can't-see-your-children crescendo, followed by a holiday after it is all over.

In some respects, a career built around creative bursts seems much closer to a career in the preindustrial age. In *Jobshift*, Bridges uses long-distance transport to illustrate the shift from the prejob world to the world of jobs and then to the dejobbed world. In the eighteenth century, when the primary means of transport was the ship, there was little permanent employment (you were hired for each voyage). At sea, although the day was divided into watches, most tasks were accomplished by people working together (e.g., pulling down the sails). Although the boat's owner was usually a landlubbing merchant, almost all the practical decisions had to be left to the captain. Then came the railway, which required far more organization. Schedules and prices were set by the head office.

Workers had specific jobs (conductors did not shovel coal). The airliner then introduced further change. At the start, the world of jobs was much the same. Now, young carriers are stealing a march on their older peers by letting their staff do a variety of jobs (at Southwest Airlines, the pilots or "team leaders" help people with their baggage). That leaves the space shuttle, Bridges's most appropriate example of the dejobbed future, where, although each crew member has his or her own specialty, the most important skills will be team ones.

## Men in the Middle

On balance, Bridges may be straining the analogy with the space shuttle. Most companies are still very much at the airliner stage—and likely to remain so for some time. (After all, Southwest does not let its baggage handlers fly the aircraft.) Although many companies have reorganized to some extent along project-based lines, few have gone as far as Microsoft or Intel. Besides, there is something of a backlash in favor of a more structured approach to work. Nothing typifies this correction more than the attitude toward middle managers.

Until recently, most companies reacted to middle managers the way that Stalin responded to the Kulaks. Middle managers were the bureaucratic class of time servers who sat awkwardly between the shop floor and the factory, who impeded the swift flow of information, and who account for a fifth of all the jobs lost in America since 1988. As Tom Peters put it: "Their goose is cooked."

Yet fashions change. By the mid-1990s, theorists had begun to talk of middle managers' bringing a "midlevel" perspective to a company's work. They are the sergeants—the only people who know enough about the shop floor and the customer to be able to tell strategic thinkers in the upper ranks how their ideas can be put into practice. Steven Floyd of the University of Connecticut and Bill Wooldridge of the University of Massachusetts, who studied management at 20 American firms, claim that companies that gave middle managers a say in forming strategy performed better than those that did not.[14] Far from being barriers to innovation in big companies, middle managers are often champions of it: they are the only people who know how to get things done in big organizations. Frances Westley of

McGill University points out that middle managers are also skilled networkers, forever making informal alliances with colleagues from other companies.[15] And middle management is a vital part of the career ladder: it gives workers at the bottom something to aim for, and it provides a few years of training in which high-fliers can get their balance.

The question is not whether to have middle managers, but how to use them without letting them indulge their weaknesses for hierarchy building and paperwork. Some firms, such as Digital and 3M, have tried to turn middle managers into entrepreneurs whose job is to invent good ideas and persuade senior managers to back them. In Japan, a country that has long looked on middle managers more kindly than the West, Honda developed its Civic model by giving middle managers a general goal (make it youth-friendly and fuel-efficient) and letting them do the rest.

The result of all this talk is that even big companies that pride themselves on being lean have been forced to reinvent middle managers—albeit under titles such as "facilitators," "boundary spanners," "process managers," and "employee coaches." As with most other things connected with the modern workplace, big companies are changing—but not by as much as the pessimists predict.

### Enslaved or Empowered?

Anybody who accepts the notion that work is changing (at least, a little) is immediately plunged into two fierce debates. The first revolves around the question of whether the new work culture liberates or enslaves the working man or woman. Does it tip the balance in favor of the employer or the employee? Are people going to live more fulfilled lives or are they destined to be racked by anxiety? The second debate, which tends to be greatly colored by the diagnosis of the first, turns to prescription. What should be done to make jobs more liberating experiences? What should a manager demand from his or her employer?

Tom Peters gives the impression that the personal computer will perform much the same role for managers that William Wilberforce did for slaves. Managers, he suggests, are on the verge of a new, empowered age. "Forget loyalty. Or at least loyalty to one's corporation. Try loyalty to your Rolodex—your network—instead."[16] To work nowadays, argues Peters, is to résumé (yes, he does turn yet another noun into a verb): everybody should become an independent contractor or think of themselves as one. "Powerlessness is a state of mind," declares Peters.

By contrast, many other gurus reckon that "powerless" is exactly what most managers are. The most downbeat are the "end-of-work" crowd. But a gloomy prognosis of the future of work (and a corresponding need to regulate the market, which will cause this distress) has become a staple of left-wing politics everywhere. Both America's labor secretary, Robert Reich, and Tony Blair, the leader of Britain's Labour Party, have talked about the rise of "the anxious class," most of whom hold jobs but are justifiably uneasy about their lack of security and fearful of their children's future.

A third group of people, including Charles Handy, seem to hop from one side of the fence to the other, sometimes celebrating those who have the necessary skills and knowledge to flourish in the new economy, sometimes sympathizing with those who will be left behind. Rosabeth Moss Kanter, for instance, divides people into "New Cosmopolitans" rich in the 3 Cs ("concepts, competence, and connections") and "locals"—her equivalent of Handy's "portfolio workers" and "somebodies."

Everyone seems to agree that there is a growing division. The mistake the pessimists make is to assume that most people in the Western world fit into the losing camp. There is a big, and growing, group of workers who should gain from the technology that is making it easier for people to set up on their own. You do not have to be one of John Kotter's Harvard MBAs to seize the opportunities presented by the modern economy. Wander around a Denver suburb or even a Cotswold village and you will find any number of moderately qualified people working for themselves—and usually being paid more for it. Similarly, the move toward small businesses seems to help workers. Many small companies everywhere are expanding so quickly that they find it difficult to find "good people." A quarter of the small American businesses surveyed by *Business Week* in October 1995 rated "a lack of qualified workers" as one of their three biggest problems (a proportion that has risen annually).

As for those who remain inside big companies, flatter management structures mean that bright people can now bound to the
top more easily.

That said, there is also a class of people who are doomed to
lose out from the changes in the workplace. This group certainly
includes some managers who are down on their luck: for example, the middle-age manager, delayered out of a job, who is now
more expensive to rehire than a fresh young college graduate. In
the aggregate, however, there does not appear to be a shortage of
managerial jobs. For instance, most people read *Executive Blues:
Down and Out in Corporate America* (1995), an autobiography of
a manager named G. J. Meyer coming to terms with unemployment, as a primary example of a new sort of "work-horror"
genre: "In Edvard Munch's *The Scream,* a solitary empty-eyed
figure stands in a roadway clutching its head, mouth open wide,"
proclaims the self-pitying author. "I hope that's not what I look
like as I walk the streets of Manhattan." At the end of *Executive
Blues,* however, the author has to admit that he has found "a job
that I like very much with a company that I like very much on
the outskirts of Cleveland."

The real losers are the unskilled poor, who are now more
likely to spend their lives drifting between short-term jobs, or
perhaps dropping out of formal work entirely. In 1995, 46 percent of Europe's unemployed had been out of work for longer
than a year. As Jeremy Rifkin has pointed out, when an early
wave of automation began taking its toll in America's manufacturing sector in the 1950s, the hardest hit were unskilled workers—particularly Blacks. By 1964, Black unemployment had
reached 12 percent, against a previous postwar high of 8.5 percent. By contrast, White unemployment crawled up from 4.6
percent to 5.9 percent.[17] The same appears to be happening
again. Virtually everywhere, "the inequality gap" between the
rich and poor has widened.

### The Paranoid Manager

The preceding remarks suggest that managers should be
worried about the poor and not themselves. However, the winners and losers in this new world of work should be judged in
psychological as well as material terms. Here managers fare
less well. For all the talk of empowerment, most are scared and

anxious creatures. Any number of factors could account for this insecurity: the recent waves of downsizing; the fact that managers are conservative people who tend to dislike change, even if it is beneficial, and who like hierarchies, even if they are restrictive; the practical difficulties of being a portfolio worker (try arranging a mortgage if you are only on a short-term contract); even perhaps the relentless propaganda about the end of the job-for-life.

The main contribution to this psychological unease is probably overwork. One of the developing world's biggest problems (and one for which management theory should take part of the blame) is that modern economies seem to combine rising unemployment with longer working hours for those in jobs. On balance, Handy's rule (about half the number of people being paid twice as much to do three times as much work) looks like an exaggeration; but, even if they are working only one-and-a-half times as hard as they used to, most workers feel shattered.

In *The Overworked American* (1992), Juliet Schor, an economist at Harvard, calculated that her countrymen spent the equivalent of four weeks more a year on the job in 1989 than in 1969. The average American now works 52 hours a week—46 hours in the office and a further 6 at home. Commuting times have grown longer and holidays shorter. Work-related ailments, such as repetitive strain injury, are on the rise. According to one study by MIT, depression costs the American economy $47 billion a year. In Japan, where people work some 400 hours a year longer than most Europeans, they even have a word for death from overwork: *kaoroshi.*

Managers are nearly always the hardest working of the lot. Once again, management fashion is partly responsible. Delayering reduces the number of managers available to do jobs. Reengineering forces managers to take charge of an entire process: suddenly you are no longer just another R&D manager; instead you are in charge of a whole "new product development" process, responsible for people from sales and production as well as your familiar team of white-coated scientists. If a company reduces the number of job specifications from 1,300 to 32—as did one electronics firm visited by Rosabeth Moss Kanter—there is bound to be an increase in a manager's workload. Each manager at the company now looks after 24 workers rather than just 12.

To add to these psychological strains, the fashion for long hours has gone hand in hand with the fashion for flexibility. Workers often devote themselves to their companies almost to the exclusion of their social lives. Poring over reports takes the place of hobbies; networking on the telephone takes over from normal socializing. People disrupt their family lives in order to take foreign postings. They also make many of their strongest friendships at work. But then suddenly the firm is reengineered, and they become surplus to requirements. The thing that has filled their days and given their life purpose is taken away from them. The overworked company man suddenly becomes just another anomic citizen.

One day, this may change. Companies may employ more people and make them work less. Workers will agree to work at strange shifts in exchange for working fewer hours and getting paid the same. A few companies, including Hewlett-Packard, have experimented along these lines. But most companies would rather work their existing workforce to the bone and reward them accordingly. A study of British Telecom managers by Britain's Society of Telecom Executives showed, perhaps unsurprisingly, that those who worked 50 to 60 hours a week were much more likely to get one of the top two grades in their annual reviews than those who did not. The whole system of incentive pay is geared toward persuading staff in general—and managers in particular—to work ever harder.

In other words, the new work order is producing not "the unemployed manager," but the paranoid manager. The probabilities remain firmly in his favor (it is still predominantly "his" rather than "her"): he will keep his job; even if he loses it, he will be reemployed fairly quickly; he has more opportunities than ever before to decide where he wants to work; he will probably be given more power earlier; and he should be worried about his unskilled colleagues rather than himself. It is not the probabilities that have unhinged him, but the possibilities: the possibility that he could be one of the minority of managers who get sacked and are not employed again; the possibility that technology will replace his job rather than just make it easier. As he commutes back to his home in Pasadena, the paranoid manager does not find the idea that his new neighbor is a consultant who works from home and earns more money than he does encouraging, but frightening. And his own company plays on this insecurity by telling him that he will only be paid more if he works harder. What can be done to make him feel more secure?

## The New Moral Contract

The social contract between the individual and society has been a mainstay of philosophical debate for centuries. Management theory's equivalent is the dispute over the responsibilities a company owes to its workers. Some people talk about "a new moral contract" between employer and employee. But what does a company owe its workers? Management theory has proposed a number of answers, ranging from "nothing except a good pay packet" to "employability" or "a stake in the company."

For many bosses, employee–employer relations can be brought down to a single word: pay. Not only is this what most workers want to talk about, but there is often a clear trade-off between job security and the size of a pay packet. Nobody pities a bond trader who accumulates several million dollars in a few years before being sacked. Many people go into the bond trading business with exactly that aim. Nowadays, even the most humdrum jobs can be "incentivized." Roughly 6 out of 10 American companies have a system for rewarding their employees for performance.

Pay is an attractive solution, particularly to economists fascinated by risk–return models. But it is not a complete solution. One of the most irritating things about middle-class angst is that it often springs from exactly the same sort of people who decided to go into, say, marketing rather than teaching because they thought that the latter was too secure and badly paid. Moreover, incentive pay remains a blunt tool, particularly lower down in any organization. In many cases, incentive pay tends to increase paranoia rather than soothe it. If a group of people do extremely well and are rewarded with 96 percent of their possible bonus, the likely response of the recipients will be that somebody has stolen 4 percent of what they deserved.

So something more is needed. Does the promise of "a job for life" fit the bill? A fair number of companies still reap the rewards from offering workers secure employment. For instance, before a jobs-for-life pledge was introduced at a Range Rover factory in the early 1990s, barely 11 percent of the employees bothered to enter an annual "suggestions" competition because they were worried that improved efficiency might cost them their jobs; afterward, the proportion rose to 84 percent. One proposal alone saved the company £100 million—enough to employ one or two surplus workers. Japanese and German companies have long looked at this trade-off and reached a similar conclusion, which led them to keep jobs at home long after strict economic logic would have dispatched them abroad.

As both the Japanese and the Germans have discovered, the problem is that such promises are often not sustainable. In 1995, Sony reached a landmark decision when it reluctantly stopped making televisions for export in Japan. Over the past five years, Mercedes-Benz and BMW have relentlessly increased production outside Germany, always assuring their expensive German staff that the new cars are for export only. One day, perhaps, Range Rover, too, will regret its promise. Its current models may be successful, but it is impossible to guarantee that the same will be true in 2010. A jobs-for-life pledge in retail banking or computer production is not worth the paper it is printed on.

### Employed or Employable?

At first glance, the concept of "lifetime employability" looks like a poor substitute. For instance, when IBM's director of employee relations announced in the mid-1990s that "unconditional lifetime employment is no longer the name of the game; instead it's lifelong employability," he was only facing facts. After all, Big Blue had laid off 175,000 people since 1986. But it is surely better to tell workers the truth than to offer them a job for life and leave them unprepared for any other employment.

During his tenure at Apple Computer, John Sculley offered staff a "new loyalty" pledge: "Apple can't promise you a job for life. Not even for five or ten years. Maybe not even for a couple of years. But what Apple can—and does—promise is that, whether you're aboard for three months, six months, six years, or, unlikely as it may be, sixteen years, you will be constantly learning, constantly challenged. At the end you will be demonstrably better positioned in the local or global labor market than you would have been had you not spent time with us."

"Training" is a word often invoked by companies that talk about "employability." Raychem, an industrial products company based in Silicon Valley, has made it clear that none of its employees has a guaranteed job for life, but it has guaranteed the opportunity to learn. The firm even has an in-house careers center to help employees get new jobs either in other parts of the company or outside the firm.[18] Ford offers its staff up to $3,100 a year to spend on approved courses. Andersen Consulting spends 6 percent of its gross revenues on training, and the average employee spends 135 hours each year in a classroom. ISS, a Danish cleaning contractor, sends all its employees on a short training course before giving them their mops and brushes.

One would imagine that being "for" training is like being "against" wife-beating. There are many good reasons for a company that does not care about the emotional state of its staff, let alone their long-term employability, to invest in their education. However, American companies spend the equivalent of only about 1.4 percent of their payroll on educating their workers.

Such statistics are always seized on by the training industry to goad employers and governments into providing more courses. However, knowledge, on its own, is not quite the guarantee of employability that some people suppose. The problem is that a good deal of knowledge is specific to the company you work for: the fact that at McDonald's you know the finance director really well does not help you much if you move to Burger King. Knowledge is also job-specific, not company-specific. If you are employed by General Electric's television arm, NBC, it is doubtful that your Rolodex will be much help if you are moved to its turbine-making division. Even when the jobs are more similar, it often takes people time to settle in. Many a Unilever brand manager who has been good at selling ice cream has flopped when it came to fish sticks.

By the same token, it is not always in the company's interest to move people around just to improve their employability: it can destroy the workers' main value to that particular employer (their knowledge) and their sense of being a team member. Employability is as much the employee's responsibility as the employer's.

## Unions and Stakeholders

Naturally, knowledge workers are in a stronger position to expand their Rolodex and renew their education if they have some power over their employer. In theory at least, companies are "empowering" workers just about everywhere. MIT reckons that 80 percent of employers in America participate in some kind of responsibility or empowerment program. Not surprisingly, workers are not entirely convinced. They want structures as well as words. The traditional response to powerlessness has been to band together in unions. However, from Japan to Scotland, unions are in retreat. Only about 1 in 10 of America's private sector workers belong to a union. Even in Scandinavia, where union membership has held up reasonably well, young people are only half as likely to join unions as their parents. Worse, there are doubts about whether unions for knowledge workers even make sense.[19] The battle lines are certainly far from fixed, with the opposing sides divided by class and money. Unions tend to be male, manufacturing-oriented groups that are good at negotiating with dinosaurs such as General Motors, not small multimedia companies. Most of the knowledge worker's problems have to do with contracts, empowerment, employability, parental leave, and part-time work.

Put bluntly, unions have changed far less than companies have. Ironically, the solution to the unions' problems may be sitting in their own history books. Most unions grew out of ancient guilds of craftsmen. If they could turn back the clock, they would do much better. From this point of view, the Writer's Guild of America, the union for Hollywood's 8,000 scriptwriters, is interesting. Many studio chiefs still regard the guild as a hotbed of communism. It has also had its share of pointless strikes. However, its basic structure is oriented toward providing services for a set of individuals rather than one uniform mob. As well as negotiating fixed minimum rates with the studios for different sorts of scripts, the guild offers its knowledge workers pension and health plans and legal advice. Its lawyers have already drawn up standard contracts for multimedia programmers.

There are similar signs of more enlightened unions springing up in other places such as Italy and even Britain. But an increasing number of theorists believe that there will be no new moral contract between employers and employees without some kind of structural change. In most cases, this means a change in the corporate governance of the firm—giving stakeholders such as employees more power at the expense of shareholders.

Whether that is justified on any grounds has been discussed in Chapter 8. It is worth noting that, so far, the changes in the way that people work do not by themselves seem to warrant changing shareholder capitalism. For a start, one has to compare the dearth of futuristic knowledge industries in "kind" stakeholder Germany with the flowering of them in "cruel" shareholder America.

The fuss about the iniquities of shareholder capitalism is the last (and perhaps most dangerous) of all the panics arising about the future of work. Like the job and the middle manager, and all the other supposedly doomed characters in the plot, the company will live on—perhaps in a slightly different shape–but it will still manifestly be the same thing. Reading much of the literature about the future of the workplace, one is reminded of those books in the 1960s that used to forecast the end of the century. Each day would begin with people clambering into an all-in-one, omnipurpose suit and taking a single breakfast pill. The fact is that shirts, skirts, and ties are still around (albeit in styles and fabrics different from those of the 1960s); and so is breakfast, although we now eat muesli with low-fat milk rather than cornflakes with cream. The most horrifying thing about "the future of work" may be just how familiar it will be.

# PART FOUR

# THE WORLD IN THEIR HANDS

# CHAPTER 10

## WHAT DOES GLOBALIZATION MEAN?

EUROPE HAS PRODUCED unusually few management super-
stars. But one man who unquestionably fits the bill is Percy
Barnevik, the founder of ASEA Brown Boveri (ABB) who in
1997 moved to Investor, the Wallenberg family company. A
tall, bearded, and fast-talking Swede, with the restless manner
of a man overendowed with energy, Barnevik has won almost
every honor his profession can bestow, from "emerging markets' CEO of the year" to (twice) boss of "Europe's most respected company." His name is dropped by the management
panjandrums at places like the *Harvard Business Review* almost
as frequently as that of Jack Welch of General Electric. And the
gap is closing fast. "Our greatest rival is no longer GE," confesses one Japanese competitor. "The one we have to be most
on guard against is ABB."

For once, the hyperbole is largely warranted. There are
several reasons to praise Barnevik. To begin with, he has
shown how a company can be big and small at the same time:
ABB, which he created and still remains chairman of, consists
of 1,300 separate companies divided into 5,000 profit centers.
He has also pioneered such popular practices as internal
benchmarking, centers of excellence, and corporate parenting.

Perhaps his foremost quality has been his understanding of globalization.

Conventional wisdom has it that world markets will gradually become more and more homogeneous. In Barnevik's view, the picture will not be quite that simple. Although purely national companies will have little chance of thriving as governments deregulate and as the cost, of travel and information plummet, markets will continue to differ. Thus, it will be important for companies to keep deep roots in local markets. At ABB, Barnevik pushed for what he called a "multicultural multinational" structure—a cosmopolitan conglomerate diverse enough to respond to local tastes but united enough to amount to more than the sum of its parts.

In 1988, Barnevik fashioned ABB from two century-old companies: ASEA, the Swedish engineering group that he had run since 1980, and Brown Boveri, an equally proud Swiss competitor. Since then, the company has been involved in more than 100 acquisitions and joint ventures, expanding into Eastern Europe and Asia, and adding (after many layoffs) 18,000 workers in 40 countries.

Barnevik put a lot of thought into how to bind this disparate empire together. He forced all employees to read his "bible," a short booklet on the company's aims and values. He made English his firm's official language, although only a third of the employees speak it as their mother tongue (Barnevik himself has a noticeable Swedish accent). He moved ABB's headquarters to Zurich so that the merger would not look like a Swedish takeover. But he kept the headquarters staff small (currently, 171 people from 19 countries) in order to avoid the impression that ABB was now a Swiss company. In making cuts, he spread the burden fairly evenly, although it is said that he treated his native Sweden rather too harshly; he once needed a bodyguard there to protect him from angry former employees.

ABB has fostered multiculturalism through an elite cadre of 500 global managers, a praetorian guard that Barnevik selected carefully, paying particular attention to the cultural sensitivity of its members, and to their spouses' willingness to move from place to place quickly. Worth more than their weight in gold, according to Barnevik, these managers knitted the organization together. Another coordinating device was Abacus, an information system that is open to all the company's employees. Abacus collects data on each of the company's 5,000 profit centers and compares their performance with budgets and forecasts in both the local currency and American dollars. The company has also used the system to spread best practice, sending out a chart of the relative performance of various divisions in ABB and encouraging the worst performers to learn lessons from the best.

In the end, however, ABB's corporate glue came down to Barnevik's own relentlessness. ABBers around, the world speak reverently about his ability to get by on four hours sleep a night and his familiarity with every nook and cranny of the organization. In January 1997, in an apparent attempt to see his wife slightly more often, Barnevik yielded the chief executiveship of ABB to another energetic Swede, Goran Lindahl. Whoever runs ABB, its history so far seems to illustrate one of the paradoxes of modern management: that the more a company tries to devolve power, the more it relies on a strong leader.

Barnevik said that the thinking behind ABB was little more than common sense. Who in their right mind, he asked, would not want to be both global and local? And who on earth would think that you can triumph globally by trampling on local differences? The only tricky part of his task, he added, was managing such a complicated organization. But Barnevik undersold himself. The multicultural multinational was in fact the most sophisticated solution to emerge from one of management theory's most enduring debates: the one surrounding globalization.

## An Idea Whose Time Has Come

Of all the words in the management gurus' lexicon, none is used with quite so much relish as "globalization." Go into the business section of any bookstore, and you will see the word emblazoned on almost every other book; talk to the chairman of any big company, and, before long, you will find that it starts dominating the conversation. Globalization—and how to deal with it—is now the leading concern (some would say the raison d'être) of nearly every big multinational company. It affects where they have their offices and factories, what they make, and who they employ. It is also a growing concern for thousands of smaller firms. Even in a domestic market as big as America's,

20 percent of the firms with fewer than 500 people exported some good or service in 1994—and the proportion is growing quickly.[1]

Huge strides toward integrating the world economy have been made in the past decade. Governments have progressively lowered trade barriers both internationally, through the Uruguay Round of the General Agreement on Tariffs and Trade (GATT), and within regions, through the European Union, the North American Free-Trade Agreement (NAFTA), and Latin America's Mercosur. Governments everywhere now regard global companies not as predators to be avoided but as sources of investment, advice, and, above all, jobs. Even the Chinese government, which once promised to wipe the capitalist running dogs from the surface of the earth, now invites them to set up factories. Worldwide, over the past decade, foreign direct investment has been growing four times as fast as world output and three times faster than world trade. In 1995, multinationals invested $325 billion overseas. The fact that roughly a third of trade flows are payments within individual companies shows that most companies have production systems stretching around the world. According to the United Nations, there are close to 40,000 "transnational" companies, three times the figure 25 years ago. Together they control about a third of all private-sector assets, and their combined GDP in 1993 was $5.5 trillion—almost as much as that of the United States.

More telling perhaps than the statistics is the change in attitudes. In the old days, globalization was about a big company lazily rolling out a product across the world. Now, a relatively small company such as Microsoft can launch a relatively sophisticated product such as Windows 95 simultaneously from Shanghai to San Diego. For many managers, the business lounge of the local international airport is more familiar than their own living room. Meanwhile, even those people who manage to avoid this sort of life spend a good part of their day talking to suppliers, customers, and colleagues in foreign places. You can send a message on the Internet to Cairo as easily as to Chicago. With "the death of distance," as mentioned earlier, it will soon cost virtually nothing to talk to somebody on the other side of the world by telephone.

The notion that the world is getting smaller seems straightforward enough. Yet, in management theory, it is not so cut-

and-dried. The first problem is definition. Despite its ubiquity in management books, "globalization" has no standard meaning. One moment, it can refer to a worldwide marketing campaign; the next, to some kind of organizational matrix, or to the irrelevance of national frontiers. Globalization is not a coherent concept, but a fuzzy feeling. This might matter less were it not for people's exaggerated expectations in globalization's regard. The three ideas that people have most often plucked out of this cloud—that globalization would usher in an era of standardized "global" products; that big, global companies would triumph; and that geography would not matter— have turned out to be myths.

## The Three Myths of Globalization

Perhaps the clearest attempt at a definition of the globalization phenomenon appears in "The Globalization of Markets," an article by Theodore Levitt that appeared in the May–June 1983 issue of the *Harvard Business Review*. Levitt, Harvard's most respected marketing guru, put forward an extreme, though admirably coherent, suggestion: technology, he said, was producing "a new commercial reality—the emergence of global markets on a previously unimagined scale of magnitude." The world would be dominated by standardized products and universally appealing brands such as Coca-Cola. Christians and Muslims, went Levitt's reasoning, may worship different gods, but they still have to wash their hair—and they want the best product to do the job. Global companies that ignored "superficial" regional and national differences and exploited economies of scale by selling the same things in the same way everywhere would soon push aside not only small local companies but also the old multinational company that spent all its time trying to be "respectful" of local quirks and peccadilloes. "The earth is round," argued Levitt, "but, for most purposes, it's sensible to treat it as flat."

This future—where gigantic firms run by global managers bestrode Levitt's flattened world like so many colossi and entertained global fantasies such as putting a soft drink within arm's reach of every man, woman, and child on the planet—was exactly the sort of thing that many managers had dreamed about for years. After all, what was the point of being a big company if not to defy geography? One of the classic books on multinationals was called *Sovereignty at Bay* (by Philip Vernon, published in 1971). Aurelio Peccei, a director of Fiat, once claimed that the multinational corporation "is the most powerful agent for the internationalization of society." Carl Gerstacker, sometime chairman of Dow Chemical, confessed that "I have long dreamed of buying an island owned by no nation and of establishing the world headquarters of the Dow company on the truly neutral ground of such an island, beholden to no nation or society."

This has not happened. The idea that most of the same products can be sold everywhere in the same way has been thoroughly discredited. True, there is a global market for a few big-ticket items—jumbo jets, for instance, although anybody who visits Boeing's factory in Seattle will be given a long lecture about the fact that every aircraft is made differently in order to satisfy the firm's customers. Also true, there are a few niche products that appeal to broadly the same people in the same way around the world: one invariably cited by harassed globalists in interviews is the magazine, *The Economist*. In the broad consumer market, however, survey after survey has shown that there are only a few truly global brands, such as Coca-Cola, McDonald's, and Marlboro, and even the items in this select handful certainly do not mean the same thing in, say, Beijing (where they are all status symbols) as they do in Baltimore.

A close look at Coca-Cola's strategy shows that, for all the ubiquitous "Always Coca-Cola" advertisements, the Atlanta company exploits rather than ignores national differences. It uses independent local bottlers to get its products to local markets. It also tweaks the product's recipe from country to country—and sometimes within a country. In Japan, the southern Japanese like their Coca-Cola slightly sweeter than people in Tokyo, and the company obliges. And when it comes to selling other drinks, Coke adopts a very local strategy. Two-thirds of Coca-Cola's Japanese products are made specifically for the local market: Georgia Coffee, for example, can be seen everywhere in Tokyo but is unknown in Coca-Cola's Georgia home.

Virtually every global brand has had to make concessions to local taste in order to achieve its ubiquity. In Japan, McDonald's stumbled until it allowed a local entrepreneur to set up small snack-bars in the center of Tokyo, rather than the large suburban eateries favored by the parent company; he also ensured that burgers were made with local meat, which is much fattier than that used in America, and even changed Ronald to Donald McDonald because the Japanese have difficulty pronouncing "r." Also in Japan, McDonald's hamburgers come with optional Teriyaki sauce (just as they come with chili peppers in Mexico). Coke's old rival, PepsiCo, also adjusts both its recipe and its message from country to country. For instance, in Shanghai it has had to dispense with Cindy Crawford's charms (because the locals do not know who she is), and it has had to rename "7-Up" because, in the local dialect, the phrase means "death through drinking." Often, products can jump one border but not two: Mickey Mouse and company hurdled successfully into Tokyo's Disneyland but stumbled initially in Paris.

If anything, marketing in recent years has become obsessed with segmenting customers rather than bundling them together. Back in 1983, Levitt wrote as if he assumed that America was one market. Since then, marketing to "hyphenated Americans" (such as Asian-Americans) has been a booming business. It makes sense—when selling, say, a Jeep—to approach a farmer in Kansas, who might actually use it, in a different way from an attorney in Los Angeles, who will only pose in it. And information technology is driving marketing into ever more particular areas, using data culled from checkout scanners and credit-card receipts to pick out smaller groups of people, who are then "targeted" with direct mail and tailored products.

The firm that took Levitt's advice most seriously perhaps was Britain's Saatchi & Saatchi. Impressed by the article in the *Harvard Business Review,* the Saatchi brothers invited Levitt to sit on their board; proclaimed, "To be big is good; to be good is better; to be both is best"; and threw themselves headlong into an expansion. This suited a few of Saatchi's clients, notably British Airways, which ended up with a "global" slogan: "The World's Favorite Airline." But many customers wanted to have a wider spread of local agencies and complained that Saatchi was just offering them dots on the map. Shareholders fared even worse, as the agency greatly overreached itself. Its share price fell to a fiftieth of its previous level, and the Saatchi brothers were eventually pushed out in early 1995.

In the years since Levitt wrote his article, it has often been small companies rather than big ones that have gained most from globalization. Far from allowing a handful of giant firms to carve up the world among them, globalization has clearly subjected these firms to humbling competition. With the lowering of trade barriers, the spread of deregulation, and the plummeting of transport and communication costs, a firm no longer needs to be a huge multinational organization in order to trade in the global marketplace. In many countries, the traditional multinational's prime resources—its carefully cultivated relationships with the government and expensively accumulated knowledge of local regulatory quirks—have dwindled in value. Microsoft and Swatch manage to sell software and watches around the world despite keeping most of their employees in Seattle and Switzerland, respectively.

Other developments, too, have allowed smaller companies to muscle in on the big multinationals' territory. The deregulation of the capital markets has made it possible for more small companies to borrow serious money. Thanks to the spread of manufacturing techniques such as just-in-time production and lean manufacturing, multinationals no longer have a monopoly on managerial wisdom. In fact, an epidemic of pirating, reverse engineering, and other forms of industrial theft has crushed the monopoly even on their own ideas. And the falling price of information technology allows smaller companies to engage in the sort of information-dependent innovation that was once the preserve of the giants. Indeed, many of the giants have found themselves at a distinct disadvantage because their computer systems, expensively installed at the dawn of the computer age, have become hopeless anachronisms.

Gurus such as Peter Drucker make much of the fact that the exporters who led America, Britain, and Germany out of their recent recessions were all small companies—often specialists. One of these, a neighbor of Drucker's in California, makes special medical beepers for hospitals.[2] Drucker has long since given up being amazed by the places where the man sells his equipment. The job is fairly risk-free, says the neighbor. Ever since a nasty experience with a sterling devaluation in the 1960s, the man has billed his clients in dollars, thereby eliminating the exchange risk. "What about the language and culture?" Drucker once asked his friend after he had returned from installing a new system in Osaka. "I don't need to understand Japan," the man replied. "I understand hospitals."

Closer inspection reveals that multinationals are often much less multinational than they seem. Many of them migrate only as far as their local regions. American firms invest in Central and South America, the Japanese in a handful of Asian countries, and European firms in other European countries. An obvious reason for this pattern is that it is easier to deal with people who are just a short flight away. Language and cultural ties are another important factor. The Japanese, for example, are much happier dealing with the informal alliances and extended company networks of Southeast Asia than are Europeans. If anything, modern management techniques are reinforcing this trend toward regionalization: with the emphasis on minimizing stock on hand and delivering supplies on a need-to-use basis, suppliers now want to be located as close as possible to their clients.

### How Much Does Geography Matter?

The chief protagonists in the wider debate about the importance of geography have been Kenichi Ohmae, a Japanese consultant, and Michael Porter, a professor at Harvard Business School. Both take a more subtle position than Levitt did, although Ohmae is in some agreement with Levitt's vision of a more homogenized world. Interestingly, Ohmae flaunts his global status. His reputation in America is largely based on his ability to explain Japan in terms that people from Detroit to Dallas can understand (the *Financial Times* once unkindly compared him to Benihana of Tokyo, a restaurant chain that sells Westernized Japanese food). Meanwhile, in Tokyo, where he used to work for McKinsey, Ohmae is seen as the apostle of all things Western—such as cleaner politics and free trade.

Ohmae's books do contain examples showing how "global" firms have become insiders. In the case of Barbie dolls, sales in Japan remained poor until the local distributor reduced the size of Barbie's breasts and replaced her blonde hair with brown. Nevertheless, as the titles of books such as *The Borderless World* (1990) suggest, Ohmae believes that firms with what he calls "an Anchorage perspective" (named after the Alaskan city, which is exactly seven hours away from Tokyo, New York, and Dusseldorf) will win. He has long argued that a firm needs to be in each of the increasingly similar triad economies—America, Japan, and Europe. Ohmae's most recent book, *The End of the Nation State* (1995), introduces yet another variant on the globalization theme. Today's engines of growth, he argues, are not "dysfunctional" nation-states but "natural economic zones" that cross national boundaries such as Hong Kong–South China or Tijuana–San Diego.

Put these transborder entities identified by Ohmae together with the emerging superstates such as the European Union and the cyberstate created by the Internet, and you begin to have a case for the decline of the nation-state that sounds plausible. But it is not. Globalization is certainly forcing national governments to be less insular and more interdependent. It is also (thank God) teaching people more about each other. But there are still clear divisions. The defeat of communism has not left any shortage of things for nations to quarrel about—whether the issue is Islam, Asian values, or fishing policies. And throughout most of the world, there are recognizable nations that want to keep their traditional shapes. True, countries have handed over some economic power to trade organizations, but, the European Union aside, they have shown very few signs of wanting to yield political sovereignty. And although Western Europe may be coming together, Eastern Europe has broken up.

As Michael Porter has pointed out, this matters to companies as well as politicians, for firms owe to their local origins a remarkable amount of what makes them tick. In *The Competitive Advantage of Nations* (1989), Porter argued that different countries (and regions) have different competitive strengths: the Germans excel at high-quality engineering and chemicals, the Japanese at miniaturization and electronics, the British at pop music and publishing, the Americans at films and computers. A German engineering firm will not necessarily become any better at engineering if it becomes less Germanic and more global—nor will a Californian software company if it becomes less Californian. Each firm needs to retain its local roots if it is to find good recruits and suppliers or, what is more important, if it is to remain in daily contact with challenging competitors.

Alfred Marshall, one of the founders of modern economics, once remarked, in an analysis of steelmaking in Sheffield, that certain skills seem to be "in the air" in some regions. Some of these centers of excellence are familiar: Silicon Valley in computing, the Prato region of northern Italy in fashion and design,

Hollywood in film making. In an increasingly mobile world, such places represent stubbornly immobile resources: their skills are too bound up with the local culture to be easily copied elsewhere. Nobody has yet tried to build a cheaper Hollywood.

Far from contemptuously ignoring these geographic irritations, multinationals now bow down before them. Witness the number of Japanese electronics firms that have an outpost in Silicon Valley; witness, too, the way that firms that already have roots in centers of excellence are digging deeper, supporting schools, funding charities, and so on. John Stopford of the London Business School argues that firms should hand across what he calls their "world product mandates" to affiliates located in the right areas. Thus, America's Du Pont has moved its electronics-related businesses to Japan, Germany's Siemens has moved its air-traffic-management business to Britain, and South Korea's Hyundai has moved its personal-computer business to the United States. A few small companies have gone the whole hog and uprooted themselves entirely. TomTec Imaging Systems, a German company with a turnover of $21 million, is the world leader in one small, highly technological part of the medical ultrasound market. In 1993, conscious of the fact that many of its customers were in America, it moved from its base near Munich to Boulder, Colorado.[3]

Becoming an insider means more than just buying a few assets—however expensive they might be. On the face of it, Sony and Matsushita did the right thing by buying into the entertainment industry's "center of excellence"—Hollywood. However, both Japanese companies were utterly confused by the industry, with its temperamental personalities, free-wheeling deal makers, and reliance on "ears" or "eyes" who could predict whether an artist would sell or a film would be successful. As a result, they vacillated between giving their spendthrift employees much too free a hand (for a time, the Hollywood hills were jammed with builders' trucks and delivery vehicles winding their way up to the rapidly expanding homes of Japanese-paid moguls) and then suddenly clamping down. One reason why MCA's long-time chairman, Lew Wasserman, rebelled against Matsushita in 1995 was that the Japanese company would not let the studio expand in areas such as music and multimedia. Bertelsmann, a staid German publishing company that bought several American music and book-publishing groups, has done better than the Japanese but has not had an easy time of it—not least because its executives annoyed RCA stalwarts by conducting private conversations in German during meetings.

However, the best reason for thinking like an insider, not just a citizen of Anchorage (not one of the world's wealthier cities), is simply that you sell more products. Remember Coca-Cola and McDonald's efforts to go native in Japan. Or notice that Switzerland's Nestlé has built itself into the biggest foreign food firm in Japan by offering Japanese families products such as packaged cereals that taste like seaweed. By contrast, America's car makers made no concessions to the Japanese preference for small cars or custom of driving on the left-hand side of the road—something that George Bush's ludicrous trip to Tokyo in 1992, when he and a group of car company executives tried to force Japan to open its markets, did little to change.

## The Transnational Corporation

By now it should be clear that globalization does not portend the triumph of monolithic companies, the eclipse of local differences, or the omnipresence of global products, as many people had envisaged. At the same time, globalization is not a meaningless term. It sprang from real events: a lowering of trade barriers, and the rapid movement of ideas, people, and money around the globe. Globalization may not make much sense as a business strategy, but as a phenomenon it still presents both problems and opportunities to companies of all sizes.

In particular, a firm that can manufacture its products globally, making use of the different cultures rather than trampling all over them, looks like a very powerful one. Such a company might act as an arbitrageur between various local centers of excellence, putting, for instance, Italian designers in touch with Japanese experts in miniaturization, and then combining these various local skills with whatever global resources it can gain access to.

By the mid-1990s, there were signs that this subtler, geographically sensitive version of globalization had a lot going for it. The question, as ever, was how to construct a company that could take advantage of it. The two best answers so far are "the transnational corporation," a phrase coined jointly by Christopher Bartlett of Harvard Business School and Sumantra Ghoshal of London Business School, and "the multicultural multinational," epitomized by Barnevik's ABB. These unlovely-sounding organizations both involve playing around with the matrix systems that lie at the heart of most multinationals, where people report to both a geographic boss (such as a country manager) and a product manager (the head of the global car division).

The transnational corporation is a tidying-up entity. For most of this century, big companies were loose affiliations of national firms that happened to share the same name. Companies such as Ford and Unilever originally dealt with the problems of high tariffs, prohibitive transport costs, and stringent local-content rules by making clones of themselves in all the countries where they operated, with their own head offices, design facilities, and production plants. This was extremely expensive at the best of times. At one point, Ford had two "Escorts" on the road that had been designed and built entirely separately. Now that tariffs are much lower, many of these activities can be integrated into a global system without necessarily destroying the company's local feel.

Recently, some companies have tried giving national subsidiaries responsibility for global products or global functions, partly to disperse decision making throughout the organization and partly to capture local expertise. Nestlé, for one, has put the headquarters of its pasta business in Italy. Johnson & Johnson has given its German subsidiary a worldwide mandate for tampons. And Louis Gerstner at IBM has set up 14 broad global product groups that have reduced the power of the company's once-all-powerful national chieftains.

The most ambitious attempt to build a transnational company is the Ford 2000 plan that began in January 1995. The American car maker had edged toward building "world cars" over the previous decade, with different parts of its empire collaborating on design. But its chairman, Alex Trotman, decided it could go further. Under Ford 2000, the company abolished a score of separate national units in Europe and North America and replaced them with five product teams, some of them headquartered in Europe. Trotman admits that the project has only been made possible by the sort of technology that allows people in different locations to work on the same project. (Visit Ford's design center in Dearborn, Michigan, and you will hear Germanic voices booming out of loudspeakers, as engineers on both sides of the Atlantic haggle over the shapes appearing on the screens in front of them.) By developing one common small-car chassis and cutting the overall development time from 37 months to 24 by 1999, Ford hopes to cut its product development costs (currently $8 billion a year) by 30 percent. Meanwhile, by setting up a worldwide purchasing system and weeding out suppliers, Trotman hopes to knock $700 off the cost of manufacturing each vehicle.

Is this sort of integration just globalization by another name? The difference is that transnational companies are much more particular about which products they think they can market across borders, and far more sensitive in the way that they do it. For instance, Ford 2000 is not a global program; it applies only to North America and Europe. It also deals only with smaller cars, and, although the chassis may now be the same, the styling and marketing remain very much in the hands of local managers. Confronted by a geographic difference, a transnational company usually retreats. General Electric is only one of several companies to break with policies of dividing operations into global product lines by setting up a regional headquarters in Asia. In China, multinationals are learning quickly that Beijing likes to deal with just one local boss who can speak for all the company's product lines; hence the rush to set up "China centers."

Sometimes this sensitivity makes for some fairly confusing corporate history—as Unilever's Western European food operations show. In the early 1990s, as part of a plan code-named "Beethoven," the Anglo-Dutch giant centralized its food operations in preparation for the 1992 Single Market.[4] Then it realized that it had gone too far, so it handed back some marketing powers to its national chieftains. But it continued to centralize production. By 1996, 20 percent of Unilever's ice cream production in Europe was sold across borders, seven times the proportion in 1992; with factories being consolidated rapidly (and ruthlessly), the aim was to reach 35 percent by 1999. Unilever also divided its food business in each country in Europe into two product-based units (basically, frozen and nonfrozen). This "market locally but produce regionally" strategy might seem relatively simple but there was also a separate "master plan." It dictated that the company should try to expand in some products (basically, ice cream and margarine) and in some markets (Latin America and Asia), though not necessarily in both at the same time. Analysts expect Niall FitzGerald, its new British chairman, to push through another bout of centralization—though that, doubtless, will be followed by more fits of localization.

## Reasons to Be Global

This to-ing and fro-ing prompts a more fundamental question: why bother? The reason is the belief that a properly coordinated multinational company can devote far more resources to any particular product than either a national company or an old-fashioned multinational. In some industries, such as jet aircraft and semiconductors, companies have always needed to sell their products globally to recoup their investments. Now the cost of innovation has skyrocketed in a whole range of businesses. In the 1960s, Siemens had to capture only half of the German market to amortize the cost of developing an electromechanical switch; soon it will have to capture 20 percent of the global market. Hollywood used to think only about the American box office; nowadays it would go bust without foreign markets.

Although McDonald's insists that it is a chain of local restaurants staffed by local people and often owned by them, it also centralizes some things to cut costs. Its global team of specialists can erect a new McDonald's restaurant out of modular parts in as little as 11 days, cutting the cost of building the restaurant by a third. A global purchasing team has saved the company $200 million a year by cutting back on the number of its suppliers. IKEA has a specialized team to set up new stores. The team plans the building, supervises its construction, masterminds the launch, runs the store, and trains the local team; after a year, it hands the operation over to the locals and heads off to do the same thing somewhere else in the world.

A good "big firm" like McDonald's or IKEA can use the same basic advertising ploy to sell its product around the globe. OC&C Strategy, a London-based consultancy, has calculated that the advertising and promotion costs needed to persuade a customer to try out a new product are, on average, 36 percent less for a recognized brand than for an unfamiliar one. The cost of developing an international brand in Europe, Japan, and the United States has been put as high as $1 billion. A big multinational can also afford to experiment (if a product or a strategy fails in Sweden, then so be it).

By themselves, such economies of scale count for little, as the first failed round of globalization proved; but if they can be subsumed into a network that mixes and matches knowledge from around the world, they become much more potent. The United Nations Conference on Trade and Development, which keeps watch on transnational companies, distinguishes between two types of integration, simple and complex. In simple integration, companies keep their most sophisticated operations in their home country but contract out other production to the developing world. This tends to suit smaller multinationals. Nike, an American sportswear maker, does all its product development and marketing in its home town in Oregon, but subcontracts production to 40 other locations, mostly in Asia. Whenever the wages in the host country get too high, the firm simply shifts production to a cheaper country. Japan's Mabuchi Motors, which makes the tiny wheels that drive things like cameras and windshield wipers, has moved all its routine production offshore, much of it to China's Guangdong Province, but it has kept all its most valuable activities at home.

In complex integration, companies locate all their activities according to the logic of the market. They also disperse decision making throughout their organizations rather than keeping it in the head office. Their hallmark is the endless flow of information in all directions, horizontally as well as vertically. Xerox, an office equipment maker, is a good example of this evolution. In the early 1980s, Xerox was just a coalition of national affiliates, such as Britain's Rank Xerox and Japan's Fuji Xerox; each firm did virtually everything itself. But competition from cheaper, more flexible Japanese companies such as Canon forced Xerox to integrate its activities. Xerox has introduced global product-development teams and centralized procurement, reducing the number of suppliers from 5,000 to 400. But it has also indicated that it is a union of equals, all of which are expected to come up with ideas.

Reinventing companies to make better use of knowledge is always complex (see Chapter 7), but doing so across borders is particularly difficult. Occasionally, transnational companies have had to deal with wholesale revolts by corporate barons, as IBM did in Italy. After the failures of the 1980s, companies have become more cautious about imposing globalization plans from above. Trotman admits that, for much of 1994, Ford was run by "the second team" because he forced senior managers to spend most of their time working out how they were going to implement Ford 2000. The firm's headquarters in Dearborn has a huge board on display, signed by all its senior managers as an expression of their commitment to Ford 2000.

Despite Trotman's care and commitment to change, Ford's culture will probably take a decade to reinvent. At Monsanto, another big American company that is trying to reorganize, senior staff refer to centralization as "the C-word." In 1995, Royal Dutch/Shell, a big firm that has always thrived on decentralization, also moved to a hierarchy organized around product groups. This seemed certain to produce productivity gains, but insiders worried that these would be wiped out by "softer" losses—such as the company's famous "Shell man" culture. There is a risk, one former director admitted, of "the baby being thrown out with the bath water."

## The Multicultural Multinational

These remarks seem to underline a fundamental point, namely, when it comes to globalization, a company's people are more important than its products. This is the main reason that small firms, such as Peter Drucker's "friend who understands hospitals," have so far generally done so much better than big global firms. Look at virtually any failed globalization strategy and you will find that the company's staff did not go along with it. No matter how often the Saatchi brothers told their award-winning London agency to recommend their New York one, the copywriters and account executives in Charlotte Street regarded their Manhattan branch as a second-division outfit—and sometimes told their clients so. The words "Not Invented Here" could appear on the graves of most globalization strategies.

If multinational firms often represent the worst of all worlds, they also hold out—tantalizingly—the promise of one day representing the best of most. Their current weakness—their variety—should also be their greatest strength. A multinational has access to a much larger pool of management talent than a small firm; it is also exposed to a wider range of stimuli about such things as consumer needs, technological changes, and competitors' moves. If a multinational does not use that knowledge, then it might as well close its subsidiaries and hire subcontractors; but if it exploits that multiculturalism, the effect should be electric. It is this holy grail that Barnevik was pursued at ABB.

The hunt for the multicultural multinational begins with a health warning, however. In many cases, a firm's most valuable resource is its internal culture—the more distinctive the better. Visiting one of the world's great companies is rather like visiting a cult: people have their local heroes (the founder, the current chairman, and one or two others), their local war stories (how the founder hit upon his winning idea), and even their local language. The "HP Way" is as Californian as decaffeinated coffee. Ford workers seem to have nicknames for everything in their Dearborn headquarters.

But multinationals should not be put off by the health warning. One reason is that multiculturalism should work for companies just as it does for countries. From Hong Kong to California, there has been one surefire way to inject some vitality into the economy: immigration. America's economy pulled ahead of Europe's and Japan's in the 1980s in part because it opened itself up to foreign investment and foreign brainpower. Japanese know-how and competition helped to revitalize America's rust belt. Surely individual companies can gain from introducing alien cultures into their midst.

This seems likely, given that even imported knowledge of the most mundane sort can be a potent weapon. For example, a French company, Danone, has rapidly become the biggest biscuit firm in Asia by importing "biscuit technology" to make biscuits that do not crumble. One of Philips's most successful recent products, an up-market large-screen television, was only pushed into production when the Dutch firm's head office received a desperate memo from Jack Lau, head of its marketing team in Hong Kong, highlighting the dramatic increase in demand for such products in the region. Philips is now moving more and more of its electronics business to Southeast Asia, which is probably the world's most creative and competitive electronics market.

Most big companies will become more multicultural because they have no choice. The three pioneers of multiculturalism—Shell, Unilever, and ABB—were all the products of mixed marriages. "We were used to pushing together Dutch and English people; adding other varieties was fairly easy," points out one Shell man, noting that there are 40 nationalities in the company's head office. In Europe, the single market is making miscegenation the rule rather than the exception. Already some 150,000 Britons work for German companies; many argue that they get the best of both worlds.

Japanese companies, according to Tadahiro Sekimoto, the chairman of NEC, a giant electronics group, used to practice what he calls "radial globalization," in which overseas offices were tied to the head office at the center.[5] In the future, the norm is likely to become "an organic network that links all overseas branches." Management, he believes, must become more "holonic": that is, "each part acts independently but when viewed from the whole all is in balance." To attain this state of harmony, the vital ingredient is a company's own corporate culture. "In this age of globalization, corporate culture has become the fifth management asset that stands on a par with labor, material, capital, and information." Even in Asia, Japanese firms have discovered that treating locals as "dumb terminals" is self-defeating. Korea's *chaebol* may also be forced to reach the same conclusion: they have feuded with German employees over works councils, and there have been rumors of fistfights between locals and their militaristic superiors.

In America, the pressure for a more multicultural future is coming not only from globalization but also from domestic demographics. By the year 2000, White males will make up only 45 percent of America's workforce. American consumers, too, are changing color and gender. In 1993, a sales manager for Avon Products in Atlanta spotted an influx of Korean and Vietnamese immigrants, so she quickly recruited a squadron of Asian ladies to sell cosmetics. Avon cleaned up. It now has a "multicultural participation council" to encourage diversity among employees. Sales at Sears stores close to Hispanic areas have risen since the firm recruited Spanish-speaking workers. AT&T has built support among recent immigrants with its Language Line, offering translations in 140 languages.

There are a few signs that such intermingled American firms do better abroad. Avon, for instance, has been very successful in both China and South America. More generally, globalization gives these hyphenated Americans other kinds of opportunities: there has been a rush, for example, to find American-born Chinese to send to China. Worried about the

image of the "ugly American" (unable to speak any other languages, and brutally insensitive to cultural differences), companies have begun to put pressure on American business
schools to become more international—to recruit their staff
and students from as many countries as possible.

One result of this new sensitivity has been a dramatic
turnaround in the image of multinationals. In the bad old
days, when Vietnam protesters used to chant, "We won't fight
for Texaco," the word "multinational" was synonymous with
firms such as ITT, which tried to subvert the Chilean government and spent millions of dollars on illegal activities in Indonesia, Iran, and Italy (to name only the countries beginning
with "I"). Nowadays, multinationals have a cleaner, greener
image. They line up to endorse worthy international agreements such as the International Chamber of Commerce's Business Charter for Sustainable Development. More surprisingly,
they usually stick to them—partly because a single global standard is easier to follow, and partly because it usually makes
life more difficult for their poorer local competitors.

## The People Test

Every multinational is happy to have a better image. But images are fragile things. In early 1996, Ford faced a rumpus in Europe because it had doctored a British advertisement, replacing
all the Black faces of workers from its Dagenham factory with
White ones before letting the ad appear in Poland. Ironically, the
American car maker's excuse, though mocked in the British
press and reviled in Dagenham, would make sense to students of
multicultural multinationals: Ford claimed it was being sensitive,
adapting a global campaign to local tastes (there are not many
Black faces in Poland).

This bizarre episode shows how hard it is for companies to
keep up their multicultural reputation. Even harder than keeping up appearances is making a reality of the idea. The real test
of multiculturalism—not to mention the only lasting source of
profits from it—is how a firm uses its own people. One good
place to look is the boardroom. After all, by appointing only a
handful of foreign faces, a company can send a clear message
that the top positions are not reserved for locals only. At first
glance, big companies seem to have done pretty well. Who

would have guessed 20 years ago that Ford would be run by a Scot (Alex Trotman), L'Oreal by a Welshman (Lindsay Owen Jones), Heinz by an Irishman (Tony O' Reilly), and McKinsey by an Indian (Rajat Gupta)?

Yet, beneath the surface, many multinationals are still stubbornly ethnocentric. For all Sekimoto's talk of holonic management, Japanese firms remain the worst offenders, but American firms are also guilty. The proportion of foreign-born board members of America's biggest firms was the same in 1991 as in 1981, 2.1 percent, according to Susan Schneider, a professor at Insead. Look further down the organization and you find suspicions of national favoritism abound. Ford Assembly Operations, for example, is known as "For Americans Only" by European staff. In 1995, the International Consortium for Executive Development Research, which is based in Lexington, Massachusetts, asked 1,500 managers from 12 large companies to rank their abilities in 34 categories. "Cultivating a global mind-set" finished last.

Given these difficulties, it is not surprising that few multinationals make the most out of cultural mixing. After all, there is nothing particularly multicultural about letting American brains boss around Asian hands, as Nike does. What you want to see being produced abroad is not just sneakers but ideas. According to a study by John Cantwell, an economist at Britain's Reading University, only 9 percent of the patents issued to American multinationals in the 1980s were for work done by overseas companies. For European firms, the ratio was 30 percent—though the chances are that most of those ideas came from other European countries.

The most powerful force for change is technology—or, to be more accurate, information. Videoconferencing, software programs such as Lotus Notes, and now the "Intranet" of online company networks all allow people from different places to work on the same ideas. At its most extreme, this can mean letting German and American designers haggle online about the same engine part (as already happens at Ford). One of the best ways of using information technology is to spread best practice around the company. Many companies have star plants, like Motorola's pager plant in Florida, which they encourage everybody else to beat.

However, technology will only do so much. In the end, multicultural multinationals require an enormous amount of human effort as well. Nestlé sets up periodic internal conferences, arranging regular short-term visits and rotating key personnel at its various technical and research centers. Richard Branson invites Virgin employees, along with Virgin Atlantic's most frequent travelers (and their families), to chaotic summer picnics at his house. All the same, much of the burden falls on that old warhorse, the "ex-pat" manager. This is not ideal. Ex-pats are horrendously expensive, costing more than double what it takes to employ a local, and they are becoming hard to get hold of—particularly if the job being offered is in Beijing or Karachi rather than London or Paris. Their flexibility has also been undermined by sexual equality: the rise of the dual-career couple means that a firm often has to uproot two people to send one somewhere. However, without an international officer class of some sort, centrifugal forces take over.

## The Battle Ahead

Can multicultural organizations outwit people such as Peter Drucker's friend who "understands hospitals" or a firm using subcontractors around the world? The answer is that it is too early to say. As David De Pury, ABB's cochairman, put it in 1994: "There are very few multicultural multinationals; the truly global multicultural company does not yet exist." For every new internal information system that helps one of the monster companies become more human and flexible, there is an Internet site that allows small entrepreneurs to swap ideas about their industries.

It can be said with certainty, however, that, even though globalization and geography may be intractable problems, every company of any size has to face up to them. Furthermore, this new knowledge-based, multicultural version of globalization stands a far better chance of working with geography than its predecessor stood of vanquishing it. That is why the endless peregrination of Percy Barnevikmay, and his successors, may just be worthwhile.

# CHAPTER 11

## THE ART OF JAPANESE MANAGEMENT

IN THE WEST, paternalist companies used to be in the habit of building company towns. In Japan, Toyota has built a company city. Two hours southwest of Tokyo by bullet train, Toyota City is proof, if any was needed, of the continuing might of Japanese manufacturing. Home to 10 gigantic car plants, which churn out three million vehicles a year, the city dominates the life of the entire region. The surrounding towns exist for the sole purpose of producing parts for Toyota City's factories. It is rare to see one of the city's 350,000 inhabitants without a Toyota badge somewhere on his or her jacket or baseball cap. The whole place is, in effect, a gigantic machine, forever grinding out Toyota products.

But it is the way the machine does the grinding, rather than its awesome size, that has captured the attention of the world—and also changed it. This is a place where manufacturers of all races still come to gawk. It is also one of the few factories that can be classed as a successful showcase for applied management theory.

At first sight, this seems a strange claim. Life inside Toyota City's factories seems much like life in car factories the world over—the usual mix of clattering robots, blowtorch-wielding welders, and, of course, assembly lines. But look a little closer and important differences emerge. The armies of workers who clog the aisles around Western assembly lines are missing. Almost everybody on Toyota's shop floor is busy adding value. Missing, too, are the shelf-loads of inventory that are common in the West. Toyota's workers have only about an hour's worth of inventory at hand, conveniently stored on shoulder-high shelves next to their workstations. A constant flow of traffic—bicycles, small trucks, and even unmanned carts, playing high-pitched electronic tunes to warn of their presence—deliver material to workers so that they can lay their hands on whatever they need without keeping huge supplies of spares.

Yet, in all this haste, each worker has the power to bring the assembly line to a halt, pulling a wire above his head if he (there are no women to be seen) spots a fault. And the news of the fault is immediately flashed on one of the many electronic boards suspended from the ceiling that also tell everybody how many cars have been made and how near the line is to hitting its target. The general air is that of competitive collaboration, with each team vying to be the most efficient. One young man displays a tool he invented a couple of years ago to make it easier to insert the steering column into its shaft. The tool is now used in Toyota's factories around the world. A second worker shows off another invention (this time, from another factory): a mobile chair, suspended from the ceiling, allows him to dart in and out of the passing cars without having to clamber all over them. The management puts an unusual amount of emphasis on the workers' comfort. Robots do the back-breaking work of lifting rather than the skilled work of welding. The cars are suspended above the ground so that the workers can insert parts without bending down. Spare parts are stored at eye level for the same reason.

It is worth bearing Toyota City in mind when listening to Japan's gloomy business people. For most of the 1990s, all they have been able to talk about is the high yen's crippling effect on exporters and the recession triggered by the bubble economy. A conversation in November 1995 with the president of the Keidanren, one of Japan's leading employers' organizations, was fairly typical, and produced a long list of complaints: Japan's companies are too fat, its employees too cosseted, its population too conformist, its interest groups too powerful, the president moaned. To revive its flagging fortunes, the country needs to deregulate its industries, get rid of lifetime employment, and become more entrepreneurial.

All this is true, of course. But we should not forget just how powerful much of the Japanese economy remains. In 1996, Japan was the world's second biggest economy, after the United States. Japan created 3.2 million jobs during the recession of the early 1990s and its unemployment rate in mid-1997 was only 3.3 percent. And the country owes a lot of its success to the way that companies like Toyota have outmanaged their rivals.

## The Allure of Quality

It might seem far-fetched to think that Japan's postwar growth has anything to do with management theory. After all, the average salaryman, relaxing over yakitori and sake after a 10-hour day, does not spend his time talking about Drucker-San and Peters-San. If you let them, critics of management theory will happily point out that Japan has only a few business schools, none of them very prestigious, and that, 30 years after arriving, Western consultancies there are still struggling to make ends meet. Because they do not have to pay the consultancies inflated fees, the argument goes, companies have more money to devote to "real" investment; and because they are not following the latest management fashions, they develop coherent, long-term strategies.

The skeptics are right in one respect. Japan has so far produced only one first-division guru of its own, Kenichi Ohmae (though a generation of young pretenders is emerging). Many of the "gurus" who appear in this chapter are business people rather than professors. Nevertheless, those businessmen have thought about management just as broadly as Drucker, Peters, and others; and their names are no less associated with theories on how to run businesses.

Moreover, in their central criticism, the skeptics are plain wrong. Japan owes a huge debt to management theory—just not the precepts currently being flogged as the latest and greatest. They owe their debt to a group of American theorists whose ideas inspired the Japanese to invent "lean production." In the best study of that revolution, *The Machine That Changed the World* (1990), Daniel Jones, James Womack, and Daniel Roos present their conclusions in no uncertain terms: "Lean production is a superior way for humans to make things. It provides better products in wider variety at lower cost. Equally important, it provides more challenging and fulfilling work for employees at every level, from the factory to headquarters."[1]

Lean production was inspired by a set of American theories about quality that Japanese businesses first discovered during the postwar American occupation. After the war, the Japanese realized that their goods were hopelessly shoddy by international standards; they were also awe-struck by the might of the American economy and the sheer profusion of American products. Desperate to compete in international markets, the Japanese seized on a set of ideas that taught how to build quality into industrial products. While on the surface this sounds too obvious a concept to bear mentioning (indeed, this was how "quality" was regarded for decades in the land of its invention, the United States), in practice it was the impetus behind an industrial revolution. In a nutshell, these ideas focused on the importance of getting things right the first time rather than spending a lot of time fixing mistakes after they occurred—a notion that went against the grain of the standard corporate model of the time, which assumed that quality was something a quality department checked for after an item had been built. In postwar Japan, American gurus who were willing to visit and talk about quality were a godsend.

Having been more or less ignored in America in the early 1950s, W. Edwards Deming and his friends were given the red-carpet treatment in Japan. Whenever they lectured, the halls were packed to the ridgepole with engineers and production managers. Whatever they wrote was immediately translated into Japanese and devoured by managers the length and breadth of the country. Even today, Japanese managers speak of Joseph Juran, A. V. Feigenbaum, and, particularly, Deming in the same hushed tones that people normally reserve for a deity. Since 1950, an annual Deming prize, including a medal bearing the face of the great man, has been awarded for excellence in manufacturing, and the prizewinners are featured on Japanese television.

Beyond the need to begin manufacturing quality products quickly, there were other specific reasons why Deming's ideas seemed so attractive in Japan. Businesses in a grotesquely overcrowded country do not have the space to keep large quantities of inventory hanging around for months. After the war, Japan could not afford to waste precious (imported) raw materials on throwaway products or crummy machinery. Japan also lacked the migrant workers who provided Henry Ford with his factory fodder; and a surge of industrial unrest made it clear that Japanese workers were no longer willing to be treated as mere costs of production. Perhaps only the nation that gave sushi to the world could have grasped "just-in-time" delivery so intuitively.

## The Lean, Mean Machine

The original ideas may have come from across the Pacific, but it was two Japanese, Kiichiro Toyoda, boss of Toyota, and Taiichi Ohno, his right-hand man, who transformed them into a new system of production. They did so by turning themselves into management theorists—visiting American factories for months on end during the 1950s and studying mass production, to see what made it so successful and how it could be bettered. They found the system rife with *muda*—a Japanese term that encompasses wasted effort, wasted material, and wasted time. Nobody except the assembly worker was adding much value, they noticed, and the emphasis on keeping the line running at all times meant that errors multiplied endlessly.[2]

The two eventually put all the pieces together for an entirely new system of production—dubbed the Toyota manufacturing system by Toyota and "lean production" by almost everybody else. Its genius was to shift the focus of manufacturing from economies of scale to "economies of time." It did this in three ways. First, every employee became a quality checker, responsible for spotting errors as they happen and correcting them immediately. Instead of installing a quality department like that of its American rivals, Toyota gave workers the right to stop the production line as soon as they saw errors—hence, all those cords hanging along the production line.

Second, the Japanese introduced "just-in-time" production. In the rest of the world, manufacturers made their components "just in case" they were needed. They filled bins, pallets, and warehouses with days' or even weeks' worth of costly parts, which gathered dust until they were finally needed. The Japanese started making components "just in time," with parts arriving just as they were needed on the production line.

Third, time was also saved by following the "demand-pull" principle. Components in Western factories were traditionally delivered by "supply-push" arrangements, with goods piling up when they were not needed. With demand pull, they are made to order. At Toyota, a *kanban,* or card, is attached to every box of supplies describing its contents. Returning the card to the supplier automatically reorders a further shipment. The demand-pull system even extends to the customer. Instead of relying on customers to wander into their local Toyota dealership and express a preference for a particular car, Toyota has an army of door-to-door car salesmen. The theory is that customers will tell these salesmen what sort of car they want and the factory will then make their car to order.

This procedure challenges the entire basis of mass production, which was (and in many parts of the world still is) the dominant manufacturing philosophy. Mass production depends on economies of scale and specialization. Workers, it is supposed, need to become more and more specialized in order to do their job more efficiently. And factories need to become bigger and bigger to achieve economies of scale. As the Japanese realized, however, this system also entails two serious costs.

First, the classic mass-production system is unable to respond to rapid changes in demand. Mass producers tend to be much keener on keeping standardized designs in production than in experimenting with new products, partly because of the heavy costs of changing the production line and partly because their specialized workers are happiest with what they know. With a change in fashion, the factory may have to close down for months as machines are recalibrated and workers are retrained. Producers may also have to throw away huge quantities of expensively stored but now obsolete inventory. By the time the factory is capable of mass-producing the new product, the demand may have changed once again.

Second, the system turns out an unacceptably high rate of faulty products. Large batches make it difficult to detect defects. A defective part may not reveal itself until the finished car finally breaks down. The Japanese argued that it is easier for the next person on the assembly line to check a small batch. And a worker making only a small batch is more likely to feel like a craftsman, whereas mass production usually achieves its economies of scale by reducing jobs to drudgery. By contrast, lean production continues to engage at least some of the intellectual gifts of the workers. They can see the impact of their workmanship—good or bad—on the company's manufacturing process. Pats on the back from one's colleagues are delivered for a job well done, scowls for a job skimped.

Lean producers ram home this concept of responsibility by making everybody aware not only of what they are doing but how well they are doing it. This information is communicated in "quality circles"—sessions at which people sit around discussing their performance and the quality of what they have produced. Workers are also fed continuous information on the job—hence the lighted electronic displays that are visible at every workstation in Toyota's factories.

Lean production also means rethinking the boundaries of the firm—in particular, its relationship with its suppliers. In the West, this relationship has taken two forms. Initially, manufacturers tried to make virtually all parts themselves, in special divisions set up for this purpose. When opinion turned against such "vertical integration," Western companies opted for a system organized around competing suppliers. In this case, they provided a large number of suppliers with a detailed drawing of what they wanted and then offered a one-year contract to the supplier who could come up with the best price.

The classic form of Japanese supply-chain management, again pioneered by Toyota, works in a different way. The suppliers may be formally separate companies, or they can be members of the same *keiretsu* (a group of firms linked by cross-shareholdings). In either case, the parent company treats the supply firms as partners rather than playing them off against each other. The suppliers provide the goods "just in time" in return for long-term relationships with the main manufacturers. The manufacturers cement these relationships by sending mid-career managers to high-level positions in supplier companies or other members of a *keiretsu*. This means all parts of the supply chain can pool resources and also share information—thus once again cutting down on time-wasting. Even today, Toyota can design and build a car twice as fast as an American-owned factory in Detroit.

## Kenichi Ohmae, *Kaizen,* and Consensus

If lean production represents the core of "the Japanese miracle," two other ingredients were, until recently, also indispensable parts of it: the doctrine of continuous improvement, or *kaizen;* and consensus, especially when applied to long-term strategic thinking. The work of Kenichi Ohmae provides insight into both these concepts.

Ohmae is now best known inside Japan for his attempt to set up a new political party. But he made his name in the rest of the world through books he wrote while working as a consultant for McKinsey. Like most gurus, Ohmae is happy to pontificate on almost any subject within the realms of politics and economics. (In an interview with one of the authors, he repeatedly compared himself with Margaret Thatcher.) In some ways, this diversity fits a bilingual, Harley-Davidson-riding polymath, who could have been, among other things, a nuclear engineer. Ohmae's main contribution to management theory centers on his vision of globalization (discussed in Chapter 10) and his knowledge of Japan.

Of the two, it is his knowledge of Japan that established his reputation. For the past quarter century, outsiders, particularly American business people, have been fascinated and frightened by Japan. Ohmae has explained it to them—showering his books with good insider examples of how Japanese companies work, and usually criticizing American firms in the process. Even in his later "global" books, nearly all the memorable examples, such as the invention of a heated toilet seat with an electronically controlled bidet, come from Japan. And the best chapters tend to deal with characteristically Japanese concepts such as the business alliance.

Ohmae writes about innovation particularly well. By Japanese standards, he has a high appreciation of the maverick. He favors splitting a research budget into thirds: one for routine research (to catch up with competitors or try to make your own products cheaper), one for long-range strategic research, and one for wild-card projects. In general, Ohmae exalts the

Japanese way of producing new products through continuous improvement.

Innovation, argues Ohmae, must add value for consumers if it is to be of any use. He tends to pour scorn on big R&D projects, such as high-definition television, and revels in meeting challenges incrementally, particularly in the mundane world. Can you make a better coffee machine—not just one with lots of fancy gadgets but one that actually makes better coffee? Yes, we discover, if you add a water purifier, because the taste of coffee depends as much on the quality of the water as it does on how you percolate the beans. Can you make a better camera? Yes, if you get it to do the focusing for you (i.e., eliminate the human error that ruins most pictures) and include an automatic flash.

A strategy of churning out products with lots of minuscule improvements fits in quite nicely with lean production. After all, one advantage of a flexible assembly line is that it can be easily altered to incorporate a new insight and include a recent innovation. It also means that you can smother your market with new versions of the same old thing. One classic example of this process was the Sony Walkman, which came in hundreds of shapes and sizes. Japanese firms such as Sharp and Canon have often jumped ahead by mixing different sorts of technology, such as photography and office machines. Matsushita tests its latest camcorders in one of Tokyo's more downmarket shopping districts, to see what the masses make of them. If sales are sluggish, the products are withdrawn. This emphasis on improvement—with its rapid updating of models and clever additions, such as vanity mirrors and intermittent windshield wipers—has helped Japanese car makers outfox their rivals. By contrast, American and European manufacturers have seemed obsessed with finding "one big solution" in their research projects—the legacy, some argue, of the Apollo project.

The trick of Japanese management is to marry this relentless incrementalism in the development of products to a long-term strategy of seeking a consensus among those involved in that development. As Ohmae points out, whereas Western firms modeled themselves on the military, with its clear lines of command and rigid distinction between the officers (who do the thinking) and the rest, Japanese firms are rooted in village communes.[3]

"Grossly oversimplifying," Ohmae writes, "one could say that in Japan every member of the village is equal and a generalist." Rather than issuing orders from on high, Japanese companies prefer to put their emphasis on *nemawashi* (consensus building) and *ringi* (shared decision making). The hope is that every decision will spring from tireless discussion, since managers will be obliged to gain the enthusiastic support of their workers.

Communal decision making also affects Japan's approach to leadership. Where American bosses are brash and bullying, their Japanese counterparts are modest and retiring; and where Americans live to make decisions, the Japanese prefer to let decisions make themselves. They compare leadership to air—it is necessary for life but invisible and insubstantial. They rise up the corporate ranks by outconforming their colleagues, religiously putting the group before the individual. Once at the top, they lead by consensus rather than command. It is not unusual for leaders to sit in silence throughout much of a meeting, while their underlings debate the pros and cons of policy. The art of leadership is to divine the will of the group, not to electrify the organization with one's charisma.

The Japanese approach to long-term strategy is also different. In the West, professional strategists help formulate clear and definite goals and their means of implementation, and everything is written down in formal plans. In Japan, the strategy is loosely generated by the whole organization and expressed in terms of visions and missions rather than precise plans. To the Western mind, this is a recipe for disaster. But, according to Ohmae, the Japanese can do it because it fits in with their general system of lifetime employment. Thus, core workers identify with the long-term future of the company. The Japanese habit of rotating people between different departments forces them to think like strategists. And since everybody must start on the shop floor, senior managers are well versed in what is going on in the heart of their organizations.

### The Sun Also Sets

Lean production, consensus, and *kaizen* experienced extraordinary success. By the early 1980s, Japanese firms were beating the Americans to a pulp in everything from price to quality, and the skies of the Pacific were black with aircraft carrying managers to Japan to study companies like Sony and Toyota. Bookshops filled their shelves with titles such as *The Art of Japanese Management* and *The Intelligent Person's Guide to Kaizen*. In the late 1980s, Americans watched helplessly as Japanese companies bought Rockefeller Plaza, Columbia Pictures, Pebble Beach golf course, and other American totems. In *Rising Sun* (1992), a thriller about corporate skulduggery in Los Angeles, Michael Crichton even paid Japanese managers the ultimate compliment of demonizing them. Americans seemed obsessed by two racist stereotypes of the Japanese: they were either clever little Asians producing ever smarter gadgets, or fiendish strategists cunningly working together toward the same unstated goal. Management books—even those of Ohmae—only reinforced these myths.

By the mid-1990s, all those books on the secrets of Japanese management were in second-hand bookshops, and Ohmae was becoming better known as a critic of Japan than as an apologist for it. As Japan's firms struggled to emerge from a prolonged recession and the burden of an expensive currency, they saw that Western companies had turned the tables on them, incorporating everything they needed to know about Japanese management into their system. Now it was the Japanese who would have to learn from the West.

There is no doubt that the West—and America in particular—has caught up quickly. Three decades after he had been spurned in his own country, Deming was rediscovered in June 1980, thanks to an NBC television documentary, "If Japan Can, Why Can't We?" The day after the program was shown, Deming's phone started ringing, and he spent the rest of his life until he died in 1993 giving seminars and being feted by American bosses and politicians. In the United States, total-quality management was the most influential fad of the 1980s. In 1987, the government created an equivalent of Japan's Deming prize, the Baldrige. Motorola, one of the most successful adopters of TQM, claimed that in 1987–92 it had added $3.2 billion to the company's bottom line.[4] In 1989, the Japanese even acknowledged America's conversion to quality by giving an American company, Florida Light and Power, the Deming prize.

Western manufacturers have also learned the secrets of "lean production," largely by forming joint ventures with Japanese companies. With Ford's purchase of 24 percent of Mazda in

1979, its senior managers gained full access to Mazda's main production complex in Hiroshima.[5] (Ford now owns a controlling 33 percent stake.) General Motors formed a joint venture with Toyota in California, transforming one of its most unproductive, strike-ridden plants into a model of productivity. The ease with which Japanese "transplants" put down roots in North America and Britain proved that lean production was not something that could flourish only on Japanese soil.

And some Westerners improved on what they learned. Companies such as Motorola, Chrysler, and Marks and Spencer have formed close links with their suppliers without subjecting themselves to the rigidities that have often bedeviled Japan's *keiretsu* system. "The traditional *keiretsu* are no longer the model of best practice," says Jordan Lewis, an expert on producer–supplier links. "For this, one has to look to the West."[6] To some extent, the role of master and apprentice has been reversed: even Toyota has had to turn to Ford to discover how to improve the relations between its engineers and its shop-floor workers, and to Chrysler to learn about "value engineering"—a new way to speed up car production by using more interchangeable components in different models.

## All Too Japanese

Having given away its secrets, many argue, Japan retains exclusive rights only to those things that nobody else wants. The system of lifetime employment has kept Japanese companies far too fat, while the weakness of shareholders has allowed some firms to remain hopelessly unfocused. The country's white-collar sector is only two-thirds as efficient as its equivalents in Europe and America. Japan's overregulated economy discourages innovation and imposes high costs on businesses, such as exorbitant fuel and telecommunications charges. In "creative" industries, such as software and multimedia, which are booming in the West, Japan is way behind, isolated by language and hampered by a conformist educational system. Japan's universities are sleepy finishing schools, not vital sources of innovation; and Japan's banks are reluctant to invest in unproved companies.

What gives these criticisms added bite is that they are being made by Japanese as well as Americans. If Japan is to survive in the computer business, argues Mochio Umeda, a consultant with Arthur D. Little and a Japan-basher for the home team, management will have to give up "its parochialism, its perverse egalitarianism, its in-group orientation, and its tendency to suppress individuality and creativity." The more sophisticated Japanese managers are stocking their libraries with Western management books and littering their conversations with words like "downsizing" and "reengineering."

The Japanese are also beginning to question two of their famed strengths: *kaizen* and consensus. While Japanese companies have continued churning out ever smarter versions of the same product, American firms have been making the real breakthroughs in consumer electronics, such as the personal computer and the cellular telephone. By the mid-1990s, for all their extra widgets, Japanese cars were beginning to look the same. Indeed, the extra widgets were cluttering up production. What they needed were simpler, bolder designs.

Meanwhile, the emphasis on consensus has made managing foreigners difficult. Japan's multinationals traditionally concentrated on exporting rather than investing abroad, partly because they felt that their manufacturing system was so Japanese that it could not survive on foreign soil. Now, thanks to the high yen, fears of protectionism abroad, and globalization, they have no choice. The Nomura Research Institute has predicted that by 1998 almost 40 percent of the production of Japan's five biggest electronics groups will be offshore. In 1994, Toyota produced 48 percent of its cars overseas; by 1998, that portion will be about 65 percent.

Although the basic lean-production system has actually been relatively easy to export, merely getting people to manufacture things efficiently is often not enough. The cultural insensitivity of many Japanese managers at times makes it difficult to manage production workers. Sanyo Electric provoked an angry strike in Indonesia when it refused to allow 33 female assembly-line workers to wear traditional Muslim dress, citing safety reasons.[7] And Japanese salarymen have found it impossible to manage hairy artistic types: witness Sony's and Matsushita's nightmares in Hollywood.

Western employees have difficulty adjusting to the two-tier management system in Japanese banks: a dummy one in the host country and a real one between the Japanese management and their bosses in Tokyo. They are forever making decisions, they murmur, only to have them countermanded by a telex from Tokyo. In 1991, the Lantos Committee of the House of Representatives, in hearings on the employment practices of Japanese-owned companies in the United States, listened to a litany of complaints: that a handful of Japanese made all the most important decisions, in collusion with the head office; that a "rice-paper ceiling" stood between the non-Japanese and serious promotion; that the Japanese discriminated on the grounds of race and sex; and that the Japanese were unwilling to listen to ideas from foreigners. Consensus, it seems, is only consensual if you are Japanese.

While the rice-paper ceiling has deterred foreigners from working for Japanese firms, xenophobia has also discouraged able Japanese from working abroad. Fearing that a spell away from headquarters may handicap them in the promotion race, many salarymen refer to overseas postings as "banishment." Mothers often stay at home so that children can continue in Japanese schools, an arrangement that imposes huge strains on families. Those children who spend any length of time abroad run the risk of being ostracized at school and accused of "smelling of butter."

Japan's dithering over innovation and internationalization seems to reflect a failure, not just of particular business leaders, but of Japan's whole approach to leadership. Worshiping consensus was all very well when Japan's economy was growing by 10 percent a year. But a flat economy is testing bosses' ability to make hard choices. They have to get rid of surplus workers (or at least retire them early) and decide which line of business to focus on. Competition from tightly managed Western companies means that Japanese companies need to be able to make decisions quickly. Now that Japan is becoming increasingly involved with the rest of the world, through joint ventures and overseas operations, Japanese managers can no longer rely on a decision-making process that is comprehensible only to their fellow Japanese.

### East Meets West: The Remix

The Japanese approach to management is clearly endowed with both advantages and shortcomings. But writing off Japan would be, to say the least, premature. The country is still the world's leading center of manufacturing excellence. And Japanese businesses have a genius for turning adversity into advantage. Because Japan lacks natural resources, the government invests heavily in education. Two oil shocks and several steep rises in the yen have acted as powerful spurs to industrial and managerial innovation. Several times before, Japanese car imports to the United States have dropped following steep rises in the yen; each time, Toyota City has found new ways to make lean production even leaner and to come back to humble Detroit again.

This time, Japan's bounce-back will not be a reprise of its remarkable postwar transformations because, for the first time in 30 years, the Japanese are looking beyond their own borders for solutions. They are not just trying to improve their own management models, but to merge them with Western ones. One important thinker in this respect is Yotaro Kobayashi, the boss of Fuji Xerox, who is something of a hero to the younger generation of Japanese managers and who has spent much of the past decade insisting to his peers that his country's idea of consensual leadership needs to change.

Kobayashi, who graduated from the Wharton Business School and has spent years as head of a joint venture with an American company, argues that Japanese bosses must learn how to make tough decisions and how to "market" them, both within their firms and in the world at large, so that employees and outsiders can see the logic of unpalatable decisions. He also believes that Japanese managers need a dose of Western-style professionalism. Leaders should be carefully trained, not just allowed to emerge from the ranks. He encourages Fuji Xerox's rising middle managers to take responsibility for strategic decisions. He also likes to send a few on American MBA courses—though he is careful not to give the impression that the firm is being turned into an American colony.

Kobayashi wants to introduce a streak of rebelliousness into the salaryman's soul: Japanese managers ought to challenge their business models rather than just endlessly improve them. Kobayashi's own career was greatly influenced by a visit to the Aspen Institute in the United States, which puts on mind-broadening seminars for business leaders. He now has his own version in Japan where business people sit and listen to philosophers, as well as people like Peter Drucker, and debate issues ranging from environmental protection to methods of management.

## A Dignified Retreat

Is Kobayashi just a voice crying in the wilderness? Consider two areas in which Japanese management has been slow to change: lifetime employment and multicultural management.

At first sight, Japanese companies have tried hard to hang on to the idea of a "job for life," doing anything to find new jobs for redundant personnel. In Honda, it is even possible to find male managers serving coffee in place of the traditional office ladies. To avoid having to fire people, companies are cutting back on bonuses, preventing workers from working overtime, and freezing recruitment. Nissan used to recruit between 1,500 and 2,000 new workers a year; it hired only 55 in 1995. Nowadays, Japanese graduates anxiously study the age profiles of companies, which are published annually, to see if they have any chance of a career.

Yet there is movement. Western-style assessment procedures are creeping into big Japanese firms, and jobs are not as safe as they used to be. Despite their loyalty to the concept of lifetime employment, firms are redefining the phrase, arguing that it applies only to a proportion of workers and whittling down that proportion as far as they can. Japanese banks have introduced a system of "up or out": those who do not make the grade by the age of 40 are sent away to run local banks. Toyota has taken to moving 50-year-old managers from supervisory jobs to "individual work." And a few are introducing "voluntary" early retirement for their lifetime employees. Nissan cut its workforce by 5,000 in 1993–95, with the majority of the losses falling on white-collar workers. Toshiba, an electronics company, reduced the size of its headquarters staff by 30 percent between 1992 and 1997, delegating more power to front-line workers as it did so. ("Small, simple, speedy, strategic" is its latest motto.) Toyota claims to be reducing its white-collar workforce by 20 percent, though the secret of this reduction seems to be shuffling people between departments.

As for the problem of dealing with foreign staff, the best Japanese companies have certainly begun to talk like "multicultural multinationals." NEC is putting all its products "into a global perspective in order to determine the most appropriate locations for design, manufacturing and sales."[8] Matsushita, once one of the keenest defenders of its home base, has now decided that it is a "multilocal" and talks about being a "global network manager."[9] Nissan is keen on creating a "global team spirit" and talks about using the entire world as a "knowledge base."

There are signs that this is more than just talk. More blue-chip Japanese companies are bringing foreign managers to Japan. Toyota now holds shareholder meetings outside Japan. Toshiba is reorganizing every bit of its work, from accounting to technology management, on a worldwide basis, partly to get rid of duplication but also partly because there is no longer any such thing as a purely Japanese business problem. The Japanese are also establishing global networks, in which people from "third countries" act as missionaries for Japanese management. Toshiba sends Thais to its plant in Malaysia, which has been operating for 20 years, in order to introduce them to Japanese production techniques.

The two-way flow of ideas is already producing results. Both Canon and Toshiba, for example, have made breakthroughs in audio technology by setting up laboratories in Britain. Honda rebounded from a bad stretch in the late 1980s with the Honda Accord, a car that it designed in part by organizing a contest among studios in Japan, the United States, and Europe.[10] The company also moved 60 American production engineers and their families to Japan for two years.

One of the leaders of the multicultural approach (and another ally of Kobayashi and Ohmae) has been Minoru Makihara. Makihara was born in London, educated at Harvard University, spent 22 years serving abroad, and speaks perfect English. He is so at home in the United States that his two children work for American companies and he is known by the nickname Ben. In 1992, he was drafted from abroad (an unusual move in a Japanese company) to become president of Mitsubishi Corporation, the biggest of Japan's dozen or so trading companies—or *soga sosha*.

In the past, a trading house could survive as an importer-exporter, acting as an agent for foreigners in Japan and for Japanese firms abroad. As markets open up, however, this role is dying. Mitsubishi's future, if it has one, is as a more proactive global deal maker, using its contacts and its people to set up things like power stations and cable television networks around the world. Ever since Makihara's surprise appointment, he has tried to force his colleagues—not always successfully—to think in the same way that he does. One of his first moves was to ask all his senior managers to write him letters of resignation (so that he could use them if necessary); he also fines them if they address him as president.

Makihara has tried to promote non-Japanese in the company. And, like Kobayashi, he is a keen supporter of letting Western thinkers into the company. But it is a hard slog. Western employees in Mitsubishi complain that they are on short-term contracts, while their Japanese colleagues have a job for life.

For the moment, people like Kobayashi, Makihara, and Ohmae remain the exceptions rather than the rule. But they have three things going for them. First, Japan's economy is becoming ever more global. Second, their strongest supporters are among the younger, more flexible generation of Japanese managers, who were bred on Disney and Nintendo and are now coming of age. And, finally, they are offering something new. Japanese management can change without merely becoming Western.

## What Japan Can Still Teach the West

Two of the greatest problems facing managers everywhere are actually dire needs: to cut costs and to manage knowledge more effectively. Although Western firms have been making most of the progress in these fields, Japanese managers can still teach the West a trick or two.

On the cost-cutting side, Western companies are wearying of brutalist management fads such as reengineering, downsizing, and delayering. So far, Japanese companies have been noticeably more successful than their Western peers at controlling costs without tearing out the innovative heart of a company. This is not just a matter of having sacked fewer people. Japanese firms have encouraged the entire workforce to help in reaching cost-reduction targets. In many companies, the walls are decorated with posters showing progress in cost control. At Topcon, an optical company, the slogan is "The budget is God."

This communal spirit has clearly benefited from the self-sacrificing attitude of senior managers in Japan. By contrast, executive salaries in the West have risen relentlessly in recent years, regardless of the performance of the company or the riskiness of the business. The public furor over this practice threatens to create a less friendly political climate for business in general. In Japan, companies believe that when the going gets tough, bosses should be the first people to sacrifice their bonuses and salaries, before they start restructuring the rest of the company.

Similarly, the Japanese reluctance to sack middle managers willy-nilly may also rebound in their favor. Yes, Japanese firms have often been slow to separate the wheat from the chaff. But, in Japanese eyes, the middle manager is not just an expendable link in the chain of command but a possessor of a valuable perspective on a company's business. In particular, the middle manager knits together two visions—the strategic view of senior managers and the detailed operational view of front-line workers.

As for suppliers, there seems little doubt that big Japanese companies treat them more roughly than they used to (and much more roughly than their own employees). There is even a name for the new trend—*shitauke ijime,* or "subcontractor bullying." Small and midsize businesses shed nearly two million jobs in 1989–94, with many businesses going under. Otaku, east of Tokyo, once a bustling area of tiny workshops, is now a shadow of its former self, as business after business has been squeezed to death. "We just sweat and sweat until we're all skin and bones," one of Matsushita's subcontractors told *The Wall Street Journal* on July 25, 1995. "Subcontractors like us are becoming weaker, while assemblers like Matsushita are amassing strength." On the other hand, what was remarkable about the *Journal's* story was that it *was* a story. In Europe or America, suppliers are used to being battered. In Japan, they have until recently been protected.

It may seem strange to suggest that the Japanese can help Western firms manage knowledge, given that Americans have been the leaders in so many knowledge-intensive industries, from software to entertainment. Nevertheless, a new generation of Japanese management thinkers, particularly Ikujiro Nonaka and Hirotaka Takeuchi of Hitotsubashi University, argue that the Japanese still have certain advantages. Western companies, they admit, are well ahead of the Japanese in managing the sort of formal, explicit knowledge that can be faxed or

E-mailed. (At Microsoft, front-line employees receive an average of 50 E-mail messages a day, and Bill Gates receives 200; at many of the best Japanese companies, E-mail has still not been installed.) But, they add, the Japanese are better at managing tacit knowledge—the informal occupational lore generated by workers grappling with everyday problems and passed on in cafeterias.

This skill allows companies to tap into the insights of the bulk of their employees and ensures that one man's hunch can become an entire firm's competitive advantage. The most important trick is to encourage workers to spend as much time as possible together, informally as well as formally. Companies routinely divide workers into teams, often expecting them to stick with the same colleagues for years on end. New recruits work closely with "mentors" or "team leaders," learning far more from them than they do from formal training courses. After-work drinking sessions and country retreats play an important part in promoting informal understanding. Some companies talk of "nommunication," a word that is made up of the Japanese word for drinking *(nomu)* and communication.[11] Honda and Canon both make frequent use of "brainstorming camps"—informal meetings in country inns in which project-development teams (and anybody else who wants to contribute) work intensively on a project, but also drink sake, share meals, and even bathe together in hot springs.

These sessions are useful not only for promoting trust among workers but also for sparking bright ideas. It was at one of these sessions that a team from Canon, trying to make a mini-photocopier, hit upon the solution to a problem that had been troubling them for months: what to do about the expense of repairing the drum. After a morning spent puzzling over this problem, the team leader sent out for some beer. As the group drank the beer, the conversation turned to the question of how much it costs to make a disposable can. This sparked off an idea: why not equip the photocopier with a disposable can-shaped drum.[12]

Sources of informal knowledge exist outside the company too. The head of a team at Matsushita, trying to develop an automatic breadmaker, decided that the best bread came from the Osaka International Hotel. So she apprenticed herself to the head baker and watched the way he worked. After weeks of study, she realized that the secret of making perfect bread was not just kneading the dough, but also twisting it. She made certain that her machine could imitate this combination of movements.

The point about tacit knowledge is that it is always there: a company does not have to create it but rather must remove barriers that prevent it from flowing around the place. Kao, a chemicals and cosmetics company, holds all its meetings in the open, allowing anybody to drop in. Half the floor space on the executive floor is given over to a "decision-making room." Kao's quarterly R&D conference regularly attracts some 1,800 people (out of a workforce of 7,000). The company encourages customers to phone in with suggestions and complaints; it receives some 50,000 calls a year. It also set up a computer network that gives all employees, however lowly, access to all but the most sensitive personal information. Even the president's expense account is on public view.

One problem with implicit knowledge is that it is difficult to transfer across borders even when people share the same language. (As any Englishman who has lived in California will tell you, irony barely travels across the Atlantic and has never crossed the Rockies.) Although Japanese companies have been fairly weak at extracting ideas from their foreign subsidiaries, they have proved to be fairly capable teachers—particularly of tacit knowledge about manufacturing. In places as far apart as Derbyshire and Tennessee, local workers are using "Japanese" methods to produce Toyotas and Nissans for their domestic markets, and they often give plants in Japan a run for their money when it comes to quality and efficiency.

## Turning Japanese

Although ideas like tacit knowledge might sound vague and unfamiliar at the moment, Western managers would be foolish to ignore them. In some ways, the world is becoming more like Japan, not less so. Even the most successful Western companies can no longer dominate entire markets in the way that General Motors or IBM once did. They are also finding that they have less and less time to make money out of a new product. By contrast, the best Japanese firms are used to overcrowded markets and instant imitation. Japan has nine car companies whereas the United States has only three. Nothing remains secret in Japan for long: word leaks out at school reunions and through meetings with suppliers. Japanese firms have always lived in a world of what some management thinkers call "hypercompetition."

But this is no time to go back to the crude Japan worship of the early 1980s, with their "quality circles," morning calisthenics, and thrice-yearly pilgrimages to Toyota City. Japanese companies are too bloated and too inept at the "off-the-wall" thinking that seems to go on in America's most inventive companies. But they are clearly learning fast, under the tutelage of men like Kobayashi and Ohmae; and there are some things that they do much better than their rivals in the West. As Westerners have learned in the past, it is always worth keeping at least one eye on the East.

# CHAPTER 12

## A NEW MODEL IN ASIA?

ANYBODY WHO DOUBTS how much China has changed should spend an afternoon eavesdropping on interviews for the 20-month MBA course at the China Europe International Business School (CEIBS).[1] The school, hidden away in Shanghai's sprawling industrial suburbs, claims to be the fastest growing in the world. Although the course costs $4,000 (or nearly twice the average annual income in China), its 65 places attract 4,000 applicants. Most of the interviewees are in their mid-20s and exhibit a drive that would make the average Harvard MBA blush. Asked "What are your weaknesses?" one replies, "I am too successful." Several of the young entrepreneurs have applied to CEIBS before and been rejected for poor English; despite apparently working from dawn to dusk, they have still found the energy to cram in nighttime language courses. Many of the best candidates are women: one, a tiny birdlike figure who works for a local textiles company, bosses around the panel of professors in a way that Margaret Thatcher's cabinet ministers would have found familiar.

However, the most memorable candidate is a tall young man—call him "Deng." He explains that his career has been carefully divided into three stages, each suited to make the most out of modern China. The first was university, where Deng finished at the top of his class. The next stage was a prized job at a foreign-trade organization, chosen for its "complicated" work; pushed to explain what he means, Deng says that there is a lot of corruption, though (here he shows a momentary sign of self-doubt as he fingers an expensive watch) obviously nothing that involved Deng. Now he wants to go to a business school that teaches Western ideas: "China needs managers more than anything else."

Deng is on to a sure thing. By 1996, there were some 80,000 foreign joint ventures in China. If each requires four managers, then even this small sector of the Chinese economy needs nearly a quarter of a million managers, but China currently produces a mere 300 MBAs a year. Even adding in those Chinese students who study overseas and the American-born Chinese that some Western firms have tried, usually unsuccessfully, to import, there is a dramatic gulf between demand and supply. Salaries for managers in Shanghai rose 10 times between 1992 and 1996; the turnover rate for managerial jobs at some foreign joint ventures is about 30 percent a year.

Chaotic China's thirst for management may be an extreme example. However, even in hyperorganized Singapore, Nanyang Technological University, which can offer only 125 places in its MBA course, has taken to selling prospectuses at $25 each to hold students at bay: it still gets 900 applications. McKinsey's fastest-growing practice is in India. Elsewhere, most of McKinsey's clients like to keep quiet about the fact that they have called in consultants; in India, McKinsey has to plead with its clients not to buy advertising space to proclaim the fact that they have secured its services. Open an Asian newspaper and, where you might have expected a full-page advertisement foretelling the imminent arrival of the Rolling Stones, you find instead a similar spread announcing that "the world's most competitive man," Michael Porter, is on his way. On the other hand, on a continent where news agents actually put publications with names like *Supply Chain Management News* on top of *TIME* and *Playboy*, an evening with Porter seems quite an event.

## Why Asia Matters

From the perspective of Western management theorists, all this implies that non-Japanese Asia is simply another slightly overenthusiastic pupil waiting to be taught. In fact, developing Asia has management ideas of its own, and, over the next decade, these ideas will have an enormously powerful effect on management theory. The comparison to bear in mind (even if it is one that, in the end, looks unlikely to be fully realized) is with Japan. When Japanese cars and radios first began to appear in America, American managers presumed that Toyota and Sony were beating them just because they had cheaper labor or because they worked harder. The reality, as pointed out in Chapter 11, was that they were being outmanaged.

Nowadays, American bosses are grumbling about cheap imports from the likes of Thailand, China, India, and South Korea. Are they in for another surprise? The glib answer is "not of the same scale." On the whole, developing Asia still has more to learn from established Western management theory than the other way around—something that was partly proved by the pounding the region's stockmarkets and currencies took in the autumn of 1997. And even if Asian companies do push all before them, it will not be because they were sticking to some easily imitable set text, such as Toyota's manuals. The new management "theories" that are emerging in non-Japanese Asia are instinctive rather than intellectual.

Yet the region demands attention on at least two scores. The first (general) reason is the underlying power of its economies and the opportunities that they are throwing up. According to the World Bank, the world's fastest-growing country in 1985–94 was Thailand (which sped along at an annual rate of 8.6 percent), followed by South Korea and China (both 7.8 percent), and then Singapore (6.1 percent). Those rates may be harder to achieve after the correction of 1997, but, as the region opens up its domestic markets, it is becoming something of a cockpit of competing capitalisms, with a dozen or so different sorts of companies battling away. These include not only readily recognizable beasts, such as Western and Japanese multinationals, but also less familiar local creatures, ranging from China's state-owned companies to South Korea's *chaebol*.

This brings us to the second (particular) reason why developing Asia demands attention: the business networks created by the overseas Chinese. Although these owe little to Western management ideas, they have so far managed to trounce all comers in many of the world's most vibrant markets. As we shall see, the strength of the overseas-Chinese empires has a lot to do with history and connections. In other respects, however, such as their ability to build entrepreneurial networks, they are as "modern" as any other nation on the planet. From some angles, the best of them offer a glimpse of how the loose "virtual" companies so beloved of Western management gurus might turn out.

Why focus on the overseas-Chinese companies and not on, say, South Korea's *chaebol*? After all, many more Westerners have heard of Samsung, Hyundai, and Daewoo than have heard of Robert Kuok or Li Ka-shing. There are also many more case studies. The answer—and this, once again, is a generalization—is that the other management structures in developing Asia look like pale (or refined) versions of ones already discussed in this book. For instance, the *chaebol* are impressive enough, but structurally they resemble Japan's *keiretsu*. The South Koreans are even following the Japanese into the same industries: cars and electronics. Similarly, the big Indian businesses, now emerging from several decades of protected markets, follow a sort of bureaucratic version of Western management theory. This may change—India is the one country in Asia that is stocked full of managers, and it has a particularly sparkling set of middle-size companies—but as yet nobody is looking to India for ideas.

By contrast, the entrepreneurial "bamboo network" of family businesses created by the overseas Chinese is not just another interesting variant, but a full fledged alternative model—and one that looks intriguingly powerful. Most Westerners already know that Taiwan, Hong Kong, and Singapore are all heavily populated with entrepreneurial Chinese. Now they are beginning to realize just how powerful those entrepreneurs have become. In the Philippines, the overseas Chinese make up only 1 percent of the country's population but control over half the stock market. In Indonesia, the equivalent proportions are 4 percent and 75 percent; in Malaysia, 32 percent and 60 percent. Hellmut Schütte, a management professor at Insead's Euro-Asia Centre, reckons that by 1996 the 51 million overseas Chinese controlled an economy worth $7 trillion—roughly the same size as that of the 1.2 billion mainlanders.

These paragons of capitalism are desperately hard to pin down. No single Chinese family firm appears in the world's 100 biggest by market capitalization; yet probably at least 20 of these families are worth $5 billion or more (America, by contrast, can muster only 10). Like commercial icebergs, most Chinese families exhibit only a small portion of themselves to the outside world. In early 1996, Robert Kuok, a Malaysian Chinese who may well be the most powerful of them all, controlled the Shangri-La hotel chain (market capitalization: $3 billion) and the *South China Morning Post* ($1.1 billion), but most of his assets in China, Hong Kong, and around the Pacific Rim were squirreled away in a network of private companies. In November 1995, the *Singapore Business Times* calculated that the seven biggest investors on the Kuala Lumpur Stock Exchange were all ethnic Chinese. The richest of them, a gambling magnate called Lim Goh Tong, owned $5.2 billion worth of shares in Kuala Lumpur alone. Previous estimates of his wealth by *Forbes, Asiaweek,* and others had put his total wealth at barely half that figure.

This lack of information extends to management theorists. So far, there are only a handful of thinkers who know much at all about Chinese family capitalism: Gordon Redding at Hong Kong University is the leader; Henri-Claude de Bettignies, who teaches a course in Asian business at both Stanford and Insead, is another much mentioned name. The most comprehensive book on the overseas Chinese so far was put together by the East Asia Analytical Unit of Australia's Department of Foreign Affairs.[2] Already research teams from the Harvard Business School are working hard to catch up. Most of the existing work encourages the idea that the overseas Chinese exhibit all the networking and entrepreneurial skills that Western companies lack, such as "trust" and "flexibility": they can be big or small, local or regional according to need, using their ready-made network of allies to dart in and out of markets. One of the more recent books about the overseas Chinese, *Lords of the Rim* (1995) by Sterling Seagrave, begins with a quotation from Sun Tzu: "Be so subtle that you are invisible. Be so mysterious that you are intangible. Then you will control your rival's fate."

Are the overseas Chinese really that good?

## All in the Family

Consider a typical tale of Chinese family capitalism. In 1994, Richard Savage, a Singaporean businessman, met some officials from North Korea. He passed on these contacts to his brother, Ronald, who works at Loxley, a Thai firm controlled by the Lamsam family. Loxley's business lines include, among other things, environmental engineering, brewing, electrical appliances, power plants, health food, chemicals, cellular telephones, entertainment, property, and six computer companies. North Korea was assigned to Boonyakit Tansakul, a younger Western-educated member of the family. In October 1995, following a successful dinner where senior members of the Lamsam family met various North Korean politicians, Loxley won a controversial contract to build an international telephone system for North Korea's new Rajin Sombong free-trade zone. By early 1996, although Lamsam had yet to see a dollar out of the hermit kingdom, Boonyakit was convinced that within a decade Rajin Sombong would become the "Singapore of the North."

Such entrepreneurial chutzpah is typical of overseas-Chinese capitalism. Its roots lie in the families that migrated from various mainland provinces—usually coastal ones such as Guandong, Fujian, or Hainan—about 100 years ago. As with Jewish entrepreneurs, family ties have been tempered by persecution. It is only 30 years since the last anti-Chinese pogrom in Indonesia; Malaysia's 26-year-old New Economic Policy favors ethnic Malays over ethnic Chinese. "It is not greed that drives the overseas Chinese," argues Simon Murray, who used to run Li Kashing's empire in Hong Kong. "It is fear—and the yearning for the protection that money will give you."

In this insecure world, clans have proved almost as important as families. In most cases, the funds to start businesses came from fellow clan members. Even today, a fair chunk of Southeast Asia's food business is controlled by Chinese who speak the same regional dialect. One Cantonese banker confesses that he still has to make a point of spending twice as long on the telephone with non-Cantonese clients, to reassure them that he is not discriminating against them. The long-standing informal alliance between the two richest men in Malaysia and Indonesia, Robert Kuok and Liem Sioe Liong, owes much to fact that both are Hokkien Chinese, as are two other allies, Khoo Kay Peng (who founded Malayan United Industries) and Mochtar Riady (who set up Indonesia's Lippo group).

Chinese managers like to boast that, in contrast to their legalistic Western peers, their businesses are based on negotiating relationships, not contracts. The chief assets of an overseas-Chinese business are usually its *guanxi* (or connections). In a time when many Western management theorists are exalting the importance of "tacit knowledge," "supplier-provider relationships," and the like, this makes the overseas Chinese look refreshingly modern. In fact, many of the most important *guanxi* are political ones. In the late 1940s, Liem Sioe Liong, the founder of the Salim Group, was working for his uncle's peanut-oil business in Central Java when he struck up a friendship with a local army quartermaster who went on to become president: Raden Suharto. The people of Bangkok joke that the Charoen Pokphand group, which is controlled by the Sophon-Panich family, has employed so many Thai politicians that it could hold a cabinet meeting.

The idea of loose entrepreneurial networks based around "trust" is the sort of thing that tends to make researchers from Harvard go all gooey—often to the amusement of the networkers themselves. ("I can't think of an organization where in-fighting is more rife," says one well-connected Chinese businesswoman.) In truth, most overseas-Chinese firms only work because they are centralized dictatorships: the head of the family makes nearly all the decisions. This helps in businesses such as those dealing in property, where one handshake can buy a building. It also allows firms to change direction quickly. In Hong Kong, industries making wigs, flowers, and radios have sprung up, profited, and then disappeared.

In China, such nimble-footed network building has brought quick rewards once again. The overseas Chinese account for half the foreign direct investment in China. By 1996, Charoen Pokphand, which first entered the mainland in 1979, could claim revenues of $3 billion from China. It owned some 80 agribusiness companies in China, stretching all the way from breeder farms to fast-food chicken shops, not to mention other businesses, for example, in beer, property, and motorcycles. How on earth could a food company get hold of a motorcycle plant when most of the Western car industry is clamoring to get into China? The answer, as usual, is through *guanxi*. Charoen then bought the skills it needed by forming an alliance with Honda, just as it has done in retailing (with Holland's Makro) and telecommunications (with America's NYNEX).

## Unexportable

On a small scale, Chinese family management is as good as anything the West has to offer. Up to a certain size, Chinese management can cope with virtually any problem, particularly in the fast-growing markets where it is based. The flexibility of such companies often puts Western companies to shame. Many of the healthiest businesses in Europe and America are small and family-owned too, but they tend to operate in only one industry and only one country. The glory of the bamboo network is that it spreads across a variety of companies and industries, seizing opportunities as they present themselves.

But once the companies begin to reach the same size as Western multinationals, the comparison with foreign companies is less flattering. Unlike the Japanese, the overseas Chinese have had little success outside Asia. Most simply have not tried. Those who have, such as Li Ka-shing, have often run into trouble (although in the mid-1990s he finally found a winner with Orange, a British cellular telephone network). Henri-Claude de Bettignies, of Insead, says that he advises Asian companies to learn how to manage across cultures first: "You cannot be an amateur in America or Europe," he says flatly.

For critics of Chinese capitalism, the failures outside Asia, not to mention the region's economic trouble in 1997, mean that people should cast a more critical eye over the successes at home. Their first charge is that most overseas-Chinese fortunes have not come from outmanaging their opponents but from gambling in a casino where, until 1997, it seemed that nobody could lose: Asian property. This charge rings particularly true in Hong Kong, where, for example, several Cathay-Pacific pilots are now multimillionaires simply because they bought a small flat in the Mid-Levels, now one of the most sought-after parts of town, in the 1970s. Most of the local billionaires, including Li Ka-shing, have made most of their money from bricks and mortar. But easy pickings from property may be a little harder to come by in the future. Offices in booming Asian cities are now more expensive than offices in the West. Also, Hong Kong's unique position as the only gateway into China is slipping. Already several Western companies have leapfrogged straight into Beijing or Shanghai, ignoring the established practice of setting up a base camp in Hong Kong.

By itself, the charge that the overseas Chinese are just overgrown property magnates is not entirely true; although property is usually their main business, they have also been successful in other fields. Other, less blunt criticisms have also been voiced. Trevor MacMurray, a consultant at McKinsey, argues that too many overseas-Chinese businesses are "structurers" as opposed to "builders," meaning that they chase after franchises of one sort or another (e.g., running the Philippines long-distance telephone system or the Macao ferry) rather than trying to create internationally competitive products or services. Many of the more profitable franchises are being worn down by deregulation and competition, so the firms' weaknesses as builders can be expected to be exposed.

In most overseas-Chinese businesses, manufacturing still means applying cheap hands to borrowed technology. Gordon Redding argues that the problem has as much to do with organization as with ideas. An old-style family company is constitutionally incapable of building something like Toyota's Lexus, he argues, because sophisticated car making requires coordination, decentralization, and bosses who trust their employees. "You need to have departments, such as marketing, production, and design, rather than just vague areas given to Number-one son."

Another growing weakness is people. Few bright managers want to work for an organization where they can never become the chairman, and where career ladders tend to be vague. Too often, respect for authority (and age) means that criticizing the boss is unacceptable. One survey in Hong Kong found that Chinese professionals preferred to work for Western and Japanese managers (anybody, in fact, who is not Chinese). Another survey, this time of 1,000 executives around the world by Britain's Cranfield School of Management, found that those working for Hong Kong businesses felt most out of line with their companies' thinking.

## Why Jimmy Lai Is Half Right

Owing to these problems, some experts say, overseas-Chinese capitalism belongs to the past, not the future. As

evidence, they cite the progress made by many Western companies in most of Asia's consumer-goods markets. One of these
cynics is Jimmy Lai, Hong Kong's best-known publisher. He argues that "*guanxi* are dead. They were important as long as
business meant striking deals with only a few politicians or relations. They count for nothing in consumer markets. You have to
make good products or offer good services. In fact, connections,
particularly corrupt ones, will count against you soon—even in
China." He gives the example of one well-known Hong Kong
businessman and his connections with the Chinese leadership.
All those connections, argues Lai, depended on Deng Xiaoping,
who died in early 1997.

Lai's own career shows he is half right. As the founder of the
enormously successful Giordano, the first Asian retailing chain
where staff deliberately said "Good Morning" to customers, and
as the publisher of *Apple,* one of Hong Kong's fastest-growing
publications, Lai is living proof that giving people what they
want is a sure way to make money in modern Asia. However, Lai
has also been forced to sell off his stake in Giordano because he
criticized the Chinese government in his newspapers, and he
needs round-the-clock protection against Hong Kong triads
whom he has also offended. As for the well-known businessmen
whom Lai criticizes, his contacts in Beijing seem to go considerably deeper than the Deng family.

Overseas-Chinese companies, no less than any other sort,
are the product of their environment; and as that environment
changes, so do they. "We have never had big home markets," explains Raymond Ch'ien, who admits that Lam Soon, his Hong
Kong food company, like many of its peers, had to change the
way it did business when it went into the mainland. Virtually
every big family group is experimenting in one way or another
with importing Western ideas. The question is how committed
they are to change. The most common response has been to
pack off all the children to Harvard and Stanford. Unfortunately, when these young MBAs return, they usually rush off
and do deals rather than try to build or reorganize businesses.

Another slightly panicky reaction has been to recruit more
managers, particularly Western-trained managers. Virtually all
the general managers at Robert Kuok's Shangri-La hotel chain
are Westerners (as are several of his closest advisers). But this
enthusiasm for management often needs to be taken with a

pinch of salt. Usually, the Western adviser's role is not dissimilar to the (non-Italian) "consiglieri" in the Godfather films: a useful administrator but the first person to be excluded when the family does anything important. Outside investors, too, are treated like second-class citizens. Even though family stakes in public companies are seldom more than 40 percent, they usually act as if they own the whole thing. Board meetings often last only 15 minutes, and assets are brazenly shuffled between private and public companies. This will gradually change as Asian companies issue more capital (some $36 billion of new shares were issued in 1995), but there is considerable resistance. Transparency, like branding and human-resource departments, is regarded as "Un-Asian."

### Full of Western Promise

The idea that management theory is somehow "un-Asian" is twaddle. There is little, for instance, that any Western carrier can teach Singapore Airlines about service or marketing, even though the airline has a distinctly Asian character. But then Singapore Airlines, unlike most Chinese family companies, has a marketing department, an advertising budget, and several sophisticated training programs. In early 1996, David Li, the chief executive of the Bank of East Asia, one of Hong Kong's biggest banks, warned Asian business people not to assume that there was a uniquely Asian way of doing business. He pointed out that Confucius (a name usually invoked rapidly in any argument about Asian business) actually had no time at all for merchants. Rewarding employees well or building up a core of professional managers, argued Li, is not "Western"; it is simply good management.

That does not mean that Western management theories can be grafted onto Eastern structures at random. In the West, for instance, "business process reengineering" has been used to cut flab in mature industries. In markets growing as quickly as Asia's, a little slack is often necessary. Nevertheless, a "kinder" version of reengineering seems to have worked extremely well in Asia. Both Thai Farmers Bank (which, like Loxley, is controlled by the Lamsam family) and the Bank of East Asia claim enormous increases in productivity from embracing the fad—though neither has sacked anybody in the process.

A similar gradual approach also looks appropriate when it comes to concentrating on core competencies. As noted earlier, outside Asia companies do best if they build up scale and expertise in one or two specialist areas. Within Asia, diversification has not yet proved a weakness: after all, in a country like Thailand where nobody has any telecommunications experience, why shouldn't a chicken-food company like Charoen Pokphand grab a license? Indeed, it has often made sense for families to diversify their risks. In some fast-developing countries such as China and Vietnam, this scattershot approach may still yield dividends. In general, though, companies that want to be internationally competitive will have to focus on a few core businesses.

### The Hereditary Defect

There is one final compelling reason why even those Chinese entrepreneurs who never want to leave Asia need to reorganize their management: succession. At present, because they are unable to separate ownership from management, all Chinese companies wobble when command passes from one generation to another. In some cases, empires have actually been split up: Sir Y. K. Pao, a Hong Kong billionaire, divided his empire so that it could be run by his four sons-in-law. In other cases, fights have broken out. In 1992, the Soeryadjaya family lost control of Astra, Indonesia's second biggest firm, because of enormous losses at Bank Summa, which had been run by one of the sons. Until 1995, Winston Wang looked certain to inherit Formosa Plastics, Taiwan's biggest industrial company; then, following reports of an extramarital affair, he appeared to have fallen out with his father, Wang Yung-ching.

One old Chinese proverb says that wealth never survives the third generation. But succession is a problem for family businesses everywhere. The difference is that, outside Asia, successful family businesses—Mars, Ford, Sainsbury, and so on—have turned into dynastic corporations, where there are clear divisions between the family and the firm, so that the competence of the children is less of an issue. Korea's *chaebol* have just begun to grapple with this problem. In January 1996, Hyundai broke with tradition by announcing plans to bring in outside directors; it is also trying to promote nonfamily members inside the company.

## Shih Who Must Be Obeyed

The temptation with overseas-Chinese management is simply to leave it alone, on the grounds that the overseas Chinese have come up with an extremely sophisticated way of running small companies, but that they will never mature into large worldbeaters in the same way that, say, Honda and Toyota have. And where is the harm in that? The real strength of overseas-Chinese management lies in its ability to keep on building these networks of fast-moving small companies and its capacity to cope with uncertainty. Provided that the stodgy old empires do not get too much in the way, this looks like a recipe for prosperity. As long as there are Chinese business people who believe a small godforsaken piece of North Korea can become "the Singapore of the North," Chinese capitalism does not need management theory.

However, a few Chinese companies have begun to mix Western and Asian ideas to create something new and exciting. Consider two fairly dingy offices, one in Taipei, one of the world's most hideous cities; the other in Kowloon, the overcrowded finger of land still considered the wrong side of the harbor by those who live on Hong Kong Island.

The first office belongs to Stan Shih. Not even his friends would describe Shih as a snappy dresser, and his office feels like a 1970s Holiday Inn suite. Nevertheless, Shih is the brains behind one of the world's most interesting companies. Like many Taiwanese technology companies, the Acer group first appeared in the 1980s as an equipment manufacturer, making computer parts for better-known Western and Japanese companies. By 1996, it was still making computers for Hitachi and components for a host of other big technology companies. But Acer had also become the seventh biggest personal computer maker in its own right and was planning an assault on the consumer-electronics market as well. Shih was confidently predicting that Acer's revenues—which in 1995 alone rose by three-quarters, to $5.7 billion—would reach $15 billion by the end of the decade.

A visit to Acer's main factory in the Hsinchu Science Park, Taiwan's technology showcase, seems at first to confirm every Westerner's prejudice that people like Shih get ahead by uniting cheap Asian hands with Western technology. To the left sit hundreds of imported young Filipinas assembling

Apple Powerbooks; to the right, a robot transports integrated circuits and plays a noisy electronic version of "Camptown Races." There is a little truth in this prejudice, but not much. As the Filipinas prove, Shih is just as short of cheap labor as anybody else. Besides, the real point about Acer is that it is not just a component supplier; its manufacturing organization is also world-class. Acer has clearly passed Gordon Redding's Lexus test—as Redding admits.

Shih's achievement, in other words, has as much to do with management and organization as it does with technology. Shih's philosophy has been colored by two experiences. In the 1970s, he worked for a technology company owned by an old-style family, but the business collapsed—in part because it was extremely difficult to criticize any decisions made by the family even when they were obviously wrong; and in part because the company's profits were siphoned off into the family's private companies. Shih's wife has always helped him at Acer, but he refuses to let his children join him there. The second experience was a crisis at Acer in the late 1980s, caused when the head office forced different businesses to follow one central strategy of expansion. Shih, who tendered his resignation at the time, has since tried to decentralize power in a way that few Chinese families (or American chief executives) would countenance.

Acer is split up into a network of different companies, all with their own bosses, personnel systems, and salary structures. (By 1996, only two had stock market listings; Shih plans to list 19 more by 2000.) When goods pass from one division to another, they do so at market prices, and no division is under any obligation to use the other's services. Shih's own role is to organize the headquarters, which employs 80 people. Its revenues come from dividends, and from charging the other groups for its legal and accounting services. Shih insists that he would not object if any division left the group. His only stipulation would be that the departing company could not carry the Acer name.

In other words, Shih has taken all the best features of the Chinese family business—speed, entrepreneurialism, networking—and institutionalized them into a meritocratic system. In so doing, he has created an organization that would seem fresh even if it was based in San Jose instead of Taipei. Indeed, Shih's federation of small independent firms could be the answer to the problems some Western companies are experiencing. IBM's businesses, for instance, will probably never develop personalities of their own as long as they remain divisions. But if Big Blue was divided up in the same way that Acer has been, some of that hidden talent might emerge.

Interestingly, other entrepreneurial Asian technology companies seem to be taking the same tack as Acer. The networks of small specialist exporters that populate places like Hsinchu Science Park and Bangalore (India's "Silicon plateau") tend to have the same pick-and-match attitude toward Western and Asian management styles, probably because most of their founders once worked for Western companies. Another Hsinchu Park company, Microelectronics Technology Inc., a pioneer in satellite communication, was founded by Patrick Wang, an exile from Hewlett-Packard; Morris Chang, the founder of Taiwan Semiconductor Manufacturing Corporation (TSMC), the world's biggest chip foundry, worked at Texas Instruments for 25 years. TSMC employs 50 engineers who have had more than 10 years' experience in the United States. Twenty-six of its managers have been to business school (10 of them in America). "It's like working for an American company," says Donald Brooks, TSMC's president.

## Kowloon Rising

All this seems to indicate that if you want to survive in a business as global as the high-technology industry, you have to embrace some Western management ideas. However, our second dingy office from Kowloon shows that Western management ideas can also be applied to that oldest of Chinese family businesses, the trading house. Once again, the result is a hybrid.

The office in this case belongs to William Fung—and to be fair, it is slightly smarter than Shih's. Pride of place is given to a picture of Fung's class at Harvard Business School—an institution his brother, Victor, also attended. It was shortly after they left the school in the 1970s, when they were both working in America, that the Fung brothers were summoned back to Hong Kong by their mother, who was worried about their father's health. In the best Chinese style, the brothers were ordered to take over the management of Li & Fung, a trading house founded in Canton in 1906 by their grandfather, Fung Pak-liu. Trading houses act as middlemen for importers and exporters, taking a cut along the way.

The two brothers began by examining their family business as if it were a business school case study. Their first two decisions, both of which their father acceded to, were that the company should give up employing all their cousins; and that it should float on the stock market, not so much to raise cash as to bring in outside advisers and to give the cousins a chance to sell out. The idea was to make the business as transparent as possible. The Fung brothers also toyed with the idea of introducing another Western custom—sacking people to cut costs. This time, their father stopped them, persuading them that this would make recruiting other staff difficult.

Li & Fung has redefined the role of a trader as "a network manager." It specializes in labor-intensive industries, such as toys, shoes, and handbags. In all these businesses, the assembly part of production tends to move to wherever hands are cheapest: bags that used to be sewn together in Malaysia are now made in China and may one day move to India. The other characteristic of the Fung businesses is that many of the components are made in different parts of Asia. Show William Fung your briefcase, and he will say that the leather was probably tanned in Korea, the metal studs (that you had never noticed before) came from Japan, and so on. Li & Fung makes nothing itself; instead, its core competence, as Fung puts it, is to act as a "value-chain coordinator," linking the different arms together, designing products, finding customers, and sometimes financing business ventures.

In 1995, Li & Fung bought the Hong Kong trading arm of Inchcape, an old British company, for HK$475 million—a deal that doubled Li & Fung's sales to HK$12 billion. The Fung brothers egg on their managers with performance-pay structures; and staff are encouraged to criticize their managers. Nevertheless, for all the American business school pictures on the office walls, Li & Fung is still identifiably a Chinese company. It survives by doing deals; and even if it is no longer run as a family employment center, it is still run by two family members, whose word, in the end, is law.

### Coming to a Town near You

If nothing else, our quick look at management in developing Asia shows that management theory remains a living science: at a time when many things in the West have a sense of déjà vu, developing Asia has uncovered new questions and seen perhaps the glimmer of new answers. Over the next decade, Western management readers will hear much more about companies such as Li & Fung and Acer, and about overseas-Chinese companies in general. The basic struggle that the overseas Chinese face—how to achieve a balance between organization and entrepreneurialism—is exactly the same one that most big Western (and Japanese) companies face. The intriguing difference is that whereas big Western firms are trying to graft entrepreneurial skills onto organizational ones, most developing Asian companies are doing the reverse. As this chapter has made clear, on balance the overseas Chinese have more to learn than they have to teach. Yet there is also a strong feeling of "Back to the Future." When Tom Peters orders tired American managers to obliterate every structure in sight, the sort of virtual company he envisages is not that far from those on display in Asia.

How important is the overseas-Chinese model? It is hard to imagine it sweeping across the West in the same way that "Japanese" ideas such as lean production and quality did. In the immediate future, even in their home markets, overseas-Chinese companies will have to change as Asia's economy, particularly its property market, slows down and more Western companies begin to compete. Research and development, marketing, branding, command structures—in other words, the sorts of things that most people refer to as management—will all become more important. On the other hand, there is plainly something there. Overseas-Chinese business cannot just be written off as a fortuitous mixture of hard work and connections. Even if what might be called the overseas-Chinese model ends up being subsumed into what might be called the Western one, it will still bring something with it. The new hybrids that are emerging, such as Acer and Li & Fung, are genuine mixtures of two traditions.

All this leaves "Deng," the young ambitious student at CEIBS with whom we began this chapter, supremely well placed. Providing that Beijing's politicians do not interfere, he should have the best of all worlds: an entrepreneurial nature, a knack for making contacts (remember that gold watch), and a grasp of management ideas. Visit any big Chinese family company and you see organizations in need of management. That does not mean that Deng needs to reengineer the whole lot of them. But there is undoubtedly room to reorganize their manufacturing and to set up organizational structures that allow workers a clearer career. In Hong Kong, Shanghai, or Bangkok, the words "Human Resources Department" no longer sound like a terrible offense to the English language; they sound like progress. Deng will follow in their wake.

# PART FIVE

# NEW FRONTIERS

# CHAPTER 13

MANAGING LEVIATHAN: THE PUBLIC SECTOR

"OF COURSE YOU HAVE to be a quality organization nowadays—but that's not enough. We are reengineering all the key processes and empowering the front-line people so that we can perform for our customers." Any journalist sitting down to lunch with William Bratton, the commissioner of the New York Police Department (NYPD) from 1994 to early 1996, who expected to discuss the truth about the Mafia or heroin smuggling was in for a disappointment. Bratton's tenure at the NYPD was as much a crusade against mismanagement as against crime. Bratton was probably the first commissioner ever to explicitly equate reduced crime with profits and the population of the city with customers. "We've already had some interest from Harvard about a case study," he said enthusiastically at one point; at another, he described the executive breakfasts where the likes of Jack Welch of General Electric and Ralph Larsen of Johnson & Johnson came to discuss management with Bratton's officers.[1]

Bratton's penchant for management theory dates back to his previous position as police commissioner in Boston, where he used to pop in for lectures at the Harvard Business School. When he took over the NYPD job in January 1994, he made a great fuss about introducing the sort of basic office computer technology that most companies would have long since taken for granted. However, his biggest changes had to do with organization and accountability. Bratton devolved power to his 86 precinct commanders and set demanding performance targets. This was unusual enough in itself; but what made the move particularly noteworthy was the sort of performance targets he set, which all revolved around preventing crime rather than just reacting to it. Bratton made it clear that he was less interested in the "response time" to an emergency call than why the call had been made in the first place. The "profits" he sought were the general well-being of all New Yorkers, which he measured not just in terms of the crime rate but also in terms of things like the number of businesses setting up in the city.

Every week, Bratton hauled in his top officers to an early morning meeting and examined the statistics that all his new computers were generating for each precinct. At one such meeting in 1995, Captain Michael Gabriel was questioned closely because murders in his Brooklyn precinct were up 62 percent when those in the rest of the city were down 32 percent. The center of the murders was a single street in which 44 shops were fronts for drug dealing. Gabriel had only managed to close down 9. He was told to put more pressure on securing court orders.[2]

In Bratton's two years in command, crime fell sharply. In 1995, some 1,000 fewer New Yorkers were murdered than in 1990. Bratton's crime-busting efforts attracted the interest of government officials from countries as far afield as Saudi Arabia and South Africa. Yet many New Yorkers argue that other changes—such as the 7,000 new cops on the force—must have had an effect too. They also point out that Bratton's reengineering exercise had much less success in reducing corruption within his force. Quibbles, perhaps. What really exposes the gap between Bratton's rhetoric and reality is a comparison with other attempts to put management theory into practice. By the standards of most corporate reengineering exercises, the NYPD's experience was so mild that it barely qualifies for the name. Bratton did not change the number of precincts; nor did he contract out many parts of the NYPD. Although Bratton sacked a few poor performers, he did not motivate the good ones with performance pay.

This is not so much a criticism of Bratton as a demonstration of the difference between the private sector and the public sector. Bratton's "failures" are the kind that usually stem from the intricacies of either the law or city politics. For instance, he could not bring in cheap outsiders to do the NYPD's paperwork, partly because there are strict rules about what work has to be carried out by police officers. Bratton's real customer was also Rudy Giuliani, the mayor of New York (who is widely believed to have forced Bratton from office in 1996), who has no wish to offend the city's powerful police unions. In other words, for all Bratton's bold talk about "profits" and "customers," management theory fit the police department like trousers fit a chimpanzee—almost, but not quite.

## A Soldier's Prayer

Bratton is not the only public servant to have fallen in love with management theory in the past few years. On becoming Speaker of the U.S. House of Representatives, following the Republicans' triumph in the November 1994 elections, Newt Gingrich supplied his troops with a reading list. As well as the usual suspects, such as Tocqueville's *Democracy in America,* the list included Peter Drucker and Alvin and Heidi Toffler. Not to be outdone, President Clinton spent his holiday holed up in Camp David with two motivational gurus, Anthony Robbins and Stephen Covey. Al Gore can barely open his mouth without talking about reinventing some part of government. This enthusiasm has been copied around the world, from Sweden to Singapore, and it has been embraced by socialists as well as conservatives. In October 1995, Tony Blair, the leader of Britain's Labour Party (who went on to become Prime Minister in 1997), sent his entire shadow cabinet to Templeton College, Oxford, to spend a weekend learning about management theory.

Indeed, it is hard to walk down any corridor of power nowadays without hearing a new and hideous language—"managing by objectives," "outsourcing noncore functions," "negotiating performance measures," and the rest of it. Even generals and admirals are "downsizing their human resources" and "benchmarking their competitors." "Of course this benchmarking is only a rough guide," admits one Pentagon bureaucrat. "The ultimate benchmarking exercise is war."

Peter Drucker has been arguing for half a century that the place where management theory is most needed is in the public sector. In most cases—the NYPD is a good example—even cynics have to admit that management theory has hardly made the public sector worse. Yet, to many people—Drucker included—management theory in the public sector has proved a disappointment. Many of its easiest victories have come from privatizing parts of the public sector that should never have been public in the first place. When management theory has been applied to areas that have to remain within the public sector—notably, health and education—its results have often been patchy. The peculiar circumstances of the public sector have only exaggerated the contradictions within private sector management theory, and there has been precious little new public sector management theory that could be called good. Victories have been won, but they have often been Pyrrhic.

## How They Met

In the United States, the love affair with management theory started with lower-level bureaucrats who were increasingly frustrated by the foot-dragging of the public sector. In the early 1980s, Bob Stone, deputy assistant secretary for installations at the Department of Defense, was furious with the way that bureaucratic regulations were producing lousy services for his troops. For Stone, *In Search of Excellence* (1982), by Tom Peters and Robert Waterman, was a revelation. Using the book that he still describes as "a bible," Stone tried to get rid of all the rules that kept him from staying close to his customer. He handed power to front-line managers, condensed thick Pentagon manuals into page-long mission statements, and turned one outpost into a "regulation-free" installation modeled on a store he had read about in *In Search of Excellence*. He also invited Peters to give lectures to the top brass.

At roughly the same time that Stone was discovering excellence, total-quality management (which can mean anything from reorganizing workers into teams to paying attention to customers) became a quasi-religion among local government officials. One of the first nationally known figures to join the movement in the 1980s was Bill Clinton, then governor of Arkansas, who took to making speeches praising W. Edwards Deming and other quality gurus. By 1992, consultants at

Coopers & Lybrand could count more than 200 local-government "quality initiatives" in the United States.

By the late 1980s, the federal government too had become a convert—albeit in its own ponderous way. In 1988, Executive Order 12,637 ordained a government-wide TQM program and established a Federal Quality Initiative housed in the Office of Personnel Management. Four years later, a 28-volume report on federal management problems appeared. But public sector management theory really went into overdrive in March 1993, when Bill Clinton established the National Performance Review under Al Gore's leadership. One of its first hires was Bob Stone, the disciple of Excellence. The Clinton Administration has also established a public sector equivalent of the Baldrige Award for quality.

Regardless of who first sponsored them, management ideas are now an institutionalized part of government worldwide. In Britain, Australaia, Canada, and Scandinavia, the public sector's love affair with management theory started at the top. In Britain, for example, Margaret Thatcher and her ministers set up a succession of powerful bodies, some of them staffed by businessmen and consultants, to improve the management of the public sector: the Efficiency Unit (under Lord Rayner, head of Marks and Spencer), the Financial Management Unit, the National Audit Office, and the Audit Commission. Thatcher also introduced a wide range of "market-oriented" reforms, including privatization (a word that Peter Drucker supposedly invented). British civil servants can win awards called Charter Marks for things such as successful staff suggestions. Britain has also established a public sector MBA to ensure that civil servants are *au fait* with the latest in management thinking. There are even special Internet sites where civil servants of all nations can log on to discuss subjects such as "TQM for public servants."

All this has proved a bonanza for management consultancies. In America, the public sector has proved such a lucrative client that most big consultancies now have several departments devoted to its needs: one firm, CSC Index, even has a special center that concentrates on federal customers, such as the Department of Defense and NASA. In mid-1995, John Major's government admitted, in a series of parliamentary questions, that it had spent at least £320 million on management consultants—almost certainly a fraction of the real figure. British consultancies are doing so well out of the public sector that they have started hiring former council members to give them advice. Margaret Hodge, once head of the notoriously badly managed Islington Council, became a consultant to Price Waterhouse before returning to politics as a Labour member of Parliament.

## Fatal Attraction

To the cynical eye, this may look like conclusive proof of a honey-trap. Talk to many consultants privately and they will admit that governments have offered them a wonderful chance to resell (expensively) products and theories that they have already dished out to the private sector. Yet they will also insist that they were relatively late to realize its potential: on the whole, most of the enthusiasm for the affair has come from the public sector, which has shown a blind affection for management theory that is rarely seen in the private sector.

That obsession has three roots. The first is a crisis in faith in the public sector and a resurgence of faith in the private sector. In the United States, Ross Perot, who founded an entire presidential candidacy on the notion that only a businessman such as himself could restore sanity to the federal government, is only the poster child for this movement. It is virtually impossible to imagine any candidate for local or national political office nowadays (particularly a Republican candidate) *not* touting his or her private sector skills as one, and sometimes the only, qualification for holding public office. In the 1994 elections, political neophytes, among them cardiac surgeons and real estate tycoons, swept into office promising to make government run like a business. One unsuccessful candidate for the Republican nomination in 1996, Lamar Alexander, rooted his campaign in his private sector experience, downplaying as much as possible his terms as secretary of education under George Bush, and as governor of Tennessee.

Nor is the Clinton Administration much of a slouch when it comes to entrepreneur worship. If nothing else, Hillary Rodham Clinton's appetite for commodity trading and the Whitewater investment scheme has shown that the Clintons have never frowned on the quick buck. The Clinton family has always had strong ties to Arkansas businesses, notably Wal-Mart, Tyson Foods, and the Stephens financial empire. Al Gore has been spotted doing all the right things—touring Southwest Airlines and General Motors's Saturn factory, and holding seminars with business luminaries such as Vaughan Beals, chairman of Harley-Davidson, and Jack Welch of General Electric.

Liberals are often most passionate about management theory because they think it will help salvage government from public disillusionment. By the mid-1990s, only 19 percent of the American public trusted the federal government to "do the right thing," compared with 76 percent 30 years ago. Elaine Kamark, Gore's chief policy adviser, blames this on the fact that the public sector is stuck with a 1950s' attitude toward its customers: workers continue to treat customers with surly indifference, whereas the private sector is increasingly competing on the basis of "customer satisfaction."

The second reason that governments of all persuasions are obsessed with management theory is a common desire to do "more with less": to continue to provide reasonable public services without spending a higher proportion of GDP on the state. Politicians have noted that companies have been cutting their workforces while producing more and better products. Watchdogs like Britain's Audit Commission and the U.S. Office of Management and Budget have repeatedly detailed public-sector inefficiencies. It is only natural for politicians to conclude that they can put off making hard decisions about raising taxes or cutting services by managing things better.

In the United States, Al Gore has said that agencies will have to "justify why they should continue to exist at all." In 1993–95, a Democratic presidency cut the federal workforce by 100,000. Britain has slimmed its civil service to a central core and contracted out everything else to some 100 agencies, which operate on short-term contracts, or to the private sector. Throughout the world, local government is a particular target. "Inside every fat and bloated local authority is a slim one struggling to get out," Nicholas Ridley, one of Thatcher's favorite ministers once proclaimed.

Many politicians, including the late Mr. Ridley, have been fascinated by California's "contract cities," which buy in most of their public services. The usual model is a city called Lakewood, which, when it was first incorporated in 1954, supposedly needed only three employees to monitor the contractors who provided its 70,000 inhabitants with their hospitals, police, and so on. Nowadays, Lakewood is a little less streamlined—it employs 160 people and the council has to meet every two weeks, rather than once a year—but independent studies suggest that per-capita spending on public services in contract cities is roughly half that in towns where the local authority provides the service itself.[3]

The third reason that governments have turned to management theory is a vague feeling that, regardless of the need to cut budgets, the public sector must move with the times. Just as the private sector has to take account of the spread of information technology and the emergence of much fussier, value-conscious consumers, so must the state. Al Gore once complained that Americans suffered "from a quill-pen government in the age of Word Perfect." Many high-ranking officials in Washington have had extensive experience in the private sector as it turned itself around in the 1980s. Listen to Newt Gingrich talk about Drucker or Alvin Toffler, and even his worst enemy would have to admit that the Speaker's enthusiasm for change in the public sector is motivated by more than just a desire to cut welfare.

### Any New Ideas?

Is there something, then, in what the consultants say: that, by and large, the politicians' feet have been so firmly on the accelerator that the management industry has usually been happy just to be taken along for the ride? This applies particularly to the gurus themselves, who, by and large, have failed to produce new ideas tailored to the public sector. Tom Peters, usually on his toes when it comes to selling his ideas, initially ignored it. It was not until 1989 that he produced a film about "excellence in the public sector." All the gurus pay lip service to Drucker's idea that the public sector is crying out for good management, and, as a group, they have begun to include a few more public-sector case studies in their books. But, from Drucker onward, their interest has largely been in the big picture rather than the niceties of how to run particular government organizations.

A case in point is the guru who has most obviously involved himself in the public sector: Michael Porter of the Harvard Business School. He first became interested in the public sector in the 1980s, when Ronald Reagan asked him to sit on the President's Commission on Industrial Competitiveness.[4] At the time, business-magazine wisdom held that the globalization of trade was making nations less and less important. Robert Reich, then Porter's colleague at Harvard, put the case in its most sophisticated form in *The Work of Nations* (1991), arguing that education and training were the only real source of national competitive advantage, because labor is the least mobile of all the factors of production.

As the commission deliberated, however, Porter became impressed by the huge role that nation-states and national differences play in determining the success of companies. The result of this conversion was *The Competitive Advantage of Nations* (1989). Over 800 pages long—lavishly illustrated with charts, cluster maps, and the like, and littered with details about British biscuit makers and Korean piano companies—the book is a general inquiry into what makes national economies successful, and how governments should act to improve their country's competitiveness. The book, which was read (or at least bought) by aspiring intellectuals everywhere, led Porter himself to do consulting work for a large number of governments, and to write reports on the competitive positions of New Zealand, Canada, and Portugal. Following similar assignments in local government, Porter produced reports entitled *The Competitive Advantage of Massachusetts* (1991) and *The Competitive Advantage of the Inner City* (1995).

The real subject of *The Competitive Advantage of Nations* is globalization (see Chapter 10). But it also shows why it is legitimate for business people and business thinkers to worry about the state's role. National environments have always played a central role in making firms successful, Porter argued. Now, as globalization and free trade expose firms to ever more competitors, the effect of national peculiarities on companies counts for more, not less.

A colleague of Porter's at Harvard, Rosabeth Moss Kanter, has examined, from the other way around, the relationship between public policy and what some would call "the business community." As globe-spanning firms move operations from, say, Massachusetts to Manila in search of better workers, they force (or should force) politicians to rethink public policy. *World Class: Thriving Locally in the Global Economy* (1995) looks at the impact of globalization on local communities. She insists that the best way for any region to thrive is to become a world-class operation in one of three activities: thinking, manufacturing, or trading. According to Moss Kanter, it is pointless to fight globalization; far from preserving local communities, nativism condemns them to disintegration.

There is a good deal of common ground between management theory and the public sector. But it is hard to see how Porter and Moss Kanter are much help to, say, a postmaster general trying to redesign the mail service. Both Porter and Moss Kanter seem fired up about issues that have more to do with general economics and political philosophy than the nitty gritty of public sector management. The same could be said for Kenichi Ohmae and his crusade to reform Japanese politics, or for Charles Handy and his concern for the quality of British public life, or for any other of the first-division gurus.

This lofty disdain for detail has left room for a new breed of management gurus who specialize in the public sector. The most influential of these are David Osborne, a public policy consultant, and Ted Gaebler, a former city manager. Their *Reinventing Government: How the Entrepreneurial Spirit Is Transforming the Public Sector* (1992) reached the top of the best-seller lists, spawned an influential pressure group (the Alliance for Redesigning Government), and provided the first Clinton Administration with something of a model. The book was originally going to be called *In Search of Excellence in Government,* in tribute to Peters and Waterman; but in the end they decided to name it after another management tome, *Reinventing the Corporation* (1985), by John Naisbitt.

As their fascination with private-sector gurus hints, the problem with Osborne and Gaebler's book is that, for all the details, it is really about recycling old ideas rather than creating new ones. *Reinventing Government* simply explains how private-sector management theory can be applied to the public sector. In practice, the real "gurus" to emerge from the public sector are the practitioners—usually politicians implementing what they think management theory should be. Al Gore's report on reinventing government, which also reached the *New York Times* best-seller list, reads rather like a self-conscious attempt to do for the public sector what *In Search of Excellence* did for the private: inspire readers to follow the example of

America's best organizations. Bill Creech, a four-star general who made his name for his innovative approach to running Tactical Air Command, including condensing a 440-page rule-book into an 8-page guidebook, has become a guru in his own right, with his *Five Pillars of TQM* (1994).

As soon as retired generals start writing about the five pillars of TQM, sensible people brace themselves for a back-lash. All the same, it is often such earthy types who do the original thinking in the public sector. When giant retailer Wal-Mart was thinking of introducing pharmacies, the firm looked around to see who was best at designing queuing systems for large numbers of customers, and found, to its surprise, that the answer was Air Combat Command. The U.S. Army is one of the leaders in getting poorly educated people from different ethnic backgrounds to work together. In 1995, Charles Handy cited the British Army as an example of a "high commitment" organization that has really reengineered itself since the war by slimming down to a fighting force of 60,000 men—an organization, he noted, that was now smaller than Royal Dutch/Shell.[5]

## The View from the Trenches

On the whole, though, cases of "best practice" springing out of the public sector are rare. In general, all the public sector does is borrow ideas from the private sector. It often seems like a bureaucratic version of Chinese Whispers, with one group of people applying what they think another group of people has said.

Many governments are introducing what Peter Drucker once called "management by objectives": mission statements (laying out broad objectives), fixed contracts (specifying what employees are expected to do), and performance measures (measuring how well they do it). An even more common idea currently making the rounds of the public sector is the notion that "the customer is king"—something Theodore Levitt preached to the private sector in the 1960s and Tom Peters repreached in the 1980s. Now, the Danish and Canadian governments are trying to persuade civil servants to treat their clients like private-sector customers; so is the British government, with its Citizen's Charter initiative. Even the Chinese government has sent out orders instructing its bureaucrats not to be rude to its citizens.

In one way, this is a little fatuous. Phrases such as "Remember that the customer always has a choice" do not make much sense in an unemployment office in Santa Fe, let alone Beijing. But governments are putting some substance to this rhetoric by offering people compensation if service falls below a certain performance measure. Even such notoriously customer-hostile organizations as the U.S. Internal Revenue Service and London's Underground have adopted "customer service standards." And, like many other things to do with management theory, merely going through the motions can be revealing—even if largely in the category of curiosity value. One of the few reasons that the White House now knows there is an "eagle parts program," which collects dead eagles partly to supply bits of them to Indians for ceremonial purposes, is that the practice was cited by managers in the Department of the Interior as an example of innovative, customer-driven government.

Moreover, just because an idea is old does not necessarily mean that it is a bad one. Most companies treat customer service as a starting point; there is no reason why the taxman should not do this too. The same goes for another "old" management technique: employee motivation and performance pay. In Britain, Australia, and New Zealand, the heads of civil service departments are appointed for limited terms and rewarded, in part, on the basis of their performance. In Sunnyvale, California, city managers can achieve bonuses of up to 10 percent if their agencies exceed agreed targets.

London Underground now publishes information about the performance of various tube lines, both against targets and against each other. The state of Oregon has introduced 270 benchmarks, measuring everything from cutting teenage pregnancies to cleaning up the environment, and has moved to performance-based budgeting. Telling people how well or badly they are doing can have a dramatic effect. Southwark Council, traditionally one of the poorest and most left-wing boroughs in Britain, divided its housing department into 19 neighborhood offices and then pestered them with information about how well they were doing, both with respect to each other and to other councils. The council also made all the comparative data publicly available. By 1995, Southwark was processing housing benefits quicker than any other London council except Kensington and Chelsea, a far wealthier area.[6]

All this customer service is fine enough, but, from most civil servants' point of view, management theory is synonymous with one thing: delayering. The NYPD apart, reengineering has often been brutal in the public sector. One victim has been Britain's Treasury, which is now urging the discipline on other departments. Al Gore would eventually like the U.S. federal government to hit Tom Peters's target of one manager for every 25–75 employees.

As in the private sector, downsizing and cost-cutting programs are increasingly accompanied by an appetite for more modern, "soft" management techniques. Some American government officials carry around small gold business cards that "empower" them to make decisions without first going to their superiors. Some departments are even giving out "forgiveness coupons," which forgive people in advance of their mistakes, in order to encourage them to adopt a less rule-bound approach to government. One division of the National Forest Service, at Ochoco National Park, Oregon, has introduced "Grue Awards," named after an employee. Employees can give these awards to each other as tokens of appreciation for outstanding work.

This affection for mixing hard and soft management theory reaches right into the White House. When he is not thinking up ideas for slimming government, Al Gore is coming up with visions, or handing out "heroes of reinvention" awards. No sooner had Bill Clinton been first elected president in 1992 than he organized a bonding weekend, designed to encourage more effective team building, at which two "facilitators" tried to get everybody to confess to some hidden secret. (Warren Christopher, the Secretary of State, admitted that he enjoyed jazz and piano bars.)

Although it is hard to imagine Jack Welch or Rupert Murdoch tolerating this sort of thing, Clinton's infatuations are fairly normal inside the Washington Beltway. Hazel O'Leary, President Clinton's first energy secretary, proclaimed herself a student of Stephen Covey, who she claimed, allowed people to break the "ring of fear" that prevented them from hitting their peak performance. Nor are the Republicans immune. Their leaders now hold a "management retreat" at the beginning of every year to help them set the agenda. Newt Gingrich argued that his Contract with America was primarily designed as "a management-training document that was politically useful, not simply as a political document."

## The Backlash Begins

At the 1995 meeting of the Academy of Management, Henry Mintzberg treated the attendees to a coruscating attack on the influence of management theory on the public sector. The *Harvard Business Review,* he argued, should have a skull and cross bones stamped on the cover with the warning "not to be taken by the public sector."

In the same year, Peter Drucker wrote a long article for the *Atlantic Monthly.* It began by ridiculing parts of Al Gore's reinventing-government crusade, such as the consolidation of "the application process" in welfare offices in Atlanta into a "one-stop shop" (which was management-speak for getting phone calls answered) and the reinvention of the Export-Import Bank, which, Drucker dryly noted, "is now expected to do what it was set up to do all of 60 years ago: help small businesses get export financing."[7]

Like Mintzberg, Drucker puzzled over why the government had to think of people as customers in order to do things that should come naturally. But his core complaint was that most public sector management theory came down to two strategies that had already failed to work in the private sector: either end-lessly patching up services, or downsizing. Worse, these reme-dies were being applied to fossilized organizations that had changed little since the Herbert Hoover era. What was needed was to "rethink" the public sector, to ask basic questions of each part of government, such as "What is your mission?" "Is it still the right mission?" and so on. Why, wondered Drucker, did the Veterans Administration run 300 hospitals itself, instead of con-tracting out the job to the private sector? And why did agricul-ture deserve its own department when it provided work for only 3 percent of the population? The point, argued Drucker, was not to shrink government for the sake of shrinking it, but to make it more effective.

Mintzberg and Drucker's frustration is nothing compared with the fury of those who have been affected by the "manage-mentization" of government. In Britain, where management the-ory has probably been applied most enthusiastically in the public sector, the idea has become something of a public joke, an easy way to get a laugh on television or in a newspaper column.

The charge sheet against management theory in the public sector begins with its expense. Fancy new management systems usually involve sophisticated computers, to speed up the flow of information, and well-groomed managers, to handle the additional paper work. Government departments frequently have to hire expensive consultants to advise on "change management" and "personnel management," as everything that used to be done by instinct is now done on the basis of "flow charts" and "action plans." In the United States, cities often spend 20 percent of the cost of a contracted-out service on managing the contract.

Public-sector employees and politicians have been more enthusiastic than sophisticated in their use of management ideas. One of the reasons that the Clinton White House turned its first 100 days into a disaster was that Clinton hastily moved to "downsize" his staff by a quarter without rethinking the jobs of those who remained. Politicians are no less addicted to fads than their private-sector equivalents—the only difference is that public-sector fads seem to lag behind private-sector fads by about five years.

Similarly, because politicians and administrators have failed to distinguish among the different sorts of management theory, they are often most exposed to its contradictions. The three most popular public-sector fads—downsizing, reengineering, and total-quality management—are, on many points of substance, mutually incompatible. Downsizing argues that workers are expendable; TQM sees them as an invaluable resource. Reengineering depends on ripping up the organization and starting again; TQM is a doctrine of continuous, incremental improvement.

A typical public-sector management reform involves keeping the old departmental structure, but hoping to do it with fewer people; worse, it introduces a performance measure in the crudest possible way. These days, academics may be promoted for writing a lot of articles despite the fact that they are all bunk, and doctors can be demoted because too many of their patients die, without accounting for the fact that a typical cardiac surgeon sees more critically ill patients than the typical dermatologist. Most "normal" companies now do much of their creative work in self-governing teams, but the public sector has largely ignored this—as it has ideas such as networking. It was not until November 1995 that Michael Heseltine, a successful publisher in the private sector, persuaded his colleagues in John Major's cabinet to welcome in Cab-e-net, an online information system.

However, the idea that the public sector has ignored most conspicuously is trust. One of the more interesting things about the government shutdown inspired by the budget skirmishes between the Republican Congress and the White House was the light it shed on the character of federal employees. Americans are in the habit of regarding federal bureaucrats as, at best, a cancer on the free functioning of democracy; lazy, inefficient, and indifferent. Once the government ceased all but essential operations, however, the press and public were surprised to discover many "inessential" bureaucrats who continued to work despite the furlough. Other government employees spoke eloquently of the shabby treatment they were receiving at the hands of their employer, and it became clear that these were not people who did not care about their jobs, but instead were eager to do their best.

Mintzberg argues that the growing obsession with measurement and accountability is bringing governments into conflict with all that is best in the public-sector ethic. Civil service professions have traditionally exercised control through shared values, inculcated through long training; now it is assumed that their only values are financial. (Mintzberg once heard a business manager proclaim, in all seriousness, that "through control, we can prevent people from falling in love with their business.")

Management theory has not merely been misapplied by bureaucrats. Examples of private-sector managers' meeting with unaccustomed failure in the public sector abound. Perhaps the most celebrated example was Hillary Rodham Clinton's attempt to reform America's health-care system. To help her, Mrs. Clinton hired Ira Magaziner, head of a management consultancy, Telesis, and erstwhile adviser to dozens of America's leading corporations. Magaziner acted like Molière's vision of a management consultant, intent on producing a perfect plan and blind to the demands of democratic politics. He set up gigantic committees, composed of hundreds of experts from around the world, to consider the problem. He assembled documents and reports from around the country. The work of the committees, was, of course, conducted in strict secrecy, without bothering to include or even brief any of the members of the Congress who would eventually vote to adopt or reject the plan.

In the end, Magaziner produced a gigantic blueprint for an entirely new health-care system. The blueprint was unveiled by President Clinton in a nationally televised address in prime time on a weekday evening. It bore a troubling resemblance to the diagram for a sophisticated computer circuit. Bob Dole, the Senate majority leader, lost no time in ridiculing the arcane system America's finest Democratic minds had devised. The plan unleashed an unprecedented torrent of lobbying, backroom maneuvering, political posturing, competing plans, and public hysteria. In the end, Congress voted against the plan in favor of doing nothing about a problem widely regarded as one of the gravest facing the United States.

Or take the example of Renato Riverso and Roberto Schisano, successful managers at, respectively, IBM and Texas Instruments, who in 1994 were given the job of turning around Alitalia, an Italian airline. They increased operational efficiency and tried to push through a restructuring plan; but they failed to cover their backs politically; by March 1996, after heavy lobbying by the unions, both of them had resigned. Speaking to Riverso, an IBM veteran, one got the impression that he simply could not believe some of the practices he encountered— such as an Alitalia cabin crew refusing to let people with confirmed paid-for tickets on the aircraft so that their friends and relations (needless to say, traveling cheaply) could have the seats. On the other hand, his critics say that he was naive to expect anything different.

Such disasters hint at a more fundamental argument preached by Mintzberg (though not by Drucker): that there are such fundamental differences between the public sector and the private sector that management theory from one will never be applicable to the other. One of Mintzberg's starting points, for instance, is that we are not customers of governments but citizens. A citizen cannot opt out of the social contract in the same way as he or she might a commercial one. In the name of the common good, reluctant citizens can be conscripted into the army.

In other words, "government" and "management" are not interchangeable concepts. Private-sector managers live under the threat of bankruptcy if they shirk tough decisions; politicians usually have the option of printing money or raising taxes. Private-sector managers are answerable to just one dictator, the bottom line. The public-sector manager, as Roberto Schisano and Ira Magaziner learned painfully, are answerable to everyone and no one. As John Kay, a professor at London Business School, has pointed out, "Where there is ambiguity about responsibility, there is no real accountability. And where there is neither accountability nor responsibility there is inefficiency and incompetence."[8]

Nor are such dilemmas confined to expensively imported bosses. Normal civil servants have to serve the party in power without degenerating into party functionaries. They have to bear in mind that large numbers of people did not vote for the government, and that an opposition party, with different policies and priorities, may soon take over. It is rather like running a firm that has several sets of contradictory accounts and lives on the edge of a hostile takeover.

Public-sector managers also live in a world of rules and regulations that limit their freedom to control both their employees and their budgets. Employment laws mean that sacking public workers is expensive (because senior staff have to be given expensive retirement packages) or counterproductive (because the first to go are the youngest and brightest). When America's Department of the Interior cut the staff of its computing facility by 20 percent, for example, it was forced to dismiss all its youngest employees—that is, the ones who actually knew something about modern computers. When private-sector managers are brought in to redesign this or reinvent that bit of the public sector, they are repeatedly shocked to find that they must meticulously obey laws and regulations, and that they are answerable to the legislature for their actions.

Nor are these necessarily bad things. The public-sector must shield taxpayer money from abuse. Too much "flexibility" can easily be turned into a national scandal by the press, forcing civil servants to reintroduce rigorous top-down controls. There is a limit to how much we can "empower" government employees. After all, the list of "empowered" individuals includes not only

Oliver North but also Robert Citron, the former chief financial officer of Orange County.

## A Disappointment, Not a Mistake

Many of the disappointments of public-sector management are really just a horrible reminder of two problems that plague policy making of all kinds. The first is that the state is an incredibly blunt instrument: it gets hold of one idea and imposes it without any sensitivity to context. The second is the desperate craving of politicians for a magical solution: management theory is expected to restore people's faith in government, allow governments to cut taxes without reducing services, and square every circle in its path.

The public sector seems to have subscribed to the notion that a problem can be fixed merely by managing it well. No amount of managing can make sense of America's Medicare program or Europe's common agriculture policy. Drucker blames this short-sightedness on political theorists who, since Machiavelli, have neglected "what the proper functions of governments might be" and "what governments should be accountable for." Even leaving aside Drucker's narrow reading of history (Hegel and John Stuart Mill had certain widely discussed ideas about the proper limits and functions of government), the idea that it is all political theory's fault looks like passing the buck. Management theory has remarkably strong views about what companies should and should not do, and it should play a role in working out the core competencies of the state.

## Is There a Doctor in the House?!

It is perfectly fair to castigate management theorists for their failures in the public sector. But proportionately: management theory has been a disappointment, not a failure. Most of its critics tend to ignore the state of the public sector before the theorists arrived. For example, the charge that management theory has "destroyed" staff morale forgets that there has been a "crisis in the civil service" in most countries in every decade since the Second World War. (A book by that name was much discussed in Britain in the 1960s—a period now revered by the traditionalists as a golden age.)

The most obvious example of management theory improving the public sector is privatization. Look at the performance of any privatized telephone service from Buenos Aires to Birmingham and you discover that, although people moan about the profits being made by the new owners, few want to return to the days when (in Buenos Aires, at least) you had to bribe an official just to get your phone connected. One reason for the problems of public-sector management in America is that local politicians (with a few notable exceptions such as Steven Goldsmith, the mayor of Indianapolis) have been nervous about moving services into the private sector.

What about those parts of the public sector that have remained public: schools, hospitals, and so on? It is in this area—the heart of the public sector—that the list of disappointments lengthens and public dissatisfaction is most obvious. It is worth saying one thing at the start: that critics of management theory are often heroically blind to what would have happened without it. In general, management theory has often been introduced ineptly and for the wrong reasons; it has also wreaked havoc with the morale of the organizations concerned. However, on balance, it has brought progress—perhaps not as much as it could have, but certainly more than in the muddled world that preceded it. It has basically won the political argument, in that its opponents want to adapt its reforms rather than reverse them. As a case study to support this thesis, we offer one that opponents of public-sector management theory would probably also choose: the British National Health Service (NHS).

To outsiders, the NHS has been the jewel in the crown of Britain's welfare state. To insiders, however, it has been a managerial nightmare. This is partly because of its size—for most of its history, it has been the second largest employer in Europe after the Red Army—and partly because it has long seethed with discontent. "One of the most striking features of the NHS," noted Enoch Powell, minister for health in 1960–63, "is the continual, deafening chorus of complaint which rises day and night from every part of it, a chorus only interrupted when someone suggests that a different system altogether might be preferable. . . . It presents what must be a unique spectacle of an undertaking that is run down by everyone engaged in it."

In theory, an unhappy institution should welcome change; the NHS never has. The staff are convinced that, however bad things are, they will only be made worse by meddling politicians. And there is a dangerous mismatch between the power of the employees (who are concentrated and visible) and the interests of the customers (who are unorganized and dispersed). Nevertheless, the Conservative Party eventually decided to shake up the National Health Service in the late 1980s; and it decided to do so along lines suggested by a management theorist.

Its guru was Alain Enthoven, an American disciple of Robert McNamara. Having worked for his hero at the Defense Department, he discovered a second career as a health economist, holding a chair at Stanford University and becoming a key figure in the Jackson Hole Group, a collection of health-care specialists who meet at the Wyoming resort every year. In June 1985, after a tour of the English National Health Service, Enthoven wrote an article for *The Economist* (arguing for a comprehensive reform of the NHS) that was widely circulated among the radical right of the Conservative Party and was the basis for the eventual reforms.[9]

Enthoven argued that the NHS structure "suffers from a lack of real incentives for good performance. It relies on dedication and idealism. It is propelled by the clash of the interests of different provider groups. But it offers few positive incentives to do a better job for patients." Enthoven's solution was an internal market, based around three big structural changes.

The first was a division between the buyers of health care (usually, health authorities) and a range of competing providers (hospitals and the like). In the old-fashioned NHS, doctors made all the most important decisions about allocating resources; the result was pots of cash for high-tech surgery and peanuts for preventive medicine. In the market-based NHS, the job of the buyers would be to assess the health needs of the population and to meet them as efficiently as possible; the providers would compete to produce the best combination of service and cost.

The second change was to introduce prices. In the old-fashioned NHS, resources were allocated by historical accident and administrative fiat. This meant that too much money went to fast-emptying inner cities (which boasted ancient hospitals) and too little to the flourishing suburbs. It also created an efficiency trap. Successful hospitals attracted more patients without attracting more resources; unsuccessful hospitals lost patients without losing resources. In the new NHS, money would follow patients.

The third change was to devolve managerial decisions to the lowest possible level. The problem with the old-fashioned NHS was that it gave doctors few incentives to improve their efficiency but every incentive to lobby for more resources. The best way to solve a problem was to complain about underfunding in the hope that you might be given more money. Enthoven wanted hospitals to be self-managing.

This idea seemed calculated to appeal to Margaret Thatcher. In fact, her instinct was to stay well clear of the "political heffalump trap," as she called the NHS. Her policy was to spend more money—real expenditure on health increased by 33 percent between 1979 and 1987—rather than ask fundamental questions. The 1987 election manifesto, which included ideas like privatizing water, contained nothing but platitudes on the NHS.

All this changed in the winter of 1987. No sooner had Mrs. Thatcher won the 1987 general election than the NHS seemed to fall apart. Hospitals up and down the country closed wards for lack of funds. Newspapers overdosed on stories of hole-in-the-heart babies killed by penny-pitching Thatcherism. Once again, Thatcher tried to buy peace: she handed the NHS an extra £100 million. But to no avail. Eventually, on a television program, "Panorama," she was so needled by an interviewer that she announced plans for a prime ministerial review of the NHS, taking everybody by surprise—civil servants, ministers, and even herself.

It is hard to claim that an idea born of panic was the result of long-term planning. Yet, in other ways, the NHS Review represented a triumph of management theory. Traditionally, British government reviews had been more like job-creation schemes for the great and the good, addressing vague problems and taking years to appear; the NHS Review was much more like something a management consultancy might be happy with. The reviewers met in secret, and consisted only of the prime minister and four cabinet members.

Enthoven's idea of an internal market was rapidly adopted. At first, some right-wingers wanted to encourage people to "opt out" of the NHS, taking their tax contributions with them.

This idea was squashed by Kenneth Clarke, the new health secretary and a formidable politician whose belligerent manner obscured his centrist, pro-welfare-state sympathies. Clarke also adapted Enthoven's internal market to British circumstances, handing more power to general practitioners, the most popular part of the NHS.

This was the blueprint for change that appeared as a White Paper in 1988. However, in politics, drawing up a plan is the easy part; selling it is the real challenge. In the private sector, all you need to do is persuade the chief executive. He or she can then impose the restructuring on the organization and fire all those who disagree. Politicians not only face an organized opposition, but they need to carry the public with them.

It soon became clear that the two things that had made the NHS Review relatively efficient—speed and secrecy—immediately counted against it in public relations. The vested interests felt snubbed as well as threatened. And the Tories failed to explain what was wrong with the NHS: that hospitals kept patients waiting for scarce beds but sat on acres of land in the middle of booming cities; that health authorities complained that they could not afford expensive drugs but failed to use their buying power to drive down prices from all their suppliers; that the concentration of resources in London short-changed people in the growing provinces.

The Labour Party seized its perceived political advantage hungrily. "By God, the government is going to get it in the neck," said Labour's health spokesman, Robin Cook. The Tories had spent the last decade privatizing everything from gas to water. Why not health? Why make hospitals self-governing if you do not plan to push them into the private sector? Repeated opinion polls revealed that the majority of voters believed that the Tories were bent on privatizing the NHS.

Even more effective than the Labour Party's campaign was that of the British Medical Association (BMA). Its footsoldiers, the doctors, who saw hundreds of thousands of patients a day, littered their waiting rooms with BMA leaflets and aired their grievances to anyone who would listen. One middle-ranking minister, on a routine visit to his general practitioner, was subjected, before he could get his shirt off, to a 25-minute harangue on the evils of the reforms.

With more than three-quarters of voters opposing the reforms, Margaret Thatcher panicked. In May 1990, just a few
weeks before the NHS bill was due to become law, she decided
that the restructuring of the health service should be put on
hold until after the 1992 election. Instead, a compromise was
reached. The reforms were to go ahead, but there was to be no
"big bang." The internal market was to be carefully controlled
from the center. The new buzzwords were "soft landing," "no
surprises," and "smooth take-off."

In fact, this compromise proved the saving of the reforms.
The government persuaded a surprisingly large section of the
medical profession to opt into the new reforms, partly by offering generous incentives to participate. In December 1990, 57
hospitals became self-governing trusts, and in April 1991, 306
general practices, containing 1,700 GPs, became "fundholders."
But the government also kept its foot firmly on the brake. The
new health contracts did little more than redescribe traditional
relations in newfangled language. The move to funding health
authorities on the basis of the number and health needs of the
population was slowed down so that the London regions, with
their well-connected teaching hospitals, enjoyed more generous
resources than they deserved.

But what really saved the reforms was the replacement of
Margaret Thatcher with John Major. The voters never thought
the NHS was safe in the hands of a woman who boasted that
she used private health care to make more room in the public
(hospital) wards; under Major, Labour's talk about the government privatizing the NHS sounded less convincing.

As a result, the NHS reforms stumbled through their first
test, the 1992 election, which Major won against all predictions. Majors government then gradually took its foot off the
brake. In April 1992, the Department of Health created a hundred more trusts and 300 more GP fundholders. This meant
that a third of GPs were fundholders, and trusts accounted for
more than a third of the total NHS budget. The Department of
Health also moved nearer to basing funding on patient numbers
rather than just on tradition (although London was always
something of an exception) and instructed purchasers to shop
around for the best care at the best prices in negotiating their
contracts.

## But Was It Worth the Candle?

There must have been many times during the introduction of the NHS reforms when the Tories wished that it had never heard of Alain Enthoven and his "internal market." The policy makers were constantly confronted by two serious criticisms of their efforts. The first was that, far from galvanizing the NHS, the reforms have demoralized it. As already pointed out, the NHS has never been a particularly happy ship, but with the management theorists at the helm, morale plummeted. Six years after the reforms were first introduced, the medical profession was still up in arms—about overworked young doctors, underpaid nurses, ancient hospitals that faced closure despite overwhelming local support, and the proliferation of bureaucracy. The government might have expected a rough ride from nurses' unions. However, there were also plenty of doctors who would normally vote Conservative and who ought to have felt "empowered" by their new opportunities, but complained instead that the new system meant that they now had to waste their weekends doing paperwork.

The second criticism was that the reforms have encouraged the worst sort of managerialism. The number of NHS managers leapt by 18,000 between 1989 and 1994—a period in which the number of nursing staff fell by 27,000. The average annual pay of trust chief executives (as the heads of hospital trusts insisted on calling themselves) had risen to £65,000 in 1995 (and was growing at twice the rate of that of nurses). The total managerial pay bill for NHS managers rose from £158.8 million in 1989–90 to £723.3 million in 1994–95. Before the reforms, administration in all its guises took up around 6 percent of all NHS spending. In 1996, the total stood at about 10.5 percent, according to the Audit Commission, the public services watchdog.

Not only did the managers seem overpaid; they were also leaden-footed. The NHS "Value for Money" unit was responsible for producing a 200-word definition of a familiar piece of hospital equipment. It begins: "Bed: a device or arrangement that may be used to permit a patient to lie down"—noting that the joke would be even funnier if it were not actually true. Nor were beds the only object of concern. In 1996, health chief executives received an "urgent" three-page memo dealing with the wrongful use of chairs.

To some extent, the problems to do with both morale and managerialism proved self-correcting. A growing number of health-service workers of all sorts eventually committed themselves to the reforms. By April 1996, when the final wave of changes took place, more than half of all doctors had been, inadvertently or deliberately given control of their own budgets, and the majority of hospitals had become self-governing. The government also did its best to combat the excesses of the new managerial class. Stephen Dorrell, the secretary of state for health until May 1997, won wild applause at the 1995 Conservative Party Conference when he announced that he intended to cut spending on management by 5 percent over the next year.

By the mid-1990s, dispassionate observers noticed, the reforms had begun to produce some of the organizational results that were hoped for. A few of these successes had been fairly rapid. The proportion of children being immunized against various diseases rose from 75 percent in the fiscal year 1989–90 to 90 percent in 1990–91, thanks to the introduction of an element of performance-related pay for doctors who performed the injections. By the mid-1990s, most statistical measures of efficiency showed notable improvements. For instance, despite an increase in the number of people being treated, waiting lists had declined. By the end of 1995, the number of people waiting for more than a year for an appointment at a hospital had fallen to 31,600, down from 200,000 five years earlier. In 1994, studies by both the King's Fund, a think tank specializing in health care, and the London School of Economics found that resources were being more closely related to needs than ever before.

The two most important parts of the internal market—the new independent trust hospitals and general practitioner fundholders—also proved to be more of a success than broad opinion polls might suggest. In 1994, a survey of hospital trusts discovered that 48 percent of patients thought services had improved since their hospital had become a trust, and 60 percent thought they got more punctual service. Only 7 percent thought they had got worse. Opinion was even more favorable among staff. In 1994, the LSE's Julian Le Grande discovered a surprising amount of support for the reforms among NHS employees: "If forced to choose between the new quasi-legal market NHS and the old command economy NHS, they would unhesitatingly prefer the new."[10]

Meanwhile, GP fundholders were so aggressive in forcing hospitals to treat their patients that Labour criticized them for it. In 1995, one survey of fundholders found that 96 percent felt that the quality of the service they offered had improved, and 81 percent claimed to have introduced new services for patients. Many doctors have used their increased freedom to improvise, adding physiotherapists and chiropodists to their practices. This reflected a wider concern within the NHS with prevention rather than cure—thanks in part to the various health targets the reforms introduced.

Such progress has won the NHS reforms a fair number of admirers abroad. What impresses foreign observers is that the health-care reforms have managed to combine two elements that elsewhere have proved incompatible. On the one hand, the NHS continues to be paid for by the taxpayer and to be (largely) free at the point of delivery. But within the NHS, market mechanisms are used to ensure the swift and flexible distribution of resources. A report of the Organisation for Economic Co-operation and Development, in 1995, held up the British system as a model for how to use market mechanisms to improve the efficiency of a public service, the goal Hillary Rodham Clinton failed to reach from the opposite starting point of America's largely private health-care system. Throughout Europe and Australaia, governments are trying to introduce into their health-care systems a division between purchasers and providers. The New Zealand government, which has gone furthest in the British direction, encourages regional health authorities to purchase health care from both public hospitals (rechristened Crown Health Enterprises) and private ones.

But what about the political payoff? To be judged successful, all public-sector management theory has to pay off at the ballot box. From this point of view, the NHS reforms have not been a vote winner. On the other hand, the reforms have not quite proven the self-inflicted wound that people have predicted. Throughout the whole debate, the Labour Party has been put in the unenviable position of having to say what it would do instead. One example of this was the 1992 election. Yes, there were a few problems for the Tories: two NHS trusts—Guy's in London and Bradford General—created a media debauch when they used their newfound freedom to sack hundreds of surplus staff. But as it became clear that, whatever they were doing, the Tories were not privatizing the NHS, the Labour Party had to come up with a new policy of its own. After much dithering, the Labour spokesman, Robin Cook, came up with an enfeebled version of the Tory idea: an internal market without the engine. He accepted the purchaser–provider split. But he refused to accept the case for NHS trusts or GP budget holders (despite the growing success of both). The only really firm ideas Cook produced were about introducing minimum wages and getting rid of compulsory-competitive tendering—in other words, handing money over to the public-sector unions.

Tony Blair went even further than Neil Kinnock in accepting the Tories' reforms. Throughout the May 1997 election, he put paid to any idea that Labour would return to its previous role as a catspaw of the health unions. True, in public he accused the Tories of closing hospitals and underfunding the health service; but in private he made it clear that he intended to preserve most of the ideas behind the reforms, including hospital trusts, GP fundholders, and the split between purchasers and providers. The paradox is that, if the reforms ever do yield a political dividend, the beneficiaries will not be the Tories, who courted unpopularity by implementing them, but Blair's Labour government.

Management theory in the public sector has clearly not lived up to the exaggerated claims of its acolytes. Politicians have demanded that the theorists achieve all sorts of impossible feats: cut expenditures while improving services, or boost morale while slashing workforces. The more unscrupulous theorists have played on these self-contradictory fantasies by overselling their products. Yet, for all the inevitable disappointments, management theory has clearly brought more good than harm to the public sector. Thanks to the gurus' ideas, organizations are leaner, lines of authority are clearer, and objectives are more clearly defined. The future lies in pushing ideas like delayering and contracting out farther still, not in returning to the old world of theory-free administration.

# CHAPTER 14

## A WALK ON THE WILD SIDE

IN THE HEARTLAND of management theory, there is usually either an established debate or one that gradually emerges after a slog through the literature. However, once you wander off toward the frontiers of management theory—the wilder areas where it mixes with self-help, philosophy, futurology, or downright quackery—this structure disappears. Like Oakland, there is often no "there" there. These unmapped regions are often where the greatest fortunes are to be made. Present your publisher with a long, well-argued treatise on supply-chain management and, with luck, you may be able to build a new kitchen. Shave off your hair, cobble together a few thoughts based on what your last girlfriend shouted at you or on an article you read about population trends, come up with a catchy title ("Unhinge Your Soul," "Supertrends 2010"), and, with a bit of luck and a lot of nerve, you should be able to buy your own island. Or so it seems.

This chapter is a brief survey of the strange but annoyingly wealthy creatures who are at home in this terrain. It is, to be honest, a bit of a rag bag, stretching as it does all the way from the former English rugby captain to Alvin Toffler and Bill Gates. Is it also a rogues' gallery? Not entirely. Yes, in many cases the marketing is more interesting than the product. Yes, the thinkers' appeal rests to an unusual extent on the fear or greed of their audience. But, there is occasionally something of value in what they are saying. Moreover, the gap between orthodox management theory and its flakier fringe seems to be narrowing. Consider first the man who has made a fortune by mixing together America's three great obsessions: management theory, religion, and self-help.

## A Very Effective Person

In the early 1970s, flush with cash from *Butch Cassidy and the Sundance Kid,* Robert Redford started to build his own small chunk of paradise 50 miles north of Salt Lake City amid several hundred acres of soaring rockfaces, giant redwoods, and iceclear streams. Redford still uses one part of the Sundance estate as his own base; the rest of his mountain retreat has become a resort, offering trekking, riding, skiing, fishing—and, of course, self-improvement.

The ranch's best client is the Covey Leadership Center, an organization set up by Stephen Covey, an earnest bald-headed Mormon and sometime professor of management at Brigham Young University. Throughout the year, high-flying executives, politicians, and public servants flock to the ranch to attend week-long seminars. They watch films of the Berlin Wall collapsing. They read "wisdom literature"—books by the likes of Plato, Confucius, and Ben Franklin. They discuss the problems that prevent their companies from attaining peak performance and their personal relationships from going smoothly. They learn how to husband their time and order their priorities by using Covey's patented personal organizer. They climb the mountain and rescue each other from various contrived calamities. Above all—for this is America and these are "high-potential individuals"—they break down and weep.

Most of the Leadership Center's activities take place 20 minutes' drive down the mountain, in Provo. Despite its straight-laced Mormon roots, epitomized by Brigham Young University, Provo is now one of the world's liveliest technological centers. Almost every young person you meet seems to be working for Novell or for some small software house—or for Covey. One might well look at the town as an archipelago of small islands of Coveyism: in one building, Covey's lieutenants plan his campaign in the American South; in another, they wonder how he will conquer the Asian market; in yet another, they produce books, magazines, videotapes, and personal organizers. Soon all these operations will be bundled together in their own brand new "campus" on the outskirts of Provo.

By 1997, Covey's management training business, founded in 1985 with a staff of two, employed 700 people and had revenues of close to $100 million. Its clients include more than half of the Fortune 500 companies—among them, AT&T, Ford, Xerox, and Merck. The center works with 2,900 school districts and was helping 10 of them, including, extraordinarily, Detroit, Dallas, and the Bronx, to become "principle-centered places." Covey's ideas have also been embraced by institutions as diverse as the Idaho Minimum Security Prison and the Oneida Indian Nation, which was keen to break its economic dependence on legalized gambling.

The foundation stone of this gigantic business is a single management book, *The Seven Habits of Highly Effective People,* which has sold about five million copies since it was published in 1989. The message of the book is simple enough: in order to reach your full potential, you have to build "character." Unlike other self-help creeds that just provide a set of excuses for people's failings, Coveyism is actually quite a tough discipline: people have to take responsibility for their actions, not blame them on others.

Unfortunately, this rigor does not extend to the book's style. The first six words of *The Seven Habits* are: "To my colleagues, empowered and empowering." Worse is to come. The first of Covey's seven habits is "be proactive"; the sixth is "synergize." (In conversation with Covey, "synergy" vies with "paradigm shift" as a favorite phrase.) He is forever referring to "emotional bank accounts" and "deposits of unconditional love."

This is disturbing territory. How can you respect a man who restates Aesop's fable about the goose that laid the golden egg as "the P/Pc Balance" (for production/production capability)? Can you really take seriously a man who claims, straight-faced, to have identified "the universal value system of all mankind"? The instinctive response of any cynical British journalist, or perhaps just anybody whose bank account (either financial or emotional) is a little less plentiful than Covey's, is to reach for the critical hatchet.

In fact, this reaction, while wholly excusable, is not entirely fair. (To begin with, there are plenty of people who are considerably flakier than Covey—as we shall see later.) The best way to appreciate Covey is to consider exactly why he has been so successful. The first reason is simple enough: he means it. Whatever its weaknesses, Coveyism's emphasis on personal responsibility comes from the heart. Covey's own Mormonism has been lifelong and unflinching. He keeps a family mission statement on the wall of his sitting room, and he has never smoked or drunk alcohol. He cultivated his skills as a public orator, and his habit of getting people to learn by teaching, through five years of missionary work in England and Ireland. He is the sort of man who can say without a hint of embarrassment or self-consciousness: "We are not human beings having a spiritual experience. We are spiritual beings having a human experience."

Nor is Covey some cone-headed fanatic from the sticks. He studied business at both the University of Utah and Harvard Business School, before moving back to his local university, Brigham Young. While doing his PhD dissertation ("American Success Literature since 1776"), Covey discovered that, for the first 150 years of the Republic, most success literature concentrated on questions of character. But shortly after the Second World War, people became more interested in superficial things such as appearance and style. Covey started to preach that people needed to get back to the ancient discipline of character building. Soon his classes at Brigham Young were attracting hundreds of students. In 1985, he gave up his professorship and gambled everything he had on the Covey Leadership Center.

The second explanation for Covey's success is that he runs an extremely efficient business. Covey is unapologetic about wanting to turn the center into the world's biggest multinational self-help organization. In Provo, for instance, Covey has removed himself from the day-to-day operations of his company, handing power to a loyal cadre of lieutenants, many of them from his own huge family, so as to give himself more time to concentrate on "high-leverage opportunities"—dealing with company bosses, giving broadcasts by satellite, and mixing with politicians. Meanwhile, on the ground, *The Seven Habits* has ingeniously spawned its own sales force. Rather than just treating the book as a quick emotional workout, readers are urged to put the structures and systems in place to make those changes into permanent habits. The best way to turn good intentions into habits is to start teaching what you have learned. The result is that, all around the country, Covey's acolytes are organizing reading groups, becoming trainers, acting as coaches—and spreading the word.

Nor is there any shortage of products for this pipeline to suck up. The center already has two other best-sellers on its hands, *Principle-Centered Leadership* (1992), and, prepared with the help of Convey's brother and aimed at *The Seven Habits of Highly Effective Families* (1997) targeted healing the American family. It is also expanding its personal-organizer business, teaming up with Microsoft to produce a software version. (The point of a Covey organizer as opposed to a normal one is that, each week, it forces you to set priorities as well as to organize your appointments.)

But Covey is determined to push the business in two directions. The first is overseas. Covey bridles at the thought that his ideas are peculiarly American, let alone Mormon. *The Seven Habits* is available in 28 languages and 35 countries; almost as soon as it was translated into Korean it sold 650,000 copies, and demand is swelling in both Japan and China. The second expansion will be deep into America's troubled public sector. Here Covey has powerful allies. Hazel O'Leary, the former energy secretary, caught the Covey bug when she was vice-president of Northern States Power. She went on to offer training in the seven habits to all the employees of the government's tenth largest department. Bill Clinton (who spent Thanksgiving in 1994 holed up in Camp David with Covey) told a conference on the future of the American workplace that American productivity would soar if people would just read *The Seven Habits*. Nor are the Republicans keen to be left behind: Covey penned a chapter in Newt Gingrich's book on American civilization.

Perhaps mixing management, religion, and self-help guaranteed a gigantic audience; after all, Covey is delivering the American dream—both economic success and spiritual salvation in one go. His ideas have attracted plenty of desperate people who think that reading a book and buying an organizer can transform them from time-wasting slobs into models of efficiency. But

Covey has also persuaded many respectable companies to part with their money too.

Put another way, merely meaning what you say and knowing how to sell it does not mean much if the message itself does not have some unique selling point. The third reason that Covey has been successful is that, underneath all that frightful talk about enabling, his ideas actually have some relevance to mainstream management theory.

Most management thinkers are obsessed with corporate organization and its systems of control and reward. From Frederick Taylor to the reengineers, there has been a long tradition of thinking about people as if they are soldiers on the parade ground: the theorists have concentrated on trying to put them into the most effective patterns. Even the "human relations school"—thinkers such as Douglas McGregor, who had a big influence on Covey when he was a student at Harvard—has mostly been concerned with improving career ladders and giving workers a stake in the company. Coveyism starts with individuals—and sets out to improve them before slotting them into their place. Coveyism is total-quality management for the character, reengineering for the soul.

Cynics argue that Covey serves the needs of corporations that want to shift the responsibility for coping with job turbulence to the citizenry at large. Jeremy Rifkin, the author of *The End of Work,* has criticized Covey for creating the psychological conditions for "just-in-time employment." Instead of spending the time between one short-term job and another drinking and going to seed, Covey's pupils spend it "sharpening the saw"—his phrase for improving their mental and physical health. It would be interesting to know how many of the AT&T managers who scampered around the mountains with Covey were later downsized in the telephone giant's huge restructuring—and even more interesting to know how many returned from Provo to plot that restructuring.

All the same, "character" does seem to be a valid topic for management theorists to discuss. One of the attractions of Covey is that he has tried to rescue "character" from both the simple-minded purveyors of self-help (who imply that you can change your character as easily as your underwear) and the social-service establishment (which ignores questions of character by blaming everything on "the system"). Meanwhile,

Covey's basic idea—that businesses should think about how individuals feel as well as about the organizational structures in which they work—is gaining ground. Witness the firms now sending reengineered employees on motivational courses; or the business schools offering courses in such soft subjects as ethics and leadership.

## Improve Yourself

One reason that Covey has won over organizations like IBM is that, by the standards of his area of management theory, he seems alarmingly well qualified. Consider one of his main rivals, Anthony Robbins, a school janitor turned "peak performance coach" who makes $50 million a year from his seminars alone (according to his own estimates) and whose clients include Bill Clinton, Andre Agassi, and the Princess of Wales. "Diana admires his drive, energy and optimism," commented her biographer, Andrew Morton, "while the American millionaire lecturer has sensed that beyond the suffering and sadness lurks a brave, strong woman."[1]

Robbins is an even more arresting sight than the spectacularly bald Covey—he is almost 7 feet tall and a dead ringer for Superman—and he shows none of his rival's self-restraint when it comes to enjoying the fruits of his labors. He divides his time between his castle in San Diego, California, which comes complete with a helicopter pad, and his island in Fiji. The essence of Robbins's message, laid down in books such as *Awaken the Giant Within* (1991) and *Unlimited Power* (1987), is that you can achieve anything you want just so long as you adopt the right attitude: just think and it will be yours. To drive home his case, he uses a blend of homespun wisdom, positive thinking techniques, uplifting case studies, and out-and-out showmanship.

Meditation and chanting, argues Robbins, can be used to unlock the creative capacities of the "right brain." However, the main way to unleash one's power seems to be opening one's wallet to attend an *Unleash the Power Within* seminar, given by Robbins. These attract thousands of people and are a cross between an evangelical sermon and a magical extravaganza. The high point comes when some members of the audience walk barefoot across thousands of burning coals, protected by nothing other than the power of positive thinking. (It is not known whether Clinton or Princess Diana completed this feat; their power was unleashed in private.)

If Robbins has any relevance to the wider world of management theory, it has unfortunately passed us by. However, one attraction of the Robbins package (and, for that matter, of the Covey package too) is that they are both one-stop shops for self-improvement. This gives them an edge over their peers in the self-help industry, who usually offer to improve just one aspect of our performance. The market has become hopelessly segmented. For instance, Morris Shechtman, a "corporate psychotherapist" (and another of Newt Gingrich's admirees), specializes in reducing the "trauma and distress" caused by corporate restructuring (he has been to the Capitol to help Republicans understand "the impact of [the] grieving process on public policy"). Another part of the management industry claims that you can radically improve your productivity simply by organizing your desk properly—and the United States has a National Association of Professional Organizers to prove it.

One of the most fertile segments might be described as mental gymnastics. Here, the uncrowned king is Edward de Bono, the father of lateral thinking. De Bono is not short on self-confidence: the subtitle of one of his books is *From Socratic to de Bono Thinking*. De Bono's books are full of clever puzzles designed to make you realize that the best way to approach a problem is often from the side: "the mind must wobble before it can leap," argues De Bono. Nevertheless, the most notable thing about the modern Plato is his ability to plow a single furrow long after lesser men would have wobbled into a different pasture out of sheer boredom. De Bono has been writing books and giving seminars on lateral thinking since 1967. Though lateral thinking has often been treated with disdain by academics, it has provided de Bono with both wealth and influence. From his private island in Venice, he dispenses advice to giant corporations and the educational bureaucracies of Venezuela, Singapore, and Bulgaria.

Today's most pervasive self-improvement philosophy comes under the New Age rubric. New Agers disagree about technical questions, endlessly debating whether hand-holding, meditation, or chanting is the best way to get on in life; but they all seem to agree on the awfulness of something called "the Newtonian paradigm." Isaac Newton is condemned for legitimizing an atomistic approach to the world, in which things can be looked at in isolation. New Agers—a category that includes Peter Senge (see Chapter 6)—are much more impressed by quantum physics, cybernetics, chaos theory, cognitive science, Eastern and Western spiritual traditions—or indeed anything that reveals that everything is interconnected with everything else: that you cannot change one bit of the world without affecting another.

This may all seem a long way away from management. But management consultancies peddling New Age cure-alls of one kind or another seem to be doing flourishing business. Some consultancies help managers clarify their "business visions" by persuading them to dance; others by dressing them up as druids and witches and setting them off on the mythical quest for "Dungeons and Dragons." The Esalen Institute, located at Big Sur in California, helps people do everything from reducing their stress to enhancing their creativity. A British company, Decision Development, uses the American Indian Medicine Wheel to help managers discover their inner selves. In Japan, an alternative think tank, the Mukta Institute in Tokyo, helps companies tap into Buddhist modes of thought. Predictably enough, the Maharishi Foundation has set up a school of management that specializes in "training managers to bring unfailing success and continuing progress to their companies" through meditation and levitation.

These gurus all preach the same seductive message: that we achieve far less than we are capable of achieving; and that we can close the gap between promise and achievement if we understand ourselves, set appropriate goals, remove inner blockages, and transform fear into strength. They also preach their message in more or less the same ways. They are forever drawing up lists. Covey has "seven habits"; Robbins has "five keys to wealth and happiness" and 365 lessons in self-mastery, of which the 364th is "remember to expect miracles . . . because you are one." They are also addicted to metaphors, which they repeat throughout their writings and dwell on in loving detail. Covey likes metaphors from the natural world; at times, he seems worryingly like Chancy Gardiner, the character played by Peter Sellers in the film *Being There:* "The sequential leadership development can be likened to a tree."

## Surfing the Wave

Unleashing all this hidden power is not much good unless you know where you wish to ride with it. As already noted, one of the most highly prized abilities among the gurus is the ability to see into the future. Most mainstream management theorists have concentrated on trying to work out the best ways for companies to cope with a changing world (see Chapter 7) rather than trying to predict what will happen. However, there is also a fringe school of futurologists.

Nearly all the futurologists are technological determinists, convinced that the motor of history lies in steam engines and computer chips. Futurology is full of excited talk about the transition from a mainframe society to a PC society, with the attendant collapse of giant bureaucracies and triumph of small, nimble organizations. On the whole, the genre is irredeemably pessimistic; there is a lot of talk about the inevitability of workers being pushed out of the way by machines (which we have dealt with in Chapter 9). The nonarrival of each disaster does no more to kill the genre than the nonarrival of the end of the world kills cults that preach it.

All the same, it is noticeable that the more optimistic authors often do best. For instance, John Naisbitt, author of *Megatrends* (1983), which has sold eight million copies, and sundry spin-offs, including *Megatrends Asia* (1995), admits that the future may have its problems—governments in particular will be left in the dust by the quickening pace of technological change; but, in general, he says the future will make us all a good deal better off. This jaunty optimism has helped turn him into "one of the world's top social forecasters." Reading his books, however, one is hard-pressed to think of anything in them that has not been said before—or anything that is not already established wisdom. Even a fleeting visit to, say, Bangkok should be enough to show the Asian megatrend: "people moving from the villages to megacities." Similarly, a quick dinner with any Asian economist could have unearthed the megatrend that many Asian industries are changing from "labor-intensive to high technology."

While Naisbitt's chief skill is as a packager, Alvin Toffler is a little more daring. His first book, *Future Shock* (1970), opened with a bold statement: "In the three short decades between now and the twenty-first century, millions of ordinary, psychologically normal people will face an abrupt collision with the future." In Toffler's case, this collision took the form of gigantic amounts of money pouring into his bank account. The book sold in its millions and turned Toffler (and his wife, Heidi) into a regular feature on the international lecture circuit. It also paved the way for two follow-ups, *The Third Wave* (1980) and *Powershift* (1990).

Toffler's appeal lies in the impression that he understands the broad sweep of history. He started life as a Marxist (an appropriate beginning for any technological determinist); he organized civil rights protests in the South and worked for years in a car factory. Nowadays, he is worshipped by the libertarian right: he was invited to dinner in the White House by both Ronald Reagan and George Bush, has given a keynote address to a meeting of Republican governors, and (inevitably) is worshiped by Newt Gingrich.

Toffler divides history into three stages (or waves): the agricultural, lasting to the eighteenth century; the industrial, lasting to the present; and, now, the information age. The information age is bringing the end of some of the most familiar features of the industrial age—massification (mass production, mass markets, mass political parties, mass media) and conformity (company man and his Stepford wife)—and is ushering in a very different world. The computer chip is simultaneously bringing globalization (killing distance by putting us all at the end of the line) and demassification (dissolving crowds into tiny interest groups). Toffler is quite interesting about the future shape of commerce (he follows Drucker's line on the importance of knowledge workers and virtual companies). But his more original thoughts tend to be political. For instance, he suggests that majority rule should be replaced with a "minority-based, twenty-first-century democracy," relying less on elected assemblies than on electronic referendums, and less on central than on local government.

Appropriately, by the mid-1990s, the technological determinists were being pushed to one side by the technologists—a new group of "digital gurus." Most of these people seemed to have been born with a computer in their hands. The classical digital guru is Nicholas Negroponte, the high priest of multimedia who works at MIT's media lab. But the group also includes Kevin Kelly, the executive editor of *Wired,* the party organ of the digerati, and George Gilder, an economist who seems to know more about computers than most people in Silicon Valley. The digital gurus are preoccupied with working out what the microchip, PC, and Internet mean for the rest of us. Their attraction is that they are much closer to the cutting edge than people like Toffler and Naisbitt—and consequently far more original. Gilder, for instance, was one of the first people to realize the importance of computer networks. Yet this affection for technology can also be a weakness: they often seem to believe that nothing ill can come of it.

This unabated optimism is certainly more convincing than the murmurings of the dreary "End-of-Work" crowd. But the technologists can seem irrepressibly upbeat—none more so than their most recent recruit, Bill Gates. *The Road Ahead* is Gates's guide to the information highway (a phrase he rightly dislikes). Although he spells out a few problems for particular groups of people, his tone is optimistic. Yes, "friction-free capitalism" on the Net will put many intermediaries, such as travel agents and retailers, out of business. But the consumer will gain—and different sorts of travel agents and retailers will arise. Yes, more rich people will work at home in the country, but that does not necessarily mean that ghettos will cease to be. The book comes most alive when Gates talks about gizmos that will make our lives easier, such as small computers that will act as phones, wallets, and diaries.

But is there any link with management theory? Not really. Gates makes the interesting prediction that, although the computer revolution has generally helped small companies so far by putting at their fingertips information that was previously only available to larger companies, the next networking phase of the computer revolution may help big ones by providing a way to bring a large number of people together; but he does not really follow it up. Books such as *The Road Ahead* tend to fall into a category that runs parallel to management theory but never quite meets it. Guessing what the future will be is a very profitable (and entertaining) game. But management involves decisions in the present. Even if you know what the future will be, you have won only half the battle. You then have to put together an organization to take advantage of it.

### Come on Down

In two respects, Gates is not a typical new guru: he has no need of money and he knows how to run a company. Over the past few years, management theory has begun to resemble a town in the middle of the gold rush: not only are you overwhelmed by the stench of greed, you also run into the most extraordinary people. Walk into a bookshop and alongside Drucker's *The Concept of the Corporation* you can find titles such as *Jesus CEO: Using Ancient Wisdom for Visionary Leadership* and *Make It So: Leadership Lessons from Star Trek: the Next Generation,* not to mention a menagerie of books with titles like *Swim with the Sharks* and *Roaring with the Lions.*

One clearly discernible group is the philosophers. The recent boom in studying ethics, fueled by worries about corruption, pollution, and the escalating salaries of bosses, has encouraged business schools to invite philosophers across for the day to speculate about the link between their trade and management. Now they are leaving their ivory towers (with their low pay and bitchy politics) and selling their skills more directly. Europe boasts more than a hundred "philosophic practices" staffed by refugees from academia who are willing to offer advice on subjects ranging from the changing nature of work to the right to be lazy.[2] The first such practice was opened in Germany in 1989, but the country that has the greatest affinity for the approach is the Netherlands, with 20. France, the home of the *philosophes,* only has three.

The second group (which really ought to know better) is the original "unacknowledged legislators of mankind": poets. A few modern bards have felt the calling of the corporate checkbook. David Whyte, a Yorkshireman now based in Seattle, has written *The Heart Aroused: Poetry and the Preservation of the Soul in Corporate America.* His "lectures" to corporations consist of recitals of poems and folktales, intended to stir managers' creative juices. He has consulted for AT&T, Boeing, and Dana. Poets have been joined by novelists. One of the best-selling management books of the past few years is Elie Goldratt's *The Goal*

(1989), which tells of how a production manager grapples with the complexities of total-quality management.

A third and much bigger group is composed of sports people. Perhaps this meeting of minds was inevitable, given the enthusiasm of managers for sport and the fondness of management writers for sporting analogies. But the latest management fads, with their emphasis on coaching and team-building, have been an open invitation for aging sports figures to turn themselves into management gurus. Needless to say, coaches are in particular demand. In March 1996, *The New York Times* asked several conventional management writers to assess the content of two recent best-sellers, *The Winner Within: A Life Plan for Team Players* (1993) by Pat Riley, and *Sacred Hoops* (1995) by Phil Jackson.[3] The general conclusion of the audit was fairly unsurprising: that most of what the coaches were saying about the importance of goals and teamwork was familiar motivational stuff but that the coaches had an undoubted talent for getting their message across through memorable examples.

The fourth group of management interlopers might be described as intellectual traders—people who import ideas wholesale from other disciplines. For instance, chaos theory (which has already migrated from physics to financial economics, with mixed success) pops up from time to time in management theory too. Some people argue that companies should no longer try to form strategies, because strategies are an artifact of linear thinking, and we now live in a nonlinear world, where tiny events can cause gigantic triumphs or disasters. Recently, however, biology rather than physics seems to be in the ascendant.

The most prominent thinker in this field is Ichak Adizes. He argues that companies have life cycles; just like individuals, they endure the normal difficulties of each stage of development and run the risk of such human ills as infant death and premature aging. When young, they are flexible but overemotional; when old, they have their emotions under control but tend to be set in their ways. They are ideal when they are in their prime. Although this does not seem like a particularly startling insight, Adizes sells it with astonishing panache, through dozens of books, tapes, newsletters, an Adizes Institute in Bel Air, and a network of "certified Adizes Professionals" all around the world.

## My Generation

One could argue that there is nothing new about the likes of Covey, Robbins, or Adizes. Half a century ago, Napoleon Hill made a fortune out of a book entitled *Think and Grow Rich* (1937). Hill's capacity to make money was only equaled by his ability to lose it. Still, he also drew up plans to found "the world's first university-sized success school" on his ranch in the Catskills and acted as a consultant to major companies. And his influence reaches beyond the grave: Newt Gingrich lists *Think and Grow Rich* as one of the books that most influenced him.

The difference is that, these days, the gap between the latter-day Napoleon Hills and respectable business theorists seems to have narrowed. Take for instance, Gemini, a well-known consultancy that lists some of the world's biggest companies among its clients. In 1995, two of its leading consultants, Francis Gouillart and James Kelly, produced a book intended to demonstrate the firm's intellectual credentials. However, no one picking up *Transforming the Organization* comes away reinvigorated by the rigor of its arguments; rather, you feel as if you have wandered back through time to a tent at Woodstock:

> It is time to replace our mechanistic view of business with a more organic one, and to endow the recently discovered biological nature of our corporations with a new spirituality that recognizes the sanctity of individual human life and has compassion for individuals.[4]

The authors urge companies to forget about dominance and preeminence and become "loved and respected institutions." But the path to this desirable end is not easy, they advise: "Like people, corporations become more whole and more credible when they embrace both the hero and the villain within themselves, both their soul and its shadow."[5] They talk about breaking through "walls of reluctance and denial"—a feat that they hope to accomplish with the help of something called bioreengineering.[6]

Picking on the men from Gemini is a little unfair. Conventional management thinkers of all kinds are increasingly looking at touchy-feely themes that make it difficult to be intellectually

rigorous, even if you want to be. Many of the ideas preached by
the gurus of the 1990s might have been invented in Haight As-
bury: shifting from command and control to flat organizations;
handing power down to workers; dreaming up visions rather
than planning strategies; thinking globally rather than just nationally. Besides, the thinkers are only responding to their market. Companies feel that they have reengineered the soul out of
their organizations—and that they need to restore that soul by
sending their workers off on a spiritual quest.

The temptation to "let it all go" is all the greater, seeing that
some of the most profitable companies of the past few years have
had a decidedly "new age" flavor. "Lighten up . . . feel your
bliss," implores a large sign in the reception area of the Body
Shop in Littlehampton, on England's Sussex coast. Workers
stroll around the place wearing T-shirts proclaiming "Extinct is
forever." Body Shop trucks bear slogans like "Practice random
kindness and senseless acts of beauty." Employees attend "values meetings," where they discuss what makes the company special to them. The in-house phone list is alphabetized by first
names: it is Anita, not Mrs. Roddick.

Interest in this approach is spreading beyond the fringe. In
the United States, a New Age think tank, Global Business Network, is underwritten by companies such as AT&T, Volvo, and
Nissan. Procter & Gamble and Du Pont are offering their employees "personal growth experiences," to encourage them to
be more creative and give them a deeper sense of "ownership"
of company results. AT&T has sent hundreds of middle managers on courses at Transpective Business Consulting, a company in Woburn, Massachusetts, which, for $1,650 a person,
offers to help people become better leaders by getting them to
tune in to themselves. IBM's "fit for the future" seminars introduce employees to I Ching, a Chinese oracle. Lotus Development Corporation has a "soul committee" that makes sure the
company lives up to its values. Even old "Neutron" Jack Welch
babbles about wanting people to be rewarded "in both the
pocket and the soul."

In 1991, TV-AM, a British breakfast television station,
adopted a new-age strategy in its effort to regain its franchise
when it was auctioned. Bruce Gyngell, the company's Aus-
tralian chairman, arranged a "personal growth seminar and development workshop" for his staff, at which they were invited

to focus their spiritual energy and inner peace, with a view to renewing not just themselves but their franchise. Unfortunately, the franchise went elsewhere. Nor are such high jinks confined to the private sector. The U.S. Army's current slogan, "Be all that you can be," is borrowed from the human potential movement. Every Wednesday, at the World Bank in Washington, a group of bank employees sits in a semicircle and tries to "connect."

In part, the gap between the fringe and the mainstream is narrowing because the generation that came of age in the 1960s, when Timothy Leary was regarded as a serious thinker, is moving into senior positions in business, consultancy, and academia. Members of this generation are much more open to wacky ideas than their more cynical (or sensible) seniors. They have also reached a stage in their lives when they have built up successful careers, had several children, and started looking for the deeper meaning of life; even Hillary Rodham Clinton, as hard-faced a lawyer-cum-politician as you are likely to find anywhere, has taken to talking about the "politics of meaning," a concept invented by another 50-something, Michael Lerner.

This is all very well—except for two things. First (as the Gemini book shows), when management theory wanders off into these new territories, it seems to lose whatever structure and coherence it had in the first place. And, second, these fringe areas rely even more extravagantly on marketing rather than content. The fringe figures are far more unrestrained in the fears they conjure up and the hopes they promise to satisfy. The hallmark of men such as Covey, Robbins, Toffler, and Adizes is marketing panache. Nobody has ever accused Stephen Covey of buying up copies of his own books in order to propel them to the top of the best-seller list. He has no need to.

# Conclusion:
# An Immature Discipline

INSTEAD OF GOING on ordinary holidays, the most fanatical managers relax by taking tours of the world's best-run companies. Experienced tourists have already visited Toyota City in Japan, to see lean manufacturing in action, or Walt Disney World in Florida, to learn the late Uncle Walt's "pixie dust" formula for managing people. Now, the hardened backpackers in their ranks crave ever more exotic attractions such as Springfield ReManufacturing, a maker of diesel engines that shows its employees all its financial figures, and Johnsonville, an American sausage maker renowned for its ability in team building.

Our own tour of management theorists has been a bizarre experience. Drop in on Michael Porter or Michael Jensen at the Harvard Business School and you catch sight of the theorist as a respectable academic, churning out articles for learned journals, arguing over the finer points of econometrics, and even doing the regular grunt work of marking students' papers. Visit Stephen Covey's leadership center, and you can see the theorist as therapist, encouraging his clients to talk about their innermost feelings. Buy a seat at any Tom Peters seminar to observe the theorist as preacher, telling his audience that the latest buzzword can mean the difference between bankruptcy and unimaginable riches.

In few other academic disciplines do personal peccadilloes play such a large part. In writing about management, many of the gurus are simply writing about themselves—and their decidedly abnormal lives. Believing in portfolio workers is so much easier if, like Charles Handy, you are one already. Imagining that the future belongs to those with a global "Anchorage mentality" comes easily to a bilingual Japanese, such as Kenichi Ohmae. If Tom Peters had ended up in the Ruhr Valley rather than Silicon Valley, the world might have ended up with *Thriving on Order*.

Even a brief encounter with the world of management theory leaves two immediate impressions. The first is of enormous commercial success. When not ministering to their students, the Harvard professors are jetting off to conferences or offering advice to giant companies. Covey's Leadership Center vies with leading software companies as the most successful enterprise in Provo. Speakers of the caliber of Peters can earn as much giving a seminar for a day as many middle managers earn in a year. One casual conversation between the authors and one of the best-known gurus on the subject of who was the greediest theorist produced too many suspects to name.

The second impression is that management theory is a mishmash. The books of tenured professors rub spines with those of out-and-out charlatans. Management consultancies can spend a small fortune on some worthy piece of research and then demean themselves with an exhibition of needless hucksterism. In conversation, every guru can move in a flash from a point of genuine insight or scholarship to one of extraordinary banality.

The gurus' enormous commercial success and the variability of their output are linked. So far, management theory has produced, at most, one "great" thinker: Peter Drucker. However, even Drucker has found it impossible to come up with breakthrough ideas year after year, as the industry now demands that he should. Lesser writers face an even harder task. Many jumped opportunistically to management theory from other academic disciplines. Their first or second book included perhaps one genuine insight. Now, surrounded by the paraphernalia of their trade—their own consultancy, the speaking tours, the book contract, the mortgage payments on their third home—they are obliged to churn out material, hoping to stumble across the next big idea. Even if they were capable of finding another insight (which in many cases looks unlikely), they have little chance of stumbling across it this way.

## The Case for the Gurus

The existence of so much junk has understandably led many people to dismiss management theory, lock, stock, and barrel. Scott Adams, the cartoonist who invented Dilbert and Dogbert, has made millions out of poking fun at management theorists and their works. "A consultant is a person who takes your money and annoys your employees while tirelessly searching for the best way to extend the consulting contract" is one of his gentler judgments. By mid-1997, his book, *The Dilbert Principle,* had been near the top of the *Business Week* best-seller list for more than a year. *Dogbert's Secret Management Handbook* had also become a best-seller; and Mr. Adams's cartoons were syndicated in more than 1,500 newspapers around the world. In writing this book, we have repeatedly come across the same reaction: How can you waste your time on such rubbish? We have listened to a long list of complaints, often delivered with striking vitriol, about management theory: that it is an apology for an academic subject, methodologically sloppy and a slave to fashion; that it causes huge harm to companies by persuading them to engage in perpetual revolution; and that its practitioners are charlatans of the worst sort, charging gargantuan fees for nothing more useful than translating common sense into grotesque jargon.

The first point we hope to have made in this book is that there is a discipline worth calling management theory: that general lessons can be extracted from what companies do and can be used to help other companies operate better. Successful management ideas are not just bits of local knowledge, fixed by culture and circumstances. They can travel and, suitably modified, can be used to reproduce that success elsewhere—in other countries and industries. The Japanese, for one, took American ideas about quality control and used them to create lean production; the Americans then reimported lean production and used it to galvanize their faltering car industry. The public sector has borrowed ideas from the private sector; good companies have borrowed ideas from management pacemakers, such as Motorola, Toyota, and McDonald's. And, in most cases, they have improved the institutions concerned.

The second point is that management theory is not entirely devoid of intellectual content. The best theorists tackle big subjects that touch all our lives, from globalization to how to husband intellectual capital. Indeed, political argument and popular debate might be improved if "normal" people had a better grasp of management theory.

Third, so far, the results coming back from management theory's continuously experimenting laboratory are broadly positive. Industry leaders such as Motorola, Merck, and 3M (just to name American firms beginning with "M") have all made a point of taking management theory seriously. Not all the ideas work, but those that do, such as quality in Motorola's case, tend to give them an advantage. Microsoft is showing every sign of following suit. In Europe, Japan, and Asia, the most admired company in each country—be it Acer in Taiwan, Toyota in Japan, or Marks and Spencer in Britain—is frequently a pioneer in management theory. Contrast two companies in broadly the same business—such as America's General Electric and Westinghouse or Citibank and Chase Manhattan—and you will often find that the company that has pulled ahead—General Electric and Citibank—is the management junkie.

This may even be true of countries too. There are many reasons for Japan's emergence as an economic power, of course, but one of them was surely the way that its companies studied and adapted management ideas. Management theory plays at least a small role in explaining the relative states of American and German industry. During the 1980s, American business restructured furiously, trying to keep up with the latest fashions like core competencies and outsourcing. German business people stood arrogantly aloof from such "fads," believing that good technology and craftsmanship would see them through. By the mid-1990s, the Germans felt conspicuously outdated. They have now embraced the ideas they earlier rejected.

### Teenage Angst

So why does a discipline that contains so much sense contain so much nonsense as well? One answer is that management theory is a young discipline; its canonical texts and defining methodologies are still being developed. As we explained in the introduction, management theory feels as if it is around 100 years younger than disciplines such as economics. This teenage period is likely to go on for some time—if only because the enormous financial success and influence of the discipline have created a cocoon around the gurus.

Rather than fretting about management theory's excesses, perhaps we should be grateful that its adolescence has not been stormier. Poor management theories have cost people their jobs; they have bankrupted companies; they may even (who really knows?) be doing irreparable damage to public organizations such as Britain's National Health Service and Argentina's telephone system. But set alongside the chaos and suffering caused by communist economics, management theory's encounter with puberty seems relatively benign.

A second explanation is that management theory's audience demands instant solutions. Anxious managers grasp at management literature as a panacea for all their worries. Many firms turn to management theory only when they are desperate. Their minds clouded by panic, they start out with exaggerated expectations, put the theory into practice for a few months, start to despair when it fails to produce results, and then turn to a new theory. Two years and 20 theories later, the business may well be bankrupt. But who is to blame: the theorists who failed to save the firm or the managers who got it into trouble in the first place?

The third explanation is less charitable: the discipline, no less than astrology, is a magnet for charlatans. The fortunes that can be made by the successful gurus are gigantic, and there are virtually no barriers to entry. And even people who are not out-and-out frauds seem to suffer from all sorts of problems, from an inability to write English to a compulsion to jump on the latest bandwagon.

## How to Choose a Witch Doctor

How can we distinguish between the charlatans and the rest? There are a few initial rules-of-thumb to follow. The first is that anything that you suspect is bunk almost certainly is. Similarly, beware of all authors who emblazon the covers of their books with their academic honors, or who argue entirely by analogy.

It would have been nice to come up with an approved list of good gurus, but, as we have shown, even the best theorists tend to be hit-and-miss, and even the worst ones sometimes have something to say. Most of the ideas covered in this book fall into the broader category of "good" management theory—concepts that every manager should think about. That still leaves the question of which ones a manager should implement.

The trite but truthful answer is: Be selective. Nothing is more witch-doctorish than the suggestion that one magic potion will cure all ills. By all means, reengineer your distribution system; but think twice about your research-and-development arm. By all means, empower your workers, but think what you are giving them power over. One of AT&T's many attempts to turn around its NCR computer subsidiary involved "empowering" salespeople to approve contracts; this only meant that the salespeople, eager to add to their quota, started taking on low-margin business that NCR would normally have rejected. And always remember that the cure can be worse than the disease. The short-term gain from axing a small percentage of your workforce may well be eradicated by the long-term effect on morale; your wonderful new "global" product may save money on packaging and advertising, but it may not appeal to the customers.

Choosing between the different medicines is not easy, particularly when so few of the witch doctors' products come with any kind of health warning. As we have already mentioned, the management theory industry is peculiarly devoid of self-criticism. Duly declaring our vested interest, we would like to point out that one glimmer of hope in this respect is the business press. Even though many media empires have a growing financial interest in promoting the gurus, a sufficient number of journalists seem to have kept their critical faculties. *Business Week* exposed CSC Index's manipulation of the sales of *The Discipline of Market Leaders*. It has also written some admirably tough reviews of books in which consultancies have invested a good deal of their credibility, notably Kelly and Gouillart's *Transforming the Organization*. In general, the reviews of management books are finally beginning to reflect the frustrations of readers.

There are signs that this more critical attitude is spreading to other areas of the industry. Management consultancies used to be able to get away with a lack of transparency that would have been impossible in almost any other profession. Now, clients are subjecting consultancies to much more probing interrogations before taking them on. They are also forcing them to share in the risks of major restructurings by paying them according to performance. Business schools have also become much more sensitive to criticisms from students, alumni, and employers, thanks to the rankings that now appear in magazines such as *Business Week*.

## Contradictions and Anxieties

This more critical attitude is commendable. But there are a number of problems that seem, if anything, to be getting worse. The first, which has come up time and again in this book, is the tendency of management theory to make today's contradictory corporation more contradictory still. As the pace of business increases around the world, the theorists are pulling companies in different directions, either by abandoning one nostrum for its opposite or by preaching completely contradictory things. Quite apart from the illogicality of trying, say, to force an organization to be more flexible (by sacking people) while at the same time teaching the virtues of trust, such fad surfing has an effect on companies' culture.

To be thrown to and fro has never been good for organizations of any sort at any time. Before any boss starts reinventing his (or her) company one more time, he should dismiss the consultants for the afternoon, unplug his telephone, lock the door, and study Gaius Petronius's description of a period of rapid change in the Roman Empire:

> We trained hard to meet our challenges but it seemed as if every time we were beginning to form into teams we would be re-organized. I was to learn later in life that we tend to meet any new situation by reorganizing; and a wonderful method it can be for creating the illusion of progress while producing confusion, ineffectiveness and demoralization.[1]

The second growing problem is management theory's insensitivity to language. It is hard to think of a subject in which sloppy writing is so prevalent. The average management book reads as if it had been translated from German, with nouns used as verbs and sentences that meander this way and that. Words like "reengineering" have a pseudoscientific air, meant to suggest that companies are machines, which can be retuned by clever technocrats. The peculiar illiteracy of management theory matters. Increasingly, institutions around the world are being run by people who have been trained in business schools. And the language of the "global cosmopolitans," as Rosabeth Moss Kanter dubs the new elite, is managementese. In *The End of History* (1992), Francis Fukuyama pointed out that all the big arguments about politics and economics have been won by democracy and free markets. That may be something of an exaggeration; but a growing number of arguments are all about management of one sort or another. It is no small thing if the language in which these debates are conducted is deformed. An idea communicated poorly, or in ways only the elect can understand, is more often than not poorly thought out, or eager to hide what it is actually about.

The third problem is management theory's insensitivity to the wider effects of its ideas. Back in the 1940s, Peter Drucker's pioneering work on General Motors treated the company as a social organization. Nowadays, only a few thinkers see the big picture. Charles Handy is increasingly preoccupied with the idea that companies are political communities, and that the best way to look at them is through the prism of political theory. Rosabeth Moss Kanter, a sociologist by training, has an acute eye for the social dynamics of companies. So, too, does Jay Forrester, an engineer by training. But most gurus are insensitive to the fact that businesses are social and political communities, with their distinctive mores, power struggles, and social dynamics.

A quick look at this wider social context brings home a number of unpleasant lessons. Thirty years ago, most Americans—particularly the managerial class—expected the future to bring increased leisure and certainty. On the whole, management theory has forced companies and public-sector institutions to become ever leaner. Millions have been downsized out of jobs; millions more work harder. These may be unavoidable things, but they often have been presented in such an inarticulate way that few workers of any description understand what is going on. It is hardly surprising that as the contradictory corporation pulls itself in opposing directions, fewer and fewer

Americans trust either their employers or their politicians. Like all the best witch doctors, management gurus have predicted a future of chaos and uncertainty that only they understand, and that their own work has only made more likely.

This is not to say that we are joining the popular clamor in favor of stakeholding. Shareholder capitalism makes it possible for companies to make difficult but necessary adjustments that its stakeholder brother fudges; downsizing, delayering, and reengineering a company is better than allowing it to die of obesity. But managers should remember that firms exist on the sufferance of their host communities. Downsizing may be necessary—but it is dangerous to raise the chairman's salary at the same time as you are laying off thousands of workers. Reengineering may be essential—but it is essential, too, to realize that, however powerful, the company's engine will not work unless it is fueled by the enthusiasm of the company's employees. The alternative is a popular backlash against big business (of the sort Pat Buchanan has tried to unleash in the United States) that could lead to draconian restrictions on management's freedom to manage. A good management theorist is something of a political theorist too.

## Up, Up, and Away

Whatever the discipline's problems, there is no doubt that it will go from strength to strength. Look at the income of the consultancies, the sales of management books, or the intake of business schools—all the trends are up. Most managers in the West have realized that, in a world in which new products can be copied instantaneously and wages can easily be undercut, the only lasting source of advantage is superior management. This realization is spreading to the East too. The founders of business empires in places like Hong Kong and Singapore might have been able to rely on personal connections and political influence to build their empires. But their successors need more formal management skills to prevent those empires from falling apart or stagnating.

But there is an even more important reason why the witch doctors will enjoy an ever-expanding demand for their services. Even if managers do learn how to thrive on chaos or control their destiny, they will still be confronted by that most intractable of all problems: the cussedness of human nature. Managers are constantly embracing techniques that promise to control the uncertainty at the heart of their jobs—and constantly having to embrace new techniques when their charges refuse to do as they are bid. In looking at the fate of managers and their pitiful predilection for magic cures, we are reminded of David Hume's insight: "In proportion as any man's course of life is governed by accident, we always find that he increases in superstition."

# Notes

## Introduction: The Unacknowledged Legislators

1   Financial Times (London), 29 December 1994, 4.

2   "America's Economic Anxiety," *Business Week,* 11 March 1996, cover story.

3   "The Downsizing of America," *New York Times,* 3–10 March 1996.

4   "Corporate Killers," *Newsweek,* 26 February 1996.

5   "Losers Feel the Stress of Playing Executive Games," *Daily Telegraph* (London), 4 January, 1995, 1.

6   Lucy Kellaway, "Volumes in Learning—Take It as Read," *Financial Times* (London), 12 September 1994.

7   Mauro F. Guillen, *Models of Management: Work, Authority and Organization in Comparative Perspective* (Chicago, 1994), 120.

8   Bain & Company, Planning Forum, "Management Tools and Techniques. Survey Results Summary," London, 1995.

9   J. A. Byrne, "Business Fads: What's In and What's Out," *Business Week,* 20 January 1986.

## Chapter 1: The Fad in Progress

1   "Re-engineering," *Wired,* August 1995, 125.

2   "The Struggle to Create an Organization for the 21st Century," *Fortune,* 3 April 1995.

3 "At Wharton, They're Practicing What They Preach," *New York Times,* 5 March 1995, F7.

4 Michael Hammer, *The Re-engineering Revolution: The Handbook* (New York, 1995), xii.

5 "What You Really Think about Re-engineering," *CFO Magazine,* May 1995.

6 "When Slimming Is Not Enough," *Economist,* 3 September 1994.

7 "Thanks, Goodbye," *Wall Street Journal,* 8 May 1995, 1.

8 "GTE to Reduce Staff by 17,000," *Financial Times* (London), 14 January 1994. Cited in *Financial Times Handbook of Management* (London, 1995), 234.

9 CSC Index, "Business Reengineering, The CSC Index Approach to Achieving Operational Excellence." Pamphlet.

10 The Lloyds case study is drawn from interviews by Micklethwait; parts of the story also appeared in "The Black Horse Goes to the Vet," *Economist,* 22 July 1995.

11 "The Pain of Downsizing," *Business Week,* 9 May 1994.

12 "Charles Handy Sees the Future," *Fortune,* 31 October 1994.

13 Gary Hamel and C. K. Prahalad, *Competing for the Future* (Boston, 1994), 5.

14 *California Management Review,* vol. 37, no. 4.

15 National Opinion Poll Survey of 801 union workers for Trade Union Conference, released September 1995 (*Daily Telegraph* [London] 11 September 1995).

16 The Corning case study is drawn from interviews by Wooldridge; parts of the story appeared in "Re-engineering, With Love," *Economist,* 9 September 1995, 92.

## Chapter 2: The Management Theory Industry

1 Figures are taken from Adrian Woolridge's survey of management consulting in "The Economist" for March 22, 1997.

2 John Kotter, *The New Rules: How to Succeed in the Post Corporate World* (New York, 1995).

3   Ronald Yeaple, *The MBA Advantage: Why It Pays to Get an MBA* (Boston, 1994). The discounted figures are from "The MBA Cost-Benefit Analysis," *Economist,* 6 August 1994.

4   "Leaping the Lectern," *New York Times,* 8 September 1995, D1.

5   "Survey of Asian Business," *Far Eastern Economic Review,* 14 September 1995.

6   Jean-Philippe Deschamps and Ranganath Nayak, *Product Juggernauts: How Companies Mobilize to Generate a Stream of Market Winners* (Boston, 1995).

7   Examples taken from *Business Week,* 18 September 1995.

8   Thomas J. Peters and Robert Waterman, *In Search of Excellence: Lessons from America's Best-Run Companies* (New York, 1982), 56.

## Chapter 3: Peter Drucker

1   Quoted by Carol Kennedy, *Guide to the Management Gurus: Top Level Guidance on Twenty Management Techniques* (London, 1991), 41.

2   C. S. George, *The History of Management Thought,* cited in David Clutterbuck and Stuart Cramer, *Makers of Management* (London, 1990).

3   "Pioneers and Prophets," *Financial Times* (London), 19 December 1994.

4   Lyndall Urwick and EFL Breech, *The Making of Scientific Management,* quoted in Clutterbuck and Cramer, *Makers of Management,* 8.

5   Mauro F. Guillen, *Models of Management: Work, Authority and Organisation in Comparative Perspective* (Chicago, 1994), 45–46.

6   Pauline Graham, ed., *Mary Parker Follett: Prophet of Management* (Boston, 1995), 27.

7   Guillen, *Models of Management,* 224.

8  Peter Drucker, *The Concept of the Corporation* (New York, 1983), 3.

9  Ibid., 78.

10  Quoted in Kennedy, *Guide to the Management Gurus,* 41.

11  Drucker, *Concept of the Corporation,* 132.

12  Interview with Charles Handy, 10 October 1995.

13  Breakfast with Bill Gates, 17 October 1994.

14  "Megachurches," *New York Times,* 18 April 1995.

15  Drucker, *Concept of the Corporation,* 241.

16  Ibid., 185.

17  Peter Drucker, *Managing in Turbulent Times* (London, 1980), 104.

18  Ibid., 226.

## Chapter 4: Tom Peters

1  Example taken from Economist Conference Unit, "Tom Peters: The Pursuit of Wow!" 27 October 1995, London.

2  Interview with Tom Peters, 27 October 1995.

3  For examples of this sort of argument, see "Europe Outgrows Management American Style," *Fortune,* 20 October 1980, 147–48; "Don't Blame the System, Blame the Managers," *Dun's Review,* September 1980, 88.

4  Thomas J. Peters and Robert H. Waterman, *In Search of Excellence: Lessons from America's Best-Run Companies* (New York, 1982), xxii.

5  Ibid., xxv.

6  Peter Drucker, *Frontiers of Management* (New York, 1986).

7  David Clutterbuck and Stuart Crainer, *Makers of Management: Men and Women Who Changed the Business World* (1990), 218.

8  Thomas J. Peters and Nancy Austin, *A Passion for Excellence* (London, 1985), Foreword.

9  Ibid., chap. 7.

10  Thomas J. Peters, *Liberation Management* (London, 1992), 612–14.

11   Homa Bahrami and Stuart Evans, "Flexible Re-Cycling and High-Technology Entrepreneurship," *California Management Review* 37, no. 3 (1995): 62–89.

12   "Tom Peters Seminar: The Pursuit of Wow!" London, 27 October 1995.

13   Tom Peters, "Maybe the Theories Need Re-engineering," TGP Communications, 1995.

14   Peters and Waterman, *In Search of Excellence,* 215.

15   Ibid., 270.

16   Ibid., 106–7.

17   Ibid., 30.

18   For a classic statement of this position, see Peter Drucker, *The Practice of Management* (New York, 1954).

19   John A. Byrne, *The Whiz Kids: Ten Founding Fathers of American Business—and the Legacy They Left Us* (New York, 1993).

20   Peters and Waterman, *In Search of Excellence,* 48.

21   Ibid., 55.

22   Ibid., 75.

23   "Corporate Culture: the Hard-to-Change Values That Spell Success or Failure," *Business Week,* 27 October, 1980, 148–60.

24   Anthony Sampson, *Company Man: The Rise and Fall of Corporate Life* (London, 1995), 196.

25   Letter from Tom Peters to authors, 30 October 1995.

## Chapter 5: Rethinking the Company

1   Anthony Sampson, *Company Man: The Rise and Fall of Corporate Life* (London, 1995), 221.

2   Tom Peters, "New Products, New Markets, New Competition, New Thinking," *Economist,* 4 March 1989, 27–32.

3   This argument has been made most persuasively by Bennett Harrison, *Lean and Mean: The Changing Landscape of Corporate America* (New York, 1994).

4   "The Case against Mergers," *Business Week,* 30 October 1995.

5   Harrison, *Lean and Mean.*

6   "The European Economist," *Wall Street Journal Europe,* 30 October 1995, 4.

7   N. C. Churchill and D. F. Muzyka, "Entrepreneurial Management: A Converging Theory for Large and Small Enterprises," Insead Corporate Renewal Initiative Working Papers, 2.

8   William H. Whyte, *Organisation Man* (New York, 1956); and David Riesman, *The Lonely Crowd* (New York, 1950).

9   The best example of this is Sampson, *Company Man.*

10   Sumantra Ghoshal and Christopher Bartlett, "Building the Entrepreneurial Corporation," *Financial Times Handbook of Management* (London, 1995), 41.

11   Jordan Lewis, *The Connected Corporation* (New York, 1995). See also "Holding the Hand that Feeds," *Economist,* 9 September 1995.

12   William Bridges, *Jobshift: How to Prosper in a Workplace without Jobs* (London, 1995), 20.

13   "Jack Welch Lets Fly on Budgets, Bonuses, and Buddy Boards," *Fortune,* 29 May 1995.

14   Quoted in Carol Kennedy, *Managing with the Gurus: Top Level Guidance on Twenty Management Techniques* (London, 1994), 30.

## Chapter 6: Knowledge, Learning, and Innovation

1   "Your Company's Most Valuable Asset: Intellectual Capital," *Fortune,* 3 October 1994.

2   See Phil Hodgson, "The Learning Organisation," *Financial Times Handbook of Management* (London, 1995), 691.

3   Dorothy Leonard-Barton, *Wellsprings of Knowledge: Building and Sustaining the Sources of Innovation* (Boston, 1995), 21.

4   Ibid., 24–27.

5   Ibid., 159–60.

6   John Kao, *Jamming: The Art and Discipline of Business Creativity* (New York, 1996), 52.

7   Leonard-Barton, *Wellsprings of Knowledge,* 156.

8   Ibid., 75–8.

9   "Tom Peters Seminar: The Pursuit of Wow!" London, 27 October 1995.

10   Leonard-Barton, *Wellsprings of Knowledge,* 70.

11   Ibid., 79.

12   Fred Moody, *I Sing the Body Electronic: A Year with Microsoft on the Multimedia Frontier* (New York, 1995).

13   Quoted in Michael Treacy and Fred Wiersema, *Discipline of Market Leaders* (New York, 1995), 95.

14   Jean-Philippe Deschamps and R. Ranganath Nayak, *Product Juggernauts: How Companies Mobilize to Generate a Stream of Market Winners* (Boston, 1995).

15   Quoted in Tom Peters, "The Pursuit of Wow!" conference booklet, 27 October 1995.

16   "The Mass Production of Ideas and Other Impossibilities," *Economist,* 28 March 1995.

17   John Seely Brown, "Research That Reinvents the Corporation," in *The Learning Imperative,* ed. Robert Howard (Boston, 1993), 89.

18   *Forbes,* 7 November 1994. Quoted in Peters, "Pursuit of Wow!"

19   Quoted in Tom Peters Seminar, 27 October 1995.

20   Gary Hamel, "The Prize that Lies in Foreseeing the Future," *Financial Times* (London), 5 June 1995.

## Chapter 7: Strategy

1   Michael Porter, "The State of Strategic Thinking," *Economist,* 23 May 1987, 21.

2   Henry Mintzberg, *The Rise and Fall of Strategic Planning* (New York, 1994), 21–23.

3   For a brief history of strategy, see John Kay, *The Foundations of Corporate Success* (Oxford, 1993).

4   Mintzberg, *The Rise and Fall of Strategic Planning,* 46–47.

5   Ibid., 62–63.

6   Porter, "Strategic Thinking," 22.

7   Michael Goold, Andrew Campbell, and Marcus Alexander, *Corporate-Level Strategy: Creating Value in the Multibusiness Company* (New York, 1994), 54.

8   Ibid., 100.

9   Amar Bhide, "How Entrepreneurs Craft Strategies That Work," *Harvard Business Review* (March–April, 1994): 150–61.

10   Ibid., 258–9.

11   Quoted in "The CEO Agenda," *Strategy & Business,* Fall 1995.

12   Jean-Philippe Deschamps and Ranganath Nayak, *Product Juggernauts: How Companies Mobilize to Generate a Stream of Market Winners* (Boston, 1995), 131.

13   Stephen Rudolph et al., "Emerging Technologies: A Novel Approach to Envisioning Their Development," *Prism* (Fourth Quarter, 1994): 105–12.

14   Mintzberg, *The Rise and Fall of Strategic Planning,* 295.

15   Noel M. Tichy and Stratford Sherman, *Control Your Destiny or Someone Else Will* (New York, 1993), 11.

16   Gerard Tellis and Peter Golder, "First to Market, First to Fail: Real Causes of Enduring Market Leadership," *Sloan Management Review* 37, no. 2.

17   Goold, Campbell, and Alexander, *Corporate-Level Strategy.*

18   "Hammer Defends Re-engineering," *Economist,* 5 November 1994, 96.

19   "As Sculley Leaves Apple, Image Lingers of a Leader Distracted by His Vision," *Wall Street Journal,* 18 October 1993.

20   Gates quoted in *Financial Times* (London), 17 November 1995.

## Chapter 8: Storm in the Boardroom

1   Noel M. Tichy and Stratford Sherman, *Control Your Destiny or Someone Else Will* (New York, 1993).

2   David Packard, *The HP Way* (New York, 1995).

3   Breakfast discussion with Bill Gates, 17 October 1994.

4   Napoleon Hill, *Think and Grow Rich* (United Kingdom: Wilshire Book Company, 1937).

5   Mark McCormack, *What They Don't Teach You at Harvard Business School* (London, 1984), 207.

6   Lee Iacocca with William Novak, *Iacocca* (New York, 1985), xiv.

7   Doron Levin, *Behind the Wheel at Chrysler: The Iacocca Legacy* (New York, 1995).

8   Carol Kennedy, *Managing with the Gurus: Top Level Guidance on Twenty Management Techniques* (London, 1994), 98.

9   "Secrets of the Survivors," *Business Week,* 9 October 1995.

10   Warren Bennis, *On Becoming a Leader* (1989).

11   "The CEO as Coach," *Harvard Business Review* 73, no. 2 (1995): 70.

12   Peter Drucker, *Post-Capitalist Society* (New York, 1993), 71.

13   "Britain's Boardroom Anatomy," *Management Today* (London), October 1995.

14   "How High Can CEO Pay GO?" *Business Week,* 22 April 1996.

15   "Are They Worth it?" *CFO* Magazine, November 1995.

16   "Are These Ten Stretched Too Thin?" *Business Week,* 17 November 1996.

17   "France Puts Her 'Affaires' in Order," *Financial Times* (London), 12 December 1994.

18   "France's Hierarchy Must Change to Stop Scandals," *Evening Standard* (London), 5 December 1995, 36.

19   Joseph L. Badaracco and Allen Webb, "Business Ethics: The View from the Trenches," *California Management Review* 37, no. 2 (Winter 1995), 8.

20   "A Company Possessed," in Charles Handy, *Beyond Certainty: The Changing Worlds of Organisations* (London, 1995), 105.

21   Drucker, *Post-Capitalist Society,* 73.

22    Quoted in "America's Most Admired Companies," *Fortune,* 6 March, 1995.

23    "Watching the Boss," *Economist,* 19 January 1994.

## Chapter 9: The Future of Work

1    Jeremy Rifkin, *The End of Work: The Decline of the Global Labor Force and the Dawn of the Post-Market Era* (New York, 1995), Introduction, xvi–xvii.

2    See the excellent article on technology and unemployment, "Technology and Unemployment" (not written by the authors), *Economist,* 11 February 1995.

3    Figures from U.S. Bureau of Labor Statistics, *Study of Job Growth in Different Sectors, 1992–2005* (Washington, D.C.).

4    "The Country: For Work, Rest or 'Play,'" *Financial Times* (London), 14 October 1995.

5    Charles Handy, *Beyond Certainty: The Changing Worlds of Organisations* (London, 1995).

6    "Handy Guide to Corporate Life," *Financial Times* (London), 17 August 1995.

7    "Temporarily Ahead of His Time," *International Herald Tribune,* 13 October 1995.

8    "The Temp Big Boom: Why It's Good," *Fortune,* 16 October 1995.

9    William Bridges, *Jobshift: How to Prosper in a Workplace without Jobs* (London, 1995), 9.

10    Philip Burgess and Paul and Sarah Edwards, *Workshifting,* Center for the New West Special Report (Denver, Colo., June 1995).

11    "Special Envoys," *Financial Times,* 8 September 1995.

12    "The New Workplace," *Business Week,* 6 May 1996.

13    "Tales of the Office Nomad," *Financial Times,* 29 May 1995, 7.

14    "The Salaryman Rides Again," *Economist,* 4 February 1995.

15    Ibid.

16   *The Tom Peters Seminar* (London, 1994), 91.

17   "What Do You Expect after the Work of Millions Is Wiped Out?" *International Herald Tribune,* 16 October 1995.

18   "Rethinking Work," *Business Week,* 17 October 1994.

19   "Adapt or Die," *Economist,* 1 July 1995.

## Chapter 10: What Does Globalization Mean?

1   Survey of 750 companies by Arthur Andersen and National Small Business United. Quoted in "It's a Small (Business) World," *Business Week,* 17 April 1995.

2   Interview with Drucker's neighbor.

3   "Fast Track," *Financial Times* (London), 6 March 995, 11.

4   "Munching on Change," *Economist,* 6 January 1996.

5   Tadahiro Sekimoto, "Corporate Challenges in the New Century" (Paper prepared for UK-Japan 2000 Group Conference, 17–19 March 1995).

## Chapter 11: The Art of Japanese Management

1   Daniel Jones, with James Womack and Daniel Roos, *The Machine That Changed the World: The Story of Lean Production* (New York, 1990), 225.

2   Ibid.

3   Kenichi Ohmae, *The Mind of the Strategist* (1982), 221.

4   Carol Kennedy, *Managing with the Gurus: Top Level Guidance on Twenty Management Techniques* (London, 1994), 222.

5   Womack et al., *The Machine That Changed the World,* 237.

6   Jordan Lewis, "Western Companies Can Improve upon the Japanese Keiretsu," *Wall Street Journal,* 12 December 1995.

7   "Japan's New Identity," *Business Week,* 10 April 1995, 37.

8   Tadahiro Sekimoto, "Corporate Challenges in the New Century," (Paper Prepared for the UK–Japan 2000 Group Conference, 17–19 March 1995), 3.

9   Ikujiro Nonaka and Hirotaka Takeuchi, *The Knowledge-Creating Company: How Japanese Companies Create the Dynamics of Innovation* (Oxford, 1994), 115.

10   Ibid., 17.

11   Ibid., 151.

12   Ibid., 144.

## Chapter 12: A New Model in Asia?

1   For a more detailed discussion of business in Asia, see a survey by John Micklethwait, "The Search for the Asian Manager," *Economist,* 9 March 1996.

2   Australia, Department of Foreign Affairs and Trade, East Asia Analytical Unit, *Overseas Chinese Business Networks in Asia* (Canberra, 1995).

## Chapter 13: Managing Leviathan

1   Interview with William Bratton.

2   "A Safer New York City," *Business Week,* 11 December 1995.

3   "California's Contract Example," *Financial Times,* 13 November 1995.

4   Michael Porter, *The Competitive Advantage of Nations* (London, 1989), xii.

5   An Interview with Charles Handy, *Strategy & Business,* Fall 1995.

6   "Benchmark in Southwark," *Financial Times,* 13 November 1995.

7   "Really Reinventing Government," *Atlantic Monthly,* February 1995. Reprinted in Peter Drucker, *Managing in a Time of Great Change* (New York, 1995), 285–301.

8   John Kay, "Sharing Responsibility for Passing the Buck," *Financial Times,* 17 November 1995.

9   "Some Reforms That Might Be Politically Feasible," *Economist,* 22 June 1985, 19–21.

10   Quoted in Simon Jenkins, *Accountable to None: The Tory Nationalization of Britain* (London, 1995), 81.

## Chapter 14: A Walk on the Wild Side

1   Andrew Morton, "A Working Princess," *Sunday Times* (London), 13 November 1994.

2   Max Berley, "A Move toward Management by Philosophy," *International Herald Tribune,* 12 February 1996.

3   "Business Advice from the Sidelines," *New York Times,* 6 March 1996, D1.

4   Francis J. Gouillart and James Kelly, *Transforming the Organization* (New York, 1995), 4.

5   Ibid., 278–79.

6   Ibid., 19.

## Conclusion

1   "Overview of Re-engineering," *Financial Times Handbook of Management* (London, 1995), 231.

# Bibliography

Ansoff, Igor. *Corporate Strategy.* Harmondsworth: Penguin, 1968.

Australia, Department of Foreign Affairs and Trade. East Asia Analytical Unit. *Overseas Chinese Business Networks in Asia.* 1995.

Bartlett, Christopher, and Sumantra Ghoshal. *Managing across Borders.* Boston: Harvard Business School Press. 1989.

Bennis, Warren. *On Becoming a Leader.* London: Hutchinson, 1989.

Bennis Warren, and B. Nanis. *Leaders: The Strategies for Taking Charge.* New York: Harper & Row, 1986.

Blanchard, Kenneth, and S. Johnson. *The One-Minute Manager.* Glasgow: Fontana/Collins, 1983.

Bridges, William. *Jobshift: How to Prosper in a Workplace without Jobs.* London: Nicholas Brealey, 1995.

Byrne, John. *The Whiz Kids: Ten Founding Fathers of American Business—And the Legacy They Left Us.* New York: Currency Doubleday, 1993.

Carling, Will, with Robert Heller. *The Way to Win: Strategies for Success in Business and Sport.* London: 1995.

Champy, James. *Reengineering Management: The Mandate for New Leadership.* London: HarperCollins, 1995.

Champy, James, and Michael Hammer. *Reengineering the Corporation.* London: Nicholas Brealey, 1993.

Clutterbuck, David, and Stuart Crainer. *Masters of Management.* London: Macmillan, 1990.

Cooper, Robin. *When Lean Enterprises Collide: Competing through Confrontation.* Boston: Harvard Business School Press, 1995.

Covey, Stephen. *The Seven Habits of Highly Effective People.* 1989.

_____. *Principle-Centered Leadership.* New York: Simon & Schuster, 1992.

Cragg, Claudia. *The New Taipans.* London: Century, 1995.

Creech, Bill. *Five Pillars of TQM.* New York: Dutton, 1994.

Crosby, Philip. *Quality Is Free.* New York, McGraw-Hill, 1979.

Deschamps, Jean-Philippe, and Ranganath Nayak. *Product Juggernauts: How Companies Mobilize to Generate a Stream of Market Winners.* Boston: Harvard Business School Press, 1995.

Drucker, Peter. *The Practice of Management.* New York: Harper & Row, 1954.

_____. *The Age of Discontinuity.* 1969.

_____. *Management: Tasks, Responsibilities, Practices.* London: Butterworth-Heinemann, 1974.

_____. *Managing in Turbulent Times.* London: Butterworth-Heinemann, 1980.

_____. *The Concept of the Corporation.* New York: Mentor, 1983. First published 1946.

_____. *Innovation and Entrepreneurship.* London: William Heinemann, 1985.

_____. *The New Realities.* London: Heinemann, 1989.

_____. *Adventures of a Bystander.* New York: Harper & Row, 1994.

_____. *Post-Capitalist Society.* New York: HarperBusiness, 1993.

_____. *Managing in a Time of Great Change.* New York: Truman Talley, 1996.

Emmott, Bill. *The Sun Also Sets: Why Japan Will Not Be Number One.* London: Simon & Schuster, 1989.

Farkas, Charles, Philippe De Backer, and Allen Sheppard. *Maximum Leadership: The World's Top Leaders Discuss How They Add Value to Companies.* London: Orion, 1995.

Feigenbaum, A. V. *Total Quality Control.* New York: McGraw-Hill, 1983.

Flannery, Thomas, David Hofrichter, and Paul Platten. *People, Performance, and Pay.* New York: Free Press, 1969.

Florida, Richard, and Martin Kenney. *The Breakthrough Illusion.* 1990.

Fukuyama, Francis. *The End of History.* New York: Free Press, 1992.

_____. *Trust.* New York: Free Press, 1995.

Gates, Bill. *The Road Ahead.* New York: Viking, 1995.

Gertz, Dwight, and Joao Baptista. *Grow to Be Great: Breaking the Downsizing Cycle.* 1995.

Goldratt, Eliyahu, and Jeff Cox. *The Goal.* Aldershot: Gower, 1989.

Goold, Michael, Andrew Campbell, and Marcus Alexander. *Corporate-Level Strategy: Creating Value in the Multibusiness Company.* New York: John Wiley & Sons, 1994.

Gouillart, Francis, and James Kelley. *Transforming the Organization: Reframing Corporate Issues, Restructuring the Company, Revitalizing the Spirit of Enterprise, Renewing People.* New York: McGraw-Hill, 1995.

Graham, Pauline, ed. *Mary Parker Follett: Prophet of Management.* Boston: Harvard Business School Press, 1995.

Guillen, Mauro. *Models of Management: Work, Authority and Organisation in Comparative Perspective.* Chicago: University of Chicago Press, 1995.

*Financial Times Handbook of Management.* London: FT Pitman, 1995.

Hamel, Gary, and C. K. Prahalad. *Competing for the Future.* Boston: Harvard Business School Press, 1994.

Hammer, Michael, with Steven Stanton. *The Re-engineering Revolution: The Handbook.* New York: HarperCollins, 1995.

Handy, Charles. *Understanding Organisations*. London: Penguin, 1976.

_____. *The Future of Work*. Oxford: Basil Blackwell, 1984.

_____. *The Age of Unreason*. London: Arrow Books, 1989.

_____. *Beyond Certainty: The Changing World of Organisations*. London: Hutchinson, 1995.

_____. *The Empty Raincoat*. 1995.

Harrison, Bennett. *Lean and Mean: The Changing Landscape of Corporate America*. New York: Basic Books, 1994.

Harvey-Jones, Sir John. *Making It Happen*. Glasgow: Collins, 1988.

_____. *Troubleshooter*. London: BBC Books, 1990.

_____. *Troubleshooter 2*. London: Penguin, 1993.

_____. *Managing to Survive*. London: Heinemann, 1993.

Heller Robert. *The Naked Manager for the Nineties*. London: Little, Brown, 1995.

Hill, Napoleon. *Think and Grow Rich*. United Kingdom, Wilshire, 1937.

Hofstede, Geert. *Cultures and Organisations*. Maidenhead: McGraw-Hill, 1991.

Howard, Robert, ed. *The Learning Imperative*. Boston: Harvard Business School Press, 1993.

Huczynski, Andrzej. *Management Gurus: What Makes Them and How to Become One*. London: 1993.

Hurst, David. *Crisis and Renewal: Meeting the Challenge of Organisational Change*. Boston: Harvard Business School Press, 1995.

Hutton, Will. *The State We're In*. 1995.

Iacocca, Lee, with Bill Novak. *Iacocca: An Autobiography*. London: Sidgwick and Jackson, 1985.

Jenkins, Simon. *Accountable to None: The Tory Nationalisation of Britain*. London: Hamish Hamilton, 1995.

Jones, Daniel, with James Womack and Daniel Roos. *The Machine That Changed the World: The Story of Lean Production*. New York: Ranson Associates, 1990.

Kanter, Rosabeth Moss. *The Change Masters: Corporate Entrepreneurs at Work*. London: Allen & Unwin, 1985.

_____. *When Giants Learn to Dance: Mastering the Challenges of Strategy, Management and Careers in the 1990s.* London: Simon & Schuster, 1989.

_____. *World Class: Thriving Locally in the Global Economy.* New York: Simon & Schuster, 1995.

Kay, John. *The Foundations of Corporate Success.* Oxford: Oxford University Press, 1993.

Kennedy, Carol. *Guide to the Management Gurus.* London: Century Business, 1991.

_____. *Managing with the Gurus: Top Level Guidance on Twenty Management Techniques.* London: Century Business, 1994.

Kidder, Tracy. *The Soul of a New Machine.* Boston: Atlantic/Little, Brown, 1981.

Kotkin, Joel. *Tribes: How Race, Religion and Identity Determine Success in the New Global Economy.* New York: Random House, 1992.

Kotter, John. *The New Rules: How to Succeed in Today's Post-Corporate World.* New York: Free Press, 1995.

Laserre, Philippe, and Hellmut Schütte. *Strategies for Asia Pacific.* London: Macmillan Business, 1995.

Levin, Doron. *Behind the Wheel at Chrysler: The Iacocca Legacy.* New York: Harcourt Brace, 1995.

Levitt, Theodore. "Marketing Myopia." *Harvard Business Review* (1960).

_____. "The Globalization of Markets." *Harvard Business Review* (May–June 1983).

Leonard-Barton, Dorothy. *The Wellsprings of Knowledge: Building and Sustaining the Sources of Innovation.* Boston: Harvard Business School Press, 1995.

Lewis, Jordan. *The Connected Corporation.* New York: Free Press, 1995.

Lorenz, Christopher, and Nicholas Leslie, eds. *The Financial Times on Management.* London: FT Pitman, 1992.

McCormack, Mark. *What They Don't Teach You at Harvard Business School.* London: William Collins, 1984.

McGregor, D. *The Human Side of the Enterprise.* New York: Mc-Graw-Hill, 1960.

MacKay, Harvey. *Swim with the Sharks without Being Eaten Alive.* 1995.

Meyer, G. J. *Executive Blues: Down and Out in Corporate America.* New York: Franklin Square Press, 1995.

Mintzberg, Henry. *Mintzberg on Management.* New York: Free Press, 1989.

_____. *The Rise and Fall of Strategic Planning.* Hemel Hempstead: Prentice-Hall, 1994.

Monks, Robert, and Nell Minow. *Watching the Watchers: Corporate Governance for the 21st Century.* Cambridge, Mass.: Blackwell Business, 1996.

Moody, Fred. *I Sing the Body Electronic: A Year with Microsoft on the Multimedia Frontier.* New York: Viking, 1995.

Moores, James. *The Death of Competition: Leadership & Strategy in the Age of Business Ecosystems.* New York: HarperBusiness, 1996.

Naisbitt, John. *Megatrends: Ten New Directions Transforming Our Lives.* New York: Warner Books, 1983.

_____. *Reinventing the Corporation.* New York: Warner Books, 1985.

_____. *Megatrends Asia.* New York: Simon & Schuster, 1995.

Negroponte, Nicholas. *Being Digital.* London: Hodder & Stoughton, 1995.

Nonaka, Ikujiro, and Hirotaka Takeuchi. *The Knowledge-Creating Company: How Japanese Companies Create the Dynamics of Innovation.* Oxford, 1994.

Ohmae, Kenichi. *The Mind of the Strategist.* Harmondsworth: Penguin, 1982.

_____. *Triad Power.* New York: Free Press, 1985.

_____. *The Borderless World: Power and Strategy in the Interlinked Economy.* New York: HarperBusiness, 1990.

_____. *The End of the Nation-State: The Rise of Regional Economies.* New York: Free Press, 1995.

———, ed. *The Evolving Global Economy: Making Sense of the New Global Order.* Boston: Harvard Business School Press, 1995.

Osborne, David, with Ted Gaebler. *Reinventing Government: How the Entrepreneurial Spirit Is Transforming the Public Sector.* 1992.

Packard, David. *The HP Way: How Bill Hewlett and I Built Our Company.* New York: HarperBusiness, 1995.

Pascale, Richard. *Managing on the Edge.* Harmondsworth: Penguin, 1991.

Pascale, Richard, and Anthony Athos. *The Art of Japanese Management.* Harmondsworth: Penguin, 1992.

Peters, Thomas J. *Thriving on Chaos: Handbook for a Management Revolution.* London: Macmillan, 1987.

———. *Liberation Management.* London: Macmillan, 1992.

———. *The Tom Peters Seminar: Crazy Times Call for Crazy Organizations.* New York: Vintage Books, 1994.

———. *The Tom Peters Seminar: The Pursuit of Wow! Every Person's Guide to Topsy-Turvy Times.* New York: Vintage Books, 1994.

Peters, Thomas J., and Nancy Austin. *A Passion for Excellence.* London: Collins, 1985.

Peters, Thomas J., and Robert Waterman. *In Search of Excellence: Lessons from America's Best-Run companies.* New York: Harper & Row, 1982.

Porras, Jerry, and James Collins. *Built to Last: Successful Habits of Visionary Companies.* New York: HarperBusiness, 1995.

Porter, Michael. *Competitive Strategy.* New York: Free Press, 1980.

———. *Competitive Advantage.* New York: Free Press, 1985.

———. *The Competitive Advantage of Nations.* London: Macmillan, 1989.

———. *The Competitive Advantage of Massachusetts.* 1991.

———. *The Competitive Advantage of the Inner-City.* 1995.

Reich, Robert. *The Work of Nations.* New York: Alfred Knopf, 1991.

Reicheld, Frederick. *The Loyalty Effect.* Boston: Harvard Business School Press, 1996.

Rifkin, Jeremy. *The End of Work: The Decline of the Global Labor Force and the Dawn of the Post-Market Era.* New York: Putnam, 1995.

Robbins, Anthony. *Unlimited Power.* New York: Simon & Schuster, 1987.

_____. *Awaken the Giant Within.* New York: Simon & Schuster, 1991.

Rohwer, Jim. *Asia Rising: Why America Will Prosper as Asia's Economies Boom.* New York: Simon & Schuster, 1995.

Sampson, Anthony. *Company Man: The Rise and Fall of Corporate Life.* London: HarperCollins, 1995.

Schor, Juliet. *The Overworked American.* 1992.

Seagrave, Sterling. *Lords of the Rim: The Invisible Empire of the Overseas Chinese.* London: Bantam, 1995.

Senge, Peter. *The Fifth Discipline.* New York: Doubleday, 1990.

_____. *The Fifth Discipline Handbook.* London: Nicholas Brealey, 1994.

Simon, Hermann. *Hidden Champions: Lessons from 500 of the World's Best-Unknown Companies.* Boston: Harvard Business School Press, 1996.

Steiner, George. *Top Management Planning.* 1969.

_____. *Strategic Planning: What Every Manager Must Know.* 1979.

Tichy, Noel, with Stratford Sherman. *Control Your Destiny or Someone Else Will: How Jack Welch Is Making the World's Most Competitive Corporation.* New York: Currency Doubleday, 1993.

Toffler, Alvin. *Future Shock.* New York: Random House, 1970.

_____. *The Third Wave.* New York: Morrow, 1980.

_____. *Powershift.* New York: Bantam, 1990.

Treacy, Michael, and Fred Wiersema. *The Discipline of Market Leaders: Choose Your Customers, Narrow Your Focus, Dominate Your Market.* New York: Addison-Wesley, 1995.

Vernon, Philip. *Sovereignty at Bay.* 1971.

Warner, Malcolm. *The Management of Human Resources in Chinese Industry.* London: Macmillan, 1995.

Waterman, Robert. *Frontiers of Excellence: Learning from Companies That Put People First.* London: Nicholas Brealey, 1995.

Whyte, David. *The Heart Aroused: Poetry and the Preservation of the Soul in Corporate America.*

Whyte, William. *Organization Man.* New York: Doubleday, 1957.

Zuboff, Shoshana. *In the Age of the Smart Machine: The Future of Work and Power.* New York: Basic Books, 1988.

# Index

# About the Authors

John Micklethwait, the New York bureau chief of *The Economist,* has written for the *Los Angeles Times,* and has appeared on National Public Radio. Winner of the Winscott Award for financial journalism, he lives in New York City.

Adrian Woolridge, the West Coast bureau chief of *The Economist,* has written for *The Wall Street Journal* and *The New Republic.* He lives in Los Angeles.